A MAN OF THE WORD

Life of

G. CAMPBELL MORGAN

JILL MORGAN

WIPF & STOCK · Eugene, Oregon

Wipf and Stock Publishers
199 W 8th Ave, Suite 3
Eugene, OR 97401

A Man of the Word
Life of G. Campbell Morgan
By Morgan, Jill
Copyright©1951 by Morgan, Jill
ISBN 13: 978-1-60899-465-6
Publication date 3/22/2010
Previously published by Fleming H. Revell Co, 1951

G. Campbell Morgan Reprint Series

Foreword

If it is true that the measure of a person's greatness is their influence, not only on his own time but on future generations, G. Campbell Morgan must be regarded as a great person. His greatness is seen not only in the wide impact of his ministry on both sides of the Atlantic, but in the fact that his books are still read and studied sixty-five years after his death. Named one of the ten greatest preachers of the twentieth-century by the contributing board of *Preaching* magazine, Morgan made the Bible a new and living book not only to the congregations who listened to him, but the vast multitude of persons who read his books.

Fox sixty-seven years Morgan preached and taught the Scriptures and served churches in England and the United States. What is remarkable is that his commentaries and expositions of the Bible still speak to persons of a new millennium. There have been many changes in the world since he faithfully preached and taught the Scriptures, but the wide appeal of his books testify to the timelessness of his message.

Although he held pastorates in the Congregational and Presbyterian denominations, he had an ecumenical appeal to persons of all denominations and traditions. The mystic

Thomas á Kempis once wrote, "He to whom the eternal word speaks is delivered from many opinions." In one of his sermons, he referred to the words of Amos that there would be a famine for hearing the word of God (Amos 8:11). The timeless work of G. Campbell Morgan addresses that hunger, as his books enable his readers to get beyond opinions to the living Word.

Wipf and Stock Publishers have rendered a great gift to the religious world in reprinting dozens of Morgan's books. This growing collection makes his books more available, so that readers have an option other than searching the internet for used, and often expensive, copies. Among this collection is the classic *The Great Physician* and commentaries on the Gospel of Matthew and John. Persons seeking a living faith and a meaningful encounter with God would profit from reading any of these Morgan books.

Near the end of his ministry, in a sermon entitled "But One Thing," Morgan commented on how Portugal changed the words of a coin after Christopher Columbus discovered America. No longer did the inscription say, *Ne Plus Ultra* (nothing more beyond) but *Plus Ultra* (more beyond). It is the hope of the G. Campbell Morgan Trust that the reprinting of these books will bring readers to the "more beyond," and an even deeper encounter with the Word in Scripture.

THE MORGAN TRUST
Richard L. Morgan
Howard C. Morgan
John C. Morgan

FOR UNCLE TED
AND AUNTIE EDITH

Contents

	PAGE
PROLOGUE	13

PART I

CHAP.

I 1863-1876. BIRTH TO 13 YEARS 21
Birthplace—Home—Parents — Childhood — Bereavement—School—The First Sermon.

II 1876-1888. 13 TO 25 YEARS 35
Evangelistic Services—Year of Eclipse—Teaching—Moody and Sankey—Tent Meetings and Popular Lectures—Albert Swift—Leaving the Jewish School—Hull Mission — Salvation Army — Rejection by Wesleyan Ministry—Marriage.

III 1889-1897. 26 TO 34 YEARS 65
Stone — Rugeley — Birmingham — First Visit to the United States.

IV 1897-1904. 34 TO 41 YEARS 104
New Court, Tollington Park — Northfield Extension Work in the U.S.

V 1904-1917. 41 TO 53 YEARS 137
Westminster — (Bible School — Mundesley — B.T.A. Cheshunt—War.)

VI 1917-1919. 53 TO 55 YEARS 221
Mildmay (Y.M.C.A.)—Highbury Quadrant.

VII 1919-1932. 55 TO 69 YEARS 238
The Itinerant Ministry in the United States and Canada.

VIII 1926-1932. 62 TO 69 YEARS 262
Cincinnati — Los Angeles (B.I.O.L.A.) — Philadelphia (Gordon College, Boston).

IX 1933-1945. 69 TO 81 YEARS 284
The Second Westminster Ministry—Retirement—The End of the Pilgrimage.

THE MEMORIAL SERVICES

PART II

INTRODUCTION 339

X THE LARGER CIRCLE 343

XI THE SMALLER CIRCLE 365

XII THE INNER CIRCLE 382

THE PLACE OF POWER 397

List of Illustrations

G. CAMPBELL MORGAN	*Frontispiece*
	Facing page
G. CAMPBELL MORGAN—1897	104
NANCY	105
WESTMINSTER CHAPEL	144
DR. MORGAN—1914	208
THE RECLINING PHOTO	288
MRS. G. CAMPBELL MORGAN	384

Prologue

DURING Dr. Campbell Morgan's lifetime two books were written about him. A biography by John Harries, entitled, *G. Campbell Morgan, The Man and His Ministry,** was published in 1930. This book commemorated the fortieth year of official ministry, and was remarkable in that the author received very little help from the subject himself. Dr. Morgan never showed any interest in the writing of his life story. He brushed aside any suggestion that he write his own autobiography, and made no conscious attempt to do so. Yet those most familiar with his books and recorded sermons know how repeatedly he used the experiences of his own life to illustrate his theme. 'Experience is a hard teacher,' we say, and there are those who never learn. Life had not reserved a gentle touch for Campbell Morgan, or bestowed upon him at birth those privileges and advantages which some take as their due. Yet he wrested from experience the discipline which governed his life, and made his teacher his servant. To cull from sermons all the references to his own life—childhood, youth, and maturity—one can obtain an autobiography of sorts.

It cannot be said that Dr. Morgan welcomed or spurned Mr. Harries' decision to write his biography. As a friend, Mr. Harries was welcomed into the home, and extended all the hospitality for which it was always noted. He took advantage of every opportunity to talk with his subject. Albums of newspaper cuttings were placed at his disposal. Miss Howell, Dr. Morgan's able secretary, was generous with her assistance, as also was Mr. A. E. Marsh, his colleague at Westminster Chapel. Mr. Harries corresponded with friends all over the world, and many sent him letters and items of interest. From Dr. Morgan's own sons and daughters he

*Published by Fleming H. Revell Co., 1930.

received letters which, as intimate personal testimony, are eloquent of their father's understanding of childhood and youth, and reveal the price which children pay who must forfeit their father's presence and companionship for long periods at a time.

Perhaps Mr. Harries would say that Mrs. Morgan helped him most. Though her letters were masterpieces of prose (for she knew instinctively how to express a thought with the most engaging brevity, and had a gift for discerning the wheat from the chaff), she never wrote for publication. But she always felt that her husband's life story should be written, and one can well imagine her telling it, 'here a little, there a little,' as she busied herself with the household tasks, and in her turn unconsciously drawing her own portrait as wife and mother which Mr. Harries has so lovingly and faithfully included in his book. For that's the way it is. We write our own stories, intentionally or not. Dr. and Mrs. Morgan's stories are living to-day in their own sons and daughters, than which they could have paid no finer debt to posterity.

About eight years after Mr. Harries' book was published another one appeared, entitled, *Campbell Morgan, Bible Teacher*,* by Harold Murray. Mr. Murray, a religious journalist of some forty years' experience, says in his opening chapter that his book is not a biography of Dr. Campbell Morgan. He calls it 'A Sketch of the Great Expositor and Evangelist—a little tribute which he, who cares so little for the praise of men, will suffer for the sake, not only of those who know and love him, but for the sake of those all over the world, who are interested in his life work.'

When the life and works of great artists are published it is always fascinating to study the sketches which are gleaned from their notebooks. Mr. Frank Salisbury, who painted the portrait of Dr. Morgan which now hangs in Cheshunt College, Cambridge, tells us in his autobiography how he was commissioned from time to time to commemorate the

*Published by Marshall, Morgan & Scott, 1938.

great national events of contemporary English history. The book contains among others a reproduction of the painting of the impressive ceremony of the burial of the Unknown Soldier in Westminster Abbey, and with it the artist's first sketch, showing how, with a few strokes, he captured the pose and grouping of the key figures. So Mr. Murray uses his journalistic pencil to give us a 'sketch' of one whom he calls 'no dry-as-dust theologian.' In brief and telling lines he has caught the spirit and essence of a living and breathing personality.

Devotion and understanding have undergirded both these literary efforts, and those who desire it will find in these volumes the essential facts of Dr. Morgan's life story.

Since his home-going, in 1945, it has been the growing conviction of Dr. Morgan's family that there is a need for an additional work on the life of their father. The first consideration of any such book is its readers. Who will read it, and what do they want to know? Apart from those who hold a personal acquaintance and friendship for Dr. Morgan himself are those who, at one time or another, sat at his feet, and to whom he 'opened the Book.' Some of these availed themselves of this opportunity over a period of months and years. Many a treasured Bible is dog-eared around the covers and marked up on the inside as a result of its regular attendance at the Westminster Friday Night Bible School. There are others who could only be occasional listeners—'whenever Dr. Morgan came to Keswick,' or 'Birmingham' (without the 'h') or 'Birming*ham*' (which means Alabama!) or 'Toronto,' or any one of hundreds of other towns and cities in Great Britain, the United States, or Canada. There are those fortunates who look back with nostalgia to the days of the great summer conference at Mundesley, on England's east coast. Others remember Dr. Morgan at Northfield, Massachusetts, Winona Lake, Indiana, Massanetta Springs, Virginia; Stony Brook, Long Island; Montreat, North Carolina, and other great rallying grounds for Bible students in the United States. Even greater numbers have met Dr. Morgan only within the covers of his books. Theological professors and students alike in all parts of the world are his readers. To these may be added the missionaries of the Cross in the far-flung reaches of earth and sea—that lonely, gallant army for whom Dr. Morgan had a very special love and remembrance. All these and many more pass in constant review before the eyes of those who hold themselves responsible for this book.

Dr. Morgan's published works hold the key to his manner of interpretation, his expository skill and his analytical method. This is rather an attempt to answer the question that is asked in one way or another about every public figure. What was he like when you really knew him? What factors went into the making of his character and his success? What did he think about his family, and his friends, and what do they think about him? What is known in journalism as 'human interest' is the story people want to know about their heroes. We feel that Dr. Morgan's admirers are no exception to this rule. For this reason his sons and daughters wished to supply in some measure the answers to these questions, and called upon some of their father's friends to help them.

It was evident from the beginning that someone must be authorized to undertake the assembling and planning of this material, and be entrusted with diaries and other sources of information invaluable for reference and research. The fact that they commissioned their sister-in-law to this task was certainly not because of any professional experience or skill. Her persistent plea that the work ought to be done by *somebody* resulted in the importunate pleader being given the assignment!

I do not remember when I first met the subject of these pages. He seems to have been always there, and when my own father passed away in 1919 he promised to 'stand in the gap'—and that is exactly what he did. There were months, sometimes years, when I did not see him at all, and while a covenant once made by him never failed, these separations made it more possible to see him objectively, and a certain perspective developed which is not so easily discerned in constant, daily contact.

In the early days of this writing a most timely word of advice came from Dr. F. A. Robinson, of Toronto, whose reminiscences of Dr. Morgan appear on a later page. He said: "Your dear Dad would, I think, be among the first to say in his oft-quoted words relating to Cromwell, 'Paint me, warts and all.' . . . He preferred a likeness to a picture that has been mercifully over-retouched." If, then, in the eyes of some, any flaws or shadows appear in his character through this narrative, it is because those of us who have devised it have tried in all honesty to show that a truly great man is always very human and better loved because of it. He himself never troubled to conceal those habits of life or convictions of conscience in which some did not see eye to eye with him, and would not wish them to be erased by others. They were part of the composite whole of a positive character, too strong and forceful, as one of his friends said, for everyone to agree with him all of the time. The fault is rather in the writing if it fails to show that in Campbell Morgan the sacred and secular were never at variance, but that to him life, and what it has to offer, is to be used and enjoyed to the glory of God.

Help has been gleaned from many sources, each one lighting a different phase of Dr. Morgan's life or a certain aspect of his character. Many of his contemporaries have passed on 'into the light.' Those who have contributed to these pages —friends, strangers, and members of the family circle, are representative of a much larger number who, because of their diversity of interest and thought, serve to emphasize how wide and catholic was Dr. Morgan's appeal to all classes and conditions of people. To all of these we wish to express our appreciation and gratitude.

Shall we say that a dozen different artists go to look at an object of strength and beauty and dignity, and are then asked to record their impressions To begin with, they approach their subject from different angles and at different times in the day. One sees its beauty best in the morning, another prefers the strength cast by the shadow in the strong sunlight. To another the clouds and the threatening storm only serve to throw into stronger relief its grace and dignity. Yet another comes in the dusk as evening softens the lines and contours with her healing fingers. Each expresses in a different and distinctly personal way his impressions—and seeing them all the spectator says: I only saw him like this . . . I never knew him like this. . . . Now I understand him better than I ever did before. J.M.

Taft, Texas, 1950.

PART 1

CHAPTER I

1863-1876: Birth to 13 years

BIRTHPLACE — HOME — PARENTS — CHILDHOOD —
BEREAVEMENT — SCHOOL — THE FIRST SERMON

IT is given to some to step from obscurity and become great in their chosen fields of endeavour; but it is not given to all of these to return at the last to the place where it all began. The path of achievement often leads far afield. For the subject of these pages it led from the little village of Tetbury in Gloucestershire, through the country towns of Stone and Rugeley in Staffordshire, and the city streets of Birmingham, to the metropolis itself—London, the mecca of all Englishmen. Like many of his countrymen, too, he crossed the seas. Towns and cities of another continent became known to him, and he to them. Distinction as a pulpit personality, and as Bible scholar and teacher, found him in England, and followed him to the United States and Canada. East, West, North and South, the Western Hemisphere saw and heard him. Busy years passed swiftly, and at last Home called again. To London he returned—a London which had looked so often upon warriors and arms, approaching the greatest conflict in her long history. Yet, before the blackouts, the bombings, the terrors by night and day, came the last peaceful years of the 1930's—the lull before the storm. In those years, for this record, the cycle was completed.

During the summers immediately preceding the war, Dr. Campbell Morgan spent a period of his holidays travelling by car through the lovely English countryside, exploring the highways and lanes of the West Country—Devon and Cornwall, Gloucester, Hereford and the Wye Valley. In the course of these unhurried 'trundlings' (to use his own word), he revisited the scenes of earlier days—the cities and little towns, Birmingham, Rugeley, and Stone; the little

Methodist chapel in Monmouth which had been the threshold to 'this one thing I do,' and Tetbury, to 'the house where I was born.'

It seems fitting to begin the record with one of these journeys into the pageant of the past, bringing to remembrance as such adventures must, events and experiences so long forgotten.

In the summer of 1939 Dr. Morgan, accompanied by Mrs. Morgan, his son, Howard, and a friend, Dr. Margery Blackie, drove to the little village of Tetbury, in Gloucestershire. With a thousand years of history behind it, Tetbury is picturesque and unspoiled; fragrant in summer of wild roses in the hedges, and the massed loveliness of its cottage gardens, and dignified with centuries of quiet simple living. The car stopped before a brick house whose colouring has been weathered by many seasons. It was No. 12 Cutwell St.

His son tells what took place on this occasion. "Dad went up to the house," he says, "and rang the bell." A lady opened the door. The visitor informed her that he just wanted the members of his party to see the birthplace of Dr. Campbell Morgan. 'Ah, yes, indeed!' she said, 'we are very proud of this house,' and proceeded to relate many complimentary and laudatory things about the local celebrity. Dr. Morgan looked unimpressed. 'Oh, I don't know about all that,' he said, deprecatingly, 'you see, I happen to know the old gentleman very well!' She was rather nonplussed by such an affront, and was about to take up the challenge when she saw the look of mischief in the eyes of her visitor, and amusement on the faces of those who accompanied him. 'Would it be Dr. Campbell Morgan himself?' she exclaimed, and graciously invited them into the home. One can imagine her pleasure in relating the experience afterwards to the neighbours, and the way in which such a choice piece of news would gather momentum as it was repeated at church and social gatherings! Nothing pleased Dr. Morgan so much as 'a bit of a joke.' Not for the first, nor for the last time, had he left behind him a smile and a warm memory in the heart.

At the time of the birth of his son, the father, Rev. George Morgan, had recently come to Gloucestershire from Herefordshire where he had been the minister of a Baptist Church. He was a strong personality, whose unconventional and unrestricted spirit forbade any hesitation in severing denominational connections if his conscience decided him so to do. This he *had* done in resigning his Baptist pastorate, having been influenced by the teachings of the Plymouth Brethren, especially by one of their number, George Müller, who contended that the temporal and spiritual needs of his life could be supplied by faith and prayer, and supported two thousand orphan children in Bristol on the strength of it. In like spirit, George Morgan hired a hall in Tetbury, and preached there 'according to the dictates of his conscience.'

He had the makings of an ideal Pilgrim Father, not only in moral courage in the quest for religious liberty, but in contempt for worldly enticements, coupled with a love of adventure and the simple life. Like those hardy pioneers, his Bible was literally his entire library. "My father never read a novel in all the eighty years of his life," said Dr. Morgan. "In that he was different from me. I think fiction has its place. We agreed to differ on that point. He was a man of one Book in the sense that I never was, and should not desire to be; but he knew his Bible." He was tall and spare, with a fine head, black curly hair which turned snow-white in later life, clear, piercing eyes, an aquiline nose, and a mouth and jaw which, despite the beard, showed themselves to be firm and determined. He seemed to thrive on austerity, and the devil, in whom he firmly believed, must have found in him a doughty foe. One day, so the story goes, he took his long clay pipe out of his mouth and looked at it. "You are becoming my master instead of my servant," he said, and snapping it in pieces, he threw it into the fire. For years he never smoked again. Even nature, in its most violent form, found an affinity in him. An experience of later life which he thoroughly enjoyed, was an Atlantic crossing in weather so rough that all passengers except he and one other were confined in their cabins. He walked the decks in the teeth of the gale, glorying in God's wonders in the deep. It would not be difficult to imagine him in Pilgrim garb at the prow of the *Mayflower*, the clean salt wind blowing back his hair and beard, his eyes searching the western horizon. He seemed to live his life with a Bible in his hand, and his face toward a better world.

His wife, Elizabeth Fawn Brittan, was small, dainty and fastidious in her personal habits, and his counterpart in religious fervour and integrity. Her grandchildren remember her with real affection as their first tutor and monitor, and the untiring reader to them of such books as *Alice in Wonderland*, *Robinson Crusoe*, and *Westward Ho!*, for it seems that she did not wholly share her husband's aversion for fiction. "It was into that home," said Dr. Morgan, "that I was born."

As a child he was physically frail, and for this reason was not sent to school at the usual age, but taught at home, first by parents, and later by tutors. For companionship there was a sister Lizzie, four years his senior. Until her death, at the age of twelve, the pair were inseparable. The affection she lavished upon her little brother and the complete satisfaction they enjoyed in each other's society, must have been very strong. Time heals childish hearts quickly, and the years soften and obliterate the sense of loss; but in this case the scar always remained. When the boy of eight lost his sister and only playmate, his grief was so acute that he could not be comforted. All his life he remembered the night that he ran from the house to lie weeping on her grave, desiring nothing more than to join her in death. Pneumonia was difficult to fight in those days, and aided by physical frailty and little will to survive, almost claimed another victim. But God had a special need of this child, and like Samuel, he was called from sleep to the consciousness of a mission. Never again would he 'preach' to Lizzie and her dolls, but the experience which had been play, was even then beginning to crystallize into a burning resolve. In the years immediately following Lizzie's death he began to put away childish things. Yet he never lost the sensitivity of a child.

Those who knew him best, as father and grandfather, loved, in Dr. Morgan, his understanding of children. His love for his own children was yoked to a keen sense of his duty toward them which, especially in the case of four obstreperous boys, full of all the exuberance and mischief which his own childhood lacked to such a large extent, provoked him at times to 'take steps'—sometimes drastic ones—in situations with which their mother could not cope, and ended by sending them all off to boarding school. With his girls, who came after the boys, he was exceedingly tender and indulgent, partly because an older daughter had died at the age of two and a half, and also because he enjoyed their teasing, and ability to wind him around their fingers— a familiarity to which the boys never dared to approach. His grandchildren he frankly spoiled. "That's my privilege," he would say, "let their parents bring them up!" All children loved this tall man who spoke their language without pretence or condescension; who shed his pulpit dignity at a moment's notice to make funny faces at them, or play games on the floor. He who had known so little of childhood's right to fun and laughter, never seemed to have enough of it to satisfy the hunger of the early years. During the closing days of his life he was reading again the eternal stories of childhood— *Alice in Wonderland, Through the Looking Glass, Peter Pan;* and loved to listen on the radio to *The Children's Hour.* If life had robbed his youth of its proper due of carefree hours, it had recompensed him with the rare gift of a childlike heart, and a child's zest every morning, for the adventures of the day.

A new companion in the person of Frank Fifoot, aided the recuperation from illness. His coming helped to alleviate the sense of loss, and the boys formed a friendship which was to remain until Mr. Fifoot's death more than sixty years later. Capacity for friendship was one of Campbell Morgan's greatest attributes, and to this there are a cloud of witnesses.

Like John Buchan, he 'kept his friendships in good repair.' No life was richer in friends than his, and every life was rich which could claim him as a friend.

The Morgan family had, by this time, moved to Cheltenham, and George was enrolled in a boy's school as a day pupil.

School opened up a new vista of life for him. The need for association with boys of his own age was gratified, and to have his time almost completely filled with studies and outdoor sports was a new experience. In these days of modern education the schedule would be considered heavy, the discipline rigid, and the system severe; but to the boy who had been too closely confined, and too much saturated in adult thinking, it all came as refreshing and thirst-quenching. The spirit of mischief, and love of fun and jokes which had been, to a large extent suppressed, found expression. The young headmaster was but fifteen years his pupil's senior, but he was a teacher with a profound understanding of boys. He belonged to that generation of schoolmen whose code was based on the principle that plain living and high thinking, administered with austere justice, resulted in the highest possible degree of character. Few of the 'old school' are left, though they have worthy successors in our day, but their influence lingers in the lives of those they taught—those who, in their turn, have become famous in national and professional life, and in the lives of a multitude of others who have made up the bedrock of their contemporary society.

Mr. Joseph Leonard Butler was Principal and Headmaster of 'The Douglas Collegiate School for Young Gentlemen,' known in Campbell Morgan's time as 'Gratton House,' at Cheltenham in Gloucestershire. He was what is sometimes referred to as 'a born teacher,' which meant, in this case, that he was only really happy when he was teaching boys. It was said of him by those who *should* know best, that he was always in the most pleasant humour at the beginning of the school term, and became more and more difficult to live with as it neared its end, only surviving the vacations himself because he had set his pupils a 'holiday task.' This usually involved the reading of one of the novels of Dickens or Scott, and would provide the opportunity to start off the new term with an 'exam!' The fact that the boys' happiness in the process of education was not commensurate with his own, is not to say that they reached maturity unappreciative of his wise methods and unrelenting thoroughness.

Why they nicknamed him 'Johnnie' is shrouded in mystery. As has been intimated, he was quite a young man when Campbell Morgan went to him as a pupil, but even then, the authority of his calling vested him with dignity and set him apart. He thoroughly disapproved of any camaraderie between boys and master that bordered on familiarity. "You never took liberties with Johnnie," Dr. Morgan used to say, "—at least, not more than once!"

He sensed the waywardness of his youthful flock even when his back was turned upon them, an instinct which gave him, in their eyes, a most unfair advantage. Dr. Morgan sometimes referred to some of his own encounters with Mr. Butler, in which he admitted he came off second best. On one occasion he suggested to a group of boys that the placing of some beeswax on Mr. Butler's chair might have interesting results. The boys were not slow to concur in the scheme, and when Mr. Butler entered the classroom and took his seat, his class bestowed on him an unusual degree of interest and attention. At last the long expected and half dreaded moment arrived, and Mr. Butler, rising from his chair, discovered that the chair was rising with him! After separating himself from it, his eyes surveyed the rows of heads, bent in diligence over their books, and came to rest by some uncanny intuition upon the instigator of the crime. Dr. Morgan has said that he would rather have suffered physical punishment than the shame he felt at the quiet words of the master's censure. "Morgan," he said, "I am not surprised, but I am *very* disappointed." In that moment the very last thought in the culprit's mind would have been that, some day, he would entrust to this man, the education of his own four sons.

"As long as these boys live," Dr. Morgan used to say of them, "Johnnie Butler will never be dead!" One of life's enigmas is this—that the teacher who demands in our youth a respect amounting to awe, becomes the friend who will be held in affectionate memory as long as his pupils live. Wherever they congregate he is quoted and remembered, and their children are reared, for the most part unconsciously, on the traditions he established.

Mr. Butler distrusted the psychology that says that children should be praised for their efforts, and perhaps he did not realize enough that young minds are sometimes stimulated by encouragement. Be that as it may, he firmly believed in the stimulation of the mind in other ways, as one of Dr. Morgan's sons, in his day, had reason to discover. "Please, sir," he once ventured, "may I leave off Euclid? I'm sure I'll never need it." Mr. Butler took time to point out that the discipline of the mind which was stimulated by the study of mathematics, was of invaluable benefit in any walk of life. So John continued to take Euclid!

The slow and painstaking pupil received his patient and constant help, but what he called 'stupidity' was, to him, the lowest form of degeneracy. He did not suffer fools gladly, and sometimes, though rarely, caned a boy for 'impertinence.' The 'love' which 'beat on them with rods' was an affection past their youthful understanding, and the belief in 'exams', to which he adhered with almost religious fervour, they did not always share, either then or later. "I suppose exams are necessary," Dr. Morgan once wrote to a school teacher, "but I don't believe in them, and I don't think they are a revelation of knowledge."

Dr. Morgan became, in turn, one of the greatest teachers of his generation. He understood the psychology of teaching —that knowledge of one's subject is limited by the ability to impart it. He understood the patience that is every teacher's first requirement; the long waiting for results which, perhaps, he himself never sees. He knew the price paid in preparation and application, the daily discipline of the mind, the toil that precedes the achievement, the drudgery behind every success. He knew the reward of honest and enduring effort—the word spoken, perhaps years afterwards, that made him know that the labour was not in vain; the thanks in letters from all kinds and conditions of people in all kinds and conditions of places; the joy of knowing that, because of his teaching, others were teaching better, and good seed was bringing forth fruit—some a hundredfold.

Who can trace results back to their ultimate sources? We say, 'Here was a great teacher,' and sometimes forget that somewhere, and at some time the gift was discovered, and that someone else had a part in its awakening and development. Dr. Morgan, at least, appreciated this, and paid his homage to his own teacher, when, in a letter to Mrs. Butler at the time of her husband's death, he wrote: "Of your beloved husband I can only think and speak with profound thankfulness and respect, which amounts almost to veneration. He was to me one of God's great men. Surely he wore, through all the years, the white flower of a blameless life. In the unveilings of the life beyond, he will be told how great his influence has been. I owe him much, and I loved him."

* * * * * *

Campbell Morgan became the connoisseur of a good sermon at a very tender age. It was an era of great preaching. Eloquence and oratory in the pulpit were the rule rather than the exception. During the holidays the boy was taken, by his father, to hear many of those whose names, forgotten now, were then famous in religious circles. Some were Welshmen, who came out of their native hills with all the fire and intensity of the Old Testament prophets. The doctrines of the faith were expounded, and theological questions debated. Sinners were challenged and brought face to face with judgment and redemption. Congregations in those days came with good spiritual digestions, and expected to be fed with meat and not milk. The elder Morgan responded to it with every fibre of his soul, and emulated it in preaching to his own flock. Years later, in the United States, an echo of this type of preaching came to the attention of Dr. Morgan's son, Frank, who wrote to his father of the incident. He received the following comment in reply: "I am bound to say that my memory of some of the preaching of my childhood days makes me feel that it is quite likely to have happened." He said he remembered hearing his father give out with, as it seemed, perfect satisfaction, the hymn which began:

> My thoughts on awful subjects roll,
> Damnation and the dead;
> What horrors seize a guilty soul
> When on his dying bed?

An event of the greatest importance occurred in 1873, an event which moved England in her national as well as in her religious life, for it was in the summer of that year that Mr. D. L. Moody and his equally gifted companion, Mr. Ira D. Sankey, came on their first preaching mission. "I saw neither of them during that visit," Dr. Morgan says, "but, like thousands of others, came as a boy under the influence of the ministry of song." It was said of them that the vibration of their presence in any town ran through all the country. "Those vibrations found their way into our home and into my life," he continues. "I distinctly remember how my father was not quite sure of what this thing meant, but 'Ho, my comrades!' was ringing through the land in a way in which I certainly never remember any other sacred song doing. There came into our home a copy of the first little hymn book, containing twenty-three hymns. My father liked some of them, and we sang them in our home worship over and over again. That little hymn book has been long lost, much to my sorrow, but I think I could still name nearly the whole of the hymns in the order of their occurrence."

Mr Moody's preaching had tremendous effect upon England, and a great religious revival swept the country. The whole tone of preaching, too, was modified under his influence. God's hatred of sin was proclaimed with power, but with no less zeal, His unbounded love of the sinner. Dr. R. W. Dale, the great preacher and theologian, told Dr. Morgan in later years that he had known one man who, he felt, had a perfect right to talk about Hell, and that man was D. L. Moody. He stated that the reason he so felt was that he never heard Moody refer to Hell without tears in his voice.

Whatever may be the influences of his environment, a small boy soaks them up like a sponge. This child had lived his few years in an atmosphere of preaching. Plain living and an absence of almost all counter-attractions, few friends of his own age, together with a sensitive nature which had already felt the basic shock of loss, combined to make him thoughtful and introspective beyond his years. It is impossible not to believe that he possessed a natural gift for using words to express thought. He had played at preaching and found it good; not only good, but fun. "It was a great game," he once said, "and I have been at it ever since . . . not trifling . . . often strenuous . . . but it has always been playtime." Lizzie, his first audience, had paid him the compliment of her undivided attention and constant encouragement. It was a natural sequence then, that led to the next step. He must preach to people—not one, but many, a congregation of adult men and women. Somehow this desire found expression. It is to the everlasting credit of the good folk of the Monmouth Methodist Chapel that they took him as seriously as he took himself. A day was set, and a time was arranged. On August 27th, 1876, a little group of men and women, with boys and girls of his own age, took their seats on the hard wooden pews in the schoolroom of the Chapel, and gave their attention to the small figure behind the desk.

Whether it was a new sermon prepared for the occasion, or one which had been proved worthy before the home audience, is not known; but its subject, 'SALVATION,' reveals the effect of the type of preaching he had listened to so often. The Rev. Samuel Chadwick, a great preacher himself, paid this first sermon of Campbell Morgan's the compliment of saying that it was as perfect in structure as any that succeeded it. We are in debt to Mr. Harries for giving us the divisions of the message.

1. *A Great Salvation.* 'How shall we escape if we neglect so *great* a salvation?' (Heb. 2. 3).
2. *A Common Salvation.* 'I was giving all diligence to write unto you of our *common* salvation' (Jude 3).
3. *An Eternal Salvation.* 'He became unto all them that obey Him the Author of *eternal* salvation' (Heb. 5. 9).
4. *A Present Salvation.* 'Behold, *now* is the day of salvation' (2 Cor. 6. 2).

We know little more than that these simple-hearted Christians took the boy to their hearts and gave him their blessing. No stumbling-block of ridicule or indifference was put in his way, and neither did they make the mistake of trying to force a premature development by demanding more than he was able to give. It was some time before Campbell Morgan preached again. The desire had been satisfied. It was enough to know his ability, and also his limitation.

If there were a prophet in that congregation to foretell a great future for this child, it was not given to him to foresee the reward that was laid up for the little Monmouth Chapel. Sixty years later Dr. Morgan had returned to England, hailed as one of the world's outstanding Christian leaders, and as the greatest living Bible expositor. He had vindicated the promise of youth, and returned to his native land with honour. The young Methodist minister in Monmouth wrote to ask if he would come if they arranged an anniversary celebration, and preach from the same pulpit desk from which the first sermon had been delivered. The acceptance came and preparations began.

News of the coming event reached the Tabernacle Presbyterian Church in Philadelphia, Pennsylvania, which Dr. Morgan had served as minister for three years, and whose minister at that time was his youngest son, Howard. As an expression of their appreciation, and in recognition of his sixty years of preaching, the Tabernacle congregation and its pastor sent to the Monmouth Church a picture of Dr. Morgan wearing his pulpit robe, and bearing the following inscription: 'Dr. G. Campbell Morgan preached his first Sermon in this room in 1876. Presented by Tabernacle Presbyterian Church of Philadelphia, Pennsylvania, 1936.' It therefore added much to the pleasure of the Monmouth Church to learn that Dr. Howard Morgan was to be in England himself that same summer, and he was invited to attend the anniversary celebration, and to preach in the afternoon.

The adult members of the congregation of sixty years before had long since passed to their reward, and those who had been children then had gone their several ways. Only one was present who had heard that first sermon, and who remembered seeing the boy preacher standing up to deliver it. The same age as Dr. Morgan himself, he, too, had been thirteen years old upon that occasion. An honoured place was given to the old man of seventy-three, and special recognition afforded him.

The day's programme began with an afternoon service, at which Dr. Howard Morgan preached on 2 Peter 3. 18—the Christian ideal of the growth and development of life in the grace and knowledge of Christ. "I did not say it in so many words," he says, "but everyone present knew that I had Dad in mind. At one point he said 'Amen' very heartily, and afterwards commented on it—that it is possible to grow in knowledge without growing in grace."

No English celebration could be complete without 'tea,' and a social hour. As the time drew near for the evening service at which Dr. Morgan was himself to preach, the little chapel became filled to capacity, until every seat was taken, and many were standing around the walls of the building. The guest-preacher and his son, who was to read the Scripture and offer prayer, were waiting in the vestry with the young minister, when the latter said: "Dr. Morgan, as a part of our service to-night, we are having a special solo. I hope this meets with your approval."

Dr. Morgan frowned and spoke rather irritably. "I don't like vocal exhibitions," he said, "I would prefer to do without them."

But the minister valiantly stuck to his guns. "This will not be that kind of singing, sir," he said, "it is one of the young people of our own church, who, we think, has a very wonderful voice."

"In that case," said Dr. Morgan, "let us have the solo by all means."

The service proceeded until it was time for the special music. At this point the soloist, a boy of twelve, came and stood up in the pulpit. The organ began to play the introduction to the exquisite soprano solo from the *Messiah*—'Come unto Him, ye that labour.' With the first clear, high note, the bell-like voice of the boy floated in ethereal cadences to the rafters of the building, and filled it with pure melody. Every tone was true, and every syllable distinct. It was, indeed, as the minister had said, a wonderful voice. As the last lovely words: "And ye shall find rest unto your souls," died away softly into the silence, the aged, white-haired minister rose from his chair, and put his arm round the shoulders of the boy.

"Just one minute, laddie," he said, "how old are you?"

The boy replied in a round, pleasant voice: "Twelve years old, sir."

A lovely smile lighted the face that looked down into his. "Ah, yes, dear," said Dr. Morgan, "and I was just about your age, sixty years ago, when I preached my first sermon in this chapel. Be true to the gift God has given you," he continued, "and He will use you, as He has been pleased to use me."

With his arm still about the boy's shoulder, he turned to the congregation and said: "Let us pray," and prayed as only he could, commending "this lad and his talent to God for His glory." Dr. Howard Morgan in telling the incident says: "It was one of those impromptu moments which none who was present will ever forget."

CHAPTER II

1876-1888: 13 to 25 years

EVANGELISTIC SERVICES—YEAR OF ECLIPSE—TEACHING—MOODY AND SANKEY—TENT MEETINGS AND POPULAR LECTURES—ALBERT SWIFT—LEAVING THE JEWISH SCHOOL—HULL MISSION—SALVATION ARMY—REJECTION BY WESLEYAN MINISTRY—MARRIAGE

'Youth is the time of vision; of choices which create direction for all the coming days. . . . Youth is the time when life is rising to the full, when dreams are being dreamed . . . the time for building castles in the air, which precedes the actual strain and stress of endeavour; the time when holy, healthy ambition is singing its song to personality.'—(*'Great Chapters of the Bible,'* pp. 85-86).

IN later years Campbell Morgan was often cited as an example of a man who had never received a conventional education; who, never having been to College, sat upon two College faculties, and became the President of another. Yet it would be far from the truth to call the boy who graduated from Gratton House uneducated. Indeed, Mr. Butler saw to it that none of his students left him without the most thorough grounding he was capable of giving them in the basic principles of education. The examinations of the College of Preceptors in London, for which he prepared his pupils, and in which a remarkably high average passed with distinction, were no sinecure, and would be more than a match for some of our College students to-day.

This foundation, in Campbell Morgan, was yoked to a quick mind, and an insatiable desire for additional knowledge, which he acquired by reading, not only in youth but all through his life. A case in point is found in a letter in which he says: "At the age of twenty-five I was reading Wesley's Journal, and steeping myself in Kingsley, much to my advantage all my life."

A young minister once wrote him that he had difficulty in formulating his ideas and convictions into words. Dr. Morgan answered in a manner which showed his sympathy in the problem, and a desire to help in its solution. "Your difficulty is a real one. Of course, there are those who have a natural gift in this direction. Where this is lacking, a great deal may be done by reading some of the best masters, noticing carefully their method in the use of words and the formation of sentences. What is pre-eminently necessary is an enlarged vocabulary, and this such reading will help to supply. Let every new word be noted, and its true value learned. Where this is done with patience, it will be found in course of time that such words come naturally into use." The method was one which he himself had found helpful.

While still in school, Campbell Morgan realized that material circumstances at home would make it necessary for him to begin earning a living as soon as possible. He decided that his immediate destination must be the teaching profession, and began to work with this end in view. At the same time there was never any doubt in his mind that he must continue preaching also; to proclaim the Gospel seemed to him as natural as breathing itself. Mr. Butler understood this, and wisely did not deter his pupil, whenever the opportunity presented itself, from attending services in village chapels near Cheltenham, and taking part in them.

In these days a boy of fifteen who spent Sundays and part of his holidays preaching in country chapels to rustic congregations, might be considered odd—at the least precocious. It would be entirely misleading to give the impression here of a pale, bespectacled, anæmic youth, unhealthily averse to fun and exercise. Campbell Morgan entered wholeheartedly into school sports, and was the participator, and often the ringleader in practical jokes—a form of amusement which always delighted him. But there was iron in this boy's character which never let him turn aside from the goal towards which he knew he must travel. If by 'odd' we mean 'unmatched, single,' then he was odd, most certainly.

He knew himself to be 'peculiar' in the sense that Israel was God's 'peculiar' people. No pleasure could ever, for long, draw him from that which gave him the greatest pleasure —preaching. Boy-preachers, moreover, were not so uncommon in those days as in ours. The fathers of the Church took their parental responsibilities seriously. Attendance at the services of the church, Biblical training in the home, and family worship took hours out of the week. We look back condescendingly upon their age and call them narrow and bigoted. Campbell Morgan himself refers to the Victorian era as a period when 'youth was held within restrictions unnatural to itself.' But it made for high ideals, and a precocity in some natures which blossomed into an early maturity. It was not unusual for children to 'feel a call' to preach. Many of them, like hot-house plants, were 'untimely born' and soon forgotten. It is the evidence of the years which tells the story. Time was to make of this youngster —this paradox of fun and gravity, so impressionable and yet so unyielding—a man after God's own heart, an unmatched prophet with a message pertinent for his generation. For more than sixty long years, on two continents, his life was dedicated to be the sounding board of that message.

Let it not be imagined that such gifts, even in potentiality, were unrecognized by the teen-aged boy himself. He knew himself to be gifted in the use of words, and to be the possessor of a voice which was, in itself, a powerful agent in gaining and holding the attention of a group. Practice was already reaping rewards. The consciousness of power over others was like wine to him, and might have resulted in disaster, but for the instrumentality of a friend. A colporteur, David Smith by name, was considerably older than the boy he had accompanied from Cheltenham to Birdlip, a nearby hamlet, where the two were to conduct a cottage prayer-meeting.

In telling the story many years later, Dr. Morgan says: "David Smith conducted the meeting and I preached. I do not think that I dare now quote my text," he adds significantly, but he tells us that it was Isaiah 51. 6. He continues: "The walk home was by moonlight, and six miles long. It seemed longer, for David Smith made full use of it to point out to me the uselessness of speaking before people merely that they might be given an opportunity to discover my ability. I rebelled at first, but finally I was convinced. . . ." It was a stiff blow to the boy's self-confidence and pride. He returned home chastened and very thoughtful. But the kind intention and Christian spirit of his friend could not be misconstrued. Through the intervening weeks he spent much time in reflection and prayer. Some time later he returned with the same companion to the same cottage for another service. He took as his theme the words of Jesus: 'Come unto Me, all ye that labour and are heavy laden, and I will give you rest.' This time self was forgotten; the message of the text captured him so completely that he broke down, and was not able to finish. As a result, two or three of his listeners professed their faith in Christ. It was an experience he never forgot, and for which he never ceased to be grateful to David Smith.

Until he was sixteen years of age, Dr. Morgan declared it had never entered his mind to doubt the authority of the Bible. At home and in school it was held in reverence as the only revelation of truth. "I did not think," he said, "there could be any honest and respectable man who could doubt that the Bible was the Word of God. Then I went out into the work of training for teaching, and found myself plunged into a world of which I had no knowledge up to that time. . . . The whole intellectual world was under the mastery of the physical scientists, and of a materialistic and rationalistic philosophy. To quote names is enough—Darwin, Huxley, Tyndall, Spencer, Bain. I was as honest then as now, and gradually faith, while not undermined, was eclipsed. When the sun is eclipsed the light is not killed, it is hidden. There came a moment when I was sure of nothing."

A mark of this materialistic philosophy showed itself in what were called 'Secularist Halls,' which sprang up in many of the cities of England. In these halls lectures were delivered on Sundays, directly attacking the Bible and the Christian religion. Charles Bradlaugh was the leader of this movement, and a similar one, under Robert Ingersoll, flourished in the United States.

Even within the Church itself, theological and doctrinal questions were being argued with intensity and bitterness.

For three years this young man, seriously contemplating a future of teaching and ultimately of preaching, felt the troubled waters of the stream of religious controversy carrying him beyond his depth. He read the new books which debated such questions as, 'Is God Knowable?' and found that the authors' concerted decision was, 'He is not knowable.' He became confused and perplexed. No longer was he sure of that which his father proclaimed in public, and had taught him in the home.

Other books appeared, seeking to defend the Bible from the attacks which were being made upon it. The more he read the more unanswerable became the questions which filled his mind. One who has never suffered it cannot appreciate the anguish of spirit young Campbell Morgan endured during this crucial period of his life. Through all the after years it gave him the greatest sympathy with young people passing through similar experiences at college—experiences which he likened to 'passing through a trackless desert.' At last the crisis came when he admitted to himself his total lack of assurance that the Bible was the authoritative Word of God to man. He immediately cancelled all preaching engagements. Then, taking all his books, both those attacking and those defending the Bible, he put them all in a corner cupboard. Relating this afterwards, as he did many times in preaching, he told of turning the key in the lock of the door. "I can hear the click of that lock now," he used to say. He went out of the house, and down the street to a bookshop. He bought a new Bible and, returning to his room with it, he said to himself: 'I am no longer sure that this is what my father claims it to be—the Word of God. But of this I *am* sure. If it *be* the Word of God, and if I come to it with an unprejudiced and open mind, it will bring assurance to my soul of itself.' "That Bible *found* me," he said, "I began to read and study it then, in 1883. I have been a student ever since, and I still am (in 1938)."

At the end of two years Campbell Morgan emerged from that eclipse of faith absolutely sure that the Bible was, in very deed and truth, none other than the Word of the living God. Quoting again from his account of the incident: " . . . This experience is what, at last, took me back into the work of preaching, and into the work of the ministry. I soon found foothold enough to begin to preach, and from that time I went on."

With this crisis behind him and this new certainty thrilling his soul, there came a compelling conviction. This Book, being what it was, merited all that a man could give to its study, not merely for the sake of the personal joy of delving deeply into the heart and mind and will of God, but also in order that those truths discovered by such searching of the Scriptures should be made known to a world of men groping for light, and perishing in the darkness with no clear knowledge of that Will.

Just about this time, Campbell Morgan took a position as Junior Teacher in a Wesleyan School for boys in Birmingham. His term of office here was short, however, for a most important step in his own education, though he was quite unaware of it at the time, was just around the corner. Nevertheless, his association with the Wesleyan School is worth comment, in that it echoed across forty years and three thousand miles. A letter from Ottawa, Ontario, in 1924, to a member of his family, has this statement: "I am enclosing a sketch of me which appeared in the paper here on Saturday. It is particularly interesting to me because it is written by a man named Checkland, whose brother, Jesse Checkland, was a boy I taught forty years ago in the Islington Wesleyan Day School in Birmingham."

It was, indeed, a strange pathway which opened up at the turn of the road for this young man who had so recently found a new foothold on faith, and a new comprehension of 'the fulness of Christ'; the youth whose 'new' Bible was still new in regard to its date of purchase but had fulfilled a purpose which had been fore-ordained from the beginning. It had convinced him that Christ was 'the One of Whom Moses in the law, and the prophets did write.' . . . The new pathway led through the door of a Jewish school.

★ ★ ★ ★ ★ ★

E. Lawrence Levy, Principal of the Jewish Collegiate School for Boys in Birmingham, had been trained as a rabbi. When an appointment as Assistant Master in his school became vacant, Campbell Morgan, still in his teens, applied for it and was accepted. To the young student with a natural gift for teaching, any opportunity to exercise it would have been grasped with enthusiasm. There was, however, an added incentive in being associated with one who held the key to a knowledge of the Hebrew Scriptures—those very writings which he longed so much to understand. During the three years of their association, a close friendship was formed between the old Hebrew and his assistant, and Campbell Morgan's interest in Old Testament literature was stimulated and encouraged.

The school, in accordance with its tradition, and in addition to other scholastic attainments, prepared the Jewish students for their Bar-mitzvah. Under the Principal's supervision, much of the work of reviewing the home training in Hebrew law was delegated to the assistant teacher. In Dr. Morgan's volume on *The Gospel According to Luke*, and in dealing with a passage found in Chapter Two, the story of the Boy in the Temple, there comes an echo of this teaching experience. "Let us examine the picture of the Boy in the Temple," he says, " . . . The Jewish boy of devout parents at that period, comes to his Bar-mitzvah . . . bar, son; mitzvah, commandment; that is, son of the law. From that time he assumed responsibility himself. Here, Jesus, either precipitated His own bar-mitzvah by going to the *didaskaloi*, the teachers; or

else He went in as a Disciple, already a Son of the Law. . . .
They talked to Him, and taught Him, and asked Him questions.
He answered them, and they listened in amazement. Then
He did what every Disciple had a right to do—asked them
questions arising out of the religious training He had received
at home; and still they were amazed. . . . They had never had
a boy like that before."

The Great Physician, a series of sermons on Christ's method
of dealing with individuals, is a rich source of information
on Jewish custom and tradition. We find here such particulars
as the exact meaning of the New Testament phrase, 'the
law and the prophets'; the fine distinction drawn between
'Jew' and 'Hebrew'; the word 'Isra-El,' and its significance
to the Hebrew people; the careful tracing of Christ's genealogy
in the Gospels. We have read scores of times that Nicodemus
was 'a Pharisee . . . a ruler of the Jews,' but Dr. Morgan
does not allow his readers to pass over such a statement as
incidental. Nicodemus takes on a new dignity and interest
when we learn what these statements mean. We do not
normally think of the woman at the well as having a religious
background, yet Dr. Morgan explains that her references to
'the Messiah' and 'our father, Jacob,' reveal more than appears
on the surface. At this point he takes time out to review the
history of Israel, and show the beginning of the animosity
between Jews and Samaritans. The status and social position
of a publican in the days of Christ give colour to the character
studies of Matthew and Zacchæus. It is somewhat of a
surprise to be told that, though Matthew 'may have been
looked upon by his contemporaries as a renegade' because
of his occupation, 'we may safely deduce the fact that he was
a profoundly religious man.' Why? We are pointed to
his own Gospel (with which we supposed ourselves familiar!)
and shown Matthew's remarkable knowledge of the Scriptures
of the Hebrew people, not only quoting from the Old Testament more than the other three evangelists put together, but
quoting from every division of them—the Torah (or law),
the Nebiim (or prophets), and the Kethubim (or writings),

and applying this knowledge to Jesus throughout every event concerning His life and death, constantly using the phrase, 'that it might be fulfilled,' always placing His story against the background of Old Testament history.

So one might go on. Place *The Great Physician* back on the bookshelf. Pick up another book, and yet another. Illustrations, almost without number, show Campbell Morgan's intense comprehension of Jewish custom and law. Like a bright thread, it weaves itself through all his work. Like a lamp it illumines obscure texts. The dead past comes to life with a vitality which colours history as it pertains to to-day, and gives us a sympathy and discernment of the unhappy Jewish struggle for identity and recognition.

During the years of residence in Athens, Georgia, Dr. Morgan counted as his friends members of the most influential Hebrew families in that city. Orthodox Jews—one a reader in the local synagogue—were often to be found in the congregation when Dr. Morgan was preaching in Athens. It is not difficult to believe that they were drawn there by the preacher's understanding of their Scriptures, and his constant appeal to them. What an influence was exerted by his consistent iteration that the Hebrew writings find fulfilment only in Christ, may be seen in something that was said to Dr. Morgan's eldest son by one of them. "If I believed what you believe," he said, "I would not rest till I had told everyone about it!"

One can well imagine that, in his delineation of Matthew, Dr. Morgan may have had Mr. Levy, his Hebrew friend and teacher in mind when he says: "The fact that he was a Hebrew means that he was characterized by a justifiable pride, and an understandable narrowness. These things are true of all the Hebrews. It is true of the Hebrew people to-day. Every Hebrew is proud, justifiably so, of his race, his history, of all the marvellous past. It stands out as an amazing fact that whatever may be the tyranny employed against him, the neck of the Hebrew is never bowed or bent. That, in certain ways is an excellent quality. We are cursed to-day with a passion for breadth. A little more narrowness would strengthen the whole host of the people of God."

* * * * * *

1883 was the year of Mr. D. L. Moody's second visit to England, and included a three weeks' mission in Birmingham. At this time Campbell Morgan's desire to see and hear him was gratified, and no volunteer worked harder than he for the success of the mission. It must have cost much of physical and spiritual strength to teach all day in the school, attend the services of the Mission in the evening, and afterwards, as a worker in the 'enquiry room,' help seekers to find the truth. But it was work he loved and a service which was all pure joy. Mr. Sankey's contribution of song made a very great impression, as we gather from his own recollections of those soul-stirring days. "It often causes me great surprise," he says, "that so little is said of that second visit to England of Moody and Sankey. . . . Indeed, I have heard those speak of the second visit as though, by comparison with the first, it was almost a failure. I am only able to judge by participation in the second, and of that, by the work in Birmingham; and also by the fact that, in talking over the matter with Mr. Moody, he told me that in Bingley Hall, in 1883, he saw wonders wrought which in his conviction, came nearer to the happenings at Pentecost than anything he ever saw in his life.

"The hall would not accommodate anything like the multitudes that crowded together, and the Town Hall and several churches in the vicinity were used for overflow meetings. While Moody preached in Bingley Hall, Sankey went round in a cab or carriage lent by some friend, to the other meetings, singing at each in turn. He would return to the central meeting in time to help in the enquiry room, which he did with great delight and profit. I only spoke to him once or twice during those busy days, but his greeting was always hearty and affectionate. In many happy hours since we have yarned together of those great Birmingham days. The first impression made by his singing has never left me, and in after years, hearing him sing often, and over and over again in my own meetings, I never had any cause to change my estimate of him, or my conviction of the secret of his power. Ira D. Sankey was never a performer; he was a prophet in song. He was not a musician anxious to attract attention to himself; he was a minister of Jesus Christ, determined to direct attention to his Master. By nature gifted with a voice of remarkable strength and sweetness, by the grace of God that gift was consecrated and used to the glory of the Lord in ways of which he never dreamed in his earlier years."

The Moody mission came into Campbell Morgan's life at the right moment to dispel any doubts that might still remain in his mind. The months that followed it were full and happy ones. Teaching in a congenial atmosphere, conscious of the friendship of his Hebrew colleague and grasping every chance of learning from him, on Sundays and holidays he was free to preach in mission halls and country villages. "My memory goes back to the early days of my work," he wrote in 1938, "and the real delight there was in services in village chapels. Indeed, I often feel to-day a great sort of hunger to be able to do that again."

Sometime during the three years spent in teaching in the Jewish school in Birmingham, another friendship was formed which was to be of a lifetime's duration. Mr. and Mrs. Walter D. Welford, a young married couple, had just opened up a photography establishment in Birmingham. To-day Mrs. Welford lives in Brighton, on England's South Coast, and she has co-operated most helpfully by putting into writing some of her reminiscences of more than sixty years ago.

"My husband and I had recently opened a studio on the Hagley Road," she writes. "One day while there, my husband came to me and said we had a caller, a teacher from the Jewish School, asking for terms for taking photographs of the school's football groups. It proved to be an important moment in the lives of all three of us—much more important than we dreamed of. The young man, tall and spare, possessing a presence of magnetic personality, distinction and bearing, was no less than the future exponent of the Bible, Dr. G. Campbell Morgan.

"My artistic photography had attracted his attention, and we became friendly at once. Prices settled, I invited him to take tea with us, and we had a chatty tea of buttered muffins. The two boys, my husband and Mr. Morgan (as he was then), having similar tastes and outlook, seemed delighted with each other. Next day he came to give the photographic order, and again we invited him to tea, when the merry-go-round was repeated. These visits continued for four days, at the end of which time Mr. Morgan's darling little mother called to apologize for her son's trespass on our hospitality. We assured her that we were delighted. I said that the boys enjoyed each other's society, their views coincided, and I found them most interesting to listen to.

"Just about that time Mrs. Morgan opened a school in her home. Our little Olive and Ruby were too young to walk so far, so we bought them a bright little red mail-cart for two—a back-to-back affair, quite new in those days. The two little girls in their navy blue costumes brought other pupils to Mrs. Morgan's school, so attractive were the occupants of the brilliant equipage.

"We had a large garden with apple trees dotted about, and in one corner a great pear tree a hundred years old. Nearer the house was our roomy studio, nearly covering the width of the garden. My husband had a large tent in the garden with a Union Jack flying from the top. During the summer Mr. Morgan used this tent for religious services. After tea had been handed round, people took their places in the tent. A prayer would begin the meeting, followed by one of Moody and Sankey's joyous hymns. Somewhere I have a photograph of the group, every face aglow, as Mr. Morgan welcomed them, bidding them come again. The people felt he could do no wrong, even though his progressive teachings were at times somewhat startling to their orthodox upbringing. They were much impressed. One of the party made a speech of appreciation of Mr. Morgan's power of bringing out new resolves. He also paid a kind reference to our hospitality. I can see them now, gathered together praying to the heavenly Father for His blessing.

"In the nearby village of Ironbridge there was an elderly man whose name, I believe, was Williams, and who was the only grocer, draper, butcher, and seller of hardware goods. He offered meals and beds to Mr. Morgan and my husband, and allowed them to fix a tent for their meetings in his adjacent field. There it stood, a fine, big white tent, with a flag flying from the top, so attractive that it brought people to see what it was all about. It was such a novelty, and quite new to Ironbridge. The old man was very pleased about it all, and arranged for me to stay in the spotless home of a widow, Mrs. Price. She had an income of ten shillings a week, which she increased by selling oddments, such as tapes, reels of cotton, stay-laces, matches, etc., all displayed in her parlour window. On one occasion she went away for the day, and the two youths decided to have some sport in her well-ordered home. They turned all the home-made rugs upside down, all the pictures back to front, and a treasured relic—a beautiful open-work brass fender—wrong side up. The boys thought it a grand opportunity for frolicsome sport. One wonders what else they had thought to do, when I whispered: 'The Vicar is just passing the window!' The next second the portly Reverend rapped at the door and walked in. Good-mornings were said with blank faces, and then neither he nor the youths spoke a word, until at last the Vicar expressed himself on weather topics and the prospect of the coming harvest, and other items of general conversation. Eventually he left, and the task of transforming Mrs. Price's well-ordered home to rights was begun, whilst I saw that every picture was perfectly hung and in orderly fashion before she returned from her little holiday. All at once the boys rushed to the window to remove a card which said: 'Widow wants washing with Hudson's dry soap!' They had forgotten this part of their little joke, but they were just in time before Mrs. Price's return. She would certainly have considered it most unforgivable! I am sure I should have protested about their practical joke, but felt I must not put a wet blanket on their youthful spirits.

"Near to Ironbridge was a giant oak tree, which it was considered to be an achievement to climb. Nothing daunted, Mr. Morgan tackled it, and climbed to an overhanging branch. He was in holiday attire, wearing white trousers, a bright striped blazer, and a scarlet tam-o-shanter with a boss on top. While still up in the tree, my husband persuaded him to pose for a photograph, while I leaned against the trunk below.

"Never in all my long life have I met a youth who, so full of fun, was also so full of resolve to proclaim the thought of God's love. He loved the lowly in heart, and could see trust and faith in every living soul, and never made a mistake. His kindness was one of the key-notes of his fame. No matter how humble the station in life, here was a man to encourage, uplift and befriend, and he never faltered in his noble resolve. It was wonderful to watch the influence he created. His simple yet powerful words went straight to the heart. He won the confidence and admiration of all.

"Later, with great power, he conducted a huge Mission in Hull. Then he went to London, and his fame was assured. As years went by he received an urgent call to go to America. This had a magnetic effect on the U.S.A. On his return to London again he reached the height of his fame. The people loved him better than ever, and showed him this at every turn. His church was crowded to capacity, and many people had to be refused for want of seats.

"Though he spent so many years in America, and we saw him seldom, our friendship remained, up to the time of his death, as true as steel."

This happy association with the Welfords found another outlet for their combined talents. In addition to the tent services in the summer, they devised a series of popular lectures, illustrated by lantern slides, and an ingenious adjunct to the camera known as a 'pandiscope,' whereby the artist could sketch pictures on the slide. While it could not be said that they were the unwitting originators of the moving picture industry, it will be granted that they had enough originality and energy, from a copy of the bill which advertised their efforts. It is written in Mr. Welford's beautiful copper-plate handwriting on a large sheet of pink paper. The bill read as follows:

>43 HAGLEY ROAD,
>>EDGBASTON,
>>>BIRMINGHAM.

Messrs. G. CAMPBELL MORGAN and WALTER D. WELFORD are prepared to give their

POPULAR LECTURES
Illustrated by Lantern Views, and the Pandiscope
(or Lantern Sketcher)
To Institutions, Clubs, Schools, etc., also on behalf of charitable objects.

Overleaf will be found a list of their *special and original lectures*, and in addition, Messrs. Morgan and Welford can give Temperance, Scriptural, Comic Tales and Pictures, and other subjects for young folk.

Any one of the lectures mentioned overleaf will provide a *capital evening's entertainment*, and at the close, or during an interval, when the time permits, comic and movable pictures, local scenery and photographs are introduced.

Terms, which are extremely moderate, may be had on application to Mr. Welford (address as above), to whom all communications should be addressed.

A reduction will be made for two or more Lectures.
Lecturer—G. CAMPBELL MORGAN.   *Exhibitor*—WALTER D. WELFORD

('Overleaf' was the itemized list of specialities):

NOSE-OLOGY
(THE SCIENCE OF NOSES)

An interesting and amusing lecture on characteristic noses. The noses are sketched by the aid of the pandiscope, or lantern sketcher, a very clever novelty which attracts great attention wherever shown. The screen is presented dark, and the sketch unfolds itself as drawn by the exhibitor.

CHARACTERS FROM DICKENS
Illustrated by photographs from original ideal sketches, presenting some of the characters in *Pickwick Papers*, *Nicholas Nickleby*, *David Copperfield*, etc., as original conceptions. The lecture deals with the characters only.

A RAMBLE WITH A PHOTOGRAPHER
Various pictures of scenery, animals, portraits, buildings, and humorous subjects, from actual photographs taken. This is a good evening's entertainment.

CYCLING CAMP LIFE
From photographs taken at the North of England Cyclist's Meet and Encampment at Harrogate, Yorkshire. This lecture deals with the life of bicyclists and tricyclists under canvas, illustrated by views of tents, racing, early morning pictures, groups, etc.

N.B.—A Syllabus of any of the above Lectures will be provided on application.

'Nose-ology' sounds quite hilarious, but 'Cycling Camp Life,' and 'A Ramble with a Photographer,' might tend to even the balance by striking a less frivolous note. In any case, we may rest assured that those who met the 'extremely moderate terms' must have enjoyed 'a good evening's entertainment.'

* * * * * *

In 1885 Campbell Morgan began keeping a diary. It is characteristic of him that this daily record was systematically continued for more than sixty years. Time, which brings change to almost every other aspect of life, is peculiarly lenient to calligraphy. The neat and beautiful handwriting in which these first records are kept, is almost identical with that of the last. In the long narrow old diaries of those earliest years, the space allotted to each day's entry is limited, and, for the most part, the writing becomes so small as to be almost illegible without the aid of a magnifying glass—for those were full and eventful days. Teaching and supervising school sports, he returned home in the afternoon, often to help his mother with her little pupils, planning the next day's work, or correcting examination papers. Evenings almost invariably found him in some nearby chapel, at a cottage prayer meeting, or at a Salvation Army service. We find such entries as these:

"In the evening I crossed the fields and had tea with Harry B—. After this we went to the meeting, and as it was a dark night, I expected very few. But the Lord disappointed me, and we had more than we have had any week night. I spoke on 'The Grace of God,' and three precious souls found peace in believing."

"I went round this evening with a bell announcing the meetings."

"Close after midnight I went to see James B—. I remained until three o'clock when he passed away. The first death-bed scene I have witnessed, and a very solemn one it was."

There is the account of a meeting arranged for miners. "By permission of the manager I went down the shaft, a depth of eight hundred and forty feet. The men who work down there ought to be well paid."

Sundays were the busiest days of the week and the most enjoyed. Though the young schoolmaster really loved his work with the boys, and entered into their play as well, he was looking forward and planning every week for the coming Sunday, and a fresh opportunity to preach. The Sunday entries rarely recorded less than four services. One in July, 1886, notes seven Salvation Army meetings:

"Prayer meeting this morning at 7. Open-air at 10. Inside at 11. In the afternoon, open-air at 2. Inside at 3. Open-air at 5.30. Inside at 6.30. Good meetings all day. The power of God was very present with us."

One wonders how he maintained such a schedule, and is not surprised to read of continual references to colds and sore throat. The climate was not the most conducive to a programme which called for speaking in the open air, and it was during this time that a throat trouble developed which was to become chronic as the years passed, and is often referred to as 'my old enemy.' It culminated in a major operation in 1900. When this affliction prevented attendance at a service, faith had to fight against discouragement and depression. Nothing reduced his naturally gay spirits to such a degree of dejection as the cancellation of a preaching engagement. From these earliest days the stoutest thread in the pattern of character is the conviction he shared with St. Paul —'This one thing I do.' Greatness builds on obsession—

a refusal to be turned aside from the narrow path which leads to the aspired goal. 'I MUST preach,' was the motif of the symphony of his life from the very beginning. "I remained at home alone," he writes on an occasion when his father had gone to take his place at a service; but adds, characteristically underlining each word: "alone—*yet not alone.*" Never again was faith eclipsed and the sun blotted out, however dark the clouds.

But boundless energy, mental and physical, were on the side of youth. Following a period of illness in May, 1885, Mr. Levy suggested a week's leave from school for a complete rest and change, and Campbell Morgan and a friend decided to go to London. This is the first visit to 'town' of which we have any record, and it seems to have been thoroughly enjoyed.

Charles Haddon Spurgeon was at the height of his power, and to his Tabernacle they went on Sunday, later to hear Canon Holland in St. Paul's Cathedral. The week's activities included visits to the British Museum, Madame Tussaud's Waxworks, Westminster Abbey and the Horse Guards, 'a sail down the Thames,' a cricket match, and an unsuccessful attempt to attend a sitting of the House of Commons.

Dr. Joseph Parker's Thursday noonday meeting at the City Temple, as famous then as the Westminster Friday night Bible School of later years, was also included. The week's programme ended by attendance at a debate on 'Why rob the poor man of his beer?' in which "we both took part," and in the breaking of a carriage window on the return journey to Birmingham!

The boys welcomed him back at the school, and cricket became an important item on the summer programme. Saturdays found Morgan and his friends on tricycle excursions, bowling, swimming, and rowing on the river.

Vacation time again opened up the opportunity to deliver the 'Tent Lectures'; and in addition to 'Rambles with a Photographer' there were new lectures on 'Savonarola,' and 'Billy Bray,' the latter an illiterate but inimitable Cornish evangelist who exerted a great influence on Methodism in the early nineteenth century. "I spoke for an hour and three quarters on Billy Bray," he writes, "the people seemed delighted. I have promised them another lecture soon."

All during the summer of 1885 the decision to give his whole life to the Gospel ministry was being given the greatest consideration and thought. It was not easy to cut loose entirely from a steady financial income, neither was the way yet clear to do so. The autumn days of 1885 found him back in the classroom, but using every opportunity to hold evangelistic services in nearby towns and villages.

A meeting at this time with a young student, by name Albert Swift, proved an important event, because this friendship was to become, above all others, a tie which would influence all the years to follow. Swift was studying at Cambridge, but in the vacations and whenever possible the two were together, drawn to each other in that David and Jonathan affinity which is as rare as it is beautiful.

Meanwhile Campbell Morgan spoke upon every occasion which came his way, whether debating, lecturing or preaching, for all was grist to his mill. He records a debate on the subject, 'That England will decay, as the great nations of antiquity have done.' He took the negative side, but it was another friend, Tom Archer, who proved the hero on this occasion. "He made a fine patriotic speech, carrying all before him. We won by 24 to 18. Hurrah for Tommy and old England!"

As Spring wore on into the summer of 1886, the feeling that he must cut himself adrift from all other occupations and give his whole time to preaching, grew more and more persistent. It was not that he was unhappy at the school. He was popular with the boys, and his relationship with Mr. Levy was always one of mutual goodwill and harmony. Some inner driving force was goading him relentlessly to take a step from which he shrank, because he saw in it no financial security, and for which he had had no theological training. For himself he was not concerned, but for the parents who were partially dependent upon him, and would become more so as time went on. At last matters reached their climax. The dramatic scene which closed Campbell Morgan's professional relationship with Mr. Levy can best be told in his own words.

"All my Sundays, and all my vacations from school I was preaching in evangelistic work; and it was laid upon me that I *must*, that it was God's will, that I should give myself wholly to that work. I had qualifications for teaching, and might have gone on with that. I did not see any door open to me in the ministry. There came a night when, through all the hours, I was alone with God about it. The end of it was that I said, I cannot do it. I dare not do it. The future is so insecure. I cannot give myself to this work unless somehow I am forced out into it. If the door opens in any way I will do it.

"I went to school next morning, and the principal, Mr. Levy, said to me during the recess: 'I want a chat with you at the close of the morning session.' At that time I went in, and he said: 'Morgan, I am awfully sorry about what I have to tell you.' I said: 'What is wrong, sir?' 'Well,' he said, 'my school will have to be closed soon, and I am having to cut down expenses. I am sorry that I shall have to part with you.'

"That was the very morning after the night of wrestling. 'Don't hurry,' he said, 'but as soon as you can find another position, go to it.'

"I said: 'Thank you, sir. I will go at the end of the term.'

"'Don't take it unkindly,' he said anxiously.

"I looked at him. 'You are a Hebrew,' I said, 'may I tell you a story?' And I told him what had happened the night before.

"He listened attentively. Then, taking my hand in his, he said, with a voice full of passion: 'The God of Abraham is not dead. Go, and be blessed!'"

The influence of the Jewish School and its Principal can never be measured, for it not only inspired in Campbell Morgan a lifetime of research and study, but, through his own Bible teaching, prompted countless others to search and understand the Scriptures. Lawrence Levy was a Jew, and had not embraced the Christian faith, but, like the prophets of his people, he contributed to his generation, under God, more than he knew, and was willing to concede to His infinite wisdom what he could not comprehend.

★ ★ ★ ★ ★ ★

Once a decision had been made it was never Campbell Morgan's habit to retrace his steps. God had closed the doorway to academic teaching he firmly believed; the direction for the future would be shown. He thought to have discovered it, when in August, 1886, he wrote: "I here chronicle my strong determination to enter the Salvation Army."

Gipsy Smith, who was to become one of the world's most famous evangelists, had just completed a meeting in Hull. In a strategic part of the city, amid the dwellings of the poor and underprivileged, a large shooting gallery, capable of seating two thousand people, had been converted into a preaching centre for the young gipsy preacher. His own humble origin, and genuine concern and love for those in the lower strata of society, drew these people to him. He sang his way into their hearts, and won them with his sincerity, and many 'who came to scoff remained to pray.' The Salvation Army, in entire sympathy with his work, felt that it should be followed up immediately, and asked Campbell Morgan to conduct a two-week's mission in the same hall. It was not easy to follow a young man of such reputation as the Gipsy, but Campbell Morgan was fast building up a reputation of his own. His power of holding an audience, and of adapting himself to new situations was put to the test in this new challenge, and evidenced by the fact that he stayed in Hull, not two weeks but thirteen months. "Looking back on that time, I feel that it was one of the most valuable experiences of my life," he writes, "it revealed to me the power of the Gospel and of preaching. Ever since those days I have known from actual experience that there is no sin that cannot be conquered, no moral poison that cannot be eradicated by the power of Jesus Christ." The beautiful West Country with its lanes and flowery fields was a sharply contrasting memory behind this picture of misery, poverty, and ugliness in which he laboured during days which knew no limit of hours. But the spiritually hungry people who came night after night to listen, found that this young preacher had the food they wanted in the Word of God, and saw its power to salvage their broken lives. All his ability became concentrated in his work, which he performed with a zest, and pursued with an interest quite beyond his physical endurance. He learned by hard experience that the laws of health cannot be violated with impunity. Crowded services, from which hundreds at times were turned away, followed sometimes by 'half-nights' of prayer, left him physically exhausted, and lowered resistance opened the way for the 'old enemy' which attacked his throat. He learned, too, that to eat sparingly, especially before a service, was for him the best practice. "I suffered in my speaking to-night from eating a good dinner. D.V., no more of them!" he wrote in 1886, and obeyed this rule rigidly for the rest of his life.

Campbell Morgan had been in Hull four months when he met Gipsy Smith for the first time, and another friend was bound to his heart 'with hoops of steel.' He possessed an intuitive instinct for friendship and trusted it completely. It was as though the bow of his life touched the strings of other lives, and recognized those that were attune to its touch. Perhaps it will not be out of place to record here that none who was present will ever forget the words of the old Gipsy when he first heard the news of Campbell Morgan's homegoing. Quietly, and with tears in his eyes he said: "Sixty years of friendship, and never a ripple between us!"

It was natural that he should confide to this new friend his ambitions and hopes for the future, relating the events which had led him to give his life to the ministry, and the challenge of the work of the Salvation Army. There were aspects of it that appealed very strongly to him, and, on the other hand, there were conditions which he was not prepared to accept. The Gipsy was inclined to feel that Campbell Morgan, like himself, could do his best work alone, and the influence of this exchange of confidences carried weight. But it was his own little mother who was instrumental in deciding the final outcome. A few days after the conversation with the Gipsy he records, at the end of a day's entry in his diary: "I made it a special matter of prayer to-night as to my future, requesting an answer by post." The next morning there arrived in the post a letter from his mother. The contents of that letter are not revealed. All we know is that "Mother's letter is the answer to last night's prayer." Campbell Morgan revoked his first resolve to unite with the Salvation Army, because he believed that in doing so he was following the pathway of the divine Will. It must never be construed as an indication that he was out of sympathy with the Army's work, or with its great leader, whom he always held in esteem. A picture of General Booth hung in his study for many years, and whenever the occasion presented itself, he supported and aided the work, both morally and materially.

★ ★ ★ ★ ★ ★

The requirement for the Wesleyan Methodist ministry in those days was that candidates should first submit to an examination, which, if passed successfully, would authorize them to become lay preachers. The other qualifications needed, in order to become eligible for the ministry itself, involved the preaching of a 'trial sermon' before qualified examiners. Though young in years, Campbell Morgan had had an unusual amount of experience as a preacher, and the months as evangelist in Hull had demonstrated his ability to capture and hold the attention of a congregation. This latter part of the examination held no terrors for him. The former, on the other hand, brought home a consciousness of a lack of education along theological lines, but if this could be remedied by reading and study, he was willing to try.

December, 1887, was the date set for the preliminary test, and beginning in October he set himself an intensive course of reading, and stuck to it with thoroughness and determination, sometimes spending six hours at a time in study. On December 12 he sat for the 'Local Preacher's' examination and passed it successfully. The next objective—to preach the 'trial sermon.' Should the candidate pass this goal, it was then recommended that he take a course at a theological college. How the latter was to be managed Campbell Morgan did not know, for since relinquishing his teaching appointment he had no steady income. However, exceptions were made in some cases, and it might be possible, for a time, to undertake active ministerial work provided the examination could be passed successfully.

Campbell Morgan was one of a hundred and fifty young men who sought entrance to the Wesleyan ministry that year, and he was instructed to report at the Lichfield Road Church, in Birmingham, on May 2nd, 1888. It was a large building, with a seating capacity of a thousand. In the vestry, sharpening a pencil, was one of the three ministers who had been deputized to report on his sermon. It looked as though he meant business, and the young man's heart sank as he realized that this was not going to savour any of the inspiration of an evangelistic meeting. Things looked even less promising as the examiner turned to him and said: "Now I am ready for *you!*" But it was when the candidate stepped into the pulpit that the biggest blow fell. The seventy-five people before him, lost in the vast auditorium, regarded him with a critical eye which seemed to say: "Make good, or we shall make short work of you!"

All through his life Campbell Morgan was sensitive to atmosphere, and acutely conscious of numbers. The former lessened as the years passed because he became increasingly able to create his own atmosphere, and because his reputation so largely cancelled out the necessity for doing so. But the consciousness of numbers remained always with him. From the earliest days he was in the habit of noting carefully the attendance at services. A large congregation inspired him; empty pews dampened his spirit. Some would call it a flaw or a weakness of character and perhaps it was, for he was known to have cancelled an engagement because people did not seem to want him, and even left a pastorate largely because of the fact that the empty seats were an indication to him that his work was not appreciated. "Numbers are not everything, but they certainly are indicative," he once wrote in a letter, and repeated it many times in one way or another during the course of his active ministry But there was always another conviction which qualified this consciousness of numbers, and, also stated in many different ways, carried the same thought: "I am quite happy and at rest . . . feeling sure that the divine Will will be made clear about the future." "One step at a time is enough." "Everything is right which is within the 'covenant, ordered of all things, and sure.'" "I am at the King's disposal—and He will show His Will, I have no doubt." "The backward look over the mosaic of the years fills me with confidence that I shall be guided aright." If numbers were few, or the atmosphere indifferent or materialistic, the dominant factor was a desire to know, in each particular situation, the Will of God, and act upon it; and, as a consequence, he gave his best to the few, as he did to the crowds. However, when he once said: "Always I would rather address a thousand people than one," he revealed a basic feature of his character.

Certain it is that a thousand faces in the Lichfield Road Church would have largely dispelled the ominous experience in the vestry; but the sprinkling of people and the critical atmosphere only diminished what little self-confidence remained. It has been aptly said that the difference between preaching in the old Hull shooting gallery and in the Lichfield Road Church was a difference of prepositions. In the former he was preaching *to* people, and in the latter he was preaching *before* people. He always doubted whether, under similar circumstances, he could ever have been able to do better than he did. Suffice it to say that, two weeks later, in the list of the hundred and five who were rejected for the Wesleyan Methodist ministry that year, was the name of G. Campbell Morgan.

He wired to his father the one word, 'Rejected,' and sat down to write in his diary: "Very dark everything seems. Still, He knoweth best." Quickly came the reply: "Rejected on earth. Accepted in heaven. Dad." The sting of the implied rebuke was more of a spur to courage than a dozen commiserations. It was a dark horizon still, but God was riding the storm, holding in check the better things that were to be. "I thank God to-day," he said many years later, as he looked back across the years, "for closing that door of hope, because, when He turned my feet in another direction I found the breadth of His commandments, and the glory of His service."

Were we inventing the story, and the sequel in the events which occurred exactly forty years later, one might well put down the book and say "Oh, no! that wouldn't happen in real life—it's too good to be true! But, like the Bible stories of old, it came to pass, and we can tell it in Dr. Morgan's own words.

In the summer of 1928 Dr. Morgan visited England, preaching in London on Sundays, and in other towns and cities during the week. From London in August he wrote home to Glendale, California:

"On Thursday, July 19, I had a very interesting experience. The Wesleyan Methodist Conference met in Liverpool, during the time that I was taking meetings in the Central Hall, Manchester. This fact had emerged in conversation with Dr. Ferrier Hulme when he was staying with us in Glendale, and I happened to tell him that I had never seen the Methodist Conference in session. He made me promise, then and there, that if I could arrange it, I would go over one afternoon.

"Mr. Cooper, the Superintendent of the Mission, had received an intimation of this from Dr. Hulme, so I found that he had arranged to take me over; therefore, on the

Thursday referred to, immediately after my noonday sermon, he and I got on the train and went to Liverpool, arriving at three o'clock. By ten minutes past I found myself seated on the platform of the Conference among the extinct volcanoes —I beg their pardon!—the ex-Presidents!

"Now to go back a bit. It is forty years since the Methodist Church declined my offer for its ministry, and of course, that was very much in my mind. Imagine my . . . interest when I found the subject under discussion was 'The New Rules for the Admission of Candidates into the Methodist Ministry!' I sat and listened to a really great debate. . . . The two greatest speeches were made by Chadwick and Scott Lidgett, Chadwick fighting for the leaving open of a door for men who could not square up to certain academic requirements, fearing lest men of real gift and power should be discouraged, and kept out of the ministry. Scott Lidgett followed, in some senses on the other side, but with a very fine speech, arguing that Mr. Chadwick's fears were groundless. The proposal was that such men should be provided for, and that it was the business of the Church to give them a preliminary course. The difference of opinion was ultimately this:—the proposal as Chadwick understood it, declined to accept these men for the ministry until they had finished that course but he said he would be content if they would receive them forthwith, and the Church give it to them.

"Now to go aside for a moment. Another most interesting fact was that Dr. Parkes Cadman was there. He has always maintained his membership with the Methodist Church, Wellington Salop. . . . This year they elected him as lay representative to the Conference. . . . Gipsy Smith was also there as a lay member.

"To resume the story. Before adjournment, the Secretary of the Conference rose, and said that they had a distinguished visitor, who, it would be the wish of the Conference he was sure, to have presented to them. Thereupon Dr. J. W. Lightley, the President, rose, and I had to go forward. He shook hands with me and welcomed me. Of course, I cannot repeat exactly what he said, but the substance of it was that everyone there had heard me at some time or other. That I had placed the Methodist Church and the entire Christian world under a debt for the Biblical work that I had done, and so on and so forth. It was a most gracious speech. . . . The whole Conference rose and gave me a tremendous ovation. The President's speech being over, I made my bow and had retired, when a storm of shouts broke out: 'Speech! Speech!' The President signifying his assent, I addressed them for about five minutes. In substance, I said: 'Mr. President, Fathers and Brethren. I have never felt quite so envious of my friends, Dr. Cadman and Gipsy Smith as I have done this afternoon, and this because they had seats on the floor of this Conference, and had the right to take part in the debate on the Admission of Candidates to the Wesleyan Ministry. I should very much like to have taken part in that discussion to-day. (Very much laughter). Never, until to-day, sir, did I feel that I was in any sense like Moses. Let me hasten to add that there are apparent differences—for instance, Moses was meek, and I am not. But I remember that Moses came to the margin of the Promised Land and was sent back into the wilderness for forty years. Also that, at the close of the forty years, he was permitted to climb Mount Pisgah and view that land. I am glad to have come to Pisgah to-day, and for once see the Conference in session. I may say that, during those forty years and still my ecclesiastical home is in Congregationalism, but my spiritual home has been, and still remains in Methodism.'"

★ ★ ★ ★ ★ ★

Just two days before the verdict from the Wesleyan ministry was received, Campbell Morgan met one of his cousins, Annie, who had come on a visit from her home in Staunton. She was known as Nancy, and it suited her better. She was *petite* and pretty, and her eyes twinkled with merriment and good nature. This strange and ungainly cousin, she had heard, had an understanding—as it was called in those Victorian days, with another young lady. But the visit to Uncle George and Aunt Elizabeth was to prove more exciting than she had dreamed. First came the news of her cousin's rejection from the Wesleyan ministry and, almost at once, an intimation that, because of it, the affections of the young lady had cooled. Father and Mother alone would have been hard put to it to cheer the disconsolate young man, who must have felt that all the fates were against him. But Nancy was here on a visit. Appearances must be maintained; she must be entertained and made to feel welcome. She was never the kind of person it is difficult to entertain. Simple country lass as she then was, the good stock from whence she sprang gave her a natural poise, and a complete lack of artificiality. It was her nature to rise to occasions, and deal capably with them. The impression she made upon her cousin is best revealed in a letter Dr. Morgan wrote to one of his children, in May, 1943. "Your letter arrived on the anniversary of the day when I first saw your mother, that being May 15th, 1888, fifty-five years ago. I am still looking her over, and the report is quite satisfactory in every way!"

They became engaged in June, after a proposal by letter which is, in itself, a revelation of personality. "I can only ask you," he wrote, "to share the life of a wandering evangelist." "If I cannot start with you at the bottom of the ladder," she replied, "I would be ashamed to meet you at the top." To him it was imperative that she should have no misapprehension as to what lay immediately ahead. For her part she never doubted that he would climb the ladder, and that she would not hinder him by lagging behind. Upon this faith in each other they built fifty-eight years of a good life together.

It was a strangely contrasted young pair who walked into the little country chapel of Market Drayton on August 20th, 1888, to be married by the Rev. Timothy White. The groom was tall, spare, and angular, with black curly hair, high cheek bones, and a large nose which dominated his features. It was a face which could not be called handsome, but it was modelled on that good bony structure to which time adds distinction. Of his eyes it is difficult to avoid using that overworked adjective 'penetrating.' Like his father, he seemed to see a horizon which was hidden from others, whether it was on a distant landscape or in another person's soul. They could express a gamut of emotions—gentleness, sometimes anger, often kindness and understanding.

The girl who stood beside him on that wedding day was of a smallness and beauty which belied a strength and determination, partly inborn and partly the result of a staunch Christian upbringing and a simple environment. She herself had cleaned the house they were to live in. It was the first of many times that her skill was to turn a dwelling into a home. She loved it then, and loved it always, even in the days when there were plenty of servants to do her bidding. It was her way of life. Up to this time neither of them had had much of material possessions. "They were in very straitened circumstances," says a friend who was present at the wedding. When riches increased she set not her heart upon them. She enjoyed what came her way because it enabled her to help others. She believed in her marriage, and rejoiced in her husband's ability and success, but she knew that there was nothing of a material nature that could increase her happiness. No account of Campbell Morgan's life, from this day forward, would be complete without the bright thread of her influence and help as an integral part of its pattern, and he would not have had it otherwise. Of many quotations which she loved and collected, and enclosed in her letters to children, relatives and friends, one of Mrs. Morgan's favourites was composed of three words: 'DISAPPOINTMENT—HIS APPOINTMENT.' Certain it was that the year which brought to her husband one of his greatest disappointments, brought him also his richest treasure. Together they walked through life the pathway that God, in His good pleasure, had appointed for them.

CHAPTER III

1889-1897: 26 to 34 years

STONE—RUGELEY—BIRMINGHAM—FIRST VISIT TO THE UNITED STATES

THE car slowed down as it entered the village of Stone in the County of Staffordshire, that August day of 1939.

Exactly fifty years ago this month of August the Congregational Church at Stone had called a young man of twenty-six to be its pastor. To this, his first charge, he had brought the girl who, a year before, had promised to 'share the life of a wandering evangelist.' Here it was they were to set their feet upon the first rung of the ladder she confidently expected him to climb. Now, these and other memories were coming back like errant children, some with a rush, tumbling over each other, others lagging behind in the mist of forgetfulness. It was difficult, for instance, to remember just which turning to take that would lead to the Church, and 'the house we were living in when Perce was born.'

An elderly man was walking in the direction of the car. "Pull in here," said Dr. Morgan, "and let's ask this man." The driver came to a halt, and Dr. Morgan leaned out of the window. "Tell me," he said, "where is such and such a street? I used to live here, but for the life of me I cannot get my bearings."

The man looked at his questioner quizzically, and a broad smile spread slowly over his face. "It's Dr. Campbell Morgan, is it not?" he said.

"Bless my soul!" exclaimed Dr. Morgan, "you're Brown, the butcher's boy!" Turning to Mrs. Morgan in the back seat of the car he said: "Look at him! He hasn't changed a bit!" The man had been a young boy in the church when Dr. Morgan had been minister there.

For the young wife of the minister the call to the Stone pastorate offered an abiding place, after a year of following her evangelist husband from one preaching centre to another. Her contribution to that work, as far as the actual meetings were concerned, had been to distribute handbills, and sing solos at the services in a clear soprano voice. "Nancy sang very sweetly," her husband used to record in his diary. Those who knew her can imagine what it must have meant, after that probationary year, to have a home in one place, and a church where her husband could become anchored, and they could 'settle down'—a home for the first baby who came that winter as a birthday gift to his father on December the ninth, and was named Percival Campbell.

As every minister knows, there is in each pastorate, that inner circle of friends whose love and loyalty abide. The pastor must be 'all things to all men,' but he is human, too, and there are those with whom he and his wife form a special bond of friendship, with whom they correspond and keep in touch over the years, whose names flash across the memory when thoughts turn back to that particular place and congregation.

"In all these places," says Dr. Howard Morgan, in speaking of those summer pilgrimages, "we would stop in to see certain of the inner circle who had been closest to Dad and Mother. In Stone we went to call on a Mr. and Mrs. Babb, two dear old people, full of life and spirits, who addressed Dad and Mother as 'Campbell' and 'Nancy.'" Having tea with these friends, the conversation centred, quite naturally, around the events of the past, breaking up, as such talk will, into small groups. Mrs. Babb said to Howard in a confidential tone: "You know, Howard, your father was a naughty man when he was here! He used to pop in to our house for a cup of tea and a smoke, when the saints in the congregation thought he ought to have been visiting them!" Dr. Morgan was listening to more than one conversation at the same time. "What's that you are telling that boy?" he laughed. Certainly Dr. Morgan's records show a most thorough and systematic programme of Church visitation in Stone. Perhaps it *was* that fact that contributed toward making a haven of such homes as this!

The early days at Stone were also remembered for the fact that on November 30th Mr. Morgan performed the marriage ceremony of his friend, Albert Swift, now private secretary to General William Booth of the Salvation Army, to Miss Laura Slowe. "May all the blessings of our covenant God be upon them!" he wrote in his diary that November day of 1889. The names of these two, who were to become more and more dear in united work and friendship, were always a source of amusement and jokes between them.

However, on the visits of later years, it was the actual church buildings themselves that held the richest memories. Dr. Morgan would stand in the pulpit, as he did here in Stone, and say, "Ah, yes. We had great services in this place." He was remembering, too, that it was in this building that he was ordained to the Congregational ministry on September 22nd, 1890, and, next day, received into the Congregational Union. His son, Howard, says that the thing that impressed him was his father's constant references to his preaching ministry; he would talk about how the congregations would gather 'hungry for the Bread of Life.' From the very beginning his first and primary concern was to break it to them, and for this he gave hours of preparation each week. "The outstanding ability of his power in the pulpit was always there," recalls another friend of those early days, "even at the age of twenty-four he could pack any place of worship to capacity."

The new minister had not been at Stone Church long before he discovered it to be 'a house divided.' History repeated itself in the case of one of his sons, who suffered a similar experience in his early ministry. To him he later wrote: "I sympathize with your situation and understand it thoroughly. It is interesting to recall my first experience in the pastorate at Stone. In that church there were two factions, and their antagonism to one another almost amounted to a feud. It had been there for years; indeed when I last went there I found it was still in existence. This kind of thing makes the position of the minister an extremely difficult one. He is always in danger of being suspected by each side of favouring the position of the other, and that, no matter how resolutely he abstains from anything of the kind."

Neither was this the only handicap to the new minister's work. The influence of the years of evangelistic preaching was strong, and young Mr. Morgan was not content for long to confine his inexhaustible energy and activity to one field. The nearby village of Eccleshall challenged him with its need and opportunity as an outpost for Christian work. He began to go there on Sunday afternoons to hold services, endeavouring to interest his congregation at Stone in the venture. Some saw the vision and co-operated with enthusiasm, but others opposed the work as taking up too much of the minister's time. The same group objected to their pastor's not infrequent excursions to other towns in the vicinity to conduct evangelistic services between Sundays, and to a renovation and building project which was launched at Eccleshall during the second year. Campbell Morgan was a fighter for whatever he believed to be right, but he was hurt and discouraged by the hindrance of those on whom he felt he should have been able to count for help. On December 8 he records in his diary: "So ends the twenty-seventh year of my life. How many failures, and how much mercy! O for better things in the coming days!"

As neither side would give in, the rift between the minister and his opponents in the Stone Church widened. Though he was never known to compromise when he was convinced that he was in the right, Campbell Morgan learned with the years to exercise authority with tact, and temper prerogative with discretion. One surmises that there was little of either in these early days. The controversy reached a climax in December of 1891, when the minister received a letter which read as follows:

"Dear Mr. Morgan,

"The Deacons held a meeting last night to consider several strong complaints which have been made to them respecting yourself, and the outcome of that meeting was the following unanimous resolution:

"The Deacons, having received several strong complaints concerning the Pastor's repeated absence, and one of these having taken a formal shape, they are constrained to desire Mr. Morgan not to accept any further invitations to leave his pastoral duties *without their consent*, as they are fully convinced such repeated absences are weakening and dividing the church.

"Yours truly,

Secretary"

One can imagine his reaction to this missive in the notes he made in his own handwriting at the foot—notes of what he evidently intended saying to his officers at their next meeting. "First. Cannot make any such promise. Absurd. Unreasonable. Second. Illegal. No formal protest. Not a unanimous vote. Deacons no right. Third. *Not* the weakening of church."

He showed wisdom before acting, however, in consulting an older friend in another town, Mr. John Crake, and received the following letter in reply:

"My dear Morgan,

"I am sorry to hear that you have still further bother with your deacons. *I would be very careful how you act in this matter.* It looks as if they wanted to drive you into resignation— and *I would not be so driven* by anyone if I were you. The sentence underlined by you is very irritating, I must admit, but still, the ball is in your hands and *I would not throw it until you are ready.*

"We need to be careful lest we get out of the Providential path. What is now taking place, while embarrassing, suggests the need of caution as to any definite step you may take. It may well be that some clear opening will present itself in a very short time. But at any rate, don't consult your feelings only, lest you take the very step some of the deacons want you to take. I would avoid if possible giving any definite reply to the letter—it does not require one. It is simply communicating to you a resolution. In the meantime *I would scrupulously refrain from going to a single meeting outside of Stone* on any account for some weeks to come. Don't let them put you, *even in appearance*, in the wrong. I should judge they have no right to put the matter in the offensive way they have done; *still, I would not complain to them.* I would, for the present, act upon the resolution. If they are doing what I suspect, then in a short time they will be sure to put themselves in the wrong. It will be a trial to you, but I would put up with it for the present.

"As to your doing special Mission work in Methodism, I hardly know what to say. If I had had any opening that would have been suitable it might have been different. But you have a wife, and your father and mother, and for their sakes I would act with the *greatest deliberation*. To go about conducting special Missions might do for a few years, but *what about the future* and your maintenance if you broke down? Don't overlook the selfishness of religious people. No; for the present I would stay at Stone. When you do leave, *let it be on your own initiative*, and not in any sense through being forced or driven. I feel sure that in a few more months your personal influence with your people will make you more than a match for all your deacons. I have strong hopes that, with patience, the right sphere will be found for you. Anyhow, don't do anything hastily. Think this matter over for a few weeks at least."

"Old Mr. John Crake was always a good friend to Dad," says one of Dr. Morgan's sons. "I remember his kind face, framed in its short white beard. He visited our home in the London days."

It may be added here that Dr. Morgan made a practice all through his life of talking over his problems with those he could trust, and in whose advice he placed confidence. Reference has been made previously to his capacity for friendship. His choice of close companions was unerring, for none of them failed him. Many years after the Stone incident he went to talk over a parting of the ways in his life with another friend, Dr. J. D. Jones, of Bournemouth, and his advice on the question of which path to take, was to watch and study all the circumstances of life. "To the Christian," he said, "circumstances are the fingers of God." Whether or not Dr. Morgan ever referred to this publicly, he repeated it often in his own family circle, for it made a deep and abiding impression upon him.

Campbell Morgan could never be tempted or coerced into conforming to a man-made pattern. The same spirit prompted him, in the United States, to decline an offer made by Mr. John Wanamaker, the department store magnate of Philadelphia, Pennsylvania, a Christian leader in his city, and Bible teacher in the Bethany Presbyterian Church, when he proposed building a new million dollar edifice, following Dr. Morgan's own plans, if he would come to be its minister. "No," said Dr. Morgan. "I am God's man. If I did that I would become John Wanamaker's man!" The great man was not accustomed to having his philanthropic proposals declined, but he accepted the reply graciously in the spirit in which it was given. Because he was a great man, he recognized and understood greatness and integrity in others.

Acting upon Mr. Crake's advice, the minister of Stone set about to cultivate the virtue of patience, and spend more of his time in the home field. His energy found an outlet in the organizing of a group of boys who came to his home every week to sing, and discuss topics of interest both religious and secular. They debated such subjects as Drinking, Gambling, and Romanism—the latter arising out of a Town Hall Meeting in Stone 'for the purpose of discussing Roman Catholic claims in the light of Scripture and History.' There had evidently been questions asked in the community concerning some sermons being preached in England upon the claim of Peter as Head of the Church. Two papers had been read at this meeting by the pastor of the Congregational Church, and the Vicar of the Anglican Church respectively. Mr. Morgan's is a three thousand word statement, logical, reasoned, thoughtful and convincing, showing his love of word study in the careful examination of the words 'Petros,' and 'Petra,' in Matthew 16. 18.

These activities, however, did little to alleviate the strained relationship with the church officers. There were the loyal friends, as there always are, to whom he could turn, but it was his nature to demand all or nothing. With one exception, only a unanimous call to a church was ever considered, and only a united minister and congregation, he felt, could be successful.

There follows a record of frequent attacks of neuralgia and the chronic throat complaint, much of it caused by worry and anxiety. It was indeed a relief, after five months of chafing against the harness, when a call came to him from the church at Rugeley, about fifteen miles away. It was a smaller town than Stone, and offered a smaller salary, but the atmosphere was warm and welcoming when he went there to preach for the first time on May 31st, 1891. "I had a good time this morning," he wrote in his diary under that date, "and an excellent time speaking in the afternoon. This evening I undoubtedly had the greatest liberty. From this service I went into the Salvation Army Barracks and took hold of the meeting. Four came out for Christ. . . . I have much enjoyed my visit to Rugeley."

The official call came in June, and 'at an annual stipend of one hundred and sixty pounds,' Mr. Morgan took up his new residence and duties there. It was to prove a most happy and profitable association for both pastor and people, and confirmed the good advice of his friend, Mr. Crake, to wait for the divine leadership. Stone was the only church of which he was pastor that he wrote of the parting, "Very glad to get away"; and added, "we have had two years of varied experiences, some very painful, but all assuredly useful and part of the 'All Things.'"

During that same summer another parting took place which was far from being a happy one. Albert Swift and his wife sailed for the United States to take up the work of a pastorate in Ocean Grove, New Jersey.

Before leaving Stone, in 1891, Mr. Morgan had the satisfaction of seeing a prospering church at Eccleshall, renovated, reopened with a series of evangelistic meetings, strengthened by the addition of new members, and free from debt.

★ ★ ★ ★ ★ ★

"I went from Stone to Rugeley," Dr. Morgan wrote in a letter of later years, "where I found people, the fragrance of whose love will be with me to the end of my days."

Dr. Morgan, at the age of seventy-six, made a most significant observation as he stood in the church at Rugeley and glanced over the empty building. "This is the place," he remarked, "where I had those two quiet years, when I did the spade work of all my Bible studies." He repeated this as he sat out in the car remembering the old days, and one felt that this place marked the real beginning of, 'This one thing I do—' the study and teaching of the Bible to which he was to devote the rest of his life.

John Buchan has told us that, as a boy, he could imagine nothing better than the life of a country minister, "in some place where the winters were long and snowy, and a man was forced to spend much of his days and all of his evenings in a fire-lit library." He might have been describing the first winter at Rugeley, and the young minister absorbed in a study of Greek, finding a store house of fresh meaning for his New Testament. Here, he and his wife found a new circle of friends, a happy and united congregation who took their minister as they found him, who loved and appreciated his wonderful gift of expounding God's Word, and were willing to share him with others. The most precious of the memories of the Rugeley days was the coming of the first little daughter, Gwennie, who was to spend most of her short life in this country town.

Ideal though this environment was for study and quiet reading, Campbell Morgan did not allow himself to become provincial in his outlook. In addition to the study of Greek he was reading Charles Dickens, and especially Charles Kingsley, with avid interest. These contemporary writers, whose books, a short twenty years after their deaths, were becoming classics of the English language, had in common a passionate sympathy for the poor and afflicted. They did much through their writings, to influence public opinion, and initiate reforms in the fields of child labour and sanitation. During the latter part of the Victorian era the cause for the social betterment of the poor was in its birth throes, and many nonconformists entered the lists, believing this to be the duty and responsibility of the Christian.

In close proximity to Rugeley lies the thickly populated factory area of the potteries, over which hangs a constant pall of smoke, earning for it the name of 'the black country.' The crowded ways of life in these manufacturing areas contrasted sharply with the rural loveliness of Rugeley, as the minister so frequently had occasion to observe. There is no doubt that he had caught something of the spirit of Charles Kingsley, though his interest in the working classes was the natural result of a close association with them during the thirteen months of the Hull mission. He began to participate in political rallies in which the candidates stood for the betterment of living conditions for the poor. He organized in his church a club for working men, called 'The Free and Easy,' which was convened on Saturday evenings. The same group was encouraged to attend a Sunday morning Bible Class. The project met with immediate success. As always, the attendance was carefully noted in the diaries. It began with forty-one present, "a thorough success, the men seeming to enjoy it very much." Three weeks later the entry reads: "A large number of men again this evening. The place crowded and many turned away." And again: "Over a hundred men passed in and out during the evening."

1891 saw the beginning of another friendship, remarkable for the fact that the first meeting between Campbell Morgan and Mr. Gregory Mantle had taken place at the Lichfield Road Church, when the former had been the unsuccessful candidate for the Wesleyan Methodist ministry, and the latter the examiner who had been sharpening the pencil in the vestry! Mr. Mantle, serving a Methodist Church in Birmingham, had ample opportunity to watch the work being done by the young minister of the Congregational Church in Rugeley, and hear of his work elsewhere. Frequent visits to Birmingham found Campbell Morgan in company with Mr. Mantle, who later came to return the visit and hold a meeting for his friend in Rugeley.

Others have recorded the fact that in later years Campbell Morgan rendered a great service to the man whose misjudgment had barred him from a coveted goal. This gesture is not robbed of its magnanimity by pointing out that it is only part of the story. Gregory Mantle had tacitly acknowledged any error of judgment, when he recommended the man he had once considered a failure to an important city pastorate, for it was due to his influence that Campbell Morgan was introduced to the Westminster Road Congregational Church in Birmingham. A basic factor of this friendship was a mutual debt and respect which left no room for intolerance on the part of the one, or prejudice on the part of the other.

1892 was an election year in England, and Campbell Morgan was much in demand as a speaker at Liberal Party rallies, especially after his appointment as Vice-President of the Liberal Association. "I addressed a meeting (at the Town Hall) in support of Kempster's candidature." "At 7.30 went to open-air Liberal Meeting. . . . Adjourned to —— School Room where I spoke. A magnificent meeting. Hundreds turned away. Went to Liberal Club and was there till after 1 o'clock receiving election telegrams." These and similar items fill the diary pages for July, in addition to the sermons on Sundays, and other meetings of the week.

"Children's Anniversary Day, and a good day it has been. I preached this morning with joy. Had a poor time this afternoon. Felt fit for nothing prior to service this evening, but God wonderfully strengthened me and I had a splendid time. Very weary at close of day." . . . "We had sixty-eight present to-night (Thursday). I took the ninth of a series on Free Church principles—'Sacrifice, Sacrament, and Ordinance'."

Scarcely a day passed without a speaking engagement. The full schedule was only interrupted when the physical machine rebelled, usually attacking the weakness in the throat, strained by too much speaking and exposure to inclement weather. This cloud upon the horizon was accompanied by another— anxiety regarding the health of the baby daughter, who, despite her mother's constant care, was never robust or free from illness for long at a time. In January of 1893 the doctor ordered a complete respite for the entire family, and ten days were spent at Aberystwith, on the Welsh coast, during which time Mr. Gregory Mantle again preached for his friend in Rugeley.

It was the latter, as has been said, who, in March, placed Campbell Morgan's name before the congregation of the Westminster Road Congregational Church in Birmingham, with the result that he received and accepted their call in April. Dr. Morgan always spoke so lovingly of the twenty-one months of residence in Rugeley. "It was like running into a harbour of refuge after a storm," was the reference he once made to Rugeley in a letter. " . . . The most delightful people. I shall thank God to the end of my days for their love, and the new grip it gave me on my work."

★   ★   ★   ★   ★   ★

The ministry in Birmingham began in June, 1893, but it seemed advisable to postpone the Recognition Service until September. During the intervening period there was considerable correspondence with Dr. R. W. Dale, whom Mr. Morgan was most anxious to have present to deliver the address upon that occasion.

Dr. Dale was a giant in the land in an age when pulpit personalities were multiple. Especially in the city of Birmingham, where he had preached from the same pulpit at Carr's Lane for more than thirty-five years, his reputation was assured. A master of theology, he was another great nonconformist with a deep interest in civic and national progress. Humble and Christlike at heart, he was at this time so much a part of the public and religious life of his city and nation, that he was possessed of that assurance, and vested with that authority which can only spring from such a source. Indicative are his letters to the new minister of the Westminster Road Church, relative to the latter's coming to Birmingham, and his Recognition Service.

From Merioneth, on June 19th, 1893, he wrote:

"My dear Mr. Morgan,

"Your letter has followed me here. I expect to return to Birmingham to-morrow fortnight, and if it would be agreeable to you to call on me soon after I reach home, I should be glad to talk over with you the arrangements for your Recognition.

"In my judgment a Recognition should be a serious and impressive service—not an occasion for gossipy and trifling speeches. For many years I have declined to take part in any Recognition except on this understanding. Sometimes, indeed, very much to my grief and vexation, the understanding has been violated. . . ."

A meeting took place in July when Mr. Morgan accepted an invitation from Mrs. Dale to take lunch with them at their home.

It was characteristic of Dr. Dale that he took time in his busy life to welcome a young colleague to his city, not only putting him immediately at ease by the hospitality and informality of the meal, but afterwards encouraging him to talk about his early life and his hopes for the future; drawing him out by sympathetic questions to tell about his reading, his study and his preparation. It was the bigness of the new charge which was weighing upon Campbell Morgan at this time, and he confided to Dr. Dale his inadequate qualifications for ministerial work, feeling that he was untrained for it.

"Never say that you are untrained," was Dr. Dale's unhesitating reply. "God has many ways of training men. I pray that you may have much joy in His service."

It was the very word which Campbell Morgan needed at that hour as he faced the demands of the new pastorate, and he returned home resolved, with divine help, to make a success of it.

In arranging an exchange of pulpits with Dr. Dale in August, he received from him the following letter:

"Dear Mr. Morgan,

"I am willing to exchange with you on Sunday morning, September 17, but I am always obliged to warn my friends for whom I undertake services, that in my present state of health I am liable to sudden attacks which incapacitate me. Mr. B— will be in reserve either to preach at Westminster Road or at Carr's Lane as you may prefer in case of my failure. I should wish him, however to take Westminster Road.

I am,
Yours faithfully,
"R. W. DALE.

"P.S.—As you are a newcomer to Birmingham, you may not know that I object to being called *Rev*. Please announce me as Dr. R. W. Dale."

The 'attacks' to which Dr. Dale referred were the precursors of his last illness, at this time making rapid inroads on his strength. He was unable, to his great regret, to carry out his intention to preach at Westminster Road in September, but his interest never lessened. Campbell Morgan visited him often during the last months of his life. It was, indeed, a friend whose loss he sustained in March, 1895.

★ ★ ★ ★ ★ ★

With characteristic energy, Campbell Morgan entered into every phase of church life at Westminster Road. This church, in a growing suburb of a great city, had lost many of its members through doctrinal differences. From the beginning of his ministry his preaching attracted the crowds, and began to draw back much of the absentee membership. Many came from curiosity. They returned to their homes to take down Bibles, long neglected, and bring them back for reference and study. Gradually Campbell Morgan was finding in Congregationalism the foothold he had sought in Methodism. He was recognized and acclaimed by fellow ministers in the denomination, and beginning to sense their respect and affection. As the busy days passed he must have thought often of his friend's words: 'God has His own ways of training men.' Unusual as had been his, it was beginning to reap rewards as empty pews filled and the membership increased.

The training was not over, however, for there were dark days ahead of suffering and sorrow. He was to know a grief which was to lay popularity in the dust, and draw heavily on his own faith and courage, and the loyalty and affection of his friends.

The year 1894 opened full of promise for the Westminster Road Church and its pastor. He spent much time in preparation on series of Bible studies, the fruit of the 'spade work' done in Rugeley, and somehow managed to fulfil the heavy demands of pulpit and lecture platforms, and many weekly church activities. The opening pages of the diary for this year record full mornings of study, afternoons of visits and meetings, evenings of lectures or preaching, and late hours to bed. Suddenly all this is put aside for meetings in Liverpool and the Isle of Man; then back again to pick up the reins of the home charge without respite. The crowds that filled the church are mentioned more and more frequently, and always the joy of preaching, and the sense of the power of the Holy Spirit. "I had a happy time preaching," is a favourite expression. "The congregations are increasing

... the place was crowded." "Have had a very happy time in my study to-day preparing for Sunday. It is wonderful how God appears for us! Have been so pressed with work this week that I could not begin to think till to-day, and feared the result, and the whole thing came with joy." But by February the strain was beginning to tell. "We had a splendid congregation to-night and I had liberty in preaching. . . . Have worked under difficulties to-day. A dreadful headache." "I am not feeling very grand physically. All the prospects of the work here are encouraging, but almost overwhelming. However I do not doubt Him who has called me."

By March the throat trouble returned in the form of a rising on the right side of the neck, and necessitated a visit to Sir Walter Foster, one of Birmingham's outstanding physicians who had attended Dr. Dale in his illness. A three months' rest was recommended. The officers and members of the church urged their minister to obey orders, and he reluctantly acquiesced. The lovely Channel Islands off the coast of France were selected as the ideal resort for Mr. and Mrs. Morgan and the two children.

Those were ideally happy days, spent for the most part on the little island of Sark, itself a small gem of beauty in the blue and white setting of the sea, 'a most delightful place, combining sea, mountains and country air . . . a series of remarkable caves and subterranean passages.' To make the holiday perfect, Albert Swift, home from the States, joined his friends, and many were the walks and talks and 'quiet reads' they enjoyed together. On a Sunday he writes: "We went to church. The service was in French. I followed the sermon with difficulty, gaining, however, a gist of its meaning. One sentence made me 'at home'—'Jesus Christ est au milieu de nous.'"

But the neck continued to give frequent pain, and at last, on May 22, a slight operation was performed in Guernsey, from which the patient made a satisfactory recovery. This anxiety only gave place to another, for the baby Gwennie was taken ill, and it was thought best to return home as soon as both convalescents could travel. Mrs. Morgan decided to take the children to her old home in Staunton, while her husband completed his holiday in the Isle of Man.

There was no premonition or warning of the sudden illness that ended the life of the little girl he had left behind. The mother, in her own grief, thought first of her husband, and in an attempt to soften the blow, telegraphed to the friends in the Isle of Man with whom he was staying, asking them to break the news gently to him. Wonderful little mother as she was—and 'The Little Mother' that she became to the many who loved her and called her 'T.L.M.'—she was first and foremost the wife whose concern it was to ease the pathway for her husband. She had learned early (though it seems she must always have known), how to subjugate her own trouble to cushion it for others. Forgetting herself, she built up an inner reserve of strength on an unwavering faith in Him 'Who doeth all things well.'

The father took the next boat home, and arriving in Liverpool, "had a couple of hours with Mr. Crake" before travelling on through the night. How much can be read in so few words! How much can be shared in so few hours!

To the bereaved father, the memory of his little daughter was linked inseparably with that of his sister. "My Lizzie has met my Gwennie. The sorrow of twenty-three years ago and the sorrow of to-day are mingling, and out of the old one falls this ray of light on the dark cloud of to-day." That these children who had preceded him into the light, were in God's safe keeping, he believed with all the faith that is the inheritance of the Christian. He demonstrated that belief by consistent affirmation, drawing from it the hope he inspired in other lonely and bereaved hearts. Whenever one of Dr. Morgan's children was asked: "How many are there of you?" the answer was the same: "Seven. Six on earth and one in heaven." Such a natural response was an echo of the parents' belief before it became for them the expression of their own.

One of the tenderest and most poignant references to this loss was made in the sermon on 'Jairus,' afterwards incorporated in *The Great Physician*. The whole message is eloquent of the feeling of a father's sensitive heart, dwelling on the death of a child—a wound which time assuaged but never completely healed. "Those gathered round saw a dead child," he says, in reference to Jairus' daughter, "and in that, the end of life, the passing to dust and nothingness of a sweet and beautiful personality. And, than that, there is nothing more terrible in this world. Charles Kingsley, in one of his writings, declared that the death of a soldier is touched with heroism, the death of an old man is surrounded with the glory of completion; but the death of a child demonstrates something wrong somewhere. . . . Jesus . . . revealed His outlook upon that fact. He said in effect, This is not the child. . . . His outlook . . . was that of the persistence of personality beyond what we call death . . . so he said to the stricken father, 'She is not dead, but sleepeth'."

Dr. Morgan explains that 'Talitha cumi' is not Greek but Aramaic—"the language of His home, the common language of the common folk in the common things of life. We render the saying with supposed dignity as 'Damsel, arise.' . . . The word 'Talitha' is a diminutive. It means 'little lamb.' t was a word of infinite love and tenderness. . . . We see God, manifest in flesh, put His hand, the hand that guides he movement of all worlds, upon the dead hand of a little assie, and we hear Him call her 'little lamb.' With this address He uttered the word of authoritative command, Arise'."

One could quote at length the interpretation of the tender tory, as only one who had passed under the same shadows could tell it. It is inevitable that, towards the end, comes the personal reference.

"I can hardly speak of this matter without becoming personal and reminiscent, remembering a time forty years ago, when my own first lassie lay at the point of death, dying. I called for Him then, and He came, and surely said to our troubled hearts, 'Fear not, believe only.' He did not say, She shall be made whole. She was not made whole on the earthly plane. She passed away into the life beyond. He did say to her, 'Talitha cumi,' 'little lamb, arise'; but, in her case, that did not mean, stay on the earth level. It meant that He needed her, and He took her to be with Himself. She has been with Him for all those years, as we measure time here, and I have missed her every day; but His word, 'Believe only,' has been the strength of all the passing years."

Six months after Gwennie's home-going, on December 9, her father wrote in his diary: "To-day I am thirty-one years old. Surely goodness and mercy have followed me all the days of my life! There have been no accidents. All under the Father's government, and all best."

* * * * * *

Dr. Howard Morgan recalls with special interest the visit to Birmingham with his parents in the summer of 1939. "We went to see the house they were living in on St. Peter's Road, when Jack was born," he says.

The son who came the year following Gwennie's death, was given the name of Kingsley John, for it was during the months preceding his birth that the lecture on Charles Kingsley was prepared and then delivered to appreciative audiences, and Mrs. Morgan, hearing it, became herself an enthusiastic admirer of the great author and reformer. Certain it is that Campbell Morgan was profoundly influenced by Charles Kingsley. His sermons were a source of great inspiration to the young minister, and were 'read wholly, and with diligence and attention.' Kingsley's relationship with the common people, and his beautiful spirit in his dealings with them, were revealed again, and in a marked degree, in the character and life of his admirer.

The lectures on Kingsley, Garibaldi, Savonarola, and others, each requiring weeks of research and preparation on the part of the lecturer, were the means by which money was raised for renovations and improvements in the Westminster

Road Church. With enough subscribed to justify a start, the work began in June of 1895. On December 7th, 1896, he writes: "This evening I lectured to a very good audience. We managed to clear off the Renovation Debt completely, for which I am profoundly thankful."

"In each of these churches," his son, Howard, continues, "in Monmouth, Stone, Rugeley and Birmingham, Dad would insist that I go and stand in the pulpit! In two of them, Rugeley and Birmingham, Dad came and stood in the pulpit beside me. I well recall that in the Birmingham pulpit he said, looking all around the church: "You know, we had great services in this place. It used to be packed to those doors, and many times people would be standing in those aisles on Sunday nights." My impression is that, as Dad would talk about those early years, his reference was chiefly to the Ministry of the Word. How the congregations would gather, 'hungry for the Bread of Life,' and how he would be off preaching in other churches between Sundays. What I want to emphasize is this. Dad rarely referred to other events or church activities. It was always something like, 'Bless my soul! What great services we had here!' or, at Birmingham, 'This is where I first started the week-night service given to definite and systematic study of the Bible.' In other words, what finally culminated in the great Friday Night Bible School in London, began back there. Yes, *that*—and also his reference to some person, like 'Brown, the butcher's boy,' or some human interest story. While he was always the preacher to great crowds, he had an infinitely lovely personal touch with people—so often, those the world would call the 'lowly and little people!' What a great soul he was!"

Many were the 'human interest' stories told, as the car ran quietly and slowly along the country lanes. Mrs. Morgan remembered the little incidents which all mothers cherish. How they laughed together, remembering the baby Jack waking early in the morning, disturbing the sleep of his elders. His father, as is the habit with fathers the world over, resented this intrusion upon his slumbers, and shouted: "Here! Stop that noise, and go to sleep!" at which the little voice shouted back, "Oo dat talkin'?"

Of the Birmingham days Dr. Morgan told of a minister to whom he wrote, asking him to come and give an address at a Sunday School Anniversary Service. He received no reply to his letter, and in two weeks wrote again, saying that doubtless his first letter had gone astray. Dr. Morgan was himself a most meticulous and businesslike correspondent, especially in matters pertaining to an invitation to speak, always replying by return of mail, whether it was to accept, or to regret his inability to do so. His reaction upon receiving the reply to his second letter can be imagined, for the invited preacher replied, saying, Yes, he had received the first letter, but had not answered as he was 'waiting upon the Lord in prayer' to know whether he should accept or not! The reply he received must have surprised him. He was told that he might consider the invitation cancelled. They would not desire a man who lived so far away from the Lord that it meant waiting two weeks to hear His voice, to be their anniversary preacher. Dr. Morgan laughed rather ruefully as he told the story, and remarked, "I was younger then!"

Always responsive to the missionary enterprise, Mr. Morgan accepted, whenever possible, an opportunity to welcome those missionaries returning home, and speed those who were departing, keeping always before his people the necessity for a consciousness of, and vital interest in the missionary cause. This was closely akin in his mind to a consciousness of national obligation towards other peoples and races. All Christendom was stirred in 1896 because of the Armenian massacres inflicted by Turkey in Asia Minor. Mr. Morgan was one of a group of ministers in Birmingham who arranged for a public meeting in censure of this crime. Neither were problems of the community neglected. The church was aware of the unemployment and misery among the poor. As a result of this, during the long, cold winter of 1895-96 a woodshed near the church was appropriated, and a project started whereby those in need could chop wood, earning enough for their immediate needs. Church members sponsored the project and subsidized the work. The minister had a way of winning recruits for his causes who worked long and hard under his direction. Willing workers helped to systematize his visitation programme. Miss Winifred Child, one of his members then, who became a lifelong friend of the family, gave herself to this work, dividing the membership into districts, so that a complete programme of visitation might be carried out in the most efficient manner.

So much was accomplished during the busy Birmingham days, both church and minister growing in spiritual power, that it might be difficult to point to the greatest achievement, were it not for the advantage of looking back over the years. Though there is no human means of measuring the influence of any of these activities, the one which remains fresh and living to-day, and, in constantly widening circles, is touching lives the world over, is Dr. Morgan's system of Bible study, which was initiated in Birmingham.

Beginning in April, 1895, Mr. Morgan began, at his Thursday mid-week service, to take the Bible, book by book, in outline, giving what he called 'a bird's-eye view of the contents of the Divine Library.' These outlines were the nucleus of the *Analyzed Bible*, which has found its way on to the shelves of seminary and S.S. libraries, pastors' studies, and mission stations. In the Birmingham days they were printed in pamphlet form for the convenience of those attending the services, and many were mailed to friends and fellow ministers. Beginning with the Genesis series in 1895, he followed into 1896 with Psalms and Acts. Sunday School teachers from his own and surrounding churches attended in large numbers. A still wider scope was made possible when a monthly magazine was issued, as the officers of the church realized the need for a wider publicity for their pastor's gift of exposition.

From the beginning this week-night service was held in the church, even before the size of the congregation demanded it. "Our churches have too often treated that service as a side issue, and put it in a subsidiary hall," Dr. Morgan once wrote to his son, Frank. "I began to do otherwise as far back as my Birmingham ministry, and found that the venture was a success. I did the same at New Court, and, of course, at Westminster. Things treated as of lesser importance come to be looked upon as such, and people treat them accordingly."

Nearly a quarter of a century later, in giving the James Sprunt Lectures at the Union Theological Seminary, in Richmond, Virginia, he told the students: "Every church should be a Bible School, a Bible College, and its minister should take oversight of all Biblical teaching from the Primary Department of his Sunday School through every grade, and up to the oldest members of the church. Much of the detailed work he must delegate to others, but nothing of it should be outside his knowledge and direction. His charge is to feed the lambs and the sheep."

He told his Westminster Friday Night Bible School students: "If I could have my way I would make it a rule that the week-night service should be everywhere turned into a Bible School, where the Bible is taught patiently, persistently and consecutively." This was, of course, precisely what he did himself, 'patiently, persistently and consecutively' through all the years of his ministry, but it was here, in Birmingham, that the start was made.

★ ★ ★ ★ ★ ★

Early in 1896, Albert Swift, living near Ocean Grove, New Jersey, wrote asking his friend, Campbell Morgan, to come to the United States for a visit. He arranged for him preaching and lecturing engagements, in his own church first, and also in Chicago, where Mr. Morgan was to lecture at the Moody Bible Institute. The Institute was under Mr. D. L. Moody's personal supervision, and the engagement to speak there must be procured with his consent. In Campbell Morgan's case Mr. Moody broke a precedent, for it was not his custom to invite anyone to speak, either in Northfield, his home, and the site of the Northfield Bible Conference, or in Chicago, at the Institute, until he had heard him personally. Arrangements progressed satisfactorily, and Mr. Morgan adjusted his home affairs in preparation for a three months' absence.

In his customary methodical way, he wrote a 'day by day' account of the trip, from the day he left England on August 2nd, until the day he returned, October 2nd. A special notebook was purchased for this record, having its onion-skin pages alternating with a heavier grade of stationery, so that by using a carbon, one copy could be sent home, and the other kept in book form. Because of this inveterate habit of doing 'all things decently and in order,' there is preserved a most interesting account of the summer of travel. Dr. Morgan was to cross the Atlantic fifty-four times during his life. Those who have enjoyed this experience, however, know that there is something unique about the first crossing, and the first sight of the New World. Even then, it is not everyone who can carry over into words the zest and excitement of a new adventure, and etch the sharpness of first impressions of places and people.

The voyage on board the S.S. *Campania* was full of interest. On the day following the Saturday sailing, is the following citation: "The saloon passengers have had a service this morning, but no provision whatever has been made for the second class or steerage. There is a tremendous amount of ungodliness of a respectable sort on board. Here, as everywhere else, one is reminded of Heber's lines:

> Where every prospect pleases,
> And only man is vile.

" . . . we had some singing . . . in the evening. How the old hymns and tunes touched very tender chords! Imagine being hundreds of miles away from home and friends, and singing, 'Lead, Kindly Light,' 'Abide with me,' 'Nearer my God to Thee,' etc. It was a very enjoyable ending to the day. . . . This is my first Sunday . . . without work, save for illness since July, 1894, and the conditions are just perfect for rest and recuperation. I am feeling thoroughly well, and look forward hopefully to my work in the States."

In mid-Atlantic "a sailing ship in full sail" was sighted "that passed us so near as for us to give them a cheer, which we did with hearty good will. It was remarkable what excitement the nearness of those other living beings had on us all." The traditional concert on the eve of landing, for the benefit of 'The Widows and Orphans of Sailors' Society,' was "a very commonplace sort of an affair. The one good thing was a quartet by a party of Princeton students. That was very fine, but, alas for public taste, received no encore. Coarse, trashy music-hall songs, on the other hand, were vociferously applauded. . . . We have had a glorious day of brilliant sunshine. I have just sat in a deck chair and bathed in the sun all the day through, except for an interval for meals, during which I have done my share of hard work."

Upon arrival in New York, on August 7, he says: "The heat here is intense. I am sitting writing this and perspiring at every pore, and yet it is not an oppressive heat. One of the first things that greeted my ear on stepping on to New York streets was an old street piano, playing, 'Write me a letter from Home!' . . . A rather curious thing happened just as we were coming out of the dockyard. A rough-looking fellow, a porter, eyed me seriously for a moment, and then said: "Well, Guv'nor, and how's Birmingham getting on?' I replied: 'Oh, very well. How long have you been out?' 'Four years,' said he, 'and I wish I'd stayed at home.' I have no idea who he was, but he knew me. . . . Well, I am here in the New World. The very first impressions one receives are of the tremendous enterprise of these folks. . . . "

After meeting Mr. Swift, "we had a long yarn together," and proceeded by train, arriving at his home about midnight. "Of course, it being the first journey on an American railway, I was very much interested in it. The whole system, as far as the travelling is concerned, I think a great improvement on ours in the way of comfort to the passenger."

The setting of Swift's home at Round Lake Park, near Ocean Grove, New Jersey, was different to anything Campbell Morgan had ever seen in a rural community in England, and utterly in contrast to the identical rows of similarly identical brick houses which shelter the English city dwellers and most suburbanites. In writing home, he describes Round Lake Park as "a beautiful place consisting of wooden houses of almost all shapes and sizes, some of them being very handsome, and no single one, so far as I have seen, ugly. These houses are built in a pine wood, the resinous aroma from which is simply delightful. The place is not set out in regular streets, but these houses are dotted here and there, and the effect is most picturesque."

Campbell Morgan himself must have realized that this first visit to the United States would have a far-reaching effect upon his future, and it was to be of even more importance to him than he could be aware at the time. But it was not the distant future which primarily concerned him, nor even the immediate future, holding the thrill of travel and adventure. It was first and foremost to see his friend, Albert Swift, that he sailed for the United States in 1896. The daily record that was sent home during the two months' absence, is a running commentary of sights and sounds, new faces and new places, comparisons between the old world and the new. One fact predominates, however—the joy of being with the friend he affectionately calls 'Bert.' It has been said that the mark of friendship is the ability to pick up the threads, in spite of separation, and go on as though the separation had never been. There were long evenings of intimate fellowship, 'good old-fashioned talks', he calls them, and adds, "but there is so much to talk about, that it seems as though we have hardly touched the fringe of it."

Mr. Morgan's first public appearance in the United States was in the Methodist Episcopal Church of which Mr. Swift was pastor. "I preached on 'The Withered Hand,'" he says, "and had a fair time only. The folks received it very kindly indeed. I think I felt the heat yesterday more than I have at all. . . . The impression of my first Sunday is that the American congregation is much like our own. They were most reverently attentive, and quick and responsive to the truth. There is much less reserve among them personally, and one could get to feel at home with an average American more quickly than with an average Englishman."

He gave, at Mr. Swift's request, one of his popular lectures, a humorous discourse, entitled, 'Men We All Know And Wish We Didn't.' "There was a very good gathering," he says, "many more than I expected on account of the intense heat. I had a very good time, speaking for an hour and a half. . . . The people here have a very great fashion of coming up and shaking hands with you. I shook hands with a great crowd of people, lots of them from England, and many more whose fathers had come from thence, and were consequently interested in an Englishman."

Mr. Swift was determined that his guest should see as much as possible in the time available. They went to Albany, where he was shown over New York state's capital building—"it excels everything I ever saw for internal magnificence," and hurrying back to the station, caught the train for Saratoga, "the most fashionable watering-place in America. We had just an hour there, so hired a buggy and drove round. . . . We saw two of the hotels. I have never seen such hotels in England. . . . One hotel is build round an enclosed space which is delightfully laid out in lawns, trees, and fountains. A band is playing, and the folks . . . are sitting about reading and chatting. . . . I walked bang in and round, as though I belonged to the place, or better still, as though the place belonged to me!"

Before going to Chicago, Mr. Morgan went to Northfield, Massachusetts, at Mr. Moody's request, to have an interview with him, and to get a glimpse of the famous Conference grounds. The charm of Northfield has been acclaimed by many. None has described it more aptly, and yet in so few words, as Dr. Morgan himself, when he wrote in the Westminster *Record* some ten years later: "Northfield, fifty miles removed from anything like a large town, nestling among hills and in the midst of beauty unsurpassed, has an air of separateness which cannot be found, even in Keswick." Here, on the banks of the Connecticut River, is the home of Mr. D. L. Moody, the Northfield Bible Conference, and the Northfield Schools which Mr. Moody founded in order to give the boys and girls of the hills an education which they would not otherwise have an opportunity to receive. With what eager anticipation must this visitor from across the sea have looked forward to seeing the place of which he had heard and read so much, and above all, to meeting on his own native soil the man who for years he had so genuinely revered!

Mr. Morgan reached Northfield at noon, but did not see Mr. Moody until the next morning. The intervening hours were spent in getting acquainted with Northfield. He listened to Dr. William J. Erdman, Dr. F. B. Meyer, and others as they led Bible studies and discussions. He attended a question meeting on Round Top, "a little knoll crowned with trees, on the slope of which the people sit"—Round Top, the scene of so many memorable hours at Northfield, and now forever sacred as the last resting place of its founder and benefactor. The last memory of this notable day was Mr. Sankey's singing in the great auditorium; the first activity of the new summer morning which followed, was attendance at a 6.30 prayer meeting. For the first and only time he was a silent, unknown listener in the crowd, watching, noting, observing, and soaking up the atmosphere of this wonderful place. All these impressions confirmed afresh his belief in the fascination and appeal of the Bible, when people are given an opportunity to hear it proclaimed and taught. The ambition of the founder, 'that Northfield may become a centre for Bible instruction, where lectures and classes are held every day . . . ' was stamped indelibly upon his mind and heart. Years later, another Bible Conference came into being on England's east coast, at Mundesley, in Norfolk. Its centre was the beautiful estate bearing the name of 'Northfield,' the home of its founder, Campbell

Morgan, who caught, long before, at Northfield, Mass., the inspiration from which it materialized.

"Directly after breakfast," he writes of the next day, "I went down to see Mr. Moody. He had a chat with me, and then took me for a drive round in his buggy. The greatness of the man comes out in the way he acts all along . . . everywhere you see him as the managing director, strong, firm, keen, yet large-hearted, tender and kind. He drove a good way out of his course to reach a labourer in a field, to warn him to take care and not to do too much on account of the heat, saying, 'If you only get a half day's work done, I shan't complain.' A little further on he pulled up to ask a group of children if they had plenty of apples; if not, to send a basket down for filling. We talked of the old days in Brimingham . . . in his first mission there in 1874." Mr. Moody pointed out to his guest the various buildings, and told him their history. "Sankey sang that up," he said, pointing to one. It was the result of royalties from the sale of the Moody and Sankey hymn book. Passing a lovely, tree-sheltered home in the centre of the encampment, he said: 'That's the homestead where I was born. People sometimes ask me how I found Northfield. I tell them I didn't find it. It found me."

There were to be other summers at Northfield, and other drives with Mr. Moody before his death in 1899. Dr. Morgan tells of one of these in *The Great Physician*. "A memory comes back to me," he says "of how once, driving through the Northfield lanes with Dwight Lyman Moody, he said to me quite suddenly in his own characteristic way: 'What is character, anyhow?' Knowing that he had something in his own mind, I said: 'Well, what is it?' And immediately he replied: 'Character is what a man is in the dark'."

Mr. Moody himself spoke on Round Top that afternoon —"a racy, pointed address on the importance of the spirit-filled life to service, and methods of Christian work." But since the intimacy of the morning drive, one listener saw the great man with new eyes. Not only demanding respect and reverence, he was henceforth to be honoured and loved.

"After the evening meeting," Mr. Morgan writes, "Mr. Moody asked me to go down to his house to meet the other speakers. It was a picture not to be forgotten to see Moody in childlike gladness of heart, serving out ice-cream to us all, and then turning the conversation on to the needs of these great American cities, and speaking of them as a man who evidently carries the burden of them on his heart. That quiet talk was a fitting ending to a very busy and blessed day, reminding us that all our blessing is to the end that we should bless."

As he bade his host good-night, Mr. Moody told him that he was to preach in the auditorium at 10 o'clock the next morning. The announcement came as a surprise and something of a shock, but Mr. Moody's word was law. So that, instead of being on a southbound train for New York, Mr. Morgan found himself facing an audience from a platform on which had stood some of the greatest leaders in the Christian world. "I preached to a large congregation on 'The Carpenter of Nazareth'," he wrote, "and had a time of very great liberty and of much power." This sermon, the first of many he was to preach at Northfield, was published later under the title, *The Hidden Years in Nazareth*. In 1932 Dr. Morgan wrote to his son, Frank, "It is interesting that someone you have met . . . heard that address in Northfield on *The Hidden Years in Nazareth*. There must have been a lot of people there from the number who have told me they heard it in the years intervening. . . . That was my first address at Northfield."

Dr. Morgan's affectionate tribute to Mr. Moody at the time of his death has been called 'an epic in friendship'. Referring to the three years of their relationship together, he said: "If we count time by heart-throbs, then I can claim to have known him both long and well, for it was my rare privilege to have come very near to him in the ripest years of his life. Perhaps the better way to put it would be to say that he came very near to me. . . . " Of Mr. Moody's 'octagon' of qualities, he says: "That side is first which you first approach," and begins with tenderness, continuing with humour, common-sense, insight, immediateness, passion, breadth, and modesty. "Had he no faults?" concludes this eulogy. "I cannot say. Certainly I was not conscious of them. Let others pen the criticisms, this is an appreciation. The greatness of the man was such that I did not observe the littleness; the goodness so evident that all else was hidden. He was one of the most remarkable men of a remarkable age, so varied and forceful by nature that he would have been known in any walk of life. As a statesman he would have attained to the place of power. As a soldier he would have won renown. By the grace of God he was what he was, and all the powers of his being, under the restraining, directing, beautifying influences of that grace, made him of more service to his country than statesman and soldier could ever be, for his influence was exerted in the deeps of human lives, where the law and the sword are powerless to operate. We thank God for him, and think of him to-day as with the Lord, whom he so faithfully served and so gloriously set forth in all manner of behaviour."

One phrase there was also used of Campbell Morgan by Mr. Moody when he said: "He is one of the most remarkable men who ever came to Northfield." On another occasion, in introducing Mr. Morgan to an audience, Mr. Moody said: "A few years ago now, in England, the good Wesleyan brethren in that country turned him down because they were under the impression that he couldn't preach. Well, all I can say to that is, Mr. Morgan surely reaches *my* heart, and I believe him to be filled utterly with the Spirit of God."

That first visit to Northfield was an enriching and exhilarating experience, to be shared with 'Bert' in "a long chat on things new and old." Another friendship was renewed and deepened in a reunion with Dr. S. Parkes Cadman, whom Campbell Morgan had known in England before Dr. Cadman crossed the Atlantic to accept the pulpit of the Metropolitan Temple in New York City. "In appearance he is greatly changed. I do not think that I should have recognized him had I met him on the street. He used to be as thin and lank as I am myself, but now is quite fat. In other ways he has improved, and is just as free and jolly as ever, notwithstanding his great and undoubted success out here. He has a fine church . . . and is doing a capital work." Mr. Morgan preached for a week in this church to large and appreciative congregations, and summed up his further observation of his friend in words which were, indeed, prophetic, when it is remembered that Dr. Cadman became world-famous as America's first, and still, in the estimation of many, America's greatest radio preacher. Campbell Morgan said of him: "He is very fine . . . I think a genius, and will yet be much more widely known."

Mr. Morgan had no compunction then or later in applying to himself such adjectives as 'thin' and 'lank'. He was not ignorant of the fact that his appearance, especially in those earlier days, had a surprising effect upon strangers. The extreme spareness of his bony frame made him appear taller than the six feet he measured, and his clothing hung upon it in much the same way as Abraham Lincoln's is said to have done, exaggerating his gaunt appearance. Those who only knew the Dr. Campbell Morgan of Westminster and after, never saw him in clothes that were not well fitting and well pressed. They knew him as one whose criterion for dress was that it should be so right, both in comfort and appropriateness to the occasion, as never to draw attention to itself by the wearer. This was one reason why he wore clerical garb. To him it was the most comfortable form of apparel, as well as the badge of his calling. He was immensely pleased when each of his four sons, following his ordination, adopted 'clerics'. His unprofessional attire was a sartorial triumph. He loved a beautiful piece of cloth, and instantly recognized it, as when he saw some in the window of a tailor's miniature shop in the Brighton 'lanes' and said: "Ah, I want a suit of that!" and went to be measured for it there and then. He had unerring good taste, and his passion for bright colours found expression in the most livid hues of ties and socks, which had a way of looking just right on him. From the shine on his beautiful hair, freshly shampooed every morning, to the perfection of his well-fitting shoes, he was always immaculate. His hands were exquisite, sensitive, long-fingered and beautifully kept. They were (together with his voice) his most perfect assets in the pulpit and on the platform. He used good perfume sparingly. He had an instinct for sartorial propriety which was entirely masculine, and an intuition usually accredited to women, which lacked any trace of effeminacy.

However, in the early days, and at the time of his first visit to the United States, his appearance was more likely to provoke astonishment than envy. He rather enjoyed a little private joke when he noticed a bewildered expression on people's faces, knowing that, once he could get to preaching to them, all eccentricities of outward appearance would be forgotten. He tells of such an occasion in relating his visit to the Bible Conference at Ocean Grove, New Jersey, where, on Mr. Swift's recommendation, he had received an invitation to preach.

"Bert introduced me to Dr. S—" he writes, "and it was amusing to see how the dear old man was quite nervous about having appointed me for the two biggest services of the Camp Meeting. My appearance does not seem to have very favourably impressed him. Perhaps my gray suit frightened him." Dr. S— was equal to the occasion, however, and "introduced me very kindly. When I rose to speak, the whole audience of about five thousand rose, and waving their handkerchiefs (that is what they call here a Chatauqua salute), they sang, 'Blest be the tie that binds our hearts in Christian love.' This was a splendid greeting and put me straight away in good form for preaching. I had a time of great liberty in preaching about Enoch's Walk with God. . . . But I knew that I still had my biggest work before me. . . . It (the evening service) was a wonderful time. The sense of responsibility as I faced that great throng of upturned faces, the largest company to which I had ever preached, was very great. The Master was with me, and I preached for fifty minutes with great liberty, and the Word was with power. My subject was 'Gathering and Scattering', and a large number decided for Christ. It was an occasion never to be forgotten. At the close, Dr. S— took my hand publicly, and thanked me for my message, and committed me to God. Then the congregation rose and sang, 'God be with you till we meet again'. . . . I shook hands with scores at the close of the service, and should hardly have got away at all if Dr. S— had not just come along and carried me off. . . . It is most remarkable how, wherever one goes, the people are eager for the teaching of definite out and out Christianity. How is it that men are so backward in giving it? There is no more delightful part of my work than this."

The week at the Moody Bible Institute in Chicago was, for Campbell Morgan, an outstanding engagement for which he had made special preparation. Young Bible students seemed, if a distinction can be made, to come nearest to his heart. A born teacher, he gave himself to classroom work with a zest and enjoyment that was a memorable and satisfying experience for both student and instructor. For the students of the Moody Bible Institute he had prepared a series of lectures on the Book of Malachi, and was delighted with their response and appreciation, as also with the plans and methods of the Institute work, all inspired and directed by Mr. Moody. "This Bible Institute," he wrote, "is doing splendid work, not only in giving the students while here a capital Bible training, making them familiar with the Word of God, but also in using them in evangelistic work of all sorts in the city. Yesterday (Sunday) the students were scattered in all directions conducting open-air meetings, and speaking in various halls, and visiting among the people."

It was not all work, however, for an astonishing amount of sight-seeing was sandwiched in between engagements. The home folks were hungry to hear about places as well as meetings, and they were not disappointed. Letters from Chicago told of a breath-taking trip on the Ferris Wheel, "being slowly lifted to that height (220 feet) over the great city, and seeing everything grow smaller beneath you, and then being as slowly dropped, and seeing it all come back to natural proportions"; to the top of the Masonic Temple, the highest building in Chicago—twenty-two storeys high, and to the Stockyards, "a sight of a lifetime . . . but I never want to see it again!"

Perhaps the descriptive letters that were read and re-read with the keenest interest were those telling of the return trip to New York by way of Niagara Falls, Toronto, and Montreal. Those who have visited Niagara in the summer time know how many different and exciting adventures may be experienced there—the views from Goat's Island and Three Sisters' Island, the Rapids, the Whirlpool, the Caves of the Winds (under both the American and Canadian Falls), the sight of the Rainbow Circle, the ride on the 'Maid of the Mist,' and last, the view from the 316 foot Tower. He did them all, and wrote graphically of each one, finishing the long letter by saying: "In some respects this has been one of the most remarkable days of my life."

To one accustomed to seeing in all God's manifestations a deeper meaning, it was inevitable that the awe-inspiring sight of the Falls should be parabolic. Dr. Morgan used to quote Wordsworth's lines:

> A primrose by a river's brim
> A yellow primrose was to him,
> And it was nothing more,

as descriptive of those who having eyes see not, as contrasted with those pure in heart who see God everywhere. Long after the visit to which reference has been made, Niagara provided a beautiful illustration in the interpretation of a phrase in the Book of Revelation, when, in depicting the sevenfold glory of Christ, the writer says:

> 'His voice, as the voice of many waters.'★

★Rev. 1. 15.

"This is poetry," Dr. Morgan said, "but it is interpretation on the highest level. It is impossible for me ever to forget the moment when that came to me with singular power for the first time, quite unexpectedly. It was when I stood by the Falls of Niagara, and listened to the voice of the waters. As I listened, my mind worked backwards from the point of the falling of the waters to the sources whence they had sprung. Immediately behind was the great lake, pouring itself over; but further back the rivers were pouring themselves into the lake, and yet, to travel by the route of the rivers was to find them being created by brooks and rivulets, all merging in the rivers' waters, and so proceeding by way of the lake to Niagara's voice of many waters. God had spoken in times past in divers portions and in divers manners. The streams had moved on, and ever on, until at last He spoke in His Son, whose voice was 'as the voice of many waters.' We listen to the music of the streams, but nothing is finished, nothing is complete. The voices of the past through prophets, all uttered the speech of God; but finality came in the Son, in whom all the streams met and merged."

The letters reveal his constant thought of those at home, and his desire that they should share these experiences with him, especially Nancy, who is told of the loss of his wedding ring in New York on August 18th. "I have been very much grieved . . . that I have lost my ring. . . . How strange that Bert and I should both come here to the States to lose our rings! I am trying to hope against hope that it may yet turn up somewhere, but it is, I fear, very unlikely." It is improbable that Nancy needed to be reminded that it was their eighth wedding anniversary on August 20th. It was not forgotten on the other side of the Atlantic Ocean, as her husband wrote in his diary that day: "Over three thousand miles apart, Nancy and I are more one in heart and thought and purpose than ever before. To-day I waft her many a message of love across the distance, and receive many such from her. May our faithful God have her and our precious boys under His special care. He will. That is my joy, and to Him I render praise again to-day for that choice gift of eight years ago." On September 17th the ring was found, and gave much cause for rejoicing. "It had occurred to me," he said, "that perhaps I had lost my ring on the elevated railroad, so I called at their lost property office and gave a description of it, etc. They went to their books, and from thence to a great safe, and the next thing I knew was that my ring was in my hand again, safe and sound. I was more glad than I can tell."

"I feel quite reluctant to leave Bert," he wrote on the eve of departure for home. The old ties had bound them more closely together in the long talks about things of mutual interest, sometimes "comparing sermon notes," sometimes "comparing the old country with this, and the methods and manners of each." They laughed at the same things—a sure basis for friendship—and both enjoyed at times the kind of sport that is detrimental to furniture, but an outlet for animal spirits, as when "Bert had a wedding. . . . A couple came in, and he performed the ceremony in his sitting-room. . . . After they had departed . . . I tried to mob Bert for his fee, but without success!"

One night, "we sat until twelve o'clock talking. I gave him the story of my Sark experience. . . . It is good to have these long chats with him again, bringing back all the old happy days. I think he and I are more than ever one in heart."

★ ★ ★ ★ ★ ★

There was nothing lacking in the enthusiastic and affectionate welcome home by the congregation of the Westminster Road Church, where the work was taken up again with as much energy and industry as if the absence had been spent in rest and recreation, instead of work and travel. But the success of the American visit had not only preceded Mr. Morgan to Birmingham, but also to London, where the New Court Church, at Tollington Park, North London, was looking for a minister. In November he preached for them, and the opportunity of the field was placed before him.

"There is certainly an enormous sphere of work here for someone," he wrote in his diary. But in December, when the call came, it was difficult to make a decision because, he said, "I have no light whatever in the matter, and must wait." This verdict rested, not so much on a choice between staying in the congenial atmosphere of the growing church in Birmingham, and the challenge of a big opportunity in a suburb of the metropolis, as on a single desire to find the divine Will in the matter. Life was so ordered as to be unsatisfied with any other course. "I have no definite light yet," is a phrase which recurs with persistent regularity. After a few days he followed an old custom of seeking advice from trusted friends, and talked the situation over with Dr. John Henry Jowett who had succeeded Dr. Dale to Carr's Lane, and later with Mr. Frank Crossley, of Manchester, as well as with friends in the Birmingham congregation. All these conferences he calls "very helpful," adding: "I do not yet see what the result is to be, but I am more clear on certain points. . . . I am still amid conflicting thoughts about Tollington Park, but am quite at rest that I shall be led aright in the matter."

The conclusive decision was given at a church meeting on December 30th. "I . . . announced my decision *re* London. After hearing all the facts of the case, they unitedly said that I ought to go. The church meeting was a painful experience, made more so by the very fact of the extreme kindness of every word said."

A deep affection for this Birmingham congregation was reciprocated in grateful acknowledgment of all their minister had meant to them, individually and collectively, in the three and a half years of their association. The church's membership had more than doubled in that time, and renovation and enlargement of its premises had been accomplished without debt, largely due to the efforts of a pastor who, seeing the necessity of these things, never lost sight of the 'one' thing—the preaching of the Word, from which the other benefits ensued.

In the years which followed, Dr. Morgan returned upon many occasions to preach in the Westminster Road Church. He continued to contribute to the church's magazine, and 'kept in good repair' the friendships formed in Birmingham. Much credit for these long-standing friendships, however, belongs to Mrs. Morgan and her little birthday book, which, at the end of her life, was filled with names on almost every line. All over the world there were those who, on their special 'day' received a letter from 'T.L.M.', enclosing a card or a poem that seemed to have been selected for that special friend. Never a tiresome task, it took long hours out of busy days to write those little notes, enclose the right verse for the occasion, and often the dollar bill or the ten shilling note where it would do the most good. The recipient, no matter how far away, felt the warmth of her thoughtfulness, because many times she would be the only one that remembered. Thumbing the pages of that much-worn little book, which is one of her children's treasures, is to be sadly conscious of the many who would most sorely miss her remembrance and help. Dear little mother, who was wise enough to know best where her talent lay! She had the genius, so rare, yet within the reach of all, to build her memorial in the hearts of others, by

> Those little, nameless, unremembered acts
> Of kindness and of love.

CHAPTER IV

1897-1904: 34 to 41 years

NEW COURT, TOLLINGTON PARK—NORTHFIELD
EXTENSION WORK IN THE U.S.

IT is unfortunate for the New Court Church at Tollington Park that Campbell Morgan's ministry there, from 1897 to 1901, has been over-shadowed by Westminster, for that ministry was unique in itself, as to both the quality and diversity of his activity in the rôles of preacher, pastor, lecturer, and organizer. Boasting a proud and romantic history, the Tollington Park Church advanced to yet greater heights in the years that rounded the century, and held an enviable position in the religious life of London—one which can only be realized when a great pastor and a great church work together harmoniously and whole-heartedly. The man who had achieved national prominence at the age of thirty-five, and who found it impossible to fulfil all the demands made upon his time, had, to all appearances, reached the summit of his career. It was not unusual for Campbell Morgan to preach at New Court on Sunday, or deliver a Bible lecture on Wednesday evening, and go straight from the church to the station, to board a train for the West of England or the South of Scotland, the Isle of Man or the Welsh coast, where he would speak three or four times, and get back to London for the next scheduled service in his own pulpit. Many of these engagements were important Bible conferences, or services in city churches, but he liked to return, whenever possible, to the little towns of the Potteries where so much of his earlier work was done. He loved the reunion with old friends, staying in their homes, having 'quiet chats' before bedtime, noting "how many of the old faces are missing, and how many of those who were children seventeen years ago, are growing up into the places of trust."

Photo: J. Russell & Sons

G. CAMPBELL MORGAN—1897

Photo: J. Russell & Sons

NANCY

This itinerant ministry was not carried out at the expense of standing before his own congregation with any lack of preparation. That preparation was often paid for in other ways, for he rose early and retired late. Those who crowded into the church to be stirred by the wonder of the Bible, and see for the first time, or in a new way, the mighty sweep of its message, had no knowledge of those lamp-lit hours before day. This man, so dynamic and virile in the pulpit, they had not seen in a circle of light at five o'clock in the morning, with Bible and notebook spread before him. Neither had they seen him in the compartment of a train, speeding through the countryside, making notes in neat and microscopic writing, as his thoughts wandered through the labyrinthine paths of a text, exploring, analyzing, seeking for truth and ways to interpret it. The potent message, the attentive listeners, the intangible atmosphere of union between teacher and taught, was the result of arduous, concentrated toil and unremitting devotion to 'this one thing I do,' this preaching the Word—this above all. To Campbell Morgan, his paramount duty and the constant burden upon his heart, was to 'feed the sheep and the lambs.' The smallest 'lamb' in the Sunday School was as important in his eyes as the mature scholar. "I had a good time talking to the children," he would write, after many a Sunday afternoon's visit to the School. For the young people at New Court, a Christian Endeavour Meeting was held after the mid-week service, at which the pastor was a frequent visitor, and often a speaker. These gatherings were provided to give shop assistants, students, professional young people and others, an opportunity for worship and recreation. Despite the many outside demands upon his time, the pastor kept a finger upon the pulse of his church, calling deacons' meetings to discuss 'my Debt Scheme,' 'the work for next winter,' the organization of a visiting sisterhood or a missionary project. His keen interest in Missions was responsible for his election to the Board of Directors of the London Missionary Society in 1899. Religious magazines asked for his sermons; publishers became interested in the sales of the first small volumes bearing the name of G. Campbell Morgan and asked for more. Series of Bible studies and analyses were being prepared and given weekly to congregations who crowded into the building an hour before the time for the service. Dr. Charles Brown, one of London's outstanding Baptist ministers, and Dr. Morgan's contemporary in the New Court days, paid a whimsical tribute to this ability to draw the crowds, when he said at Dr. Morgan's Memorial Service at Westminster in 1945: "He came to my neighbourhood unknown in North London. I had never seen him. I had heard of him, but it was soon manifest and obvious that a new force had come to disturb the placid waters of suburban denominationalism. . . . He had flowing locks and a bubbling humour, which came into his exposition and preaching. The mobile people of our congregations would stray away when a new star appeared in the firmament, and Dr. Morgan's coming created vacancies in many congregations. These people would meet their minister, after coming to New Court and listening to Dr. Morgan, and, with shining faces, they would tell him what a treat they had had, and they would express the opinion that if all ministers preached like that, all the churches would be filled. As if any man would attempt to preach like that man, or ever could!"

Following his career in the clipped words of a hastily written record, gives the impression of breathless activity carried forward with enjoyment, and saved from distraction by poise, a keen sense of humour, and an inner solitude of spirit.

"I reached home this morning (from Newcastle-on-Tyne) and had a quiet, happy day. . . . During the evening looked towards Sunday. I am thankful to say that, notwithstanding the rush of the week, I am feeling well. 'As thy days . . so thy strength.'"

"To-night (Sunday) we had a large congregation. During the sermon we had a thunderstorm, and I had to fight with it for the attention of the people. Pretty hard work. I won because I kept on longest!"

The increasing pressure of work and correspondence made the need for secretarial help acute, and Mr. Morgan was grateful for kindly volunteers who offered their services. One of these was Miss Winifred Howell, who, with her family, was a member of the New Court Church. When Mr. Howell, a fine musician, passed away, Mr. Morgan asked Miss Howell if she would come in regularly each week and help him with his work. The offer was gratefully accepted. The inauspicious and modest nature of her advent into the home could not have seemed significant at the time. None could foresee that this tall young girl would, from this time forth, give her life's devotion and undivided loyalty to 'the General,' the name she chose to call him. Though untrained in secretarial work at the time, Miss Howell found many ways in which to be helpful. In a short time it was clear that a business course would add much to her usefulness. She gave herself to this study, and applied what she learned to the peculiar demands of a busy minister's life. To a knowledge of shorthand and typewriting she added the rudiments of library methods. With her own Christian background, and a familiarity with church life and organization, these technical accomplishments soon made her indispensable to her new employer. She was efficient and painstaking, interested in every detail of her work, and so identifying herself with it, that he was able to relegate to her judgment and execution more and more responsibility. Nor was this the extent of her activity. Mrs. Morgan became a friend to whose kindness she responded with loving appreciation. She found innumerable ways to be of service to a busy wife and mother, and spared neither time nor effort to do so. None of the children, except Percy, could remember a time when 'Winnie' had not been at hand, and the birth of 'Frank Crossley', in 1898, was usually linked in the mind of the family with her coming. "Winnie came to Dad the year Frank was born," was the way they always remembered it. On their part, the children looked upon her as being as much a part of their home as a piece of furniture, to be loved and abused in turn. She nursed them, scolded them, indulged, taught and advised them. In the unconcerned manner of children they made jokes about her hats, imitated her manner of addressing a meeting, ignored her commands, and tolerated those peculiarities which, seen in others, are always so lacking in ourselves. She saw clearly through their thoughtless ways to the knowledge that they loved her devotedly. She was content to know that she had a part in furnishing a background of security and dependability to their environment. As the older ones grew into manhood and established homes of their own, they complained to each other that she still bossed them, lectured them, and called them 'the boys.' It never occurred to any one of them to question her unwavering loyalty, so completely had she submerged her life in that of the family she served. Servants, friends and guests came for a time to join the family circle, but Winnie, like the brook, went on forever—or so it seemed. Only when, in 1924, a severe illness laid her aside, and necessitated a long absence from the home, did her adopted family realize what they had always known, that Winnie was— WINNIE, and therefore unique, and quite irreplaceable. What she meant to Dr. Morgan himself cannot be expressed in words. She was all that an efficient secretary and librarian can be. In addition, she was a charter member of his Westminster sisterhood, in which capacity she 'guarded the vestry', ushering in those who wished to see the Doctor, and often becoming, to those waiting their turn, a patient listener and sympathetic confidante. Miss Howell was, herself, an excellent Bible teacher, and as such, made for herself a wide circle of friends in each of Dr. Morgan's subsequent pastorates and places of residence, both in England and America. It is peculiarly fitting that he should have dedicated the volume published in 1938, which he called, 'THE BIBLE, FOUR HUNDRED YEARS AFTER 1538,' to

WINIFRED MARY HOWELL

> For over forty years my Confidential Secretary, Fellow Worker, and Friend; through whom the publication of this Volume has been made possible, for she reported the lectures and has prepared them for the Press. This Dedication is a small tribute to her devotion during those forty years in the wilderness with me.

There is a sense in which it may be said that her own life ended with the passing of her 'General,' though she survived him for two years. In physical weakness, and by almost superhuman strength, she felt that there was one more labour of love she must leave accomplished. Setting herself to read through sixty years of diaries, she gleaned from them all that she felt might facilitate the work of his biographer. With loving and painstaking care she typed out these notes, allowing herself, at the end, one word of self-explanation and tribute. With touching simplicity she wrote: "When the father of her family died, a grief-stricken girl found in the minister and his wife in early New Court days, help and sympathy. This led to a closer tie. For nearly fifty years after this, it was her privilege to enjoy the friendship and share the work, principally on the literary side, of her friend. Living in close touch with him and 'The Little Mother,' travelling with them, sharing their joys and sorrows, was a unique experience, the value of which, to her, can never be measured. She thanks God upon every remembrance of them both."

★ ★ ★ ★ ★ ★

During the four years at New Court, Campbell Morgan was also becoming more widely known in the United States. Mr. Moody invited him to Northfield again in 1897, at the same time asking for return visits in the two summers ahead. By 1899 Mr. Morgan's itinerary included thirteen of the largest cities in the United States and Canada. It was, in all respects, a triumphal tour, and established Campbell Morgan as a Bible expositor of the highest order. People hungry for such teaching crowded the churches where he was to speak, and spread the news of this vital and appealing preacher and teacher wherever they went. The crowning indication of success, judging from all human standards, came in an invitation to the pulpit of the Fifth Avenue Presbyterian Church of New York City, where he preached three times just prior to sailing for home. A call from the wealthiest and most renowned Presbyterian Church in the metropolis of the New World, has been declined by very few. Yet, at thirty-five years of age, Campbell Morgan declined the call. There were those critics who said of him that he 'must have his crowd'. Others asserted that money meant to him more than it should to a minister of the Gospel. There was some ground for truth in the first criticism, as has already been stated, but none in the second. "You are an extravagant man, Dr. Morgan," someone once said to him. "I am not an extravagant man," he replied, "but I *am* an expensive man." He wanted the best, and was willing to pay for it. He received large honorariums, raised by voluntary offerings. He gave away such untold sums of money in acts of kindness and charity to others as would silence any murmurings of censure, had these gifts been publicized, but they were never advertised, and rarely spoken of, even in the family circle. If fame and wealth had come first in his life, he would most certainly have accepted with alacrity the call to the Fifth Avenue Church, and settled down to a life in which both these desires would have been satisfied. New York's cosmopolitans and transients would have filled the church Sunday by Sunday where such preaching could be heard, and the salary would have insured ease and luxury of living for himself and a growing family. If he had felt it to be within the divine Will that he accept this call, nothing could have turned him from it. That it was most definitely not within the divine Will for him at this time, he proclaimed by quietly and resolutely shouldering again the needs of New Court. Among these was the material need for a new building programme.

Like Westminster Road, Birmingham, New Court owed to Campbell Morgan the initiative to renovate and remodel its premises, for the debt incurred was paid in large part by the proceeds of his lectures, and the interesting and entertaining reports of the summer visits overseas. In addition, certain hours were set aside for 'sitting at the receipt of custom in the vestry', to receive donations and subscriptions to the Debt Scheme. When a great denominational financial drive called 'The Twentieth Century Fund,' was launched, the pastor needed all his ingenuity to persuade the deacons first, and then the congregation, to see the altruism of this larger challenge, when the immediate issue was so pressing. It was one of the few times that Campbell Morgan allowed himself a criticism of a system of Church government in which he so strongly believed. "Presided at Deacon's Meeting *re* Twentieth Century Fund," he wrote. "No enthusiasm. This wretched independence!" But perseverance won out, and New Court's share in the great fund was worthy of a missionary-minded congregation.

Another project for whose sake the pastor pleaded, persuaded, and finally won over his people and obtained their whole-hearted support and co-operation was the cause of the Holloway Chapel. Mr. Morgan had been reading *Sesame and Lilies* about this time, and in his habitually thorough and systematic way, when a great piece of writing appealed to him, he investigated the author, learning all he could about him. It is not known whether he was in any way influenced by John Ruskin's interest in the Holloway Congregational Chapel, which he had established in architectural annals by calling it one of London's most perfect examples of Gothic, or whether the fact that a church, once strong and forceful, had fallen on evil days. Both these factors may have entered into Campbell Morgan's determination to relight the lamp of witness and usefulness in this place. At subsequent deacons' meetings the possibility of the reopening of Holloway Chapel was discussed, plans and suggestions were submitted, the premises were inspected, and a survey of the community was made. Some of the old members were brought together with others who were interested in the venture. In December of 1899 a group of workers was organized, some from New Court, and some from the vicinity of Holloway Chapel. Under Mr. Morgan's direction they canvassed the neighbourhood, announcing the reopening of the building for public worship. Mr. Morgan himself, and other visiting ministers preached, and attendance increased, until it seemed justified to call in the services of a pastor. On January 3, 1900, Mr. Morgan, in writing up his diary for the previous day, reported: "Edmunds reached here soon after 3.30, and we immediately drove down to Holloway Chapel to look over the premises. This evening Messrs. Wilkins, Vinter, Schofield, and Heiron* came up, and we talked the whole business over together. They left at 9.30. Edmunds and I then had some further chat together, retiring at 11.30." By October, through the joint efforts of Mr. Edmunds, the new pastor, his group of workers, and the New Court support, the Holloway congregation was reorganized, and became a self-supporting and growing force in its community. New Court continued to watch with real interest the progress of its protégé, and New Court's pastor was ever a constant and welcome guest.

Early in the New Year of 1900, and with no other warning than a sore throat diagnosed as 'tonsilitis,' Campbell Morgan's 'old enemy' returned to strike with almost deadly power. In January a consultation of doctors resulted in the sentence of 'complete silence' for two months, on which the patient commented philosophically: "Evidently I need to listen for a while—and I am content." The treatment did not meet with the expected result, however, and after some weeks of extreme pain and weakness, it was decided that an operation was imperative. On the diary page of February 13th, in Miss Howell's handwriting, are the words: "Operation—an hour and a half—Isaiah 41. 13."† Dr. Morgan often referred

---

*Deacons of New Court.

† For I, Jehovah thy God, will hold thy right hand, saying unto thee, Fear not; I will help thee.'

to the nurse whose skill and kindness had been a large factor in saving his life. Nurse Burgess was a Roman Catholic, and except for her attendance at early Mass on Sunday morning, gave her patient complete and whole-hearted devotion. There were times in preaching or giving a Bible lecture in Westminster Chapel, when every one of the two thousand, five hundred seats were filled, and it was not unusual to see a Roman Catholic priest sitting, perhaps, in the same pew with a Salvation Army lassie, that some reference might be made to the Roman faith. "I owe my life to the devotion of a Roman Catholic nurse," Dr. Morgan would quietly testify, and sometimes follow that remark with the comment that: "Whenever I see a nurse on the street, I feel I want to raise my hat to her." It would give Dr. Morgan cause for gratification to know that, at this time of writing, two of his granddaughters are graduate nurses, and a third is in training.

Five years later Dr. Morgan used the experience of this illness in speaking of the words of Paul in 2 Corinthians 1. 3-7.

"Before going to the United States it fell to my lot to be suddenly smitten down in the midst of work very dear and precious to my heart, and for three long, and in many senses, weary months I was not able to touch my work. I found out a great many things in those months. I found out what Paul meant when he spoke of the God of all comfort. God comforted me, not only directly but also through his own people. It is a great thing for a minister to suffer if it is only to find out how tender his people can be. When I got back to my work one of the first men I went to see was Dr. Parker. Sitting and talking I said to him: 'I do not know at all why God has laid me aside. I am not complaining, but some men come back from sickness and speak of the vision they have had, of the new revelation of God they have had. I do not feel that I have gained anything.' Dr. Parker replied in his inimitable way: 'Never mind whether you know or not; your people will find out. There will be a new tone in the preaching.' And I felt that day that God had answered my questionings in that little vestry behind the City Temple. It was worth while to have suffered if there should come into my life any tone that should speak for the comfort of suffering hearts."

It is of interest to learn that, after leaving her patient well on the road to recovery, Nurse Burgess returned to visit, not Dr. Morgan, but 'Jackie' the four-year-old who insisted on sitting outside his father's door when no one was allowed to enter, and whom Nurse Burgess at last carried in to be his father's first visitor.

On the morning of December 23rd, 1899, the newspapers of the world proclaimed the death of D. L. Moody. Many were to recall Mr. Moody's own words as he anticipated those headlines: "Some morning you will see in the newspapers, 'Moody is dead'. Don't believe it! I shall never be so alive as I shall be in that morning!" Campbell Morgan must have remembered those words when he opened his London paper. Appreciating their significance, he nevertheless felt shocked by the loss of the man to whom he had come so close in the three years of their friendship; whose hand he had held in farewell only a few months before, and with whom he had looked forward to a joyful reunion in the summer ahead. "A great blank," is the way he recorded it. "How past finding out are His ways! We felt that, just now, we could not do without him. Oh, the comfort of the ever-living One!"

Past finding out, indeed, when in the summer of 1900, Campbell Morgan, who, himself, had so recently lingered in the dark valley, stood upon Round Top, where the tree-shaded mound which had so often served as a pulpit for his friend, now afforded his last resting place. Stranger still, as unfolding circumstances revealed God's plan for Northfield, and the part Campbell Morgan was to play in it. In October of that year, Mr. Will Moody, the son who was to shoulder so ably the responsibility of carrying on the Northfield tradition, crossed the Atlantic for the purpose of asking Campbell Morgan to help him in the great task. Would he come and make his home in Northfield, and go from there to all parts of the United States, preaching and giving Bible lectures under the Northfield Extension programme?

"No other church in the world could have tempted me from a pastorate which is a peculiarly joyful one," he told his own people in explaining to them his reasons for his resignation. "This, I trust, was proved by my refusal last year to entertain the advances made to me by the Fifth Avenue Church in New York. In this Northfield invitation the case is different. I have long felt that God was preparing me for a ministry to the churches, rather than to one particular church. Now the door stands open for such work. It has not opened in my own country where I hoped and thought it would. . . . To wait would be to choose for myself, when I wish that God would choose for me."

Campbell Morgan ended his pastorate at New Court on March 31st, 1901, and sailed with his family for the United States, on June 12. This was the first of the 'big moves' which Mrs. Morgan and Miss Howell organized and executed with such efficiency and despatch. While Mr. Morgan personally directed and participated in the packing of his library, his time was otherwise occupied in a 'farewell' preaching and lecturing tour of more than a dozen towns and cities, including the best-loved Midland communities where most of his residential ministry had taken place.

But the religious circles of London were not content to let him go without a public demonstration to voice their sense of loss in 'loaning' one of their most gifted and eloquent leaders to the United States, to express to him their affection, and assure him of their prayers for his new work.

With the willing co-operation of Dr. Parker, the City Temple was procured, and arrangements were made for a reception, followed by a public meeting in the great church. Police aid was necessary to control the crowds who desired admittance. Dr. Parker was accustomed to seeing the building filled to capacity, but he said he had never witnessed such crowds as came for the evening meeting.

The programme carefully preserved in the pages of the diary is decorated, in the fashion of the times, with flowers, birds, curlicues, and an appropriate ship in full sail; yet these serve only to emphasize the timeless atmosphere of that memorable occasion. With Dr. Parker in the chair, the opening hymn set the tone for all that followed—'We come unto our father's God; Their Rock is our Salvation'. As Rev. E. M. Edmunds led the opening prayer, one can imagine how many in that vast congregation held membership in Holloway Chapel, or had had a part, under Mr. Morgan's leadership, in its reorganization.

The speakers of the evening represented all denominations, for Campbell Morgan's appeal had, from the beginning, superseded these barriers, and never allowed them to limit his friendships. The name of Rev. J. Gregory Mantle is of special interest. This friendship had ripened during the years, and it is evident that Campbell Morgan placed much confidence in his judgment, and consulted him on more than one occasion when in doubt about his future. Gipsy Smith's place among the speakers is a reminder of Campbell Morgan's interest in the work of the evangelist, and of his special affection for the Gipsy.

The occasion lacked nothing of loving affection for its honoured guest. There is a heart-warming message on the back of the programme which must be quoted:

> Good-bye!
> Make haste back!
> Be sure and take a return ticket!
> An affectionate Good-bye!
> God bless Wife and Bairns!
> God bless You!

Those who would miss him most—the people of New Court, said good-bye to their pastor in a Farewell Meeting on the eve of his sailing. A simpler and less spectacular gathering, he yet described it as "a wonderful time, maintained at a high level for three hours." The closing lines of one of the hymns was a prayer which was to be answered in fullest measure in the new sphere of service:

> And grant him many hearts to lead
> Into Thy perfect rest,
> Bless Thou him, Father, and his work
> Bless, and they shall be blest.

★ ★ ★ ★ ★ ★

To set down the progress of Campbell Morgan's life and work with any degree of accuracy, superlatives should be reserved for the later and maturer years; yet it is difficult to describe the period of Northfield Extension work in more moderate terms, for a bright page was written into the record of religious history in those three years of travelling ministry. Had he himself told their story, the emphasis would have fallen consistently where it belonged, glorifying the Master Who used him as an instrument in His service. In his single desire to walk in the pathway of the divine Will, he found a wellspring of peace in the midst of almost constant activity. There were contributing factors also on the earthly plane which oiled the wheels of success. A home from which to start out on a journey with confidence, secure in its devotion and surrounded by its prayers, is a home to which one returns with joyful anticipation as a haven of rest and refreshing. If Campbell Morgan's ministry was a blessing to others, it was, in large part because his own life, in this respect, was so supremely blest.

When Mr. and Mrs. George Morgan first heard of their son's decision to take up his residence in the United States, they received the news with differing emotions characteristic of them both. 'Grandma' Morgan was all eagerness to go along. She was devoted to her grandchildren, and having appointed herself their first teacher, now felt indispensable to their safe launching upon the seas of education. 'Grandpa', on the other hand, saw no reason to leave his own land for the wide open spaces and the untamed wildernesses of the New World, and declared himself to be opposed to making any change in his environment. 'Grandma' accompanied the family to America, and was soon comfortably adapted to her new surroundings, and engaged in her task of teaching Jack and Frank their figures, and the mysteries of strokes and pothooks. It was not long, however, before 'Grandpa' relented, and wished that he, too, was a part of the new adventure. Campbell Morgan's love and consideration for his parents is beautifully expressed in the fact that, during the busy days of that first American summer, he took three weeks off from his work and went back to England. He helped his father to pack up, and brought him back to the United States, not willing that the old gentleman should manage his affairs alone, or to delegate to another his filial duty in this regard. Two years later, when his mother expressed a desire to return for a visit with her sister, he acceded to her wishes, making all arrangements for her to have as comfortable a journey as possible.

The home base for the first month was in Northfield, then for a time in Baltimore, Maryland, and ultimately in Northfield again. It was in Baltimore that the fourth son, Howard Moody, was born, named after Mr. D. L. Moody and Dr. Howard Kelly, eminent surgeon of John Hopkins University, a great Christian gentleman, Bible student and teacher. The new baby had black hair and a dark complexion, so that his brother Jack, much impressed by the fact that, in America, the family employed a coloured cook, suggested to his parents that the baby was 'a little coloured', a remark to be remembered and repeated, and take its place in the family saga.

Released from the duties and demands involving upon the wife of a minister in a residential pastorate, Mrs. Morgan was now able to give herself unreservedly to the task she loved best—home-making, but she never made her home duties an end in themselves, as model housewives often do. They were but a means to an end, and that end was the welfare of her husband and the onward march of his work. Her aim was to provide a home setting which would produce, to the best of her ability, the external comforts and physical well-being that would make this possible.

It was not often now that she could accompany her husband on his travels, but it was a great treat to both of them when she was able to leave affairs at home in capable hands for a few days at a time. Sometimes she took in part of a journey, and when they were again within easy reach of home she would leave him to go on to the next engagement alone. A brief and telling comment reveals what he thought of this procedure. "At 3 o'clock Nancy left for Baltimore," he wrote; "a sort of gap is created when she does this sort of thing! Strange!!"

In January, 1902, the Morgans, with Miss Howell and Mr. Will Moody, were in New York City staying at the Murray Hill Hotel. Workmen were excavating in the street in front of the building, when, by accident, some explosives were ignited, blowing up the street, killing a number of the men, and shaking the hotel to its foundations. Mrs. Morgan and Miss Howell were in their hotel apartment, and Mr. Morgan and Mr. Moody downstairs in the lobby. As the building trembled and glass shattered in every direction, the two men ran for the stairs, mounting as quickly as possible one flight after another. They found Miss Howell slightly cut by broken glass, but otherwise both ladies were uninjured. Dr. Morgan often referred to this incident as being the time when he was most conscious of the limitations of the flesh, the physical body holding him back as he tried so desperately to climb the stairs and reach those for whom he was most concerned.

In December of the same year Mrs. Morgan was with her husband in Washington, D.C., when they had the honour of being presented to President Theodore Roosevelt at the White House. They were given a most gracious interview, and received the President's signed photograph as a souvenir of the visit.

With Northfield as a base, and the extension of the Northfield programme of evangelism and Bible exposition as a goal, Campbell Morgan's itinerary carried him and his message far afield. In consultation with Mr. Will Moody and

Mr. A. P. Fitt, Mr. Moody's brother-in-law and co-worker, plans were laid weeks and months in advance for Bible conferences during the Autumn, Winter and Spring, providing for Mr. Morgan's presence in Northfield for the summer conferences, followed each year by a few weeks in England. Thus Moody's dream which became a reality in Northfield, and made it such an outstanding centre of Christian teaching and power, widened to make these things available in far distant and removed areas of population. From England, too, there came at Campbell Morgan's suggestion, some of the finest and best of her pulpit personalities to be heard on the Northfield platform.

So many hours were spent in train journeys, that it is safe to say that Mr. Morgan could have written an entertaining book, had he so desired, on the evolution of railroad travel. Instead he wrote of his experiences in letters to Percy, at the Hill School in Pottstown, Pennsylvania, while Jack and Frank filled albums with picture postcards. More than thirty years later, Frank was sending postcards home to his own little son, pictures of places where he was speaking at Bible conferences, and wrote to tell his father about it. "What you say," Dr. Morgan replied, "brings back very clearly to memory that I used to send *you* postcards beginning, 'Dear Fatty.' Well, it need hardly be stated that I should not feel justified in addressing you in that way at present, not only because it would not be consonant with your dignity, but it would not be according to truth."

The boys loved to hear, upon every return, of their father's travelling adventures, and had to be told again and again of the time when the locomotive left the rails on the edge of a steep embankment near Baltimore; of another which began whistling in the middle of the night and could not stop; of a time when the passengers were rudely awakened and almost thrown from their berths, because another train, passing on a side track, hit the tail end of the coach, carrying away the steps; of the first trip to the West Coast when, a day's journey out of Seattle, a trestle bridge ahead burned in the night, causing a freight engine and some cars to be precipitated into the gulley, and necessitating all on the passenger train behind to walk over a temporary bridge to another train on the opposite side.

Dr. Martyn Lloyd-Jones, in later years Dr. Morgan's associate and successor at Westminster, made a profound statement when he pointed out that Campbell Morgan came to his work immediately following the great evangelistic campaigns of Moody and Sankey, when new converts needed the work of the Bible teacher to strengthen and deepen their faith. This truth is borne out in the manner in which people flocked to hear him, as though starved and hungry for every word that was spoken. Wherever he went he was received with eagerness and heard with joy. Not once or twice, but day after day, week after week, churches were thronged and people turned away with almost monotonous regularity. Of a meeting in St. Paul, Minnesota, he wrote: "To-night I preached in the auditorium to 6,000 people, and hundreds were turned away." In Wilkes-Barre, Pennsylvania, the place of the evening meeting had to be changed to accommodate the size of the crowd. In spite of rain, "the building was completely filled—2,000 people . . . a great sight." In St. Louis, Missouri, the meeting place was "densely packed" for the first services. "The interest is very great. These two addresses have not been such as to amuse, and yet these great crowds have listened for an hour in each case with the closest attention." On another occasion in this same city "the Pilgrim Church was packed as was also the St. John's M.E. Church on the other side of the road. . . . I spoke in both places, an hour in Pilgrim and fifty minutes in St. John's." Of a Sunday service in Dayton, Ohio, it is recorded that "Three times have the buildings been utterly inadequate to accommodate the crowds." A meeting in Seattle, Washington, was climaxed on a Sunday when he spoke to 2,000 men for an hour and a half in the afternoon, and 3,000 people at night. In Atlanta, Georgia, he admits that "I hardly had room to stand and preach." On the Sunday, "I preached in the Tabernacle three times. The place has been literally besieged with multitudes of people. At no service was it at all possible to accommodate the people. Some got their seats in the building, and sat it out clear through the day." The Baptist Tabernacle here referred to was the home church of Dr. Len G. Broughton, one of the most outstanding religious leaders in Atlanta's history. Dr. Morgan came here more often than to any other city, except New York and those in which he held a pastorate, for during the Westminster years he and Dr. Broughton exchanged pulpits nearly every summer. From these early days he never failed to receive a great welcome in Atlanta. "Crowds in the Tabernacle were simply enormous," he wrote on another occasion. "Thousands were unable to get into the building." Meetings were arranged for men only, for young people and for ministers, as well as for mixed congregations. The results were the same—great crowds, overflow congregations, increasing in numbers as the period of the conference progressed, often having to be moved to larger quarters.

A lovely testimony to Dr. Morgan's appeal to young people, capturing their enthusiasm for Christ, and creating a life-long love for the study of the Bible, is told by Mrs. Herbert Halverstadt of Winter Park, Florida, mother of one of the fine young missionaries who have gone to Africa under the auspices of the Southern Presbyterian Church. She writes:

"I first heard Dr. Morgan at Northfield, Massachusetts, while I was still in College. My mother and I had gone for the first time to the General Conference held there in August. I was fascinated by Dr. Morgan's Bible lectures, and as a result I became a regular attender at the General Conference for seven consecutive years. I did not meet Dr. Morgan until the second summer. He was teaching the book of Genesis, and in discussing how to study the Bible he very emphatically urged everyone to secure a copy of Strong's Concordance, adding that if anyone would get one he would show him how to use it. That was enough for me. I immediately wrote to New York and ordered one. It came in due time, and I rather timidly informed Dr. Morgan that I had secured one, and would be very glad if he would show me how to use it. He was kindness itself, and told me to bring it to their cottage the following morning. It was a hot day in August, and the Concordance somewhat resembles a Webster's dictionary, but I walked on air all the way. From that time I have used it constantly in Bible study. Next to Dr. Morgan's books it is my most treasured volume. Never before had I studied the Bible by books. It is a very common practice now, but I do believe it was Dr. Morgan who started people reading and studying that way. His lectures were so illuminating that he never failed to draw crowds wherever he went, as I can personally testify, for it was my good fortune to be in many of the cities where he conducted Bible lectures. I have listened to him in New York, Brooklyn, Atlanta, Baltimore, Pittsburgh, San Francisco, Berkeley, Philadelphia, and London. In fact I never missed an opportunity to hear him if he happened to be anywhere in the vicinity, and I never failed to get great inspiration as well as information. Certainly he made everyone feel that the Bible was the most interesting Book in all the world, and he made everyone want to know more about it. To me he was and is the teacher supreme, and his teaching is original and authoritative. I constantly refer to his books. Most of all I value his friendship and counsel over a long period of years. I shall never cease to be grateful for him."

Campbell Morgan's paramount contribution to the cause of Northfield Extension lay in teaching the Bible and showing people how to study it for themselves. Auxiliary to this, however, was the promotion of Y.M.C.A. work, especially in centres where such an organization was lacking. He not only supported this work, but urged its worth and assisted in its development. His persuasive powers of raising money for causes dear to his heart were outstandingly demonstrated in the city of Denver, Colorado, in 1903, when, in two meetings on the same day, he asked for and received $1,000 in order to place a man in the Y.M.C.A. there, 'for distinctly personal and religious work'. Again, in 1904, in Los Angeles, he met with a company of business men, placing before them the claims of the Y.M.C.A., with the result that '$3,000 was raised round the table'.

In the early days of his ministry, Campbell Morgan learned to appreciate the value of the small group gathered together for prayer and Bible Study. These groups which he called Bible Readings met in homes, and those in the neighbourhood, particularly non-Christians, were invited to them. It is a tribute to his greatness that, in the day when his presence in a city was enough to ensure the assembling together of great masses of people, he still realized the importance of encouraging these small neighbourhood gatherings. He advocated them wherever he went, and would meet with them as far as time would permit. This he considered one of the fundamental factors of the Northfield Extension work—leaving in the wake of great Bible Conferences practical ways of continuing the study of the divine literature. At his suggestion many such Bible Reading groups were initiated in different places, under differing circumstances, in the homes of rich and poor alike. In Chicago, Mrs. Cyrus McCormick opened her home for this purpose, inviting her friends to come, and asking Mr. Morgan to attend the first meetings. This he did, and the impression he received provoked interesting comment in his diary: "At 4 o'clock went to Mrs. McCormick's and gave a Bible Reading in her drawing-rooms. It is a great question how much money was represented in those rooms—certainly thousands of millions of dollars." On the two succeeding days a larger company was present. The Book which he had carried into the slums of Hull, the villages of Staffordshire, and the towns of the Potteries, proved itself of equal dynamic as it was expounded in the homes of the wealthy and influential.

During these years of high tension activity, living for weeks at a time in hotels and on trains, Campbell Morgan adopted certain rules of health and habits to which he strictly adhered. In the matter of diet and rest these rules were unrelenting, and in accordance with them he declined, with few exceptions, entertainment in private homes and invitations to meals. It was inevitable that this practice should invite criticism from some quarters, but he knew that only by protecting himself in this way could he keep up the measure and quality of his work. It was always a happy event, however, when the itinerary led through, or included St. Paul, Minnesota, for a friend of the old days, before the Birmingham ministry, now had a church here. Mr. Archer's home was, indeed, a home to his friend, and a bit of England besides. Of one of these delightful reunions he wrote: "Tommy and I had one of the old-time long talks on all conceivable subjects, from the sublime to the ridiculous, with all the semi-tones!"

Part of the working day was set aside, if possible, for recreation. People soon learned that Campbell Morgan was an ardent golfer. He also enjoyed a game of tennis, and while in Chicago for a seven weeks' period, in 1902, took up horseback riding with enthusiasm! On trains and in hotel rooms, hours were deliberately and systematically set aside for work and study. This fact cannot be over-emphasized, for it is in this habit that the secret may be found of his ability to stand before throngs of people after a long journey, fresh and relaxed and brilliantly equipped for the exacting work of expository preaching. There was never any hint that the teacher was unprepared, or that preparation had been skimped; never could the feeling be sensed that the instructor was only one jump ahead of the pupil; but always the perfect poise that accompanies complete familiarity with the subject matter.

In August of 1902, Campbell Morgan stood before the Northfield Bible Conference to deliver his first lecture on the Minor Prophets. The audience that greeted him meant business. Notebooks were opened and pencils poised, and as the singing of the preparatory hymn died away, a thousand faces were lifted, and eyes were fixed in eager anticipation upon the tall ascetic figure on the platform. There followed an introductory message, and after that a day by day discourse which brought living, flesh and blood personalities from the Old Testament pages. One could almost hear the swish of their flowing robes and the pad of their sandalled feet in the dust; see their flashing eyes and uplifted hands, as they stood up for Jehovah in the market place and on the broad highway; veritably hear the ring of their prophetic voices, warning, condemning, threatening, pleading with their hearers. It was here that Campbell Morgan used his magic art of dramatic gesture, and sounded every organ stop of reasoning and emotion, through his person and his voice, climaxing it all in driving home the living message for the present day and hour. "How does he do it?" they marvelled. "It's all there, but I never saw it before." It *was* there, for he never embroidered the Book or distorted the text. But it had come to him in long hours of reading and study. For months, as he travelled across the plains and over the mountains, as well as in quiet hours in his Northfield study, the prophets had been his companions. He had lived with them, with the result that there was never any last minute haste to remember what they said, and why. They were his friends, and he had absorbed their spirit and message. One day's comment which might be duplicated in substance many times reads: "This morning just buried myself in Habakkuk and enjoyed it." In Northfield a closed study door meant that 'Dad' was working, and none might disturb him. "Play with me, Jack," said five-year-old Frank one day. But Jack for once had business of his own to attend to, and put his brother off with the reply: "I can't. I have to work on the Minor Prophets." Such is the force of example!

Nor was this the extent of Campbell Morgan's literary activity. There were Sunday School lessons to be prepared for religious magazines, manuscripts to be corrected for the printer, and always more and more reading and learning; for here was a man who never knew what it meant *not* to feel the need to know more. On a day in Los Angeles, when the crowds had been so great that the meetings had had to be moved from the church to the Pavilion, he wrote that "after lunch I went round to the Free Library here, and looked through the article by Schmiedel in the Encyclopædia Biblica on The Gospels." Rarely did Campbell Morgan voice a caustic criticism of a fellow minister, but after hearing one man tell a congregation that he felt he had reached the place where he had no further need to study, he simply remarked: "It was palpable!"

Yet, however much work had preceded a sermon or address, it is accurate to say that Campbell Morgan never once stood before a congregation without having given an hour or more of additional preparation to the theme which had already taken so much of reading and study. Here was the secret of the freshness of approach which was always characteristic of him. One of Dr. Morgan's daughters,* who for seven years was to travel extensively with her father through the United States and Canada, bore testimony to this fact when she said: "Some of his sermons I know almost word for word, and yet they never grow stale, they are never the same. Always he makes them fresh and new, and every time he preaches them I see new light thrown upon their theme."

Itinerating work brought Campbell Morgan in constant contact with new groups. A congregation composed of strangers at the first meeting turned into friends as the conference days progressed. Always sensitive to atmosphere, he admitted very often a feeling of restraint before a new audience and in a new building. The fact that he mentions the 'spirit' of a meeting so often in his diaries, shows how much it meant to him. Sometimes it was 'a great spirit of expectation', or 'an interest that is quiet and deep'. Yet on another occasion (and this in the familiar air of Northfield itself): "I felt the wheels drove heavily, but I think the message was the right one." There were other times when the going was hard; where the richness of architecture, and the physical grandeur of a building seemed to have suffocated the spiritual realities, and made it difficult to reach through

*Kathleen.

to the congregation. But for the most part the people were waiting and hungry for the Bread of Life, and its breaking was all joy and delight.

Summer time meant Northfield Conference time and more busy days, for the programme often included lectures to the students at the Northfield schools, and week-end trips to New York City, where Dr. Morgan supplied the pulpit of the Fifth Avenue Presbyterian Church for weeks on end. But they were also exceedingly happy days, because now Campbell Morgan could enjoy his home "and all the family," as one child expressed it with much satisfaction on one of those great days in mid-summer when 'Dad' came home to stay. "It is not easy to leave them all behind," he had written, after one of the 'peeps at the family' which was about all he allowed himself during the rest of the year, "but I am ashamed to write a word about suffering in His service, so great is the joy of it, and so easy does He make my pathway." When that pathway of service led back to Northfield and home, there was much rejoicing and gladness. Scenes of the wildest excitement marked his home-coming, for he himself was excited beyond words, and impatient to be back. Therefore the first hours of reunion were occupied with 'romps with the boys', 'playing trains', and 'marking railroad maps with Percy'. He loved Northfield, too, for its own sake and for its natural beauty, and enjoyed nothing better than the country drives in horse and buggy with his friend, Will Moody. "What a glorious old earth this is even now!" he wrote after such a day's outing, "What will it be when redeemed man knows how to get the best out of it!"

To the children Northfield was an idyllic existence. After living in London where one always had to be 'dressed', to be put down in this play-time paradise, where overalls and bare feet were not only tolerated but encouraged, and where one was allowed to play with a minimum of supervision, was like a dream come true. But after England, the Northfield summer weather was extremely hot, and two small boys, left to themselves, were soon devising ways and means to alleviate the situation. At eight years of age, Jack was fully able to grasp the fact of his father's exalted position in relation to the Northfield Conference, and saw no harm in bending it to his own advantage. Frank, at five, was always ready for a new adventure, especially when the plan was explained and he understood the nature of the benefits to be derived from it. All these nice kind ladies were walking up the hill to the auditorium twice a day, just for the purpose of listening to Dad! What a golden opportunity! The two sat down beside the road to wait for the first group to pass, and were not disappointed in their victims when they asked: "Who are these dear little boys?" "We're Dr. Morgan's little boys," they replied. "We're dying of thirst. Please give us a nickel to buy a drink!"

The ladies were completely captured by the 'cuteness' of the young mendicants, and the harvest of nickels increased as other groups succumbed to the same treatment. Business was at its lucrative peak when Mrs. Will Moody came along driving her horse and buggy. She stopped to take in the small drama, and then drove on smilingly to tell Dr. Morgan in delighted tones what his sons were up to. With the suddenness that accompanies such catastrophes, the bottom fell out of the market, and business ceased abruptly and forever. It was always very funny to remember and talk about in the years to come, when Dr. Morgan could share the joke with his sons, but at the time there was a severe reprimand forbidding any recurrence of the escapade, which always called forth the remark: "We never forgave Mrs. Moody for that!"*

Christmas at Northfield was something to be fondly remembered, for 'Dad' came home again, this time to a world of white beauty, to share in sledding and snowballing.

---

* 'After reading over the MS. Frank wrote the following comment: "As to the 'Morgan boys' begging for money; Jack will bear me out when I say that our somewhat incensed feelings towards Mrs. Moody were created not so much by the fact that she told on us, but that Dad misunderstood and thought we had asked *her* for money which we had *not* done. Even in those days we were sly little rascals, for when we saw her coming we agreed we had better not solicit from her because, being so close a friend of Dad and Mother, we thought she might tell!!!" '

and drives in the sleigh behind belled horses. But mishaps befall the best of drivers. It was unfortunate that it was not the children Dr. Morgan was driving to Mt. Hermon one day, but a sleigh full of ladies. Rounding a curve the sleigh struck a snowbank, and tipped them all out! Christmas, 1902, was memorable, because it was on December 24 that the letter came notifying Campbell Morgan that the Chicago Theological Seminary had conferred upon him the honorary degree of Doctor of Divinity. That the honour was appreciated by the recipient goes without saying, but it is not mentioned in the diary. It seemed more important at the time to record "a real good, old-fashioned sort of Christmas Eve with the boys, getting apples out of a tub of water!"

Summer visits to England were of short duration during these three years, because of increasing demands in the United States, but they were important on two counts. In the first place Campbell Morgan was a good traveller. To this fact he owed much, for he could completely relax, and gain the utmost benefit from a sea voyage. He may have boarded the ship in a black or grey clerical suit, but on the first morning at sea he would appear at the breakfast table, after a turn on deck, in 'mufti', in all probability a checked suit, and very pleased with himself if a member of his party was startled enough by its brilliance to make a caustic remark about his tie. He could shed dignity and gravity as easily as he could adopt holiday attire. At all other times a sparing eater, when at sea his appetite was keen, and ship's food, which is proverbially appetizing and plentiful, he thoroughly enjoyed. Friends, who, at one time or another, crossed the ocean in his company, would agree that it had been an unforgettable experience. He rarely travelled alone, so wide was his acquaintance in the world of which he had become a part on both sides of the ocean. His was the art of remembering and telling the anecdote. One story led to another, and he enjoyed listening to those of his friends almost as much as he delighted in the rôle of raconteur. Indeed, many of Dr. Morgan's stories had been told him by others and stored up in his mind to pass on with telling effect. It was often said that in Campbell Morgan the stage lost a great actor. He had the professional's ability actually to become the character he was impersonating, and could not only imitate an accent or inflection of speech, but would often get up from his chair to act out the part he was playing with such perfect caricature as compelled his hearers to watch the tense drama with the most flattering absorption, and dissolve into helpless laughter at its climax. Congregations would be amazed could they see some of their clerical friends in their lighter moments, such as those when Campbell Morgan and his fellow-voyagers 'swapped stories' on deck. His inexhaustible energy spent itself at such times in pure fun and frolic. Those seven or eight days on board ship acted like a tonic, and renewed his vitality for whatever demands lay ahead at the end of the voyage.

The yearly contact with the homeland was also advantageous in that it kept Campbell Morgan in touch with church life there, and with religious thoughts and trends. He often spoke of Northfield, stimulating interest in the nature of his work in America. Not of least importance was his ability to interpret the New World to the old, and promote the cause of international understanding. He certainly used these visits to renew old friendships. It was consistent with his nature that, despite the honours that had come to him in the United States, he returned to the friends of past years with the same affection and interest in all that concerned them. News of the death of Mr. Wilkins, one of the deacons of New Court, came as he landed in England for one of these summer visits. He went straight from the ship to the home of the family in Tollington Park. After conducting the funeral service he said of it: "I remember nothing more difficult." On the following Sunday he attended the services at New Court with the bereaved family, afterwards going with them to visit the grave. "It is a lovely spot," he wrote. "There I leave the sacred dust of one of the best friends man or minister ever had."

Of all the busy years to this point, 1904 carries the honours as being the most eventful. Each month had its quota of incident, much of it unexpected and some unwelcome, but all memorable. April brought glad and welcome news to Dr. Morgan, when after a series of good meetings in Denver, he reached Omaha, Nebraska, to find a telegram awaiting him from the Northfield doctor: '*Rejoice and be exceeding glad—you have a daughter.*' The baby was named Kathleen Annie, and four brothers welcomed her for him, for she was three weeks' old before she met her father for the first time. Meanwhile, ever since the preceding summer in England, Dr. Morgan had been receiving communications from the officers of Westminster Chapel in London asking him to become their minister. He had received calls from three churches in the United States during these three years of residence, one in Philadelphia and two in Chicago. Each of these received his most careful consideration, but all were declined. The call from London, which persisted during the winter of 1903-04, met all Campbell Morgan's pleas of engagements ahead and plans for the future with the insistence that the church was willing to bide his time and his conviction in the matter. Dr. Joseph Parker, the most famous and influential of London nonconformist preachers, had passed away in November, 1902, and his voice was sadly missed. This factor certainly entered into the situation, and the Macedonian call to 'come over and help us' was too urgent and persuasive to be lightly set aside. Having talked the matter over with Mrs. Morgan, and also with those in charge of the Northfield work, he made arrangements to go to England in May and thoroughly investigate the situation. So important did he consider the outcome of the visit that it is not surprising to find Mrs. Morgan going with him. This was possible because the children, with the exception of Jack who accompanied his parents, could be left in expert hands and under capable supervision. Percy was away at school. Nurse Lothrop, who had been with the baby Kathleen since birth, remained to take care of her, and Frank and Howard, with the management of the household, were given into the capable hands of Miss Edith Wood, who had been brought from England in 1901 to help with the children. She afterwards married Mrs. Morgan's youngest brother, Edward, and became the 'Auntie Edith' so devotedly loved by all her nephews and nieces.

Albert Swift, back in England, had for some years been serving a church in East Dulwich, a suburb of London. The tie between these two friends had increased in strength despite separation, as is revealed by the account of a previous summer's visit: " . . . (we have been) chatting over old times and future plans. It was a quiet, delightful time with him, the like of which we cannot have now as often as we could wish, but we are both content to be in the circle of the Father's Will, for that is best." On Sunday morning, 22nd May, 1904, the ship bearing Dr. Morgan to England docked at Liverpool. The party reached London in the early afternoon. The diary completes the day's story: "Drove straight to East Dulwich Grove. Had a cup of tea and a quiet hour, and at 6.30 preached at the church. The place was overcrowded and many were turned away. I had a good time. Had a long chat with Bert over the general situation and retired at 11.30." Perhaps there had always been a hope in their minds that they would some day join forces and work together in the cause of the Kingdom. It was certainly in Campbell Morgan's mind and heart that the time had now come to do so, and it was soon evident to the officers of Westminster that he would only consent to enter upon what was a supreme venture of faith for both himself and the church, if Albert Swift would be his colleague. For four weeks Dr. Morgan filled preaching engagements in different parts of England, and wherever he met friends in whose judgment he placed confidence, "matters concerning America and Westminster" were discussed. Among these were Rev. Gregory Mantle, in London, Rev. Samuel Chadwick, in Leeds, and Mr. Frank Fifoot, in Cardiff, for he leaned heavily upon the interest and judgment of consecrated friends in both the ministry and laity. The longest and most frequent conferences were with Mr. Swift. Together they met with the officers of Westminster, discussing equipment, resources, and finances. They explored the premises from top to bottom, from the old tower to the basements; they looked into every nook and corner of the sanctuary itself; the old almshouses and other adjacent buildings were inspected—in fact they missed nothing! And what did they see? Everything to discourage the most doughty heart—that is, on the material level, for everything was not only old, but run down, dirty, and disreputable. But Campbell Morgan saw more than this, or perhaps it is more accurate to say he saw through it to the tremendous possibilities for a work after his own heart, a work centred first, last and all the time in the preaching and teaching of the Word of God. It is needless to say that this vision was fully shared by Albert Swift, and it was with the knowledge of his friend's wholehearted sympathy and enthusiastic devotion that the call to Westminster was accepted. This momentous decision was announced at the morning service, on Sunday, June 19th. It was a dramatic moment in the life of this old church as, even before Dr. Morgan had completed his remarks, Mrs. Mary Leighton, then organist, had climbed to her seat at the console of the great Willis organ and was ready to sound the opening chord of the Doxology. Unannounced and with one accord the whole congregation rose to its feet and sang the noble words, 'Praise God from Whom all blessings flow.' "It was a memorable occasion," wrote Dr. Morgan in his diary that night. To all who were present it was a mountain-top experience. To the one most concerned, no other words were needed to remind him in future days of that rare day in June, 1904.

With Mrs. Morgan and Jack, Dr. Morgan sailed back to the United States, on June 29th, aboard the S.S. *Baltic* on her maiden trip. She was at that time the largest ship in the world —24,000 tons. The nine-year-old boy had realized something of the importance of his father's visit to England. To have returned home under these conditions was going to be something else to make him the envy of his brothers! On Sunday morning aboard ship, Dr. Morgan read the Episcopal Service and Lessons for the day, and on Tuesday evening he preached in the saloon "by special request to a large and attentive audience."

July saw the family reunited in Northfield, and Dr. Morgan plunged into the busy Conference season.

As though events were not crowding each other fast enough, a crisis in the family took place in August, when three-year-old Howard was suddenly taken desperately ill. When the Conference was at its height his life was despaired of, and while his mother and Nurse Lothrop watched beside him the great assembly in the auditorium paused to pray for the child's life. Little as he was, he had lived long enough in the environment of sacred music and hymn-singing in the home to love the familiar tunes. As his mother sat beside his bed he said to her: "Sing to me about the sweet peas." When she hesitated, not knowing what he meant, he added: "*You* know—sweet peas, the gift of God's love." The sequel of the story must be told here, for this boy, for whom the Conference prayed, was the one who succeeded his father at the close of the latter's ministry at the Tabernacle Presbyterian Church in Philadelphia in 1932. Dr. Morgan himself conducting the service in Tabernacle, and announcing Howard's acceptance of the call, made this statement: "I think this congregation is human enough to understand the strange and almost mixed emotions which I have in making this announcement. I looked up my old diaries this morning in the early hours, and found an entry on August 3rd, 1904. You see how long ago that is. It is an entry that tells of a laddie who was not quite three years old who lay at the point of death in the hands of three physicians and nurses at Northfield; and of the whole Conference ceasing its considerations to pray that the laddie's life might be spared and devoted to the work of God. He now accepts your invitation. I dare not trust myself to say many things. . . . I greatly rejoice that when presently I shall lay down with more reluctance than ever I shall be able to tell, my privileges and responsibilities here, my baby boy will carry on the work. I know you will give him your loving support and sympathy. I have urged him to come when he was somewhat reluctant to face the situation; and so he comes. Forgive the personal word. Most of you are fathers and mothers, and are going to understand how a man feels on an occasion like this."

Once Campbell Morgan had reached a decision which he felt to be right he never looked back, or indulged in sentimental yearnings for 'the good old days'. For the days in America *had* been good, marked by material security and spiritual blessing, and enriched by many friendships. Now, as he set his face towards England again, and a new venture of faith, he did so in that quiet confidence which had prompted him on his fortieth birthday a few months before to write in his diary: "They have been years crowded with the goodness of my God. As to my use of them? Well, what He puts away I will not carry, and what He accepts I will rejoice in. These years are now with Him. For the rest, as I know my heart, they are at His disposal."

CHAPTER V

1904-1917: 41 to 53 years

WESTMINSTER—(BIBLE SCHOOL—MUNDESLEY—B.T.A. CHESHUNT—WAR).

'The latter glory of this house shall be greater than the former, saith Jehovah of hosts; and in this place I will give peace, saith Jehovah of hosts' (Haggai 2. 9: R.V.).

WHEN Campbell Morgan came to Westminster Chapel, Buckingham Gate, in 1904, the church was known in religious circles as the white elephant of Congregationalism. Fallen on evil days, its membership of two hundred was almost lost in the vast barn-like proportions of its shabby auditorium. Yet it had not always been so, for Campbell Morgan inherited a great tradition built by worthy predecessors.

Thirty-four years later, very near the close of his life's work, which had taken him across the thirteen years of his first ministry in Westminster, over thousands of miles of land and sea, to bring him back 'home' again at the end of the pilgrimage, Dr. Morgan told the Westminster Bible School of 1938 a story which is eloquent in its mute testimony of the 'former glory' of the church's history. "When I came to Westminster in 1904," he said, "my beloved friend, Albert Swift, being with me, we explored the building. The top gallery had not been opened for fifteen years. We found dirt and spiders there, but we found a Bible, covered with the accumulated dust of years. It was a remarkable Bible and I took it home to examine it. It was marked with a pencil mark round a verse or number of verses or part of a verse, and by the marking a date and a preacher's name. The name most often found was that of Samuel Martin, but there were other names of great preachers. A woman's name was in it, but nobody remembered her. Submitting it to careful examination I found she had been listening to sermons over forty years, and there are not many Sundays in that time that she had not listened to preaching. It was a marvellous record."

The Rev. Samuel Martin came to Westminster Chapel in 1843 as its first minister. Twice during his ministry, which covered thirty-five fruitful and beneficent years, the church building was enlarged to care for the growing congregation and to give scope to the work which was developing under his influence. His devout and deeply spiritual nature set the tone and rhythm of the church's life. Perhaps the outstanding attribute of this many-gifted personality was an inherent love for his people. " . . . no man can fully understand the place which my people have in my heart," he said, " . . . my very heartstrings have hold of Westminster." This devotion to his people led him to examine the church roll—nine hundred in his day—every quarter. Not only did he write to every member whose irregular attendance at the Communion Service suggested backsliding, but he bore them up in prayer before the Throne. A close friend once wrote of him: "He had a gift for prayer which matured as he himself was cast upon God." He formed the habit of praying for his people as individuals as well as groups. During the days of the week when the church was empty and still, he would kneel in the pews and pray for those whose names were listed there. What a picture for an artist! The golden sunshine of an English summer morning, or the cold waning greyness of a wintry afternoon catches in its shaft the lonely figure kneeling in the pew. In the white stock and black clerical garb of the mid-Victorian period, he is the only occupant of the building. We who are strangers to brush and pencil may, by imagination, convey the sense of height and capacity and emptiness in the building, the sense of loneliness and concentration in the kneeling figure, and perchance suggest a fancy which flashes through the mind, that should the white head be raised for an instant, he would find the sunshine and shadows of the outside world merged in the light of the Master's presence as 'the glory of the Lord' fills the house! In some office, some home, or in some distant city, the one for whom Samuel Martin pours out his soul in prayer is, perhaps, 'wondering how' his thoughts turn to his church home, and remind him of his duty and responsibility there.

During the next twenty-five years three others built upon this foundation of prayer—indeed, prayer was the mortar which cemented every pillar and stone, for each was essentially a man of prayer and self-dedication to his task. The Rev. Henry Simon who succeeded the Rev. Samuel Martin, was one of four brothers who all became ministers. His unique quality, according to his friends and the members of his congregation, was that 'he was one of those rare souls who could talk as well as preach Christ'. "The God he preached was not a God of long ago," wrote one of them, "he had spoken to Him that morning, and his Bible was inspiring as well as inspired. . . . Through all his preaching one effort was apparent, to tell his hearers at first hand what he had seen face to face with the Eternal, and lift them up by his own undoubting faith into a higher atmosphere."

The Rev. W. Evans Hurndall who succeeded him in 1894, and whose ministry was cut short by an accidental and tragic death after only sixteen months of service, filled those months so full that it almost seemed as though he wrote above his short tenure of office: 'So much to do! So little time to do it!' Mr. Hurndall brought to Westminster a love of the poor and lowly and underprivileged of society. He saw them with his Master's compassion 'as sheep not having a shepherd', and under him Westminster became a centre of activity in winning them to Christ, for he had the gift of inspiring others with his vision and enlisting them for service.

The man who succeeded him, the Rev. Richard Westrope, followed closely in Mr. Hurndall's footsteps, and Westminster became more and more a Christian social centre. Mr. Westrope's strongest desire was to make Westminster a lighthouse and refuge for the poor and humble whose homes and little shops crowded so closely around its doors. He was a man of enormous faith and vision. His ideal for Westminster was that it should be a 'people's church', with clubs, a labour bureau, a people's lawyer and a free medical clinic. "It was a task beyond his strength," said one of those who was drawn in to help him. "He reached for an ideal which could not be realized." How poor our world would be without the idealist! He reached beyond his grasp, and because he did the lives of many humble folk were drawn a little nearer to heaven.

All this is history, you say! Dr. A. T. Pierson drew a tremendous truth out of the grab bag of the English language when he said: "History! His Story!" If the ground had lain fallow and gone to seed for a time before Campbell Morgan put his hand to the plough, it was the same ground upon which history had sown the good seed—prayer, the love of the Bible, the passion for souls, the urge to put faith into action. The soil was ready. The atmosphere was pregnant with possibilities and promises for the future.

Toward this field in the centre of a great metropolis, the Master was leading his servant in a most remarkable way. In a statement to his people in January, 1905, Dr. Morgan told of the circumstances which had led him to the decision to accept this challenge. Characteristically he put first things first. "It is the Lord's doing," he stated, and proceeded to tell how he had first become interested in Westminster during Mr. Hurndall's ministry. At its close a friend had remarked, "Either Westrope of Leeds or you ought to go to Westminster." "That was the first word that ever connected my name with Westminster, as far as I know," commented Dr. Morgan. But first the New Court Congregational Church at Tollington Park, London, and later, in 1900, Mr. D. L. Moody and the Northfield, Massachusetts Conference, laid claim to him, and it was not until 1902 that Westminster's representative, Mr. R. C. Powell, approached him again. "I told him," said Dr. Morgan, "that I was pledged at least for another year to the States. He asked if they might approach me again in a year's time, and I said, 'Yes,' but it must be clearly understood that that did not in any way pledge me to accept, neither must it prevent the church from securing any man who might in the meantime appear. After that I carried Westminster in my heart, and earnestly hoped that the right man might be found. It was with a sense of personal relief that I learned of the call extended to Dr. Smith of St. Paul's, in 1903. When I came to England in the autumn of that year I found he had declined, and the vacancy was not filled.

"What followed is known to all. Suffice it to say I sailed for America on November 4th, with the call of the church in my pocket, and great perplexity in my heart. That perplexity was not lessened in the States, for when the American papers announced the fact of this invitation I was inundated with letters. In the course of a month six prominent churches had invited me to accept their pastorates. There was but one thing to do, and I did it. I wrote to the church at Westminster stating my dilemma, and suggesting that they wait six months till I could come over and examine the problem on the ground. I did not expect they would do so. It did not appear reasonable to ask it. They decided to wait—and thus I was pledged to come and consider. But for this action of the church it is almost certain I should never have come, for during the next six months continuous pressure was brought to bear upon me to keep me in America. Three theological colleges offered me positions on their faculties; one well known Christian man of wealth offered to build me any premises I needed for preaching and Bible Institute work, while my Northfield friends offered to rearrange my work so that I should be free to remain at the one centre, or go to any part of the world for special work, without any financial care or responsibility.

"My promise to consider Westminster bound me to keep an open mind. I came in June—and how shall I describe what I passed through? Believe me, I can never do it, and I will not attempt it. Suffice it to say, I came, I saw—God conquered, for there is no shadow of doubt in my heart that this is His doing. The vast opportunities on the other side of the Atlantic appealed to me with almost irresistible force, but the conviction that here was a strategic point in danger of slipping out of the hands of the church was too strong, and I came to be convinced that I, with the help of one other man, could hold it.

"The question was, Would he come? And when Albert Swift, my life-long friend, said he was willing to stand with me, the matter was settled. So I came. Now, by the grace of God, my heart is quietly confident, and I look for the guidance and blessing of that God Who never fails those who obey."

★ ★ ★ ★ ★ ★

None familiar with the history of Westminster will doubt that, as Campbell Morgan said: "It was the Lord's doing" that he came to the helm in 1904. There was always something irresistible to him in a lost, or seemingly lost cause. Here, on a larger scale, was a repetition of the challenge that had come during his first pastorate at Stone, in the almost extinct mission church of Eccleshall, and again in New Court days, when he had seen the need of the Holloway Chapel. He was always a champion of the underdog, whether it constituted an individual or a group. In the present case the 'underdog' had earned the added stigma of 'white elephant'. Viewing its battered and soiled appearance, one strongly doubted the suitability of the latter descriptive adjective. 'Under' it might be, but 'white' never!

The sight which would have halted one of less imaginative spirit, acted upon him as a spur to action. The vast emptiness of the interior, and especially the upper gallery, dared him to fill it—and he knew that he could. Its physical deformities cried out for money which could be channelled into building, painting and repairs. He would ask for it and get it, all of it, whatever the cost. Its neglect called for love and devotion, and spirit-filled lives of consecrated men and women. Were there not two of them to start with who were prepared to give all of these, himself and Albert Swift? And was there not that inner circle of faithful souls found in every church everywhere, which would form the nucleus of future growth? Just as it was, in all its decay and ugliness, it was to Campbell Morgan a building with character. Some who followed him in after years felt repelled by it; but from the beginning he loved it with the possessive affection which irrevocably binds the place and the man together. As it was 'Dale of Carr's Lane', and 'Parker of the City Temple', so it was to be 'Campbell Morgan of Westminster'.

In his favour was the fact that he did not come to Westminster a stranger. He had established for himself a definite place in the church life of London, and in the larger field of nonconformity in the United Kingdom in the years before going to America, and had kept his memory green in the summer visits home. Friends who had been drawn to him in former years knew his fitness for the task he had undertaken. They admired his courage and faith, and were prepared to support him with their help and their prayers.

Neither did he come to Westminster alone. Albert Swift, who had shared with him his youth and his calling in the work of the ministry, whose departure for a time had only served to strengthen their mutual affection, came forward now to join forces, and put his own broad shoulder to the wheel. His was a personality of singular sweetness and charm. His handsome bearded face radiated kindliness and good humour. Like an oak tree, he gave the impression of strength and stability, sensitive to every breath of life, yet rooted deep in the things he believed to be right. He had that intangible magnetism which is so attractive to young people. They saw in him something good and wholesome and strong, and knew him to possess that 'age-abiding life' they desired to inherit. From his experience as a pastor in the United States he brought a fresh approach and new ideas of organization. Dr. Morgan insisted from the first that they must be co-pastors. "He is not my assistant but my colleague in this work," he declared. But Mr. Swift knew that a ship can have only one captain. He identified his place in the pattern as well as that of his friend, and deliberately subjugated his own personality, making himself a supplement to his partner for the glory of God and the good of the whole.

In his first sermon as minister at Westminster Chapel in October, 1904, and again at the Recognition services which followed, Campbell Morgan reiterated a conviction which was upon his heart, and which he desired most earnestly that his congregation, and all who expected to be associated with the work in any capacity, should understand. 'We preach Christ Jesus as Lord', was the text, and the burden of the message was the Imperial Christ as the centre and circumference of the church's life and work; all its aims centred in Him and all its activities within His control. "Will you help me to realize that," he asked, "and make it true by your prayers? . . . Pray that I may know Him better. Then it shall be true—'We preach not ourselves but Christ Jesus as Lord'. Here, this morning, in all solemnity and simplicity I dedicate myself anew to Him. . . This is the beginning of a new opportunity. What God means I do not know. I know one thing—that this is His Will, and that is all I ask to know. Let this at least be remembered, that here, so help me God, Christ shall speak. No man will ever be welcome to this pulpit while I am pastor who is likely to degrade His Person, or limit His purpose, or question His power. I bring Him to you as the one Imperial Royalty, and with all subjection of heart and mind and will I give myself to Him, and pray that He may be evidently set forth, the altogether lovely One, the Chiefest among ten thousand."

It has been well noted that it would have been easy for Campbell Morgan to inaugurate at Westminster Chapel a preaching and teaching centre, having about it little or no organization, and also that this course would have resulted in greater financial profit to himself. Certainly he considered the preaching and teaching of the Word of vital importance, but he constantly reminded students that 'the teaching of the Bible is a means to an end and not an end in itself'. The wisdom of the sacred writings must ever lead the way 'unto salvation' and into service; evangelism, and then activity for Christ must be the goal of all Bible preaching and teaching. What better field of opportunity for service could be provided than the masses of London's vast population, and more especially that part of it whose homes and places of business crowded up to the doors of the church? Within a few hundred yards are the dwellings of the poor and the luxurious apartments of the rich; tiny shops tumble upon one another down narrow streets, only a few blocks removed from the residences of Cabinet Ministers. The Wellington Barracks and parade grounds lie a short distance to the west, and beyond them, across a wide avenue, rise the walls of Buckingham Palace. From an approximately equal distance to the east comes the rumble of traffic as it hurries to and fro along Victoria Street, from Victoria Station north to Westminster Abbey. Westminster Chapel, Buckingham Gate, can well claim a central place in the heart of the nation's capital, holding within its shadow a cross section of London's infinitely varied population. For months before the formal opening of Campbell Morgan's ministry, he and Mr. Swift were in constant conference together, the latter making it his special business to become fully acquainted with the needs and possibilities of the immediate neighbourhood. Mr. Frank Collier, of Manchester, to whose great Mission in that city Dr. Morgan was well known, suggested as a good working motto: 'A minimum of organization for a maximum of work'. There was no question that machinery would be needed, but it must only be set up as the need demanded. "Whatever becomes stereotyped," said Mr. Swift, "is in danger of losing its freshness and vitality." Organization must never be allowed to dominate the spiritual life of the church.

The Diaconate which Dr. Morgan found when he came to Westminster was composed of a small group of men who, representing the membership of 'the white elephant of Congregationalism', had had the faith to call to be their minister one of the denomination's ablest men, and undaunted by his apparent reluctance, had come back again and again with their demand. Now they, and those who were to be added to them, were to show their confidence in him by following his leadership and direction in the acceptance and execution of plans which were audacious in their scope and challenging in their performance.

★ ★ ★ ★ ★ ★

It has been suggested that a book might well be written about Campbell Morgan's ministry at Westminster alone. If that were so, a chapter of that book should be given to the first organization to come into being under the new order —the Sisterhood. A group of consecrated women who were willing to devote themselves and much of their time in assisting in the pastoral and educational work of the church had proved its value in other places. Such an organization had been in the minds of the new ministers of Westminster from the start, as the primary and most effective help to them in their work. By the beginning of 1905 there were five who wore the becoming and distinctive new uniform of navy blue and scarlet. They were Miss Winifred Howell and Miss Nellie Evans, the private secretaries of Dr. Morgan and Mr. Swift; Miss Alice Hulse, who had worked with Dr. Morgan in previous years; Dr. Charlotte Murdoch, of Baltimore, Maryland, who felt the call to devote her life and medical skill to Christian service, and Mrs. A. M. Gardner, who, before her marriage had served on the Sisterhood of the West London Mission, and whose husband was at this time the General Secretary of the London Missionary Society. The Sisters were known by their first names—Sister Winnie, Sister Nellie, Sister Alice, Sister Charlotte, and Sister Freda. Others came to join the ranks in the days which followed, for longer or shorter periods of time, for marriage claimed some and others retired for various reasons. Those who knew these women of singularly rich and varied talent, and watched them follow Dr. Morgan into the church on Sundays and at the Friday Night Bible School to take their places in the pew reserved for them, will, perhaps, recall them again as their names are mentioned. Others were Sister Mary who was Charlotte's younger sister; Sisters Nora and Florence; Sister Margaret who had charge of the dining room, and an unemployment bureau for neighbourhood women; Sister Josephine, who held a B.A. degree from London University, and in addition to her gifts as a Bible teacher was equipped when the need arose to teach a class in New Testament Greek; Sister Irene and Sister Emily, trained kindergarten and primary teachers; Sister Edith who accomplished a notable work in missionary education; Sister Helen and Sister Mona, the latter an artist of exceptional ability; Sister Dora who continues her devoted service as church secretary unto the present time; and Miss Amy Miller, Superintendent of Normal School work and Evangelism, who with Sister Freda pioneered in Bible Teaching extension work in other towns and cities. The Sisters, with the ministers, Mr. A. W. Hewitt, the church evangelist, the chapel keepers and organist, constituted the Westminster Staff.

Staff meetings were held on Friday afternoons, when tea together preceded a period of worship and conference. No formal order was observed for the time of worship. Prayer was offered for immediate objectives in the life of the church, for guidance in some pending national crisis, for some special meetings, such as the remarkable Welsh Revival of 1904, for the Bible School to follow in the evening. No plans were made or problems discussed without first seeking divine guidance. This period was often climaxed by the observance of the Holy Communion. It is referred to many, many times in Dr. Morgan's diaries as 'a quiet restful time', or 'a time of great spiritual refreshing', and it is evident that he derived much inspiration from this fellowship. There followed a period of conference at which weekly written reports were handed to Dr. Morgan. Future plans were made for all departments of the work, and new projects debated in the light of their need and value. Special problems and ways of meeting them were sympathetically considered. Mr. Swift's ideas for the development of the work among the young people; Mr. Hewitt's evangelistic meetings in the vicinity of the church; improvements in the present plant and new plans for future building—all were deliberated upon at the Staff Meetings. Here was the heart-beat of the church; from here flowed the life-blood which supplied every nerve and sinew of its being. Surrounded by such a group, devoted and loyal, whose sole aim was to put Christ and His Church first in their thoughts and actions, it is difficult to see how the venture of faith could help but succeed. Nothing is detracted from the characters of great men and women when it is remembered that there are many factors which contribute to their greatness. Their unique gift lies rather in their skill to choose people of the right qualities and abilities and place them where these can be most constructively used. Dr. Morgan fully realized how heavily he leaned upon the loving and intelligent co-operation of this corps of workers, and in particular these women who gave so freely of their time and talents. He paid them many tributes of appreciation over the years of his ministry at Westminster in such words as these, which are culled from the *Westminster Record* of October, 1908: 'The value of the work of consecrated women cannot be over-estimated. If we may be permitted a word of personal testimony, we do not hesitate to say that, apart from the work done at Westminster during the past four years by our Sisters, the results obtained would have been impossible. Those upon whom the burden of oversight and responsibility chiefly rests, thank God with full hearts for these women also who have laboured with us in the Gospel.' When in 1907 a volume of Dr. Morgan's sermons entitled, *The Simple Things of the Christian Life*, was published, it bore upon its dedication page the following inscription:

TO
MY STAFF
AT WESTMINSTER
WHO BY PRAYER AND LOVE EVER HELP ME
TO PREACH

Perhaps the first thing which attracts the eye of the visitor to Westminster Chapel is the big circular pulpit. This was the initial architectural change to be made under the new order. Dr. Morgan had delivered his first Bible lecture inaugurating the 'Friday Night Bible School' for which he became internationally famous, on 4th November, 1904. For these lectures, constituting analytic and systematic teaching of the Bible, he needed a blackboard, large enough and high enough to be seen, even in the second gallery. With this in mind an architect drew plans for a circular rostrum 16 feet in diameter, upon which such a blackboard might be placed. This change was carried out in January, 1905, and used for the first time on February 17.

With the organization of the Sisterhood and the immediate needs of the Bible School met, the attention of the deacons and Staff turned to the renovation of the entire plant of the church. The proposed 'Renovation Scheme' resulting from their deliberations was staggering in its proportions. Nothing had been done for so long that now everything needed attention. At the Recognition services an initial fund of fifteen hundred pounds had been raised. Dr. Morgan had accepted the call with no guaranteed salary, and day by day the faith of pastor and people had been honoured and justified. But there were no financial 'left-overs' for paint and polish. Meanwhile, repairs of such elastic dimensions as bad drains, a leaking roof, broken windows, inadequate heating, poor ventilation and a neglected organ were shrieking for immediate action.

It would have to be another long chapter in that book on Westminster to tell of the prayers and planning, the meetings and methods, the sacrifice and service which paved the way to success. A year later saw the transformation completed at a cost of twelve thousand pounds, including in addition to the above items the cleaning and decorating of the Chapel, the schools, lecture halls and offices, the building of a new house for the caretaker, and the cleaning of the exterior of all the buildings. Dr. Morgan brought back from Northfield,

Mass., that summer of 1905, sixteen hundred pounds in gifts, and other friends of Westminster in Great Britain increased this amount. But the major portion of the total sum was contributed by the membership and congregation, from the first gift of twelve penny stamps, sent to Dr. Morgan by a poor charwoman, to the doubling of large subscriptions by those who gave out of their wealth. On the second Sunday in June, 1906, "I spoke on giving," he says, "and appealed for four hundred and eight pounds to complete our Renovation Fund. Inside twenty minutes four hundred and fifty pounds was promised. We sang the Doxology full of thankfulness."

Though perhaps the largest, this was by no means the only great money-raising project which Campbell Morgan inspired and completed. He knew much about givers and gifts, as is evidenced by his cogent comments on the subject. "It is really arresting," he once said in preaching on the Widow's Mite, "how that, in looking over subscription lists when some enterprise is on hand, and subscriptions are being sent in, we find the gifts are arranged according to amounts, and then very often at the end of the list we have the words, 'Amounts under one pound—' so much, no names being given. Nevertheless it is true over and over again, within that sum total of small amounts with no names attached, there is more sacrificial giving than in the totality of the larger sums. Too often the large amounts may be dismissed under Christ's word, 'superfluity'; and within the small and apparently unimportant section described as 'Amounts under—' may be found the gifts of infinite value." 'Of infinite value' to him were twelve penny stamps, framed and hung upon the wall of the study, wherever it happened to be, from that day forward.

* * * * * *

Clean new buildings and facilities were soon being put to full use, for the membership was growing under Dr. Morgan's ministry, aided by Mr. Swift's unceasing activity among the young people, and the untiring efforts of the Staff. In addition, the Brotherhood, under Mr. Hewitt's leadership, was recruiting young men for Christian service, and holding weekly evangelistic meetings in the neighbourhood. Many of these young men were employees in stores, who 'lived in' at the large wholesale drapers in St. Paul's Churchyard and the West End. They pledged themselves to pray for each other every day, to help each other in every possible way, and to make a definite attempt every week to win another for Jesus Christ. They met early on Sunday morning, so early in fact that breakfast was provided for them at Westminster Chapel. Dr. Morgan met with them, driving a distance of several miles from his home in Upper Norwood to do so, and presided at their meetings. An observer says: "The outstanding feature of the meeting was the Doctor answering questions on Christian life and conduct."

Financially the church proceeded as it began—on faith in the goodwill and support of its membership. Because of its location, Westminster's congregations would always hold a large proportion of transients, and the church depended largely on free will offerings for its support. Campbell Morgan believed, and inspired his people to believe that God would supply all their need as long as they continued in the pathway of His appointing. September, 1905, in the midst of a remodelling and rebuilding project involving thousands of pounds, might not seem the psychological moment to suggest to the deacons that henceforth one tenth of all income be devoted to missionary work. But the diaconate was composed of business men with a vision. The 'Missionary Resolution' was passed, and Westminster became thereafter a missionary-minded and missionary-motivated church. Its missionary programme permeated every department of its life and service. The story of Missionary Westminster became a romance which must be told in a later chapter.*

While Dr. Morgan carried forward the preaching and

* See Chapter X.

teaching ministry of the Word, and Mr. Swift exercised perfect freedom in his own sphere of activity, the two worked in close association and co-operation. They made all their plans together for the weeks and months ahead, evaluating their resources and exploring every avenue of possibility. This team-work, carried on consistently and harmoniously, was largely accountable for the success which attended their efforts.

As Mr. Swift reviewed the first year's achievements he revealed something of the nature of this success. "There is a two-fold feature of our work," he said "There is a wider work, and there is a local one. That wider work very largely centres in the fact that God has given to my beloved brother and colleague a unique gift for the teaching of the Word of God, and it is our business to see to it that Dr. Morgan has the largest and fullest opportunity of using it, not only here but in every place. It means just this. We should all be delighted to have Dr. Morgan here every night in the week, attending every gathering connected with our church work. But he cannot do that and do the work he is doing. I confess to you that the whole tendency of my influence—and I am conceited enough to think that it counts for something—has been to lead him to concentrate all his time and all his energy upon his Bible work, for in that he will do for the Kingdom of God far more than if he gives himself to the more promiscuous activities to which people are for evermore inviting him. That Bible work, here at Westminster and further afield, is to be one of the distinctive features—the great distinctive feature—of our work. Its centre will be here, though it cannot be confined to this place. But apart from that we are resolved that here at Westminster there shall be a very real local work. . . ."

It was upon this 'local work' that Mr. Swift's vast store of energy and resourcefulness was concentrated. With the building up of the Sunday School and the work among young people, he held up as a goal a programme which should fulfil every need of a great city's anchorless youth. For the realization of this ideal the 'Institute' was organized for those over sixteen years of age. "Here in our locality," he continued, "there are great numbers of young people. Someone counted recently just one section of the congregation. There were 218 people, and of that number 104 were young men. They are all about us in these business houses and in these great mansions and flats. Hundreds of young men and women are in London, who yet have no home in London. Their loved ones and early influences are away back in the country. They have come to face temptation in this great metropolis, and are bereft by their coming of the influences that formerly restrained and kept them. . . . We want to provide a home for them here, where holy influences shall be all around them, in which they may grow up in a sane, strong and healthy Christian life. . . . That is the ideal of our Young People's Institute which has grown so marvellously during the year. We already have four hundred members. . . . In association with it, circling all about it, are many organizations. . . . It is not simply that we are asking them to come and study their Bibles. On the other hand it is not that we simply say, 'Come and have a good time'. We *are* saying, 'Your first and primary interest is spiritual. Come to Jesus Christ; give your life to Him; take His Word to be the light that shall direct you in all life'. Therefore, at the centre is the work of the Bible classes. The roll of the Institute is the roll of the Bible classes. Then there is the need of intellectual stimulus and social intercourse, and we have our Literary Society, our Greek Class, our Missionary Study Class, and our Hygiene Class, and any other Class it may be desirable to start, our 'at homes', gymnasia, and the like. We want our young people to give recreation and intellectual development their right place, and maintain in their life that perfect balance which alone makes true and complete and noble life. . . . We do not promote these things individually and separately, but so bring them into contact and relation with each other that there shall be the perfect balance that makes the perfect and complete life."

Years later, looking back on this period in retrospect, Dr. Morgan said: "At Westminster I had the advantage of being able to begin from nothing." He himself drew up the plan of Bible teaching in the Sunday School which was used throughout his ministry at Westminster, in itself a colossal task; Mr. Swift organized the classes and departments and put the plan into action. This plan of teaching, which is outlined in Dr. Morgan's book, *The Bible and the Child*, is based upon a thorough knowledge of the Scriptures and a sympathetic understanding of childhood and youth. Some so-called 'experts' of a more modern day have stated that the Bible is an 'adult' Book and that there is very little in it for children. Campbell Morgan maintained that the Bible has a definite message for all age groups, and based his deduction upon sound psychology. "Believing as we do," he said, "that the Bible is for all life from earliest childhood to maturest age, we feel that it is most important that we should find and use the very best methods of dealing with it in our schools." ... "One certain thing," he stated, "is that the old idea of an International Lesson which is graded to meet all in a Sunday School is utterly wrong." Neither did he swing to the extreme which 'applies' the Bible to this or that phase of individual, social or national behaviour. Rather the Bible is to be read and expounded on the presumption that it will reveal of itself individual, social and national behaviour in their relation to divine principles, and that its abiding laws will apply themselves to life in every age with the freshness of the morning sunlight.

His plan provides for a four-year primary course in which the pupil becomes familiar with the stories in the Old and New Testament within the range of his comprehension, and in this 'adult' Book Dr. Morgan finds one hundred and fifty stories suitable for the five to eight year old child. The junior ages, nine to twelve, he states, are those in which children become interested in stories with continuity, and bases for them one hundred and fifty-three lessons on the biographies of the Bible. In 'the most difficult period' of thirteen to sixteen years, the adolescent is developing a consciousness of inter-relationships. His interest, therefore may be captured by a study of Bible history. After sixteen comes the period when young life is ready for 'those great portions of the Bible which have of necessity been largely postponed, namely the didactic portions—the laws of Israel, the poetic literature, the messages of the prophets, the teachings of Jesus and the Apostolic writings'.

Under this system, and with no other text book than the Bible itself, teachers in the Church School were required to attend normal classes each week, and students of all ages were encouraged to take periodic examinations on what had been learned. All achievements were honoured by recognition and suitable awards. In the course of time a children's page appeared in *The Westminster Record* in which Bible stories were told with blanks in the text for the contestant to fill in by consulting chapter and verse. At the annual Sunday School anniversaries, a Sunday afternoon was set aside in which pupils of all departments, under Mr. Swift's direction, demonstrated to a large assembly of parents and friends what they had learned during the year. On one of these occasions a triumphal arch was erected on the rostrum, each stone and pillar symbolizing a phase of Bible study, all unified in one structure. The climax of the building came as Mr. Swift, with a tiny member of the Primary Department in his arms, mounted a ladder so that she might set in place the keystone which bore the motto: 'To the Glory of God'.

To say that the entire youth education programme at Westminster was Bible-centred is a conservative statement. It was Bible-saturated to the extent that no child or young person having any connection with it could fail to absorb the Bible content, so completely and yet so attractively was he surrounded by it. In every department children and young people were led to find expression for Christian ideals in service for others through the channel of missions at home and abroad. The Institute had as the aim of its members the carrying of these ideals into their places of business and institutions of learning. Upon its walls appeared the pictures of missionaries whom they had pledged themselves to support. Thus Westminster proclaimed one of its ruling principles—that 'a church without vigorous Sunday Schools is like a river without springs.' From these springs the church membership became enriched, as those were added to it whose training in the Church Schools had so thoroughly fitted them for leadership and active Christian service.

★ ★ ★ ★ ★ ★

A spectacular beginning does not always mean a sustained interest; the novelty wears off, and those who are only seeking for 'some new thing' fall by the wayside. But the critical second year of Campbell Morgan's ministry saw the congregations greater than before yet more earnest, including many whose hunger was for the Bread of Life, and who had found a place where their need was met, week by week. Spiders no longer found an undisturbed haven in the top gallery, for its doors had to be opened to accommodate those who had patiently lined up far down the narrow lanes of Buckingham Gate until five minutes before time for the services. By that time seat-holders must be in their places, for the ushers were instructed to fill all remaining seats on the floor and to open the galleries. The word 'seat-holders' might mistakenly suggest that a rental was required if any member wished a seat reserved in his name. Actually it was the privilege of each member to select his own seat, the 'rent' paid for it being simply his financial pledge towards the support of the church, the amount decided upon by himself alone, and known only to the deacons to whom it was paid.

The Sunday congregation at Westminster was once described by an eminent religious journalist and close friend of Dr. Morgan, Mr. F. A. Atkins, as follows: . . . "It frequently contained three or four members of the Cabinet. Lord Armistead was always there, and Lady Tullibardine (now the Duchess of Atholl); you would see Lord Acton, Lord Halsbury, and Lord Northcliffe being piloted to very bad seats by a sidesman who for the first time in his life was embarrassed by an overwhelming crowd. Journalists, judges, doctors, members of Parliament, editors, were there by the score. I have myself seen Mr. J. A. Spender (editor of the *Westminster Gazette*), Mr. W. T. Stead, two American editors, two ladies of title, and the present Shipping Controller all within an area of ten yards. Snobbishness is not one of my besetting sins, and I do not regard a peeress as of more importance than a parlourmaid—really she is not so important, seeing that a peeress is usually old, and a parlourmaid generally very young. But it is an interesting fact that Dr. Morgan's ministry attracted many people seldom to be seen in any other Nonconformist place of worship."

Mr. Atkins failed to mention a part of the regular Sunday morning congregation for which Dr. Morgan had a special regard—the girls from Miss Sharman's Orphans' Home. They were among his most attentive listeners, and his many visits to the Orphanage endeared him to them as a friend as well as a pastor. A bright new sixpence fresh from the Mint meant far more then than it does to-day, and on Christmas morning each girl received in an envelope this token of her minister's thoughtfulness.

The organ in the first gallery behind the rostrum was flanked on either side by the choir. It was a large group who volunteered to lead the services in praise. No one except the organist was paid, no distinctive dress was worn, and they were in no way conspicuous among the rest of the occupants of the gallery. There was little of 'special music' in the services at Westminster at any time, though the choir had many opportunities at social or other week-night gatherings to demonstrate its talent. On some rare occasion on a Sunday a solo might be rendered, but only because it added something important to that particular service. There was never anything in the nature of a musical performance on the part of organist and choir. Mr. Percy Foss, and later Mr. Percy Pomeroy, trained the group with the sole purpose of contributing to the service of praise. Dr. Morgan loved to hear those strong voices behind him leading the great old hymns of the church. It inspired him to preach, he said. Certainly it was difficult for anyone in the congregation, whether or not he could sing, to refrain from making 'a joyful noise unto the Lord.'

Though Friday night was set aside for definite Bible teaching, the rôles of preacher and teacher so synchronized in Campbell Morgan that his transcribed sermons as well as his lectures and analyses have become text books for teachers and students. Sunday morning sermons followed for the most part the continuous exposition of one Book of the Bible. In this way three years were occupied with the Gospel According to Matthew, and two years with the Book of Acts. These series were interrupted from time to time for some special occasion or event; even then, inspiration for it was found in the Scriptures, for topical preaching, hung upon a text, was entirely foreign to him. He believed that there is no experience of good, and no ill that flesh is heir to, that cannot be deepened in joy or lessened in pain by an understanding of the Bible. To grow in the knowledge of abiding things was, to him, the secret of the good life, and his business was to focus that knowledge upon the whole range of human experience. He was known first as a Bible expositor, and so he was. Yet his gifts were many-sided, or rather it might be said that his one great gift of exposition was like a revolving light, illuminating all the facets of a well-rounded ministry. Thus, when the occasion called for a missionary sermon, a stranger might have labelled him a great missionary statesman. Given some national event—the crowning of a new king, the stunning disaster of the *Titanic*, some social cause in which the welfare of humanity was at stake, a case of injustice across the world, where man's inhumanity to man seemed far removed from 'England's green and pleasant land', he rose superbly to every occasion. He became an expert in the avenues of his calling because he was stern with himself, spending painstaking hours in preparation and research. The office of the teacher was not hindered by the fact that he lost nothing of the fire of the evangelist as youth passed into maturity. Sunday evening sermons were preached especially with a view to leading men and women to decision for Christ. The appeal for such decision could never be to Campbell Morgan either a formal, stereotyped proceeding, or a sentimental overflow of emotion. There was no high-pressured 'salesmanship' of church membership, no reference to the 'opening of the doors of the church'—a phrase Dr. Morgan abhorred, for the church doors, he said, were never shut—no prolonging of the opportunity. Those who wished to remain and ask questions on conversion and discipleship were directed to a room where the ministers and members of the Staff waited to talk with them. There were some remarkable cases of conversion during those days, outstanding among the many who confessed themselves to be bewildered and wandering, lonely and afraid, among the temptations of a big city; frantic people on the edge of suicide, cynical young students, rich idlers and poor prostitutes. One young shop-girl was saved from a house of ill-repute because, having come to Westminster and asked for help, Mrs. Morgan took her to her own home on Friday nights and kept her there till Monday mornings until she became a strong Christian character. Dr. Morgan himself told a part of the story when, reviewing the work of the first twelve months, he said: "I had breakfast here this morning (Sunday) with a Brotherhood of sixty young men. . . . Sixty young men scattered through the business houses of this neighbourhood, every last one of them devoted to Christ and His Kingdom. Here they are, all amongst us this morning. Here are men and women who a year ago, many of them, were very reverent toward Jesus Christ; but they had not crowned Him. Blessed be God, He is their crowned Lord this morning. . . . I had a letter a little while ago from a young man in South Africa, who turned into this building one night—I quote at this point his own words—'hot from the house of sin'. He was arrested, and yielded himself to Jesus Christ; went out the very next week to that land so full of subtle and awful temptations for young life. He went, as he says, realizing that now he was Christ's, and he must take an immediate stand for Him. He writes and tells me of the struggles and beginnings of things there, of victories won, and that Sabbath after Sabbath he has been into the compounds with a preacher, and men and women have been saved through his message as he spoke to them."

These are but a few whose story could be repeated in many keys and with many variations. Thus could be written another chapter of a book which might well be called *Wonderful Westminster*, this one ending with the familiar words: 'And the Lord added to them day by day those that were being saved'.

★ ★ ★ ★ ★ ★

If it be true that the name of Westminster is written upon the heart of Campbell Morgan's life-work, there is also substantiation for the statement that the Friday night Bible School stands at the heart of his work at Westminster. This is not to minimize other phases of the work, some of which have been mentioned, and certainly not to underestimate his preaching ministry and its influence, but to underline the one momentous achievement which was unique during his time. For the Bible School was, in a special way, his own— the dream of his heart come true. When Westminster Chapel had been derelict, and those who loved it had come to him with their invitation, the factor which had been strongest in determining his decision had been his conception of what Westminster might become. "I came with a passionate conviction," he later told his people, "that the Church is renegade when she abandons great centres to the devil." This great centre, he believed, had the potentiality to become a theatre where Biblical preaching and teaching might find their perfect setting and enjoy their greatest opportunity. For this he had been prepared in ways difficult and mysterious and often not of his choosing. Now the mosaic of his life was fitting into the pattern—the home influences, the lowly beginnings, the years in which the teaching technique was being tried and proven, the period of eclipse, the first foothold of faith, the realization of a gift and the crystallization of an ambition; the climbing, working, fighting, and always the reading, thinking, praying; the genius that in finding the 'one thing' forsakes all others; the hunger for truth, never fully satisfied; the joy of knowing the ability to impart it; the culmination of years of study and experience, and the sensing of people's need and hunger to understand the Bible.

It has been said that, however well we think we know it, we can never, in imagination, visualize a whole city. It is always that particular street or landmark we know the best that springs first into our minds. Thus Edinburgh may mean Princes Street, and New York, Times Square; in Paris, perhaps, the Eiffel Tower, and in Rome the Coliseum. But there are people all over the world who, when one speaks of London, think not of Trafalgar Square or St. Paul's but of Westminster Chapel on a cold Friday night in any of those years between 1904 and 1916.

It is doubtful if such a heterogeneous assembly ever met under one roof as gathered on those Friday evenings. The attendance averaged fourteen hundred—at certain seasons of the year considerably more, at other seasons somewhat less.

They were of all age groups, though many were young, and from all walks of life. There were Sunday School workers and ministers of all denominations, not excluding those of the Roman Catholic Church. The Salvation Army was present in large numbers, and the professions were well represented. The wealthy were here, and those, too, whose lives were a daily battle with poverty. Faces could be recognized which appeared often in the daily press and magazines; missionaries from far distant places; visitors from other lands; nurses and servant girls, members of Parliament and policemen; soldiers and sailors, and those to whom these were 'under authority'. But the majority of those present were Christian workers gathered from all parts of greater London, some coming as far as thirty miles. For many of them, to be here had meant a crowded bus, or a strap-hanger's ride in the Underground at the end of a hard day at the office, or behind the counter, nursing a sick patient, or making responsible decisions of far reaching implication. They had not come here to be amused or entertained. They knew why they were here, and that they could expect to listen for an hour to a sustained and logical discourse. But the man who was to deliver it was possessed of a remarkable power to proclaim the ageless truth in a language all of them could understand.

Let memory turn back the pages and look again upon that waiting crowd. The moment comes when he appears in the doorway behind the circular rostrum, treading quickly across the red-carpeted floor and mounting the flight of steps. Ungowned, the height of his gaunt figure is exaggerated under the brilliant illumination thrown upon the blackboard and desk. In the buttonhole of his immaculate clerical suit is a flower, and in his hand a Bible and note-case. The light catches the threads of silver which are beginning to appear in his dark hair, and every chiselled line of his face, so austere in repose. He glances toward a pew near the front on his right, to be sure 'Nancy' is there. The older boys are away at boarding school now, and the younger children in bed, but she is seldom alone. There is often a guest in the home, or a friend she has brought with her to the church.

The service begins with a hymn of praise. As the organ plays the melody his eyes catch a familiar face, last seen at Northfield, perhaps, or a missionary home on furlough after years of service. On a rare occasion it may be a child, home from school for the mid-term holidays, and allowed to stay up late to accompany father and mother. Suddenly he smiles, and his face is transformed and beautiful. The congregation somehow feels included in this intimacy; without effort he has captured them before he speaks. But some special heart is warmed to be singled out and remembered. That child will treasure this moment for the rest of her life; for Campbell Morgan possessed in abundant measure the gifts that make up the elusive quality of personality.

There are some announcements and a brief prayer, and the congregation rises to sing two verses of 'Break Thou the Bread of Life'. This hymn is traditional in this service, as much a part of it as the lecture itself.

The lecture begins. The theme of it is a Book of the Bible in its entirety. In the first few moments of introductory comment the rows in the pews are restless as pages are turned and note-books opened. Then the speaker takes up the chalk and begins to write. The blackboard is invisibly grooved so that the divisional lines may be straight and true. It is very black and clean, so that the white chalk makes the writing clear. The hand that writes is fast and beautifully legible— (Mr. Butler would be pleased, and give credit to the many 'copies' neatly and painstakingly executed!). The outline is spaced into broad divisions and the theme develops. The lecturer explains and writes simultaneously, an art learned in the schoolroom, where attention must be maintained while the master's back is turned to his class. (Once, in lecturing to a group of ministers on this 'blackboard' method, he said: "I am quite convinced that, difficult as at first it may be, it is far better in the use of the blackboard to allow your students to see your diagram grow under your hand than to put it on the board first. When the whole is displayed as a chart, the minds of the students are constantly tempted to look ahead, and in doing so to miss the impact of the next thing.") He aims at simplicity, clarity and brevity in the adoption of titles and sub-titles. He uses alliteration and rhythm, repetition of letters, words and prefixes whenever they serve his purpose, for things are longer retained if they sing in the memory, or follow an association of ideas. For example, the divisions of Genesis—'Generation, Degeneration, Regeneration'; and Matthew—'The King: His Person, His Propaganda, His Passion'. "In doing this work in the process of the years," he once said, "I wrought not for myself alone, but as a teacher, in order to help those who, by reason of their daily callings, are not able to devote so much time to study as one set apart to that special work." He added that "in the work there was no careless haste," an understatement to the student who marvels at the seeming ease with which the outline progresses. He seldom refers to the page of notes which lies beside his Bible on the desk. The eraser is rarely used. Suddenly he turns with an aside which provokes a smile, relieves the tension. Skilfully he draws up the reins again, using his whole slim co-ordinated body and his expressive hands to give emphasis to a phrase. His voice is like a Stradivarius in the hands of an artist. It never jars, never becomes mechanical or harsh. For an hour it sings or thunders, monotones or whispers, but shows no strain or weariness. With consummate skill the Book and its contents reveal their part in God's plan of redemption, showing its relationship and contribution to the whole. His audience is unconscious of the passing of time. The only man with an eye on his watch is the man in the pulpit. He remembers that for many of them there is a long journey home, a day's work on the morrow. Accuracy in timing is not the least of his gifts. With no sense of incompletion or haste the lecture is ended, and he pronounces the Benediction.

These analytical outlines and explanatory comments are the content of Dr. Morgan's series of books entitled, *The Analyzed Bible*. He describes his method as "telescopic—the taking in of large areas at one view, in order to see the relation of part to part and system to system." In reviewing his own work of Biblical analysis, he says that it "is the result of a serious and honest attempt to grasp the general movement and consequent content of each book by the reading of that book without any aid other than that of the actual work of the writer, and unhindered by the usual division of the book into chapters and verses." He set for his own standard the reading of a book fifty times before putting pen to paper in preparation. "I claim no dogmatic finality for any of these outlines," he says. "In the case of any one of them I would say, Here is an outline, rather than, Here is *the* outline." Dr. Morgan warned Bible teachers of the temptation to 'preach' when they teach. "Trust your

Bible," he said, "to produce results. During seven years of Friday night teaching at Westminster I am perfectly safe in affirming that not a month has passed in which, by letter, I have not heard of Christian men and women called to higher life and nobler service, and of men and women brought into definite relationship with Christ."

In his private study and public preaching and teaching Dr. Morgan used the Revised Versions of the Bible. At Westminster he used the English Revised Version, though his preference was for the American Standard Version. "I use this," he said, "because, after careful study of the various translations of the Bible, I am convinced that, for conveying to the English reader the sense of the Scriptures, this is the most accurate. . . . I am not guilty of the folly of criticizing the work of the King James translators. I am remembering that language has changed since they did their work. . . . We now have manuscripts at our disposal which they lacked. The accuracy of their work is the perpetual marvel of the student of that great Version. Nevertheless, the honest student must ever seek that which is best and most accurate. The work of the English revisers was of great value and carried us a good way forward; but there are marks upon it of bondage to tradition and lack of courage . . . which failed to lead us as far as was necessary. The American revisers, untrammelled by this traditional cautiousness, went that extra distance, and so have given us boldly a Version than which, up to the present, there is none equal."

The appreciation with which the Bible School was received at Westminster soon created a demand for it in other centres. In October, 1905, Rev. Gregory Mantle asked Dr. Morgan to come and lecture at his Mission in Deptford, on alternate Tuesday evenings throughout the winter. This extension work met with unqualified success, and in his diary Dr. Morgan noted the attendance as averaging between seventeen hundred and two thousand, rivalling the school at Westminster. On Wednesday afternoons he met with his own Institute teachers and others to discuss the Bible lesson for the coming Sunday. Questions arising out of the Bible studies were submitted to Dr. Morgan and answered through *The Westminster Record*. In the early summer there were many requests to know when the course for that season would end and the new one begin, so that people might plan their vacations in such a way as not to miss a lecture. In response to popular appeal, Dr. Morgan also conducted a series of Sunday afternoon meetings, lecturing on a variety of subjects relative to Christian life and work, and with the close of the Bible School season in June, conducted in the summer a six-weeks' Saturday evening course—in 1906 it was on the subject of Prayer—before sailing for a few weeks to the United States —not for relaxation, save on board ship, for a heavy schedule of engagements awaited him there.

Reference has already been made to the official literary organ of the church, *The Westminster Record*. This monthly news-sheet came into being under Mr. Swift's editorship for the primary purpose of giving wider publicity to Dr. Morgan's sermons and lectures. In addition, it included current news of the church and announcements of group activities. Any month's calendar of events discloses that the church was open and busy every day except Monday, which was kept strictly as a 'rest day' for all church workers. Mr. Swift himself wrote each month for the *Record* an important and informative column entitled, 'The Social Outlook', and revealed himself as a man with a deep and sincere social consciousness. He believed that the Church should bear its witness in the national life. He followed closely all political trends, interpreting them in the light of Christian principles. He was far-seeing and often prophetic. "We are living in a period of transition," he said in the *Record* of 1906. "The old order is passing away. The material progress of the past century promises to issue in a social transformation which will be the wonder of the era upon which we have entered." In the summer of 1906 Mr. Swift attended the International Christian Endeavour Convention in Geneva, Switzerland, and was much impressed by all he saw and heard, as people speaking eighteen languages met on common ground. His comment on hearing the Lord's Prayer recited 'each in his own tongue', was, indeed, characteristic. "'Thy Kingdom come!' Yes! and while we pray, isn't it time to lend a hand?"

In this as in other matters, the ministers at Westminster were of one mind and heart. As a young man Campbell Morgan had taken an active part in national and civic affairs, and this interest was maintained throughout his life. He, too, believed that Christians must lead the way to social betterment, and saw the Church militant, 'terrible as an army with banners', upholding the right, opposing the wrong.

In 1910 the church magazine continued under the name of *The Westminster Bible Record*, because of a demand from an ever-widening public for Dr. Morgan's sermons and lectures. At that time subscribers numbered four thousand, many requesting that the magazine be sent to country manses and missionaries on the field.

* * * * * *

In December, 1907, the Trinity Congregational Church of Reading invited Mr. Swift to become its pastor. He had done a wonderful work at Westminster in the organization and development of its numerous activities and their many branches of service. Many hands were busy now, and many hearts had responded to his gentle and firm leadership. Beloved by all at Westminster, his first friend was still his most understanding, and Campbell Morgan entered wholeheartedly and sympathetically into consideration with him of the call to a new field of opportunity. When Mr. Swift decided that he must accept the Reading invitation, his loss to Westminster was felt most by his friend and co-pastor, and certainly not least by the children in the schools. Dr. Morgan expressed his own personal feeling in the matter in *The Westminster Record*, when he said: " . . . It is a great temptation to me to write, 'I only am left.' The context of the quotation makes it singularly inappropriate, but the text itself is one from which just now I could preach a topical sermon! . . . To me personally this is a genuine sorrow. But sackcloth is not the apparel of those who serve the King. I thank God for the opportunity which has come to my friend. I believe that Trinity Church, Reading, will give him a splendid sphere for the exercise of all the gifts with which he is so richly endowed, some of which, in the exigencies of this fellowship, have been lying dormant. That church has my hearty and brotherly congratulations. They have been given by the Head of the Church a rare man of God. May the union be as fruitful as has been the ministry of Mr. Swift at Westminster. More than that I cannot wish them."

It was another parting of the ways for these two, but there was no rift in the friendship. Reading was very near to London, and Mr. Swift was always available for consultation and advice, and the two were constantly together for no other reason than the delight in each other's company. It was acting upon Mr. Swift's recommendation that Dr. Morgan invited as a temporary assistant pastor a young American, Mr. Frank Weyland Pattison, who had recently graduated from the Theological Seminary of Rochester, N.Y., where his father had for twenty years held the Chair of Homiletics and Pastoral Theology. Mr. Swift introduced him to the various church organizations in which he was to assume active leadership, and his agreeable and unassuming personality found for him a way into the hearts of all with whom he came into contact.

At the end of six months Mr. Pattison returned to the United States to the deep regret of his many friends at Westminster, and once again Dr. Morgan displayed his uncanny ability of knowing how to choose the right associate for the work at hand.

Mr. Arthur E. Marsh had 'belonged' to Westminster from the start. He was of that inner circle who had welcomed Dr. Morgan in 1904 and believed in his ability to make the old church come alive. He had served in the capacity of secretary, had travelled with Dr. Morgan in some of his itinerant work in the Provinces, and had intimate knowledge of the methods of the work. He had exerted influence for good among the young people of the Institute, and his friendliness and enthusiasm had made him a popular leader. Feeling the call to the ministry, Dr. Morgan made arrangements to release him in order that he might take a two-year course of study at Princeton Theological Seminary in the United States, under Professor Charles R. Erdman. A year of that course had been completed when the call came to him to return to Westminster Chapel as Minister's Assistant and Church Secretary. He assumed this work at the beginning of August, 1908. To all who know Westminster the rest is history. For more than forty years the name of Arthur E. Marsh has been linked with Westminster and its work. Since Campbell Morgan's day many great preachers have stood in her pulpit, both as pastor and guest. Two great wars have cast their shadow and dragged their aftermath of insecurity and anxiety behind them. Through all the changes and shifting circumstances of the church's life and continuing service, Arthur E. Marsh has held a consistent and constant place of fidelity and trust. There are countless numbers who would gladly testify that Dr. Morgan's words were prophetic when, in his welcome and introduction, he congratulated the church "on the acquisition of a man loyal to Christ, and devoted to service."

* * * * * *

'Mundesley' is one of those English place-names so puzzling to the American tourist or reader. In this case it spurns the 'de' and, in unconcerned manner, pronounces what is left. As the English traveller in the United States and Canada meets up with a few tongue-twisters in the matter of pronunciation, it is expedient not to argue the point!

When, on a raw December day in 1904, Dr. Morgan first saw the old 'Hill House' in the little village of Mundesley-on-Sea, he sensed again the possibility of a dream coming true. Mundesley nestles in one of the little indentations of the sandy cliffs that characterize so much of the Norfolk coast, with its sea front open to the north. On that day, two weeks before Christmas, Mundesley held little to recommend it, and 'Hill House' even less. The wind from the North Sea met with no resistance as it howled round the empty old house. No smoke rose from its chimneys with promise of warmth and welcome within. What had once been a garden was now a wilderness of weeds. Inside the house, Dr. Morgan must have been reminded of Westminster Chapel as he had seen it a few short weeks before, only just emerging now from dust and decay. But here again he saw what Mundesley might become, and looked at it with but one question in his mind—would it serve his purpose and realize his dream? And the dream was something like this.

It is summer time, and the air is sweet and clean and full of sunshine. The song of the sea comes from a sandy beach just over the cliff. The old house, painted and clean, has come to life and is filled with bustling activity, brimming over with family and guests. Tennis courts and a rose garden are out yonder; perhaps there are chickens and dogs, and a donkey for the children—but there is far more than these. There is a large tent on the grounds, with seating capacity for a thousand people, some of whom are housed in the village, while others have come in from the surrounding towns and villages in vehicles and on bicycles. Inside the tent is a blackboard on a raised platform. It looks reminiscent of the winter Friday Night Bible School at Westminster—and that is just what it is. This is a summer conference ground, like Northfield on a smaller scale. To the Bible student the changing of a name often signifies a new beginning and a new important relationship. What new name could better be bestowed upon the old house than 'Northfield', holding promise of what the future had in store!

With the purchase of the property, Dr. Morgan entered into this new venture with the unfailing enthusiasm that was his. He again exercised his gift of picking just the right man for the job of transforming it into a place of comfort and beauty. In January, 1905, he took his brother-in-law,* Mr. Edward Morgan, to look at the house. He also was a man who saw a challenge in a difficult task, and for this one he had the ability as well as the will to succeed. In April, repairs got under way, and Mr. Edward Morgan moved in and started work on the grounds.

In June of that year the first Staff Retreat was held in Mundesley, not at 'Northfield', however, for the house was not yet ready, but in a boarding house belonging to a friend. For four days the workers met together for conference and fellowship in planning the coming winter's work at Westminster. The only guest at this first Retreat was Mr. Gregory Mantle. "Gregory gave us a very fine paper on 'Responsibility as to Missions'," Dr. Morgan wrote in his diary. "We shall none of us easily forget it, and I hope never lose the influence of it." The visitors were, of course, eager to see 'Northfield'. "Ted has worked wonders on the place since he got here," states the diary. Upon Dr. Morgan's return from the United States in September there was a wedding in Mundesley, and 'Ted and Shoody' were left in sole charge of 'Northfield'. Children have their own way of contriving names for people they love. Miss Wood, who had been a part of the family since the Northfield, Mass., days, was first 'Shoody', and then, following her marriage to their uncle, 'Auntie Edith'. She was a second mother to the younger members of the Morgan clan, and contributed much to the deep affection in which they held Mundesley and all its associations. She was a born housekeeper and homemaker, and under the combined efforts of 'Uncle Ted and Auntie Edith' the old house at Mundesley entered into its own, and the wilderness in which it had stood 'blossomed as the rose'.

For a ten day period during eight consecutive summers—1906-1914—Mundesley-on-Sea became a vital part of Westminster. America had shown the way by which a summer vacation can combine physical relaxation and recreation with spiritual study and inspiration, in its many denominational

---

* Mrs. Morgan was, before her marriage, Annie Morgan; Mr. Edward Morgan was her brother.

summer conferences. Keswick and Southport were, at the time, the nearest approaches to this idea in England. They both held short conferences each summer, attended by crowds of earnest Christian people, with the object of teaching certain important doctrines, but with no idea of building up a holiday centre which should be permeated with Christian influences. Dr. Morgan's ideas were based chiefly on his Northfield, Mass. experiences, and his ambition was to create at Mundesley a 'British Northfield'. From the beginning he placed great emphasis and importance on preparation, seeing to facilities for adequate accommodation, obtaining special cheap rates at boarding houses, and making arrangements with the Great Eastern Railway Company for reduced fares and extra coaches for the Conference visitors from London. For the first Conference a second-hand tent was rented, but it blew down in a North East gale, and thereupon Dr. Morgan decided that there must be a new and stronger tent for future years. In his visit to Northfield, Mass. later that summer, he told of this need to a sympathetic crowd who liberally contributed enough to buy a new tent for the British Northfield. Purchased at a cost of two hundred and fifty pounds from experienced tent-makers in Norwich, who supervised its erection and dismantling, the new tent seated a thousand comfortably. A platform for the speakers stood at the front, large enough for the huge blackboard. Dr. Morgan delivered his Bible lectures in the first morning hour, followed by another speaker, perhaps to preach, or to discuss some aspect of missionary work or Sunday School methods. The evenings were devoted to inspirational services, at which time a visiting minister, or Dr. Morgan himself would preach. It was a great sight on a warm summer evening, when the sides of the tent were rolled up so that many standing outside, or sitting on the grass might join in the singing of the hymns, and hear the great Bible messages. To call the roll of those who were invited to Mundesley as guest-speakers would be to name some of the most famous pulpit personalities of the day, both in England and America, and in addition there were others whose names were not known at all except in the small locality from which they came, but whom Dr. Morgan had discovered and selected because of what they had to give. In the choice of his speakers denomination and prestige meant little to Campbell Morgan. The aristocracy which he summoned to bring its wealth to Mundesley differed widely in style and emphasis, yet all had in common the badge of devotion to the teaching and preaching of the Bible, and the ability to impart its truth to others. The opening address at the 1906 Mundesley Bible Conference was delivered by Rev. J. Gregory Mantle, whose name has a way of appearing like a silver thread in and out of Campbell Morgan's life story. Samuel Chadwick, Dinsdale Young, and W. L. Watkinson, also of the Methodist Church; Charles Brown, F. B. Meyer, and John Wilson of Woolwich, great names among London Baptists; Stuart Holden, Hensley Henson, Hay Aitken, and R. B. Girdlestone of the Church of England; John McNeill and John Hutton, Presbyterians, and James Orr of the United Free Church College of Glasgow; T. Charles Williams, and W. H. Griffith Thomas from Wales, and Elvet Lewis, whose fiery Welsh eloquence brought him back to Mundesley year after year; from the Congregational Church, J. D. Jones, J. H. Jowett, Thomas Yates, Monro Gibson and the great P. T. Forsyth; William Robertson Nichol of the *British Weekly;* Carey Bonner, and Miss Emily Huntley, outstanding Sunday School authorities; Arthur Yapp, of the Y.M.C.A.; missionaries and missionary laymen, and a notable representation from the United States, including A. T. Pierson, Paul Moody, Charles R. Erdman, Len G. Broughton and Douglas Adam; some who had great stories to tell of personal testimony and experience, together with Gipsy Smith, Mrs. Bramwell Booth, and Mrs. Booth Clibborn —all of these and many more came to Mundesley during those wonderful summers, and there, in the centre of it all, the life of it all, its mentor and leader, the host of the Conference as well as teacher—Campbell Morgan himself.

It may be because people came to know him better in the intimacy of Mundesley that so many affectionate tributes to the founder of the Conference were written, some by personal letter, and others like that of a visitor whose complete account of the 1914 Conference was printed in the *Record*, and has this to say about him:

"Those who know Dr. Campbell Morgan as a great organizer, a powerful preacher, a prince among evangelists, a teacher and leader amongst ministers and students of Holy Scripture, do not really know him until they have seen him at Mundesley. The Conference is his 'child', and he is amongst his own people and altogether in his element, and all sides of his character and personality are there revealed. Exact, direct and punctual in his habits, he transcends himself when the Bible is in his hands and a fire burns in his soul . . . Alike in superintending the music . . . taking his part in the tennis tournament . . . and as a conversationalist, the breadth of his interests and accomplishments was strikingly demonstrated. It is due in no small degree to the kindly humour, the largeness of heart and the all round development of its Founder and President, that the Mundesley Conference has come to possess the sane, healthy, and thoroughly bracing character that it has always maintained."

It was not enough to Campbell Morgan to give the little village of Mundesley a larger place on the map than it had ever held before; to bring to it once a year those whose names would be immortal in the history book of the Christian Church. When only the memory of these remained there was also a practical evidence of the blessing Dr. Morgan brought to Mundesley in the complete restoration of the little Union Chapel—new furnishings and an Estey organ from Brattleboro, Vermont. For this he appealed for funds, being one of the largest donors himself, though as was always his habit, remaining anonymous.

One of the finest things that Dr. Morgan did in a long lifetime of service to others, was when he established a 'Mundesley Fund', whereby each year about fifty ministers from all parts of England, who rarely got a chance to attend outside study groups, or leave for even a short time their small, and oftentimes difficult fields of labour, might be furnished free travelling expenses and board at Mundesley, in order that they might, for those ten glorious days, enjoy these great speakers and associate with them. Mr. Swift said of them: "Some had not been away for a holiday for years, and it was good to see the wholehearted fashion in which they entered into the programme—lectures and laughter, prayer and play alike. If Mundesley did nothing else it would be worth while, for the sake of the inspiration and cheer it gives to these men." Others who gathered with them were Bible students and teachers of all denominations, and a large number of young people who had been drawn to Westminster through the Institute work. There was always a representation from the United States among the guests, some of whom came to England purposely to attend the Conference. At one season a party of more than eighty members of the Society of Friends added a most stimulating tone to the services, and, because they knew that there was a welcome for all, inhabitants of the countryside came also, to enjoy the opportunity of hearing and seeing the great preachers of their day.

Afternoons were given over entirely to recreation, this being a Medes and Persians rule of the Mundesley Bible Conference. There were picnics, cricket matches, golf, and excursions to the many beauty spots in the vicinity, including the famous Norfolk Broads; lawn tennis, bowls, croquet, and clock-golf on the grounds of 'Northfield'. Whenever the weather was kind (and it was for the most part wonderfully kind to the Conference), tea was served on the lawn. Mrs. Morgan, assisted by 'Auntie Edith' and others, sat at a table under a huge awning, liberally spread with plates of thin bread and butter and cakes, and poured tea for any who were in the grounds. Dr. Morgan would invariably be the centre of a group, not discussing some deep doctrinal question, but just having fun and swapping stories. Just as nothing was allowed to interfere with this week-day recreational programme another rule for Sundays was just as final—NO games whatever. Tennis nets and all games equipment disappeared on Saturday night, and on Sunday a Sabbath peace prevailed. No general tea was served, just a small tea in the lovely rose garden—'Uncle Ted's crowning achievement, and Dad's holy of holies', as it was called—for just the family and a few friends before the afternoon service, for there were three services on Sundays. One of the sons remembers how, at one of the later Conferences, he was asked to play the piano for a Sunday afternoon service. Gipsy Smith was the speaker, and he asked him to play, 'I would be like Jesus'. It had never been sung in England before, but that summer afternoon the sweet mellow voice of the Gipsy framed the simple words with melody and started it on its way to popularity. Many familiar Gospel hymns, especially those which Mr. Morgan had first heard in the United States, such as the beautiful 'Footsteps of Jesus', and Mrs. Will Moody's own 'Moment by Moment', were first heard in England under the 'big top' at Mundesley.

In his own inimitable way Mr. F. A. Atkins recorded his impressions of the Conference of 1912. It is so typical of them all that it seems appropriate to quote him here:

"However devoted a man may be to his work, however much he may love it and revel in it, there comes a time when he is all the better for an interval of change and rest. And not only is the worker better for it—the work itself is more efficiently performed when the worker recovers his freshness of mind and returns to his toil with a new and leaping enthusiasm. And this is quite as true of Christian service as it is of the routine of the counting-house and market-place. After eleven months of strenuous church work the mind loses some of its elasticity and the heart something of its daring, and if any man in the world needs and deserves a holiday, it is the country minister or the village evangelist or the town missionary who has stuck to his post for fifty weeks. A vacation, however, is not always refreshing and vitalizing. Everything depends on the kind of holiday. The delirious rush that would delight a bohemian stockbroker would bore and sadden a Christian worker. I submit that for tired ministers and church workers the ideal holiday is to be found in a fortnight at the Mundesley Conference.

"First of all there is the charm of the simple, unconventional life of a somewhat remote seaside village. In Mundesley there is no glare of electric light, no fatiguing amusements, no dressy promenade, no invasion of noisy excursionists—there is not even a band or a pier. But there is the infinite variety and the unfailing satisfaction of the vast mysterious sea and the friendly beautiful country, a strong bracing air that steadies the shattered nerves and restores the depleted vitality, and the ministry of silence which helps us to face our problems calmly and pray a multitude of misgivings out of the way. The difficulties that seemed so appalling when we met them at close range, shrivel and disappear when we look at them amid the quiet spaciousness of sea and country, and in Christian comradeship we are led to a deeper faith and a sunnier optimism.

"I confess that I find something that is spiritually energizing in the very atmosphere of this Conference. I miss a certain morbid pietism that occasionally creeps into the proceedings at some conventions, and I am glad to escape the political clamour that so often intrudes into the demonstrations of the Free Church Council. Here there is no clash of angry controversy. No one indulges in the cheap impertinence of defending the Bible. We are not half so anxious to disestablish the Welsh Church as we are to disestablish the devil. The speakers deal, not with cloudy and conflicting theories, but with clear and challenging actualities. Every address and sermon is closely related to daily duty and practical service. We not only count our blessings—we begin to see our obligations and recognize our responsibilities. The whole Conference is perfectly sane and intensely practical.

It means business and means it all the time, and this stimulating atmosphere is largely due to the spirit and personality of our leader.

"The Conference this year was blessed with the most amazing weather. Day after day we revelled in cloudless blue skies, radiant sunshine, and a cool sea breeze that relieved the midsummer heat. A rainy June had kept the country fresh and green, and never had it looked more beautiful. The long afternoons were given up to healthy recreation, and tennis tournaments, golf matches, bowls, and croquet were indulged in under the most delightful conditions. But no sport or pastime has ever been invented that would be sufficiently attractive to keep the members of the Conference away from the morning lectures by Dr. Campbell Morgan on 'The Pentateuch', and 'The Gospel of Mark'. The great tent seats nearly a thousand people, but every morning by 9.30 it was comfortably filled with eager students of the Bible. It was a great sight, and it must have cheered the heart of the leader, who, to tell the truth, often went to the platform after an almost sleepless night. No one knows the labour and stress which this Conference involves for its leader. He has no real rest while it lasts—no private life—no refuge of silence. He practically lives in public for a fortnight, and the risk of physical breakdown is always a source of anxiety to his friends. Some of our leading Free Church ministers who preached the evening sermons at the Conference postponed their departure the next day in order to hear Dr. Morgan's lectures, and expressed to me their deep appreciation of the spiritual power and intellectual freshness of his method.

"Mundesley has been memorable the last two years for the remarkable series of lectures by the Rev. John A. Hutton, M.A., of Glasgow. It was Mundesley that discovered Mr. Hutton in England, although for some time he had been widely popular in Scotland and the United States. His intellectual alertness and resource, his virile, fearless faith, his exuberant vitality, and his extraordinary gift of irony and humour combine to make him an ideal teacher and lecturer. He is a wonderful tonic for tired hearts and enervated minds. Under his influence things that we have been afraid to face lose their terror and frighten us no more. He fortifies the timid and heartens the depressed. This year, under the title of 'Weapons of our Warfare', he presented a careful and brilliant study of the life and progress of the Christian Church in the third century, and showed how the Church fought the despotism of the world and withstood all its subtle allurements by the weapons of her exclusiveness, her faith, her purity and suffering. Mr. Hutton gave us his very best, and what that best can be only those can tell who have enjoyed the privilege of listening to him morning after morning in the Mundesley tent. Even a verbatim report would give but an inadequate impression of the effect produced by these lectures, because the reader misses the impact of the man.

"In some respects the cool, peaceful evening hour is the most delightful of all. The sun is sinking and the glare of the day is over, the birds are singing around the tent, and in the shadow of the restful twilight we sing our evening hymn and listen to some uplifting message from a great and inspiring preacher. We shall not easily forget Dr. Len Broughton's gracious and beautiful sermon, in which he showed that the staggering power of the life and personality of Christ was only to be accounted for by the great little word—love. 'Unless you love much', he exclaimed, 'you cannot preach at all', and I think some of the ministers who heard that sermon will go back to the restless world with the old message, but with a new glow of dynamic affection in it.

"This is an impression and not a report, and I shall not attempt to catalogue the names of all the preachers who helped and taught us at Mundesley this year. But, looking back, I cannot help feeling that Sunday was the most memorable day of the whole Conference. The afternoon service was held in an almost overpowering heat wave, and yet in the drowsy air of the suffocating tent, baking in a blazing sun, not a head nodded throughout Dr. Morgan's sermon.

Everywhere I saw eager eyes, strained attention, and a wistful longing to hear the message. And what a congregation it was at night, when 1,600 people—hundreds of them standing outside the tent—listened to an evangelistic address which seemed positively overwhelming in its irresistible argument and its force of appeal. There were weather-beaten sailors, jolly Norfolk farmers, simple-minded villagers, scores of country ministers and Cambridge students, groups of godly Quakers and foreign missionaries—probably in all his varied experience Dr. Morgan had never preached to a more remarkable crowd.

"One more impression. I had been up in the Sheringham woods with Mr. D. J. Hiley, and we returned to the tent, not knowing what we should hear. To our surprise we found we were in the midst of one of the most romantic and fascinating missionary meetings we had ever attended. The platform was crowded with foreign missionaries—most of them home on furlough. One after the other these modest, valiant men and women from the very ends of the earth got up, and in sure, swift little speeches of two or three minutes, each told us with telegraphic conciseness of the triumphs of the Gospel, of great world movements, of the stirring of new life in decaying countries, of miraculous opportunities, and the tragic limitation of resources. It was to me very wonderful and very touching.

"And now we return to the turbulent activities of the city or to the monotonous routine of the village—to go forward with a steadier tread and to front life with a more open-eyed sanity and a more overcoming faith. We have seen the glory of sun and sky and sea. But we have seen more than that—we have seen Jesus. And the joy and thrill of the experience will nerve us for the day of battle and liberate us from the prison-house of care."

★ ★ ★ ★ ★ ★

Most men in Campbell Morgan's position would have counted their lives full to overflowing, even though the

Westminster routine was admirably organized, and his assistants were thoroughly trained in his methods and at one with his ideals. Yet by 1907 he was lecturing in five other centres besides Deptford—fortnightly at the West London Central Baptist Church, Westbourne Grove, and the Mildmay Conference Hall; and monthly at Trinity Wesleyan Chapel, Bristol, Roath Road Wesleyan Chapel, Cardiff and at the Central Hall, Manchester. In addition there were somehow dove-tailed into these regular appointments preaching and lecturing engagements which carried him all over the United Kingdom and even to Rome, where, that same year, in his capacity as President of the Sunday School Union he attended the World Sunday School Convention, and on Whit Sunday preached the Convention sermon to a large congregation. Why, it may well be asked, did he burden himself with such a heavy load of outside engagements? He loved his home and his church, and there was always enough literary work awaiting his pen to fill all his spare time. One reviewer has answered the question by saying that "restlessness was said to be his besetting sin." The assumption was based upon this continual urge to be on the move; but to attribute it all to 'restlessness' is a surface supposition. The "motif" of Campbell Morgan's life was to 'preach the Word'. Like the great Apostle he felt himself to be debtor to every man, and the urge to share what he had was behind the acceptance of as many invitations to preach and lecture as it was possible for him to accept. That the duty of this itinerant ministry was swallowed up in joy there is no denying, for he revelled in it. All denominations sought him and he made no discrimination. Within the space of ten days in 1909 he had spoken before the meetings of a Presbyterian Synod in Bristol, the Baptist Union in London, and the Congregational Union of Hertfordshire, and within the month had attended a union conference at the Church of England headquarters at Lambeth for deliberations upon the Congo situation. Reading, writing and studying he did on the trains to and from these appointments.

A minister once wrote to Dr. Morgan troubled because his friends, Christian people, pronounced his habit of reading his Bible in the train as 'an unnecessary parade of religion'. Dr. Morgan replied out of his own experience in these words: "I may say that I constantly read my Bible in the train, and work on it there; and it has never entered my head that anyone felt I was parading, because I certainly have never done it. If I were aiming at that I should feel that the teaching of Christ would condemn me immediately. Seeing that I am not, I am not at all sure that my action may not have been a testimony. Quite recently a gentleman who sat in the train with me, seeing me at work on my Bible with a notebook and pencil, after a while apologized, but began to talk to me about Bible study; and I think before the journey ended I had been able to help him."

So he continued during the busy Westminster years to the limit of his strength, and often trespassing beyond it. There were few who knew the physical weariness and longing for respite to which he sometimes gave expression in his diary. 'Brain-weary', 'physically and mentally tired', and similar phrases occur during these periods of exhaustion. Preaching is done under 'a sense of difficulty', though it is often true that only in preaching did he forget all discomfort and weariness. "In the morning I had a hard sort of time," he records of a Sunday, "never got free of myself—a miserable experience. To-night I had an equally good time and felt the service to be full of power." Brain fatigue resulted in neuralgic pain, sometimes becoming unbearably intense, and at times it would have been impossible for him to get through the Sunday without a doctor's help. When one of these attacks occurred in New York, in 1905, a friend persuaded Dr. Morgan to take osteopathic treatment. It gave him such relief as enabled him to continue his work, and when the doctor gave him the name of an osteopath in London, Dr. Morgan determined to consult him. Osteopathy was new in those days, and almost unknown in England. Dr. F. J. Horn was an expert in his science, and his skill completed Dr. Morgan's conversion to the efficacy of osteopathy. Many times on a Sunday afternoon Dr. Horn's treatment enabled him to conduct the evening service when he would otherwise have been unable to do so. Dr. Morgan introduced many people to osteopathy by his enthusiastic endorsement of Dr. Horn, among them members of the peerage whose influence was widespread. It is safe to affirm that Dr. Morgan helped to a considerable degree to strengthen osteopathy's early foothold in England. All his life he used it and recommended it to others.

★　　★　　★　　★　　★　　★

There were few of the Westminster years which did not see Campbell Morgan making at least one and sometimes two visits to the United States. He was good 'copy' for reporters, for it is always 'news' when people queue up for city blocks to gain admittance to a church, and when, as happened often at Fifth Avenue, the police had to be called out to control the crowds. In the Spring of 1908 Dr. Morgan crossed the Atlantic for the express purpose of going to Atlanta, Georgia, where a dream of Dr. Len G. Broughton's had been fulfilled. Next to his Baptist Tabernacle, Dr. Broughton, who was also a physician, had built a hospital, every bed being equipped with earphones (long before the days of radio), so that the patients might 'tune in' to the services. Dr. Morgan came to dedicate this hospital and hold a series of meetings in the Tabernacle. His children had good cause to remember this visit, but not all for the same reason. Early in the year, Jack went down with measles and was promptly put to bed and isolated. He called loudly upon everything that was in him to rue the day that such evil befell him, and in desperation appeal was made to his father to 'do something about it'. Dr. Morgan told Jack that if he would be a good boy and do everything that his mother and the doctor said, he would take him with him when he went to Atlanta in March. There followed such a sudden transformation of life and character as to materially hasten the patient's recovery. It made no difference to him that all his brothers and sisters succumbed to a measled state with spotted regularity. A promise was a promise with Dad, and Jack was the favoured and envied 'Joseph' when he sailed with his mother and father on the *Mauretania*. But he was to learn that in this life nothing is quite perfect. In Atlanta he was lionized by society, and the dulcet tones of feminine voices saying: 'So this is Dr. Morgan's little boy!' haunted his thirteen-year-old dreams. What was even worse, in some mysterious way the family at home heard about it, which left Jack's life with a stigma never to be eradicated.

Dr. Morgan's frequent absences from his family naturally increased the responsibility which fell to Mrs. Morgan's lot. Another April baby had come into the home in 1907 and was given the name of 'Ruth'—"Just plain Ruth," said her father, and frequently reminded the youngest of his flock as she grew up that she had the distinction in the family of bearing only one name. The oldest brother Percy, was now at 'Douglas' with Mr. Butler; Jack and Frank attended a private school in London. These two were feeling the restrictions of English life like balls and chains after the carefree existence at Northfield, and consequently gave vent to these inhibitions at home when school hours were over. Howard was now old enough to make his presence felt, and imposed himself upon his older brothers, insisting on being included in their activities. The only effective way they found to be rid of him was to scare him with 'BEARS', who were ready at any moment to jump out from behind any convenient ambush. In retaliation he shouted at them one dire word of his own invention 'YOUPIGYOUBEAS'YOUDEBIL!' Something was seriously missing in their make-up, for along certain lines they lacked anything in the nature of imagination and were cursed with a passion for realism. Once in the 'schoolroom' of the Norwood home in London, Jack and Frank, playing trains, decided to have a fire in the station. Nothing less than a 'real' fire would do, so the station was stuffed with newspaper and a match applied, causing a most satisfactory blaze and plenty of smoke. The fire brigade was called out, and loud encouragement from the onlookers caused a hasty rush to the scene by troublesome adults who, without invitation, hastily assisted the young firemen to extinguish the blaze, but unpleasantly expressed the proceedings as being 'naughty', and 'very dangerous'. Left once more to themselves they determined upon a scapegoat for this offence. A train was 'wrecked', and the miniature brakeman accused of turning the wrong switch. He was arrested and tried for murder, receiving the sentence of capital punishment. A guillotine was erected, and the executioners, not content with having decapitated the unfortunate victim, spread red ink in realistic and gory profusion over the block and its surroundings.

One of their father's favourite after-dinner stories concerned an old farmer, a devout pillar of the church, who was having trouble keeping his pigs out of the potato-patch and elsewhere —they were always rooting in the wrong place. Wildly waving his stick at them he would shout: "I'll teach you that there's a God in Israel!" The boys had a peculiar sympathy for those pigs—and for a very good reason. One Friday afternoon the parents had departed for Westminster—Staff Meeting and Bible School—leaving the children with the servants, and in charge of the 'mother's help'. Upstairs in the nursery was a plaything known as 'the swing'. It was a curved wooden contraption with a seat at each end which rocked back and forth like a see-saw. The boys often pretended it was a boat, and on this occasion determined to chart a wider course than usual by sailing through the door and out on to the landing. Reaching the head of the stairs they decided that more adventurous voyaging might be encountered if they launched out upon these 'waves'. They realized too late that the ship was sinking—and fast! It gave a lurch down to the turn of the stairs, struck the banisters breaking a portion of them, and only by wedging itself in the gap were the crew saved from being catapulted into the hall below. A horrified maid came rushing upstairs in time to avert a more serious accident, and two youngsters were hustled into bed in disgrace. But no amount of cleaning up could repair the damage to the banisters and the sight which greeted father and mother when they returned home that night. These and many less spectacular adventures became good for family jokes, but strangely enough, Dad, who was usually so quick to see the funny side of things, couldn't seem to get the point of this one until many years after it happened! For some little time he had been threatening to send Jack and Frank to boarding school. The wreck of the Hesperus decided their fate—to Mr. Butler they should go.

Education up to this point had been somewhat of an irregular procedure, with changes of schools from one side of the Atlantic to the other. On the other hand, what had been omitted in regularity had been atoned for by a liberal course of travel. At a very tender age the children became used to crossing the ocean, meeting new and sometimes important people, and above all absorbing an international atmosphere. The American way of life was as familiar to them as the British; whatever they were, they could never be described as provincial. Realizing their handicap of growing up with only occasional and spasmodic association with their father, Campbell Morgan tried to make up to them as best he could in other ways. When he was away each of them received letters and postcards from wherever he happened to be. He addressed them by the little pet names, so beloved of children because of their set-apartness, remembered to ask about whatever specially interested them at the time, referred to jokes they had shared the last time he was at home. Whatever else happened, he saw to it that he arrived home at Christmas in time to go shopping with them. In London it was always to Gamage's—that mecca of all toylands. The boys never forgot the year they thought—and hoped—he would buy them a new engine for the clock-work train, and ended up with a whole brand new set with all the trimmings! He was their hero and their idol, and it detracted from his power over them not at all that they secretly stood in awe of him. They knew by instinct, and sometimes by experience, that he had inherited from their grandfather strict ideas of discipline, and that, for all his fun and nonsense, there were limits of familiarity beyond which they could not go. Discipline was an expression of love—or so he understood his Bible, and obedience on their part must be an expression of trust in parents who held their highest good at heart. He wanted desperately to be a good father as well as a friend to his children, and none of them to-day will deny that he succeeded. However, the boys when they get off by themselves, will unanimously agree that, whereas they learned with thoroughness that 'there is a God in Israel', the girls could get away with anything with Dad!'

Percy was already at 'Douglas' as a student and assistant teacher when Dr. Morgan relegated to Mr. Butler the oversight and education of Jack and Frank, and later of Howard, with the utmost confidence in the integrity and ability of his old schoolmaster. They did not share this bland confidence of their father, but they had not been consulted or asked their opinion on the subject. Whatever loose ends there were, and whatever sins of omission, committed as regards their education and manner of life, were skilfully corrected under his stern, just rule. They may have been sceptical at times that the hymn-writer was keeping within truthful bounds when he wrote: 'Though painful at present, 'Twill cease before long'—but holidays had a way of coming round, and then they discovered that the lesson they had learned the best was that Dad and Mother were the most wonderful people, and home the most wonderful place on earth.

The boys were usually still in school during the Conference season, but they descended upon Mundesley with exuberant delight in their summer holidays. They remembered especially those of 1909, one of the few summers when 'Dad' did not go to America, but spent the holidays with them. With Percy and 'Uncle Ted' he slept out in a tent and pronounced it 'great fun', and purchased an old railway coach to convert into sleeping quarters for the boys and their friends when the house was full of guests. While a lot of his time that summer was given over to the children in games and trips, Dr. Morgan's own account, from notations in his diary, testifies that he was running true to form by spending his mornings 'working on Ephesians and Colossians', 'correcting MSS.', 'preparing the September *Record*'. His reading covered *Gladstone* and *Kenilworth;* but his only public appearances during that month of August were confined to preaching once in the village chapel and giving a week-night lecture on *Kingsley*. One Sunday evening he drove to a nearby town to church. "Heard a capital sermon with which I did not at all agree," he confided to his diary, "on a text which had no relation to the subject. Text, Proverbs 9. 5; Subject, 'Holy Communion'."

There was rarely a time in their lives when the boys ever felt that 'Dad' had 'let them down', but they admit that their suspicions on that subject were strong when they heard that he had invited 'Johnnie' and Mrs. Butler to spend part of one summer holiday at 'Northfield'. How could he do such a thing to them, they asked one another in apprehensive horror, and how could they stand it? But he could, and they did—not, to their amazement, with endurance, but with agreeable surprise. For Mr. Butler turned out to be a most pleasant and entertaining guest. Schoolroom ethics were never mentioned or even hinted at, and when he suggested that they all go out and fly kites in the meadow the boys acquiesced with alacrity, sure that in this field of endeavour at least, they knew who would be master. To their astonishment, 'Johnnie' soon showed that *he* was, by flying his kite higher and with more skill than they. "Can you beat it?" they said over and over to each other, and marvelled at his boundless patience in unravelling the string—this same unfailing patience, they realize now, which made of him such a successful teacher. One can imagine the Morgan boys returning to school in September to report on how "old Johnnie can really fly a kite! You should see him!"

* * * * * *

Two most significant outgrowths of the Westminster Bible School and the Mundesley Bible Conference deserve special mention. The first of these was the compilation by Dr. Morgan, with the help of his eldest son and others of special musical ability and fitness of *The Song Companion to the Scriptures*. This hymnal, published in 1911, was first used at the Mundesley Conference that year. While not seeking to enter into competition with any denominational hymnals, it was specially prepared to meet the demand created by the growth of the Bible School movement, and contained a large number of the choicest hymns on the Word of God, gathered together with extreme care. Its value is enhanced in that it contains some hymns and music never before published, including the only hymn that Dr. Morgan himself ever wrote, and set to appropriate music by May Whittle Moody (Mrs. Will Moody). It was sung for the first time by Mrs. Moody, on August 6, 1903, at the Northfield, Mass., Conference. Based on the words of Hebrews 3. 15, Dr. Morgan's hymn is as follows:

'To-day!' oh, blessed voice of hope
    And laden still with heaven's own breath;
The night is past—and has not come;
    Between the shades life conquers death.

'To-day, if ye will hear His voice,
    To-day, if ye will hear His voice
Harden not your heart, harden not your heart.'

Light falls around the ruined soul,
    The Wind of God blows with new lust!
        Fling back the shutters! Swing the door!
Answer God's breath upon thy dust.

Then day shall never end in night,
    But night be merged in perfect day;
        And all the forces of God's life
Control thy life with mighty sway.

> But if thou harden still thy heart,
> To-day will vanish into night;
> The Wind of God no longer blow,
> Life close in dark eclipse of light.
>
> O blessed Master of 'To-day,'
> To Thee I yield my stubborn will;
> Thou Sun of health, renew my life,
> And with Thyself my being fill!

The other important outgrowth of Dr. Morgan's Biblical ministry, especially of his work as a Bible teacher, was in the organization of the Bible Teachers' Association.

An assembly of Bible teachers was held at Westminster, in February, 1910, for the purpose of bringing together those who were teaching the Bible regularly, and were in sympathy with systematic methods of teaching. Out of the 135 present, 80 were ministers coming from as far north as the Border, and from the south and west; some from country villages and others from the great centres of population. Out of this conference emerged the B.T.A., with the following as a basis of membership:

> 'An association of men and women who teach the Bible. Those who are unable to accept these Scriptures as the full and final authority in all matters of faith and practice, cannot, in the nature of the case be eligible for membership; but no theory of inspiration nor any private interpretation of meaning is necessary of acceptance in order to qualify for membership.'

The co-Presidents of the B.T.A. were Dr. Campbell Morgan and Rev. Stuart Holden, and its Secretary, Rev. E. D. de Rusett.

The object of the Association was to train an ever growing group of Staff teachers, appointed after full consideration of their method, which must be 'systematic, analytic, and consecutive', and their ability to teach, to go out into the provinces wherever possible, holding Bible Schools of two or three days' duration.

So keen was the interest and so large the demand for

qualified teachers in the 'Westminster method', as it came to be called, that by September of 1910 over two hundred members were enrolled, and Bible schools were being held in London churches and all parts of the country. In the Spring of 1911 three hundred members attended the annual conference where the theme of consideration was *The Graded Bible*. Experts in the fields of Primary and Secondary Education gave of their experience; Mr. Swift spoke of the Bible in its relation to the 8-16 age group, while Dr. Morgan dealt with a method of presenting the whole Bible to Institute students in a period of five years.

If one of these schools might be selected as unique in its success it might be the one in Bradford. In the Spring of 1910 Dr. Morgan had spent three weeks in Bradford, then considered by ministers and laymen to be one of the most difficult fields for Christian work. The results of Dr. Morgan's series of Bible lectures exceeded all expectations, and he was requested to return for monthly lectures throughout the winter. The number of interested students was so large that Miss Miller supplemented Dr. Morgan's work during this period, when more than nine hundred students not only attended the lectures, but followed out the line of study indicated on a carefully drafted syllabus.

Fully as worthwhile as the work in the large centres of population was that carried out in the villages, and those who pioneered in this work found the method peculiarly suitable to rural areas. In response to another demand a Home and Circle Bible Study course was arranged by correspondence for any who were unable to attend public meetings. For this purpose a booklet was produced, containing an outline chart of a whole book of the Bible, and a series of lesson studies mapped out with brief notes and questions on each study.

The Mundesley Bible Conference was, of course, a meeting place for as many Staff teachers as found it possible to attend. The number of missionaries at the seventh conference exceeded that of any previous year, and the 'Westminster method' was carried into other lands, and its influence felt in a thousand ways among people unconscious of the source from whence it came. Letters from such widely separated spheres of missionary service as Algeria, Bulgaria, China, India, Peru, Madagascar and Ceylon testified enthusiastically to the success of Bible Schools. In addition to these, the *Westminster Bible Record* was able to publish in November, 1912, a list of nineteen places where active Bible School sessions were being held in London and its suburbs, and fifty-three in other parts of the United Kingdom.

★ ★ ★ ★ ★ ★

There was nothing neutral about Campbell Morgan's character, and this, perhaps, more than any other attribute he inherited from his father. When George Morgan passed away in 1907, his son wrote of his life as one "of many storms, but also with many stretches of calm and beauty." . . . "He was my first Bible teacher." Dr. Morgan once cited as an example of that early teaching, in reference to the Book of Proverbs: "My father told me that there were thirty-one chapters; a chapter a day for every longest month!" A friend who had known the father in earlier days and had not seen him for many years, wrote in retrospect: "I well remember his tall, lithe frame, a fine type of the genuine Puritan. . . . Some faces we cannot recall after a few years' separation, but of your father's my mind bears a most vivid picture. . . . He was no ordinary man, but of high principles and a willingness to make sacrifices for which, if need had arisen, he would have faced stake and prison."

His wife survived him for four years, cared for devotedly by her son and daughter-in-law, and the six to whom she was always 'little Grandma'. Mr. de Rusett expressed the thought of many when he said at the time of her passing: "Our deepest sympathy is with Dr. Morgan in this hour of sorrow. . . . What we owe to her will only be gauged when we realize what we owe to him."

"You cannot compel your child to an act of faith in Jesus

Christ," Dr. Morgan said once in preaching, "but you can make it almost impossible for a child not to exercise that act of faith. My father and my mother could not compel me to be a Christian, but as God is my witness, I had no choice because of what they did for me and what I saw in them."

The parents who had dedicated their son to God before his birth, and whose prayers had buttressed his life and all his undertakings, lived to see those prayers abundantly blessed.

★ ★ ★ ★ ★ ★

In accepting the Presidency of Cheshunt College, in Cambridge, in 1911, Campbell Morgan was repeating a pattern of his life, for the only nonconformist theological institution in this centre of learning was in desperate straits, both structurally and financially. His condition of acceptance was one to which the governing board readily acceded—that plans for the re-housing of the College be entered upon immediately. Items in the diaries of 1911 and 1912 show the direction in which some of these plans operated. There is a notation of a luncheon given by one of Dr. Morgan's closest friends and supporters, Lord Armistead, at which time he was able to meet Countess Bentwick, Lord Morley, Sir Francis Hopwood, and Mr. and Mrs. Andrew Carnegie, and solicit their interest. Sir William Lever contributed a thousand pounds to the Cheshunt fund, and others of wealth, influence, and consecrated vision on both sides of the Atlantic assisted towards the success of the enterprise. The new President was untiring in consultations with architect and builders, and compelled the attention of the nation upon this citadel of nonconformity in one of the seats of world culture and learning, by assembling to its foundation stone-laying some of the outstanding personalities of national and international life, including Viscount Haldane, Lord Chancellor of England, who laid the foundation stone, the Chancellor of Cambridge University, the Master of Trinity, and Mr. Walter Hines Page, whose first public function it was to attend after becoming United States Ambassador to the Court of St. James.

Rev. E. W. Johnson, M.A., B.D., the Resident Tutor of Cheshunt College, under Dr. Morgan's incumbency, said of him: "It is mainly to his courage and decisiveness that we owe the beautiful college buildings in which the work has been carried on since his time. If they had not been erected when they were—before the strain and the turmoil of the War came upon us—in all human probability they would never have been built at all."

This building achievement alone vindicates Campbell Morgan's term of Presidency. Some felt that he made a mistake in assuming the office, and that he was never completely at home in an academic appointment. It must be remembered that he was, at the same time, carrying the ministry of Westminster and all it involved, living in Cambridge and going to London for the Friday Night Bible School, preaching at the services on Sunday, and returning on Monday to his duties at Cambridge. None who knew him would deny the fact that some of those duties irked him. That he himself had never attended a theological college as student did not necessarily assume an unsurmountable handicap; he possessed much of scholastic experience, and was himself a teacher of that rare quality which is inborn and not acquired. Joseph Parker and Charles Haddon Spurgeon also became world famous preachers without academic training, and models for all preachers who followed them, though it should be added that their triumphs are no argument against theological colleges.

The spiritual evaluation of Dr. Morgan's service to Cheshunt leaves no room for doubt. Students whose privilege it was to learn from him, went out to their separate fields of labour bearing the stamp of his influence on their lives and the passionate love of the Scriptures in their hearts. He taught them to reach always for the stars, never allowing them to see their calling save on the highest level; and to keep their feet, also figuratively speaking, on the ground, but feet which must literally be *shod* in the morning for the work of the day, as he sternly reminded those who, early in his administration, appeared at breakfast in bedroom slippers. It only happened once!

A master is revealed best by his students, and impressions of two of them may be given. Rev. J. Stanley Perkins, M.A., writing fifteen years later, said: "As I see it, looking backward, his influence over his students was threefold: (1) He inculcated in us the fact of the central importance of preaching. The sermon class he conducted was always an inspiration, and his emphasis on the appeal at the close was unforgettable. (2) He stressed the pre-eminence of the Bible in our work. His idea of a Bible School has been copied by more than one of his students, and proved strikingly successful. (3) His big humanity appealed to us. He had a broad, sympathetic outlook with a complete absence of pettiness or donnishness. His intense spiritual earnestness and devotion to hard work never destroyed his love of a jest. The genial friendship which captivated his students has retained their affection, though three thousand miles of ocean now divide them from the man who exercised it."

At a distance of more than thirty years, Rev. J. P. Stephens, M.A., of Camberley, writes:

"At the beginning of a new academic year in the autumn of 1911, Dr. Campbell Morgan took up his duties as President* of Cheshunt College, Cambridge. His name was well known to us all. We were to know him better. We were to know him intimately.

"The majority of the students were reading for their honours degree in the Theological Tripos, and lectures for this course were arranged by the University dons. We also had our own tutors in Dr. Whitehouse and Rev. E. W. Johnson. The President took us in Homiletics and kindred subjects. Those hours were a delight. How good he was; how wise and human! His flashes of insight and humour thrilled us! Rebuke and uplift, criticism and encouragement kept company.

---

* The Head of Cheshunt is President, not Principal as with most, if not all of our theological colleges.

"He started to give Bible lectures after the pattern of his famous Westminster Chapel Bible School, and to these were invited members from other colleges. But the men's time was almost wholly taken up with degree work, and terms were irritatingly short, with the result that attendance was disappointing. Besides, the college was then housed in temporary buildings which afforded small rooms only, just sufficient for class work. Clear-sighted, the President dropped the experiment.

"When the new President arrived he asked those of us who were in our final year to meet him. I well remember his words: 'Now, you men know I am travelling in new country. It will depend on you whether I find my way or get lost. I want you to see me through. You know the ropes; kindly correct me if I drop any bricks!' At that moment he captured us; we would do anything for him. We felt he was just a big brother and one of us.

"Once in referring to the Leys School which stood across from his home in Cambridge, he pronounced it 'Lays'. Taking him at his word, I went to his room afterwards and told him that the correct pronunciation was 'Lees'—though why it should be so I had not the least idea. 'Thank you! Thank you!' he said in his charming way. That little incident was a peephole into his character. He never made that mistake again; once was enough. He had no use for blundering.

"His good humour never failed. It steered us round many an awkward corner.

"Students can be, and often are rebels. On one occasion we thought the college food to be lacking in quantity and quality, and a deputation waited upon the President. Alas, I was designated to be spokesman, and tried in my own way to express the views of the men. 'When I have eaten I have had enough', I said, 'but yet I am not satisfied. I feel full but not fed.' The interview was terminated in a non-committal way. That evening we were all invited to the President's house for a squash.* Calling me aside, my host said to me:

* Informal social.

'J.P., when you were describing the college food this afternoon I wanted to quote a text.' 'What text, sir?' I enquired. Eyeing my considerable girth with an inimitable twinkle in his eye, he quoted Deuteronomy 32. 15: 'Jeshurun waxed fat and kicked.' I registered a vow, then and there, never again to complain about college food!

"He enjoyed a joke when it was on himself. Upon occasion the nerves in his eye would twitch, giving the impression of a wink. It was said that, at one time when he was travelling by train and needing refreshment, he went into a station restaurant and asked the girl behind the counter for a milk and soda. She saw his eye twitch, mistook it for a wink, and gave him a whisky and soda! When I related this story to him he laughed and said: 'Good story! Unfortunately, it is not true!'

"Once at least I saw him angry, and he had good reason to be. We were gathered together for our weekly devotions and one of our colleagues was leading in prayer. His fellow-students considered his manner unctuous. We questioned his sincerity, and attempted to cure him by punctuating his prayer with mocking moans. Our method was ill-advised and childish to say the least. One look at Campbell Morgan's face was enough—it resembled a thunderstorm. We never heard a word from his lips about the incident, which we considered was the mark of great human understanding.

"During the year the President took each 'exit' man at different times for a week-end at Westminster Chapel. We helped him with the services, trembling at the knees at facing so many people gathered for worship. It gave us an insight into the workings of that great London church in all its many and varied activities.

"In the summer of 1912 the President invited all the senior students to be his guests at the Mundesley Conference. Here we helped, too, particularly on the social side. In tennis tournaments and golf matches our host held his own; he was an opponent not to be treated lightly. He wore the College blazer to be like us, and sang the College songs with us in the summer house and on the lawn.

"The President's house in Cambridge, 'Brookside', was open house to all. The Morgans were a happy family, and every Cheshunt student felt himself to be a member of it. Mrs. Morgan was the perfect hostess.

"Dr. Campbell Morgan was largely responsible for the magnificent buildings which now house the College. He had many important and well-to-do friends in Britain and America who responded generously to his appeal for finances. The present College is a great memorial to him.

"His knowledge of men was piercing and always sound, although he never found it easy to suffer fools gladly. There were some things for which he had no time. They made him tired. In pastoral talks with us I remember him saying that he would prefer to preach three sermons a day rather than spend half an hour at a deacon's meeting discussing who ought to keep the keys to the doors.

"World events largely dictated his resignation from the Presidency of the College in 1914. Undoubtedly the position cramped his style. He was glad to be free of it, to follow fully the line for which he was so eminently suited, and for which all his experience had fitted him—the preaching of the Word.

"As a preacher he had no superior. In pulpit and on platform he was master of his craft.

"In 1940 I found him in my own congregation. In the pew he was the best of listeners. He was a true friend, a big brother. We shall not see the like of him again."

★   ★   ★   ★   ★   ★

In 1911 the attention of the London Missionary Society, and especially of those who served it in official capacity, was directed in a peculiar way toward South America. In that year an effort was made to unite and consolidate all missionary work under British auspices carried on in various parts of that great Continent, resulting in the formation of the Evangelical Union of South America.

The E.U.S.A. attracted the immediate sympathy and

interest of Dr. Morgan. He would have endorsed it simply because all missionary activity was dear to him, but the E.U.S.A. was irresistible because it was newly launched, and struggling for support and recognition; and a worthy cause that needed a champion had never appealed to him in vain. With characteristic thoroughness he learned all he could about 'the neglected Continent', as it was called, and over a long period devoted one Sunday evening a month at Westminster to acquaint his people with all he had learned, enlisting their support of the new organization. The 'Neglected Continent' emerged under E.U.S.A. activity as the 'Continent of Opportunity'. Mr. Stuart McNairn, F.R.G.S., the active secretary of the organization since its beginning, tells elsewhere of Dr. Morgan's connection with this great work in its inception, and the part he played in its climb to recognition and success.*

★ ★ ★ ★ ★ ★

Sometimes the calendar seems to hold in a year's span, a burden of heartbreak that outweighs the measure of its joys. Campbell Morgan would have viewed 1913 as such a year, had he ever entertained for a moment the 'slings and arrows of outrageous fortune' as outside the realm of the 'all things' which work together for good.

The promising career of Dr. Morgan's eldest son was suddenly halted because of a lung condition which threatened to become tubercular. Percy's was a brilliant and scintillating personality, and he was possessed of an unusually retentive mind. He read fast and remembered what he read, and all phases of life interested him keenly, so that it seemed that without special effort, whatever he did met with success. Fingers that could play the piano with brilliance were equally at home with machinery and creative art. His mathematical sense was keen, but he was a wizard with words as well. To write a song and set it to music was as easy to him as to repair electrical equipment or invent a labour-saving device for the

* See Chapter X.

home. He gave a series of lectures entitled, 'The Evolutionary Hypothesis in the Light of the Biblical Revelation'. In spite of its title and technical subject matter it is written in a sparkling and fascinating style entirely readable to the layman, yet revealing an incredible amount of supplementary reading and study. He could have made a success in any of many fields of endeavour, for he had more than a spark of genius. The faults that so often accompany it were mitigated by an abundant kindness and generosity. He gave of himself and his possessions with a prodigality that sometimes violated reason. Certainly he never stopped to consider that his strength was limited. His call to the ministry pleased his father as much as his physical condition created anxiety. The weakness from which he always suffered was arrested in 1913, after special treatment at Cambridge, by removal to a more beneficent climate. Through the good services of friends in America a church was found for him in the mountains of North Carolina where he regained his health. He married Janet, the daughter of Rev. William Ross, one of his father's close friends.

In the midst of these domestic upheavals the news came of the sudden death of the only son—and child—of another of Dr. Morgan's minister friends. His own problems were put aside in the face of this shared sorrow. It was not his way to express sympathy by word alone if it were possible for him in any way to alleviate the hurt by deeds. Money was no object in the face of need, and if the need was that of a dear friend he never stopped to count the cost in convenience or cash. In this instance—only one which held the key to his marvellous talent for friendship—he took the bereaved parents away with him from the home of unbearable memories, and for a month he and Mrs. Morgan entertained them in London and in Cambridge, and took them for a holiday to Wales, where Dr. Morgan had preaching engagements at the time. Meanwhile he connived with the good people of his friend's congregation who changed the residence to another part of town and made it altogether attractive and new, as an expression of their affection for their pastor and his wife.

There are no comparisons in grief for each stands alone. The year 1913 closed in sorrow for Campbell Morgan, sharper because of the suddenness and unexpectedness with which the blow fell.

In 1912 Albert Swift retired from the work of the active ministry for reasons of failing health, and with the help of his wife and elder daughter had taken over the administration of a Rest Home for ministers at Littlehampton, where it was hoped he might be quiet for a time, have his garden and recover strength for more years of service.

The story is best told in Dr. Morgan's own words, spoken on the first Sunday of the New Year of 1914, to a congregation who, for the most part, knew and loved Mr. Swift, and to whom for that reason, it was easier—and at the same time more difficult—to speak of him.

"It was not to be," he said. "On Wednesday morning, December 17th, a telegram was put into my hands telling me that he had gone! I could not believe it, and rang up on the telephone and spoke to his child. 'Is it true?' I asked. She replied: 'Yes, it is true. He was on his way to his garden'. He reached his garden; but it was the garden of God, where flowers never fade, and which death never enters. It was a glorious passing. Oh, that I might pass so into the larger life and the higher service!"

The tribute—for it was one of those few occasions when the sermon was set aside—was a wondrous testimony to a most beautiful and satisfying friendship. In it Campbell Morgan reviewed the life-story of his friend, quoting another who said of him: 'He was sweet as a rose and true as steel'. He told of their earliest associations and their growing intimacy, and traced the lovableness and strength that distinguished Albert Swift's life. He said again what he said often—that without his help he would never have accepted Westminster. He dwelt with deep understanding upon the many sidedness of Mr. Swift's character, telling how each attribute was consecrated and subjugated to his Master's service. He called him a man of great visions—the vision of the Saviour, creating the passion for evangelism; the vision of the Christian citizen, and what he can mean to his community and nation and the world in which he lives; he spoke finally of the vision which completely mastered and inspired him—the vision 'of the value to the Christian Church of its young life'.

"In my hand," said Dr. Morgan, "I hold something that is very familiar to our young people; it is the badge of our Institute Department. He designed it. On the face of it is a star. At the centre of the Star are the letters 'B.S.', standing for Bible Study or Bible School. At the points of the star there are other letters: 'M', missionary; 'D', devotional; 'S', service; 'G', guild; 'R', recreation. This badge is the symbol of the fact that all the departments of the Institute are centred in the Bible School. He stood from the beginning here at Westminster, where we still stand, and where, thank God, through his influence other Institutes are now standing. We do not start societies for young people in the hope that they will join our Bible classes; but we make provision for every side of the life of the young people who join our Bible classes. I sometimes tremble lest in the modernizing of our Sunday Schools we should fail to realize that ideal. As I travel about I find again and again that societies recreative and mental are started in the hope that the young people through them may be induced to join Bible classes. This method always fails. On the other hand, if any person desires to see our young people in our Institute—which is still his Institute—they must come, not to the social hour merely, but on Sunday afternoon to the Bible classes. That is the time when they gather in the largest numbers. This conception we owe to Albert Swift; and not we alone, but the whole of the Christian Church in this country is in debt to him for his insistence upon the importance of thus putting first things first in this matter. It was his last vision. As I have said, he lived for it, toiled for it, wore himself out for it. In those

Reading days, in all parts of the country, gladly set free for the doing of it by that splendid church which was so loyal and true to him, he went here and there explaining, and pleading this sacred matter. At last the strain told upon him. Five years ago the thing began which ended last Wednesday."

It was in keeping with the entire lack of thought for himself which was a part of Mr. Swift's nature, that he had never told anyone what he himself knew—that the end might come for him at any moment. Only afterwards did his daughter find hidden in his desk a piece of paper bearing the words, *Angina Pectoris*, in his handwriting. So to the last did he shield those he loved as best he could, and for as long as he could, from anxiety and distress.

* * * * * *

The tempo of life which Campbell Morgan had set for himself during the Westminister years began, in 1914, to take its toll of his health. Only the careful habits of diet, and the vigilance of Mrs. Morgan, who did all in her power to make the wheels of domestic affairs run smoothly, had enabled him to continue the pace thus far. The determination not to lower his standards of preaching and teaching, or to overlook any duties of administration at Westminster or Cambridge; the oversight of the B.T.A. and the E.U.S.A., and the endeavour to accept as many outside invitations as possible, together with a certain emotional strain, combined to tell upon the natural resilience of a physique which had never been robust.

It was providential that early in the year Mr. Francis W. Pattison, who had already endeared himself to the people of Westminster five years before, returned from America with his bride to take up his former work among the young people and assume general pastoral oversight. This help, added to the splendid work already being done by Mr. Marsh and the other members of the staff, relieved the ministry of much of its burden. However, a ten day illness in January forced Dr. Morgan to consult a specialist, who insisted that if his patient was to avoid a complete breakdown he must confine himself to his own particular work of preaching only. This meant that he must give up his duties at Cheshunt, and he reluctantly acquiesced by handing in his resignation to the Board of Governors. It was hoped that a visit to the United States which had been planned for some time might help. Certainly the sea voyage in early February, and the absence from England during the inclement months to follow was beneficial, but the preaching schedule which had been arranged was of large proportions. He took part in a chain of Bible Conferences in some of the principal cities including Washington, D.C., Columbus, Ohio, Atlanta, Nashville, Pittsburgh, St. Louis, Springfield, Ill., and Philadelphia. Twenty speakers took part in the course of these conferences, and of these five, including Dr. Morgan, were in every city. While in the Southland it gave him peculiar pleasure to visit his eldest son and his wife in their first home. On Sunday, March 1, he recorded in his diary: "At 11 o'clock Percy preached. . . . I heard him with great delight. . . . I spoke in the afternoon. . . . Heard Percy again to-night. Even better than the morning."

During the Conference in Washington Mr. William Jennings Bryan and others prominent in the life of the nation's capital were often present in the congregation. Dr. Morgan preserved in his diary a letter from the White House, under date, February 16th, 1914:

"My dear Dr. Morgan,
"I was deeply disappointed that I did not have the pleasure of seeing you and of hearing you, or of attending any of the Bible Conferences of the past week. I was confined by illness to my room, and so was prevented from carrying out the plan I had cherished of not only seeing you but having, if it were possible, at any rate a single meal with you at the White House. Mrs. Wilson had the great pleasure of hearing you several times, and cheered me by descriptions of the services

and analyses of what had been said. May I now send you, both in her name and in my own, the most cordial greetings and the most sincere expressions of interest of the deepest sort in the great work you are doing?

"Cordially and sincerely yours,

"WOODROW WILSON."*

* * * * * * *

Back in England the uneasy grumble of approaching war was sensed by those who stood at the heart of national affairs. Dr. Morgan was drawn close to this inner circle by the group amongst them who frequented Westminster, and had come to find in their minister that strength and assurance of the spirit to which men turn in times of disquiet and uncertainty. There was scarcely a week that did not find Dr. Morgan lunching with Lord Armistead or Lady Tweeddale,† or Lady St. Hellier, and it was at the home of the latter in June that he first met Mr. Winston Churchill. The occasion was of interest because of a conversation between them which Dr. Morgan liked to relate. Mr. Churchill was an enthusiastic advocate of aviation even in its early and perilous days. At the dinner table the subject was being discussed. "You should try flying, Dr. Morgan," said Mr. Churchill. "Have you ever been up?" "No," replied Dr. Morgan, "and I never expect to until I go up for the last time." "But I shall have the advantage over you," said Mr. Churchill, "for I shall have had more practice!" Dr. Morgan never said what, if anything, he replied to that. Perhaps, for once, he did not have the last word!

In the early days of the War people flocked to the churches all over England. Especially was it true in London, 'the world's whispering gallery', as it was so aptly called, that there seemed to be a wave of religious consciousness. On Sunday after Sunday Westminster Chapel was crowded to the doors, until there was literally no more room to sit or stand.

---

* President Woodrow Wilson was a member of Dr. Morgan's congregation on subsequent visits to Washington.

† Dowager Marchioness of Tweeddale.

People lined the walls of the building, both downstairs and above in both galleries. The platform where the Communion Table stood was filled, and others found places on the floor at the feet of those seated. Even the large circular rostrum was crammed to such capacity that Dr. Morgan himself could barely make his way to the desk between the close rows of chairs on either side, and had room only to stand to preach, his own pulpit chair being occupied, and people near enough to touch him on either side.

A reviewer of the Westminster years deems that one of Dr. Morgan's greatest achievements was the series of sermons he preached in Westminster Chapel, in August, 1914. "In those days of bewilderment and alarm," he said, "when it seemed that the very foundations of our national life were shaking, Dr. Morgan's sermons with their note of confident assurance that God reigned, and that wrong would be worsted, allayed the anxieties of thousands of trembling hearts. I can recall no intervention by any preacher in a time of crisis which produced so powerful an effect. Dr. Morgan served the whole nation in that grim hour."

Miss Jane Stoddart, Assistant Editor of *The British Weekly* before her recent retirement, said: "Dr. Campbell Morgan rose to his greatest heights as a preacher on the five August Sundays of 1914, before and after the declaration of war with Germany. Incomparable service was rendered by him at that time to the people of London, to the nation and to the Allied cause."

"I have preached from this pulpit for ten years," he said on that first Sunday after war was declared, "and you who are my people know how every vestige of my nature hates war. Yet I am convinced that to have remained neutral would have been to disregard the obligations of national morality."

Characteristically, one of the first activities Dr. Morgan entered upon in connection with the war was to lead a movement to see that soldiers were supplied with Testaments.

* * * * * *

He was not himself aware that September of the precarious condition of his health. All summer he had complained of weariness, and a difficulty never before encountered in the execution of his duties. Physical exhaustion and the strain of the approaching conflict created an emotional and mental reaction. September 27 was the anniversary of his tenth year of work at Westminster. He preached that morning from Psalm 119. 96. 'I have seen an end of all perfection; but Thy commandment is exceeding broad.' As he gave out his text the congregation waited, wondering what he had in his heart to say to them. How could they have foreseen that the next Sunday he would be hovering between life and death in the throes of typhoid fever? All they were aware of was the strangeness of the things he was saying, perplexed and troubled; for the man who had literally lifted a derelict church and set it on a pinnacle was telling his people that, could he have foreseen the disappointments and disillusionment in store for him he would never have dared to come. "During these ten years," he said, "I have known more of visions fading into mirages, of purposes failing of fulfilment, of things of strength crumbling away in weakness than ever in my life before." He cited the places where he felt the church had fallen short of ideals. Unbelievably, it seemed, he had lost his sense of perspective—or so it was decided in some hasty and careless judgments. But even then his self-discipline in the matter of the study of the Scriptures would not allow him to break the text or ignore a part of its teaching.

"'But Thy commandment is exceeding broad.' This is the rest of it, and this is the best of it! During these ten years I have at least loved and sought to know and do the will of God. I may have missed the way more than once; I may often have failed to do the will; but no man shall take from me the confidence that in my deepest soul I have loved it, and have desired to do it. And now at the close of these ten years, looking back, I have to declare with great surprise and thankfulness, that I have made a new discovery of the breadth of the commandment of my God!"

Sentences and phrases of the sermon were severed from their context to make 'copy' for the religious and secular press in the days to follow. It remained for Rev. Samuel Chadwick's unerring sense of judgment, combined with his close understanding of his friend's mind and heart and his consciousness of his physical condition, to review in sane and unimpassioned words the sermon which had caused so much controversy and speculation. Those who have so much desired for this record the testimony of Mr. Chadwick concerning his friend, could ask for no finer tribute than this—not of ten years of public work merely, but of a lifetime of intimacy and affection. Surely 'he, being dead, yet speaketh'.

"On Sunday, September 27th, Dr. Morgan preached on his ten years' work at Westminster. The sermon ignored all conventional canons of pulpit speech, and was avowedly a frank, unveiling of the pastor's heart to a beloved and trusted people. It was not for strangers, but the penalty of greatness is publicity. The confidences of intimate friendship are too sacred for the public press, and unfortunately a few striking passages detached from their context found their way into the gossipy paragraphs of the religious newspapers. It is useless to complain of misunderstanding or misleading quotations, but it would have been as well if the intimate character of the occasion had been respected, and both preacher and hearers had been content to treasure the spoken word in their hearts. The sacred confidence of the deliverance was frankly stated in the opening sentences of the sermon, and the preacher took refuge in his favourite quotation from Mrs. Craik on 'Friendship':

> 'Oh, the comfort, the inexpressible comfort of feeling safe with a person, having neither to weigh thoughts nor measure words, but pour them all out just as they are, chaff and grain together, knowing that a faithful hand will take and sift them, keep what is worth keeping, and then with the breath of kindness blow the rest away'.

Photo: C. Vandyk

Dr. MORGAN — 1914

"Perhaps the most precious of all Dr. Morgan's brilliant gifts is his genius for this very kind of friendship. Where he loves he loves with all his heart, and where he trusts he confides without reserve. He talks as he ponders, and shares his shaping thoughts and hopes while they are as yet unformed. In fellowship his plans crystallize, and in expression he finds certainty. Some men think their way through in silence, but there are minds that talk and pray their way into the light. Such preachers have much more to say when they have finished than when they began. The kindling glow of speech brings inspiration, illumination, and certainty. Such preaching is always pastoral rather than pedagogic. It has the personal intimacy of closest friendship, and on special occasions its speech is too domestic for those not of the household.

"At such times no man's judgment upon himself should be taken at its face value. His speech has neither the careful balance of the judge nor the detachment of the critic. He speaks out of his heart, is influenced by the mood of the moment, and is too conscious of the personal factor to get the perspective of things. Emotion finds luxury in emphasis. Exaggeration is its normal speech. The language of penitence competes for the place of the chief of sinners, and the songs of the redeemed are always soaring into rhapsody. Dr. Morgan's Anniversary Sermon laid bare his sad broodings over years of disappointment and disillusionment. The dismal paragraphs came to those outside the immediate fellowship of Westminster with the shock of a great surprise. They gave the impression of despondency and regret, and reported him as having said that, had he known all he knew now, he would never have accepted the call. No one knew then that the virus of fever was in his blood, and that he was sickening for a long and critical illness. The printed sermon is before me as I write, and while the record of unfulfilled ideals lacks the usual buoyancy of Dr. Morgan's exuberant vitality, there is neither pessimism nor despondency in his speech. He did say that much of what he had hoped to have accomplished was still unrealized, and that, if he had foreseen the experiences through which he would have to pass, he would not have dared to come, but these are not unusual feelings in the act of review.

"Dr. Morgan came to the work at Westminster with high ideals and very definite plans. He accurately describes himself as 'a man of super-abounding vitality, of remarkable resilience, of unclouded optimism'. He was in the prime of life, and disciplined and prepared for his great opportunity in a religious experience unique in its range and variety. On two continents he had seen the goings forth of the Word with mighty power, and he had gathered wisdom in many schools. He entered upon its ministry with a sense of vocation and a solemn conviction that it was for this he was born and to this all life's paths had led. He had definite views about most things connected with the Christian Church, and he set himself boldly to realize a New Testament Church at the heart of London. Westminster was to be 'A House of the interpretations of the Oracles of God', and its fellowship was to be as catholic in spirit and missionary in practice as the Apostolic Church. He accepted Westminster as a base and not as a sphere. For years he had been associated with Moody's work in Northfield and Chicago, and he had visions of similar centres of Bible Training, with Westminster for headquarters. He is pre-eminently a teacher of the Word, and it was upon the Word that rationalistic criticism was making its fiercest assault. He was set for the defence of the Word, not by Apologetics, but by Interpretation. This was the work to which he was called; to make known again the authority, completeness, and finality of the divinely inspired Word of God.

"In this cause he spent himself with reckless prodigality. His daring faith was superb, and his courageous originality was splendid. His Sunday sermons were solid instructions in the Word. There were no ingenious devices to attract the people, no subtle philosophy to arrest the intellectual, no elaborate ritual to allure the aesthetic, and no sparkling humour to amuse the crowd. The service was reverent, simple and spiritual, and, in all, the Bible was the source of light and the test of truth. The Friday Night Bible School was a great venture of faith. Those who knew the religious life of London would have unanimously foredoomed it to failure, but for ten years it has been the most remarkable Bible School in the three kingdoms. The Bible College has never materialized, but ten years are not enough for everything, and the record of service in the decade stands, so far as I know, absolutely unrivalled and unique. It is not necessary that I should speak of the Mundesley Bible Conference, the Bible Teachers' Association, and the Bible Classes that are held almost daily. If Dr. Morgan has not done all it was in his heart to do, he has done as much as any man has a right to expect to do, and enough to fill his friends with amazement and grateful envy.

"There is one service that Dr. Morgan seems to have reckoned at less than its true value. Looking into the future he says: 'The question is being forced upon me, as to whether it is worth while to preach constantly at one centre, where it is not possible to work out the teaching into the life of a church'. That is the nomad in his blood crying out for a roving ministry. He has been greatly blessed to thousands in the brief ministry of special services, and the desire for spaciousness is strong in him. It is not for another to say which is for him the greater service, but it is difficult to imagine a greater than that of the Westminster pulpit. During the hurricane of theological controversy, he was to thousands a tower and a light. His Scriptural teaching has strengthened the faith of many, and saved not a few. Leaders of thought in all ranks of life have found in him a messenger of God. More precious still is the presence of those to whom his message has brought life and healing, strength and peace. His own people love him, as one to whom they owe their very souls. Such a ministry is always worth the best that the best can give.

"There is another ministry of the ten years, that is a

monument of industry and wisdom. I refer to the ministry of the pen. I wonder if Dr. Morgan has any idea of the number of studies in which there stands a long row of his works on the Bible. He is teaching teachers by the thousand every week. He has published books at the rate of three a year, besides all the public work of preaching, teaching, and lecturing. He says he feels as if he had grown twenty years older in the ten years; and no wonder, seeing he has lived at least thirty.

"Dr. Morgan spoke of the future. He had no plans and no panic; and it is well both were true. Within a few days he was stricken with fever, and for weeks loving hearts have waited and prayed. He gave generous praise to his helpers, and once again they have given proof of their devotion. Through the years he has passed through many sorrows, and now in the midst of the years he is stricken, but there is a sure confidence that his work is not yet done. He will come forth baptized anew for service. The vision will have cleared, and a chastened wisdom will revise the hours of the working day. The best service will come with the riper years. For him the best is yet to be. I have rejoiced in his ministry; for twenty years I have esteemed his friendship one of God's greatest gifts, and I pray with thousands that he may be long spared to expound the Scriptures, proclaim the Gospel, comfort the mourner, and lead valiantly to exploits of grace and truth."

* * * * * *

Campbell Morgan possessed an amazing amount of physical resilience, but on the few occasions when serious illness attacked him it struck with such force as seemed would be fatal. This time he had not the elasticity of youth with which to spring back, and only an indomitable will was left to help medical science fight the virulent disease. It was a long, hard pull even for a fighter, and it was Christmas time before he was able to take his place again in church on Sunday morning. He sat in the pew of a Presbyterian church in Cheltenham, where he had gone for the period of convalescence. "The preacher is their new minister, Mr. J. Macara Gardner, only two months out of college," he wrote in his diary, "but if I am not greatly mistaken he is a coming man. His sermons were fine. It was a great treat to me after being so long away from public worship."

It was February, 1915, before Campbell Morgan again took his place in the pulpit of Westminster. "I was nervous as a boy beginning, but had a good time . . . for which I am most thankful." Listeners were thankful, too, to see that the old power and magnetism of their minister was undimmed and undiminished, though in appearance he looked older and more slender, if that were possible, and there was more silver in his hair. Suffering had accentuated the lines in his face, leaving it, in repose, an added severity, and as if to make amends, something extra, too, of gentleness and charm. It is not strange that the great artist, Mr. Frank Salisbury, who often attended the services at Westminster with his wife, should at this time ask Dr. Morgan for sittings, and in 1915 painted the picture which now hangs in Cheshunt College, Cambridge. During the months of convalescence Dr. Morgan visited Cambridge to see the new buildings. "Excellent in every way," he pronounced them. "I think they are far better than I expected." Though he had been forced to resign as active Head, he remained on the Governing Board of the College, and it is fitting that Mr. Salisbury's portrait of him should now grace its walls.

Dr. Morgan felt now that even with the efficient and loving help of the officers and staff, he was not equal to the demands of Westminster, and expressed his wish to resign. But the affection of his people for him, and the remembrance of all he had done for them, and all they had accomplished and experienced together, would not allow this final step. The officers begged him to reconsider, and though he declined at first, the church was so insistent that he remain, making every concession that would ease his mind and facilitate his activity, that he consented to do so.

Was it the same as before? Is anything ever the same, or is it wise to make comparisons? Campbell Morgan's ministry at Westminster, from this point, was limited because of physical inability to carry the load, and because war, as is always its way, was harrowing its steady and relentless path through the smoothness of peacetime routine and daily living. Nothing was, or could be the same. But nothing had ever been the same. A period of accomplishment had ended when the partnership with Mr. Swift was severed, as Campbell Morgan himself afterwards declared. But another period began, and Westminster continued to grow and put out other branches of service while continuing the older ones. With his illness in 1914 it is evident that this period, too, came to completion. It would not be prudent to call what followed anticlimactic. Different, yes; but other branches of usefulness and importance, offshoots of former activities, showed fruition. 'The glory of the Lord' still filled the house, and the sunset of Campbell Morgan's first Westminster ministry reflected quiet, strong maturity and richness, gained through pain and trial. England did not have need to be dazzled, but she did have need to be steadied as war-weary months lengthened into years and saw no end. This was his mission. For three months in the Spring and three in the Autumn he preached on Sundays and conducted the Bible School as before, and the Mundesley Bible Conferences of 1916 and 1917, though held in Westminster Chapel and Llandrindod Wells respectively, because the East Coast was in the hands of the militia, were attended in large numbers and produced satisfying results.

The slower tempo of life should have provided for more rest, more leisure to read and write, spend in recreation or the enjoyment of his family—or so it might be argued. But the one who reasons thus, whoever it may be, did not know Campbell Morgan. Whether right or wrong, that was not his way. To conserve his strength beyond reasonable limits was foreign to his nature, and with returning energy he began to chafe at the prospect of inactivity. Whether or not it was reasonable at this time to accept preaching missions in Wales and elsewhere can only be decided by their results. Mr. Chadwick was right when he called Campbell Morgan a nomad, for he was ever lured by other worlds to conquer —not for himself, but for Christ; and those who loved and understood him knew that the force that compelled him, and the restlessness to be on the move had this as its primary motive. Though concerned for his health, his church took it as their duty and their pride, as in the past, to share his gifts with others, and widen his influence into these larger areas.

This itinerant ministry of 1916 was carried on as an activity of the B.T.A., an organization which, despite war and its attendant ills—or because of these circumstances—was still flourishing and spreading its influence. "'It's an ill wind that blows nobody any good,'" said a reporter. "Dr. Morgan's release from Westminster for a part of the year is not only providing him with relief from the continual strain of the church, but is giving the Association the opportunity of a forward movement such as it has not had since its formation."

The lovely poetic phraseology of Wales has a way of colouring even prosaic newspaper reporting. The following came from Swansea: "The sanctuary became a lecture-room for ministers, and the eagerness with which notes were taken brought to mind the Scripture, 'They were all amazed and glorified God, saying, We never saw it on this fashion'. . . . Old words became new, and the delight the Doctor evinced in breaking one alabaster box after another revealed one of the secrets of his fresh and powerful preaching."

The report of the conference at Merthyr had a familiar ring: "He came first to deliver the Williams lectures, and also to help a weak and heavily burdened church. As a result of this visit they have had a new lease of life. . . . In no part of the world," continues this writer, "is the Bible more a book of isolated texts than in Wales, the land of sermons and great preachers. . . . The lecture on 'How to Study the Bible' created a deep impression. The Bible will become to many a new book after that night."

A local paper in Leicester had this to report: "Leicester people have been experiencing grand times sitting at the feet of the greatest living exponent of the Scriptures, the Rev. Dr. Campbell Morgan. . . . One does not have to listen to Dr. Morgan long without realizing wherein lies his attractive power. One does not know whether to describe it as his spiritual intellectuality or his intellectual spirituality, but the attractiveness is certainly compounded out of a great brain and a great soul. . . . What charms one most is the clear way in which he is able to enunciate religious truths. His reasoning is almost mathematical in its closeness. One feels all the time that this man not only believes, but knows why he believes."

A business man in Manchester said: "A friend asked me to go with him to hear Dr. Morgan. I said I would prefer to listen to J. Pierpont Morgan. The latter might teach me something about finance. The former was, to me, an unknown quantity. Under protest I went to the Monday night meeting at the Central Hall. I went again on Tuesday night, twice on Wednesday, twice on Thursday, and to the closing service on Friday at noon. I lost some business that week, but I gained a new standard of values and a new Bible. I learned something about the coinage superscribed with a Cross, and I went back to the old Book to read it afresh for 'a message for the times'."

Dr. Morgan's gifts as a teacher appealed to a reporter in Chatham who said: "Dr. Campbell Morgan is a great teacher. He has the teacher's knowledge of the value of repetition, a teacher's quickness to know whether his hearers have grasped his meaning, a teacher's desire to make himself understood, a teacher's intuition to know when the brains of his hearers are flagging, and should be sent out to play while he tells them a story. Added to this there is the persuasive eloquence of a great, good man who speaks with authority."

In Gloucester, the county of his birth and childhood,

Dr. Morgan drew tributes from age and youth alike. An old minister said: "Can anything be finer than this?" and a fifteen year old lad in the same congregation said: "I would not have missed one of these four sermons for anything."

An editorial in the *Staffordshire Sentinel* referred to Dr. Morgan in these words: "He is one of the finest exponents of the Bible of his generation. He is a great theologian, a brilliant preacher, a wonderful teacher. All sorts and conditions of people, believers and unbelievers, crowd to hear him. He has an astounding insight, an imagination which assists him to vision things as they are in the moral, spiritual and material worlds alike, and a delightful and irresistible method, voice and delivery."

The results of war came very close to the summer Bible Conference of 1916, and it was a poignant moment when Dr. Morgan told the Conference that Principal W. B. Selbie, M.A., D.D., of Mansfield College, Oxford, who had been speaking to them with such power and courage during the first week, on 'The Ministry and the Modern World'. had lost a son in the war only a fortnight before; and that a message had been received from Dr. John A. Hutton, of Glasgow, who was to deliver the second week's lectures, saying: "I have just had news that my eldest son is killed in France. Will try to face up to the work. Will be with you."

Under such circumstances the duties of the leader are so delicate as to demand special gifts of insight and understanding. One who was present at this conference, Rev. D. Arthur Davies, said: "He showed himself a master of assemblies. When introducing a speaker he would do so gracefully, not a single fulsome or unnecessary word, always assuring the newcomer of an expectant and sympathetic audience, and so putting the speaker at once at his ease. When . . . there was a time limit given the speakers—as in the Missionary meeting—he was inimitable in the way he would remind them that their time was up. He did it with such unfailing courtesy that there was no possibility of taking offence. . . .

When leading in prayer he was always brief and to the point, never failing to take our souls with him into the very presence of God. When thanking a speaker the Doctor, with his hand on our pulse, would interpret our heart, and say the word we felt we would wish to say. At the close of Dr. Hutton's masterly exposition of a passage in Philippians, Dr. Morgan, in a tender and beautiful tribute said: 'We thank him for his great interpretation of a little but great Epistle; but he is himself, by his courageous devotion to duty in the midst of deep sorrow, the greatest interpretation of the spirit of the Epistle'."

A testimony of the influence of Dr. Morgan's Bible School work at Westminster came at this time directly from the line of battle, in a letter from Rev. H. J. Gamble, a student at Cheshunt during Dr. Morgan's term as President, and a chaplain with the British Expeditionary Force in France: "We re-opened our Bible School last week, and continued the studies we commenced on Salisbury Plain. It seems rather strange, so near the firing line, but the men are very keen. In fact we have extension work as well! The parent class meets some few miles back every Friday evening. The second meets anywhere it can, in fields, trenches, barns, though of course we are strictly limited to small numbers because of the shells and aeroplanes. In continuation of our course we are taking the Epistles week by week, and Romans has a new ring about it out here; and to read, 'Who shall separate us from the love of Christ?' amidst the noise of shells and big guns is—well, you must come here to really understand! . . . There is no question that 'God is for us', and I never believed as intensively the great truths of our faith as I am learning to here."

These are enough of many who might be quoted in testimony of Campbell Morgan's Westminster ministry in its closing days. With the end of the year he became definitely convinced that the time had come to bring his relationship with the church to an end, and the reasons for this decision he incorporated in an address at a Church meeting on January

1, 1917. Mr. Chadwick was also right when he said that Campbell Morgan could not give himself in half measures. Again he spoke to his people with such intimacy and in such a disarming manner as this time to make it impossible to use any weapon of persuasion or compulsion to influence him to change his course. "These are very poor words," he said, "but if you have got to know me well, you know how much I am capable of feeling about certain things, and how, at the utmost pressure of feeling, I break down." He spoke of his acceptance of a college Presidency while remaining as minister of Westminster as perhaps "the wildest thing to have done," but added quickly, "but I do not regret it; and long after I have passed on as to bodily presence, splendid premises will remain at the disposal of men training for the ministry which I was able to secure for that Institution."

The closing words of the address are very characteristic of its author when he was, to use his former words, close to 'the utmost pressure of feeling'.

"I shall trust you to be, in the love of your hearts, my defenders against those who misunderstand my action. I am not taking this course without thought, nor without poignant suffering. No man can put twelve and a half years of his blood and his life into work, as I have done here, and leave it easily. I hope there is no tone that is unchristian in my emphasis, but when some people say, Don't you *want* to get away from Westminster? I am angry! Get away! No! So help me God! I thought I was here for life'. But if He is proving by circumstances that there are other places for me to serve, I have no alternative other than to follow the Light. I repeat to you that the decision I have arrived at is one that has given me intense sorrow, but it has not caused me a sleepless night, for I have been determined to seek only to know His will, and I am bound to believe that He is guiding."

He had written no formal resignation, he said, for they had become so near to each other as pastor and people, that to talk to them out of his heart was best. He told them, too, that the resignation must, for the good of all concerned, take place immediately. "I cannot stand long in the midst of you, here at Westminster," he said, "knowing that I am going. Probably by the end of January I shall have passed out of your midst."

Those last public words to his people bring to mind a seemingly irrelevant comparison. Any member of the family or close friend, seeing him off at railway station or dock, will remember him saying: "Run along! Don't wait till I pull out!" He had an aversion for good-byes or backward looks, and the closer the friend, the dearer the backward scene, the more anxious was he to precipitate the parting.

The New Year was only just born. The future held much to add to the hostages of the past. A chapter is closed—but hurry! Turn the page. It is time to start living another!

CHAPTER VI

1917-1919: 53 to 55 years

MILDMAY (Y.M.C.A.)—HIGHBURY QUADRANT

TO Campbell Morgan on that last Sunday in January, 1917, the 'longest chapter' of his life was 'closed and sealed'. Too dearly loved to be lingered over, his desire now was to put Westminster behind him, not only figuratively but literally, by separating himself swiftly and cleanly from all its associations. "I may go to Australia . . . or America," he had told his people, and there was unexpressed relief in the opportunity created by these calls from over the sea, in closing the door definitely and finally, and being free of the temptation of an early return.

For the second time the invitation had come to him from the Collins Street Congregational Church in Melbourne, Australia, to fill its pulpit for a year, with freedom to do the itinerating work he loved in other towns and cities. This invitation came now, as it seemed providentially, and was gladly accepted. Dr. Morgan soon discovered, however, that owing to Government restrictions forbidding the travelling by sea in wartime of women and children, if he went to Australia he must go alone. He refused to go without Mrs. Morgan and the girls, and cabled the church, asking that they either cancel or postpone his engagement. They preferred the latter alternative, but subsequent events prevented a later visit. The same restrictions cancelled out all ideas of going to America also. It was two years before Campbell Morgan again left the shores of England.

Those two years were to be spent for the most part in London. Cutting right across the plans he had anticipated, they were to hold many contacts with Westminster, and he was to preach more than forty times from the old familiar desk on the big circular rostrum between March, 1917 and

April, 1918, while the church was without a pastor. But 'chance' and 'happenings' had no place for him in the course of human events. "This is the second year in succession," he wrote, "in which plans have been interfered with and programmes disarranged. Surely He means to teach us . . . that those who are called to teach His Word, not only must but may safely live by His will, and see it proceed to the accomplishment of all highest and best issues as apart from human arrangements. In that assurance we are at peace."

In 1917 the Young Men's Christian Association purchased from another religious group some property in Mildmay Park in North London, for the establishment of a centre for the training of its workers, especially those chaplains and others who were engaged in service with the armed forces. Sir Arthur Yapp, General Secretary of the National Council of the Y.M.C.A., asked Dr. Morgan to help in the earlier stages of the work. He promised to do so for a year, beginning in September.

As the plan developed, groups of men came to Mildmay for a two-weeks' 'retreat', one group following another in immediate succession. These groups were, of course, non-sectarian, and Dr. Morgan's emphasis on the essentials of the faith which unite all Christian denominations, and his attraction for all classes and conditions of men made him peculiarly fitted for this work. The process of indoctrination covered all branches of Y.M.C.A. activity. Dr. Morgan's office lay in the teaching of the Bible, and with the special needs of his class in mind, he chose to give a series of lectures followed by discussion on Christ's method with individuals. Some of his audience were men who had already served in the camps among the soldiers, at home and overseas; others were on the eve of going out for the first time. The former group came with a sense of relief and keen appreciation of the privilege of two weeks in retreat, during which they might renew their spiritual, mental and physical strength. The latter were glad to avail themselves of the inspiration of the lectures and fellowship with older men. Dr. Morgan participated in this enterprise with a real appreciation of its national importance, but added to this was a more personal desire to be of direct service to the armed forces, for many of the young men who had grown up in the Westminster Sunday School and Institute were now in France, Flanders or the Near East. Among them was one of his own sons.

After a period of training in Cambridge and Scotland, Frank was commissioned an officer in the Lancashire Fusiliers, and was engaged in active duty in France. Dr. Morgan learned from personal experience a sympathy for the anxious ones on the home front, as well as for the gallant host who faced the perils of the fighting front. There is rarely a page in the diary from the time that Frank entered the service, that the words, 'Frank . . . Cambridge', or 'Frank . . . Gailes', and then 'Frank . . . France', do not appear in the left-hand column where a careful record was kept of all correspondence. The list might contain a few, and oftentimes many other names, but the one occurring most frequently was that of the soldier son. In those days, it is well to remember, young officers were the expendables—the first 'over the top' in trench warfare, the largest contributors to the casualty lists, so frighteningly long, so agonizingly scanned. Dr. Morgan often quoted to ministerial students a saying of Dr. Jowett, that 'preaching that costs nothing accomplishes nothing'. Small wonder that those who passed through Mildmay testified to the power and richness of those Bible lectures.

In response to an overwhelming demand the Friday Night Bible School opened its fourteenth consecutive session in London that September, this time at Mildmay. In spite of moonlight air-raids it was well attended, a thousand people on the average gathering each week. Dr. Morgan's schedule precluded the possibility of extended Bible conferences, but it was through this year that he so frequently preached from his old pulpit at Westminster, and in between times, though *when* is an unsolved mystery, he did an enormous amount of writing for the religious press and in the interests of the Y.M.C.A.

His year at Mildmay was considered of sufficient importance for him to be selected as one of a group who, from time to time, attended the famous 'breakfasts' which Mr. Lloyd George inaugurated at 10 Downing Street, and enjoyed the confidence and friendship of the great wartime Premier. In November, 1917, representing the Y.M.C.A., Dr. Morgan went to France to see for himself the work his 'pupils' were doing in camps and hospitals and in the trenches themselves. An old Westminster boy as well as a new-made friend at Mildmay was surprised to look up from his desk or hospital duty to see the tall, slender figure of his former pastor and teacher, the familiar 'dog-collar' topping the unfamiliar khaki, and the same friendly smile beneath the incongruous 'tin hat'. This was Dr. Morgan's second visit to France during the war, the first having been made in 1915.

At the close of his year of service with the Y.M.C.A., Dr. T. R. Glover joined the staff on a similar year's appointment. A garden party was held on July 24, 1918, to bid farewell to Dr. Morgan and to greet Dr. Glover.

A characteristic glimpse of Morgan humour was disclosed on this occasion when the departing honouree was asked to address the assembly. He described an invitation card he had received requesting the presence of Dr. G. Campbell Morgan at a garden party to bid farewell to Dr. G. Campbell Morgan! He said he had anticipated a useful experience, but had not been allowed time to say good-bye to himself on account of all the kind things people had said to him. He went on to say that, a few days later, Mrs. Morgan also received an invitation to bid farewell to him. At that he drew the line!

★ ★ ★ ★ ★ ★

There were few Congregational churches in London in which Dr. Morgan had not preached at one time or another. Among those in which he felt particularly at home was the Highbury Quadrant Church in North London. At this time the church had been for fourteen months without a pastor—war months, in which an unusually large proportion of its young men had participated in the conflict, and many had given their lives for their country. Dr. Morgan supplied the pulpit of Highbury Quadrant on several occasions during his year of service with the Y.M.C.A., and brought messages of comfort and strength to the stricken congregation. As that year drew to a close the officers of the church asked him if he would come to them for a year, not as pastor in the accepted sense of that term, but to fill the pulpit on Sundays, conduct a Bible School on Fridays throughout the winter, and attend one Church Meeting a month, so as to keep advised regarding the general condition of the church. Dr. Jowett had come from Fifth Avenue Presbyterian Church in New York to be Westminster's new minister and had taken up his duties there in May, 1918. On September 1 Dr. Morgan began his year as minister at Highbury Quadrant.

The terms of the ministry made it possible for him to resume his Bible conferences in the United Kingdom, and his list of engagements filled the days between Sundays and Fridays. His ministry in Scotland was always a time of happy associations, and conferences in Wales were unique in one way at least—that, no matter how hard it rained, the enthusiasm of the Welshman for good preaching was never damped— at least, Dr. Morgan found this to be true. Perhaps his name had something to do with his popularity in Wales, for a Welshman, if not a Morgan—though a Davis, a Price, a Williams, a Jones, a Thomas, and possibly a few others might challenge the statement—can find one not too far back in his ancestry. There is a fondness, too, for the use of the double name. On one occasion during a conference Dr. Morgan stayed in the home of a Mr. Morgan Morgans!

Though the responsibility for the Sunday School at Highbury Quadrant was not included in the duties of the new minister, it was here that he began to go into action. Calling the teachers together for conference, he carefully investigated the administrative and educational programme of the school. Here again he chose a deputy, with his fine instinct for putting the right person to work in the right place. Miss Craske who had been 'Sister Edith', at Westminster, now became 'Sister Edith' at Highbury Quadrant. She combined a thorough knowledge of Sunday School methods and missionary education with tact and charm and consecration. One has only to read in the *Quadrant Magazines* of that period to see how completely she captured the devotion of those she directed. Miss Howell, too, volunteered to meet with the teachers once a week to study the lessons. In a short time an Institute Department and a Missionary School on the lines of similar activities at Westminster were organized.

Beginning with the October issue of the magazine there appeared the copy of a letter which had been written by the minister, and sent to each of the Highbury Quadrant men serving on the different fronts. These letters ranked high among the benefits of Dr. Morgan's brief ministry. Friendly without being effusive, uplifting without being pedantic, these little gems of writing filled a need for those at home almost as well as they did for those to whom they were directly addressed. The first letter and extracts from a few others are enough to show the author's aptitude in the almost lost art of letter-writing.

September, 1918.

"My dear Friend,—Letters from someone you don't know personally can never be quite so interesting or welcome as those others which you are doubtless receiving all the time. Moreover, it is not easy to write to those whom one is not acquainted with personally. However, in spite of these difficulties, I have it in my heart to believe you will care to have a few lines from me, and I am going to take my courage in both hands and write.

"I expect you have heard that the church at Highbury Quadrant has taken the risk of inviting me to occupy the pulpit there for a year, and that I have accepted. I began on the first Sunday of this month.

"Well, it is impossible for me to be brought thus into close relationship with the life of a great church, such as that with which you are so closely associated, without feeling the deepest interest in all its members. Among these, those of you who have answered the high call of duty and have gone forth for God and country hold the first place in our thoughts and love and prayer. . . .

"I am not proposing to preach you a sermon. If you get home before I am gone, you will get enough sermons. I do want you to realize that I think of you with honour, and remember you in the secret place.

"I more and more understand how little we, in the comparative quiet and comfort of the homeland, can appreciate the things you are enduring; and that creates an ever-growing desire to serve you in sympathetic and constant intercession.

"Many of you are probably continuously cut off from the means of grace. I pray you remember that you are never cut off from grace. That is always available for you. The prayer that finds no words, which is only the upward push of the soul towards God, in the place of loneliness or amid the hell of actual strife, always finds Him, and brings grace to help in the very nick of time. That, in all probability you have already proved. May it be your constant experience.

"Yours with sincere affection,

"G. CAMPBELL MORGAN."

After the signing of the Armistice he wrote:

"It is the month of fogs—and we have had some in this dear old London; but just now, in many ways, we are thinking much more of sunshine . . . we are all waiting to welcome you home, for with your coming will come the sunshine. . . . When you think of the love of those at home, remember that it is entirely beyond the control of any scheme of rationing!"

January, 1919.

" . . . If someone started a guessing competition just now as to the most interesting word in our language, I think I could get it the first time. I should go for the word—

DEMOBILIZATION! How's the voting on that? . . . Well, there is another word . . . the virtues of which we must practise. It is the word PATIENCE! Having written that I feel that it looks as though I were lecturing you. Well, I'm not. I am really talking to myself and to others here at home. . . . It is a big job to get millions of men returned to their homes. In the meantime we know that our men and boys will be worthy of their faith and devotion to the very last lap of the course, however tedious it may be.

"Things are going quietly on at H.Q. (Those letters have two meanings, both of which apply). This is my twentieth Sunday, and it is wet. That makes eighteen wet Sundays out of twenty. Still, as the weather arrangements are not in our hands—happily—we go cheerfully on. When you come home things will clear up!"

February, 1919.

" . . . Some of the men are already back at the Quadrant, and it is a great joy to have them. May the day be hastened when you are all with us again. . . . I have preached now twenty-four Sundays at H.Q. Of these twenty have been wet! I am inclined to talk about 'H.Q. weather'. I hear that some people are talking about 'Campbell Morgan weather'! We'll leave it at that, as I believe I referred to this in my last letter. The song of Spring is already in our hearts. One swallow does not make a summer, but one boy does in a home. When he gets back the 'winter of discontent' passes."

The ending of war, as was inferred, does not mean a speedy return of the soldier to the homeland. The left-hand column of the diary now bore repeatedly the words: 'Frank . . . Germany', for many, including Frank, were with the Army of Occupation. But the day came at last when, returning from a Bible Conference in Wales, Dr. Morgan stepped out of the train at Paddington Station to find Frank waiting for him, 'out', and home to stay! "Our hearts are full of thankfulness to our God for preserving him from all perils, and bringing him back to us." So reads the diary for May 2nd,

1919, and a few weeks later—"This is Frank's birthday. . . . It is good to have him with us."

There were eighty-one from the Highbury Quadrant Church and its Missions who never returned to their homes. An impressive Memorial Service, at which Dr. Morgan read every name, the congregation reverently standing, commemorated their sacrifice, after which he preached from Hebrews 11. 13.

He was keenly interested in the inception and progress of the League of Nations, having great respect for its founder, President Woodrow Wilson. It was like him to read exhaustively on this subject and then communicate his findings to his people, interpreting them in the light of the Christian revelation. Referring to President Wilson's statement that the world must be made safe for democracy, he stated that the goal was now to make democracy safe for the world. "If democracy is not right at its heart and centre, then woe to the world," he said. In his diary he expressed his thoughts on world events thus: "We have seen great things. God is revealed anew to man. Now may we walk in the light and set our house in order thereby."

Setting the house in order meant, for one thing, working toward the ideal presented in Zechariah 8. 5, the subject of his sermon one Sunday in the new year of 1919. Someone was very much stirred by this 'imaginative and original sermon', and wrote his impressions for the *British Weekly*. "In his deep and wise familiarity with the Old Testament Scriptures he is growing like Dr. Parker," said the writer. Quoting Dr. Morgan, he continued: "'The word is not praying, but playing—Children playing in the streets'. Dr. Morgan recommended a return to the prophet's ideal of a city where boys and girls play together in the streets. 'Play is preparation for work. We shall one day decide what to make of our boys by watching what they play at in childhood. I preached to my sister's dolls long before I faced a congregation. Blessed be God, it is the fun of my life to-day—and I am not going to take that word back! . . . If children are to play in the streets, the streets must be fit for them to play in. They must be emptied of impure literature, evil placards, unholy pictures—every influence that can corrupt the growing mind. . . . Christianity is not the soft and mealy thing that some imagine. It is a hurricane, a strong rage against everything that hurts the child. Christianity should sweep like a simoon through London, driving out everything that harms the bairn. . . . Remember, too, that the home life must be Christian if the streets are to be fit for children's play'."

The week following the preaching of this sermon, Dr. Morgan received the following letter:

"Dear Sir,—As a thank-offering in memory of my visit to London, I enclose one pound for the boys and girls who are playing in the streets of your great city. I very much enjoyed my visit to your church, and your two sermons. I remain, Yours truly—'A Soldier'."

Dr. Morgan translated his sermon into practice in a concrete and altogether characteristic way. The Quadrant Church sponsored a Mission in a poorer part of the neighbourhood, known as 'Britannia Row'. Though he had no more obligation towards this outpost than he had towards the Sunday School, it was not long before he had paid the 'Row' a visit. It must be evident by this time that he had no patience with the saying that 'What can't be cured must be endured.' In the days of his popular lectures he used as a title for one of them: 'Some Saw Sophisms'. It was based on outworn and contradictory proverbs, and provided some pearls of wisdom clothed in humour. The outcome of the visit to Britannia Row was a notice in the *Quadrant Magazine*, of May, 1919, which reads, in part, as follows:

BRITANNIA ROW—URGENT!

By Dr. Campbell Morgan.

"My year at Highbury Quadrant is fast drawing to a conclusion. Whatever it has been to the church, to me it has been a singularly happy one. . . . And now to the business which I have in hand. For many years Highbury Quadrant has been responsible for Britannia Row, and during this year it has been my lot to come into touch in some way with the work there. Once I went down and saw the premises and met the band of workers. . . . The result is that I have some very strong convictions about this enterprise. These I will tabulate briefly:

"1. The neighbourhood teems with glorious child-life; and from that standpoint is full of possibilities of great work for the Kingdom of God.

"2. The workers are magnificent. They are visionaries as well as workers; they see the possibilities, and are enthusiastic and splendid in their effort to realize them.

"3. The premises are atrocious. That's a strong word, but I don't withdraw it. The conditions to-day are positively unsanitary.

"These convictions have generated a desire, and it is that these premises shall be put into thorough repair. This will cost in the neighbourhood of a thousand pounds. Then, in order that this great opportunity may be taken full advantage of by these devoted workers, a debt or mortgage—what's the difference?—should be cleaned up.

"This means that I want to see one thousand, five hundred pounds provided for this work before I leave for the United States. I would rather leave this behind me as a tangible result of my year at Highbury Quadrant than anything I can think of, for I am completely captured by the greatness of the chance at Britannia Row, and by the quality of the workers there.

"The thing can be done. It needs only a systematic—and really consecrated giving.

" . . . Some promises are already made. The matter is urgent. On Sunday evening, May 11th, I hope to speak on this subject, and at the close of the service to launch the scheme. If before then each one of us will have had that time of lonely consideration in the presence of the King, I believe that we can see the venture not launched only, but sailing away under full canvas and with favouring winds towards the desired haven."

Dr. Morgan really enjoyed himself in sponsoring this cause, not only because of its worth, but because of the added element of a time limit. An invitation to join the staff of Dr. Wilbert W. White's Biblical Seminary, in New York City, had already been accepted, and in three months he planned to be on his way. Hence the King's business required haste.

On May 11th, "the church was crowded," he says, "and I had great liberty in preaching. Afterwards conducted a service of dedication of gifts for Britannia Row. Over a thousand pounds was contributed." On the last but one of the forty-seven consecutive Sundays in which he occupied the Quadrant pulpit, he reports: "To-night the place was crowded and hundreds could not get in. We had a remarkable time completing the Britannia Row Fund. Throughout the day we realized over three hundred and sixty pounds."

By September of that year the Mission premises were in the hands of the workmen, and by November the Renovation Scheme was completed. "Everywhere fresh, light-tinted walls free from damp stains," reported the exultant superintendent, "clean windows, and radiators and hot pipes carrying warmth to all parts of the building. It is something to rejoice over, and during the first week-end in November the 'Row' was 'at home' to all those who have helped towards the good work. . . . In a Service of Thanksgiving the thoughts of all present turned to him who had done so much to make it possible. . . . Truly both the Quadrant and the Row owe Dr. Morgan a great debt of gratitude."

Having decided upon his next move, Dr. Morgan began winding up his affairs in England. The most difficult was to part with 'Northfield' and all its associations.

"I suppose this means never again!" he wrote, thinking of the Mundesley conferences, and the many times between when the country home had been a haven of rest and refreshment in the midst of busy days. A Gas Company in London bought 'Northfield' for a rest and convalescent home for its employees, and Dr. Morgan left a large part of his fiction library for their enjoyment. 'Uncle Ted' and 'Auntie Edith', to whom it had been home for so long, now settled in Essex. They did not know then that, for thirty years and more, beautiful Yew Tree Farm was to take the place that Mundesley had held heretofore in the hearts of the second generation.

★ ★ ★ ★ ★ ★

When it became known that he was going to America for an indefinite period, Dr. Morgan was deluged with letters expressing regret at his leaving. He kept very few personal letters of the hundreds that must have been sent to him, so that the few that were treasured in the pages of the diaries were, for one reason or another, of special value. From those written at this time two are chosen for their beauty and originality, and for the self-portraits of the writers.

Cliff College, Calver,
Via Sheffield,
16th June, 1919.

"My dear Morgan,

"I do not know when you expect to sail for America, but I would not like you to go without a word of love and God-speed from me. Great Britain will miss you, and to your friends your going will leave an immeasurable blank, but though I sorrow more than they all, I rejoice greatly in your appointment; it is a fitting crown to a life of distinguished and devoted service. You will do more in the last decades of your life than in all the rest, for all your past will find its effectiveness in your present. It is work in which you have no peer, and work in which you will be supremely happy. God has kept the best till the last.

"I cannot tell all your friendship has meant to me. I am flattered when people bracket my name with yours, and though I know the distance at which I follow, it pleases me that they think of us together. The privilege of your friendship I reckon among God's best gifts and my chiefest joy. It would have been good to see more of you, but I have always known you were there. If sometime you can send me a line of news about yourself and your doings I shall be glad, and if at any time I can be of service I shall hail the opportunity with joy.

"With love to Mrs. Morgan and all your household,
"Yours always,
"CHAD."*

                          BENDERLOCH,
                            ARGYLL.
                             2nd July, 1919.

"My dear Morgan,

"... As our American friends would say, I simply hate to think of your leaving us and making your home elsewhere. What times we have had together, and how much I owe you! You beat them all for all the qualities I like in a man. For as St. Paul said, or as he meant to say, 'Though I speak with the tongues of men and of angels and am not all the time a kindhearted man, I am nothing but a kind of dinner gong, inviting people to what they like'!

"There is a volume of meditations of mine coming out this autumn, and whether you like it or not, it has to bear on the page succeeding the title-page something of this kind of legend:

> To
> G. CAMPBELL MORGAN,
> Known of all men
> as a preacher;
> Known to his friends
> as the kindest of men.

"I am due in America next year.... But it won't be America if I do not see you, and see a lot of you. Once more, good-bye, my dear old friend, and always think of me as one who loves you.

"Ever yours,
"JOHN A. HUTTON."

*Rev. Samuel Chadwick.

There were many who felt most strongly that his going constituted a calamity, and that an organized effort should have been made to keep him in England at a time when he was so sorely needed. The most eloquent voice raised in protest was that of Mr. F. A. Atkins. This colourful journalist, who himself loved the United States to the extent that he was once heard to exclaim: "If heaven is like America—I WILL BE GOOD!" did not resent Dr. Morgan's going there so much as he resented what he considered the lassitude of the church people of England in allowing him to leave at a time of national and social difficulty, restlessness and disquietude.

"I hope British Congregationalists will never forget," he said, "how Dr. Morgan saved one of their largest and most important churches, and made it a great centre of spiritual life and social enterprise."

He reviewed Dr. Morgan's achievements at Westminster, and like Dr. John Hutton, bore witness to his kindheartedness as a friend. "A sour critic who once saw him in a motor car said he was extravagant. So he is—with a gorgeous, exhilarating extravagance! He would empty his pockets and drain his banking account to help a friend. One day he received a draft from an American publisher on account of one of his books. He turned it over to a colleague and told him to take his wife away for a holiday."

It is true that, in certain respects, Dr. Morgan was a thorn in the flesh to some of his more circumscribed brethren, and Mr. Atkins draws attention to this with delight.

"I do not think he shines much on committees. . . . He is too impatient, too venturous for the dull routine of the council chamber. . . . I remember when I was very young, a minister who was very old took me aside and said: 'Don't be too venturesome'. It was the most deadly, vicious, and thoroughly wicked advice that could be offered to a young man! Dr. Morgan has never given such advice to anyone, but I am sure he has received it frequently from misguided deacons and timid officials. I rejoice to think that it has never had the slightest effect. But while Dr. Morgan has a daring faith and a sound contempt for outworn conventions, he is the most methodical of men. He once showed me a book, like an office ledger, in which he entered the title of every book he read . . . and what he thought of it.

". . . Dr. Morgan possesses in the highest degree a genius for friendship, and he has the blessed gift of humour. He has also a wonderful spirit of generous appreciation—that is, he rejoices in the gifts and successes of other men. I have never heard him speak an unkind word of anybody—not even of men with whose views he profoundly disagreed. Throughout the New Theology controversy with all its deplorable bitterness, Dr. Campbell Morgan never indulged in a harsh comment or anything approaching a personal attack.

"Let us make no mistake about it—we are losing our greatest expository preacher. He has made the Bible a living Book to thousands who have found it drab and difficult until this teacher came along to light up its obscure passages, reveal its romance and beauty, and declare its life-giving message. And he is much more than a Bible teacher, for all through his ministry he has preached a very definite and uncompromising social gospel. . . . No one who worships Christ can meet the dark problems of life with a dull acquiescence. As a matter of fact, the most eloquent of Labour leaders would have to give way to Campbell Morgan in his scorching denunciation of social wrongs, and his passionate advocacy of brotherhood and justice.

"Dr. Morgan has a strong, lively personality and an explosive method of expressing himself, and therefore no one is likely to agree with him all the time. . . . But he is a good man and a great preacher, and we are all profoundly sorry that he is leaving us at a time when we are uneasy and bewildered, and need every flaming prophet and every vitalizing ministry."

But Campbell Morgan had already decided his immediate future, and in view of the broadening of vast opportunities which unfolded for him on the Western Continent, who would say that he was not led by God to leave the homeland for a while; for that leading was not to be confined to one city or one institution as he supposed. At the last moment all plans were changed, circumstances making the Seminary appointment not feasible at this time. It was to be again a ministry to the people of the New World—of the United States and Canada. During the next six and a half years he would cover approximately 150,000 miles and preach more than 3,000 times in many cities, states, and provinces. A door was swinging open, and the view beyond, hidden at first, emerged to show limitless horizons

CHAPTER VII

1919–1932: 55 to 69 years
THE ITINERANT MINISTRY
IN THE UNITED STATES
By Rev. K. J. Morgan

WHEN my father stepped from the good ship *Adriatic*, on the seventh day of August, 1919, he stepped into one of the greatest and most fruitful periods of his life, a period as active and arduous and amazing as anything he was to experience in all the days of the years of his ministry. From the time he left the ship at her pier until he boarded the *Britannic*, more than thirteen years later, he packed his time to the utmost limit, never sparing himself, and not a little amused with the rest of us when we failed to keep up with him. The weather was glorious that August morning in New York City, fine, but not too hot. It suited him perfectly. He was off to a good start, and he was never one to underestimate a good beginning.

That he was not unaware of the significance of this beginning is revealed in a diary entry for October, 1919: "Thus I start out on the new journey. The old pagans would have said, 'The issue is in the lap of the gods'! We say it is in the mind and heart and will of God. That gives peace." And it *was* peace throughout those busy years, though this tranquillity of heart and mind and spirit must never be confused with indolence. Dr. J. H. Jowett once said of him: "His one aim is to let the Bible tell its own eternal message. In that kind of work he has a genius which is incomparable." With a son's rather intimate knowledge of his father I place the emphasis on the word, 'work', in Dr. Jowett's estimate, rather than upon the word, 'genius', for no man worked harder than did my father, especially during this period.

This fact made itself felt in many ways, not least in the reports of those who listened to him. One expressed it thus: "The messages are the result of hard, painstaking work and study." Another, making mention of "the marvellous simplicity and lucidity of his interpretation of the Scriptures" little realized, perhaps, the stupendous amount of 'painstaking work and study' involved in the 'simplicity' and 'lucidity' of the spoken word. Even in his reading of the Bible was noted the 'unfailing accuracy of emphasis' of the preacher. That his reading was impressive is beyond dispute, but it should be remembered that behind such reading there had been much time and thought and preparation.

The years of itinerant ministry were the rapids of his life, and he shot them well and truly and with never a backward glance. There were of course, the more leisurely episodes through which he passed between the summer of 1919 and the close of 1932, but taken as a whole the period was one of perpetual motion from one place to another. The list of towns and cities visited makes interesting reading, and looks for all the world like a railway time-table alphabetically arranged. There's Atlanta, Baltimore, Chicago, Detroit, Evansville, Findley, Grand Rapids, Harrisburg, Indianapolis, Jackson, Knoxville, Los Angeles, Miami, New Orleans, Orlando, Richmond, Seattle, Tacoma, University (Va.), Washington, and Youngstown, to list but a very few. Practically every State in the Union was visited for a series of meetings, among the notable exceptions being Texas, the largest of the forty-eight. But Texas is not completely missing for, watching the view as the train sped across the Lone Star State, a diary note reads: "The scenery is monotonous. Still, it is interesting as showing man's determination and ability to compel the desert to serve him, and also the fact that the desert has resources, if man knows how to get at them."

Thousands of miles he travelled and scores of places he visited, and always with one single aim—to break the Bread of Life to the waiting, eager, expectant multitudes. Nor were they disappointed, for Campbell Morgan ever gave of his best, and as Mother would say, 'fed them'. The crowds *did* wait for him, and not infrequently a service would begin thirty minutes or more before its appointed time, the building being packed to the doors and many turned away. They were eager to see and hear him, some perhaps from mere curiosity, but many more because they were after that which is only found within the pages of the Book, and 'there is only one', as Sir Walter Scott said. They were expectant, for whatever had been said about this man it had never been said that he did anything but preach the Word, and the fact that he did so at considerable length never seems to have deterred them. North, South, East, and West it was always the same; great crowds, buildings overflowing, and a message lasting a full hour, sometimes well over the hour. On Sundays there would be two sermons, and quite often an 'after-meeting' at night in which an invitation would be given to follow Christ and become His disciple. There was no fuss about it, nor were any who stayed for the meeting made to feel afraid, still less was there any smell of brimstone. Those who had received the message were invited to receive the Lord of the message, to take Him into the heart and life and crown Him. The appeal was quite simple and as dynamic as it was simple. "Just raise your hand, no need to keep it up"—that was all and it was enough. A verse or two of Charlotte Elliott's searching hymn, 'Just as I am', during the singing of which momentous transactions transpired. These after-meetings were not confined to the Sabbath, for they were not confined to anything. None could say at the beginning of a service whether there would be a second service, certainly not the preacher himself. But of one thing there is no doubt at all, scattered over the length and breadth of the United States are multitudes who have good reason to rejoice because their names are written in heaven, and this as a result of hearing the unsearchable riches proclaimed.

Outstanding among early engagements was Dr. Morgan's visit to Richmond, Virginia, to deliver the James Sprunt Lectures at the Union Theological Seminary. His theme for these lectures, peculiarly his own, was *The Ministry of the Word*, a series in which, as stated by the author himself in his prologue, he was "desirous of considering the subject of the Christian Ministry solely from the standpoint of New Testament ideals." In reviewing the lectures a writer to the *Christian Observer*, having referred to Dr. Morgan as "the pre-eminent expository preacher of our time," continued: "At Union Seminary where the chief aim has always been the making of effective preachers, we are glad to have a man presenting this subject who has shown so conclusively that the minister can do his best work by simply preaching the Word in its purity and fulness."

The itinerant years in the States were often marked by the unexpected. In a Southern city, just before time for the evening service there was a torrential and tropical rain and thunderstorm, yet the church was completely filled. That the preacher had 'a somewhat hard time through the storm' is not as surprising as was the great congregation on hand.

Though never one to berate the weather, he was most susceptible to the spiritual temperature in which he worked as is clearly revealed in a diary entry reading: "I had a fair time to-night, but the theological controversies which have been waged in this city have made the whole atmosphere very difficult. Everyone is on the *qui vive* in a fighting sense. I hate it!" and 'hate' was indeed the right word!

There were times when news would reach him in the midst of busy days, news that affected him profoundly. He was in California on the first Sunday in February, 1924 when, thirty minutes after his service had commenced, word was handed to him telling him that President Woodrow Wilson had passed away. "I abandoned my sermon," he wrote; "read Joshua 1. 1-2, and spoke out of my heart for half an hour." Just a month later, in Chicago, he received a cable from England giving the news of the passing of Sam Nutton, one of his dearest and closest friends. But the work went on, and we could almost hear him saying: "Ah, well, dear old Sam! I'll see him in the Morning."

In December, 1923, he reached his sixtieth birthday, which fell on a Sunday. He preached twice, and expressed his reactions in his own inimitable way: "So the sixtieth milestone is passed, the three score years are gone. What remains? Who knows? Who cares? God does, and therefore I need not and I don't! Cheerio! Carry on!"

That his messages were repeated is true enough, though there is a most necessary qualification in this respect. He never repeated himself in the same place, indeed, he abominated the very idea. In a letter sent home he wrote: "It is always an amazing thing to me how a man can go back to the same town and repeat messages delivered there except, of course, under exceptional circumstances where some series is requested. I think the trouble with a great many men is that when they begin to go about they cease working." That Campbell Morgan went about in an almost incredible way is something which is known and remembered by most people who knew and remember him at all. What is not so generally known is the stupendous amount of sheer hard labour involved. Throughout the strenuous years it was always the same, whether preaching in the Cathedral of St. John the Divine in New York City or in a little town almost buried away in the red hills of Georgia. Everywhere he gave himself completely in his work, and it cannot, therefore, be a matter for surprise to find him described as 'an impressive speaker with an enthusiasm and devotion that likens him to St. Paul', and by another as 'speaking with a power that must be akin to that of St. Peter's on the day of Pentecost'. Those of us who knew and loved him best were oftentimes appalled at the pace he kept, for he outpaced us all. Though there were times when we ventured to remonstrate we knew perfectly well it would be of no avail, and we were not surprised or even disappointed, for we knew he could not stop, so great and glorious was his conviction that what he was doing was 'within the Will' for him. Occasionally, very occasionally it is true, there would be a free Sunday, and though we rejoiced in the fact, we also knew he would not share our delight, as witness this illuminating diary entry for Sunday, December 30, 1928: "I suppose my last idle Sunday for some time, and I hope so. I hate them." And he did! An idle Sunday could disturb the 'even tenor of his way' as perhaps nothing else.

Many rich tributes have been paid to the itinerant ministry in the United States. From them the following have been selected because they are representative.

The *Presbyterian Standard*, of Charlotte, North Carolina, now united with the *Presbyterian Outlook*, of Richmond, Virginia, described Dr. Morgan as 'a Prince of Preachers', and makes an observation that has found an echo in the hearts of many of his hearers: "Under the skilful handling of truths they take on a new meaning, and one wonders how he himself, though reading the passage hundreds of times, could have failed to see the same."

Rev. William E. Hudson writes of the Bible Conferences at Massanetta Springs, Virginia:

"Dr. G. Campbell Morgan, world famous Bible teacher, appeared on the Massanetta Springs programme in 1923. He was at the peak of his fame and was at his best. His eloquent expositions of the Bible sparkled with wit and humour but above everything else, his exhaustive and profound study of the Bible in its original language and his grasp of history and the philosophies of the world made him a teacher in whom everyone showed the greatest faith and confidence.

"In each of his sermons he held the rapt attention of his great audiences. He won the hearts of everyone. . . .

"On the last night of the Conference he preached on the text, 'If any man thirst, let him come unto Me and drink', after which an appeal was made to the audience to stand if they wished to dedicate their lives afresh to the Master and be channels of living water to others. To this appeal some four or five hundred people rose to their feet, making a most profound and impressive spectacle. . . .

"Dr. Morgan returned to Massanetta in 1930, and on this occasion again captivated his audiences by his clear exposition of the Word of God and his unanswerable logic in presenting its divine truths. During this week he was associated with a team of speakers unbeatable at that period of American Church history. . . . Campbell Morgan was in a class by himself and stood out as a most popular and convincing expositor. He was said to be the preacher's favourite. . . .

"Massanetta reveres his memory and is proud of the fact that he honoured the Institution with his presence for three summers."

Dr. Walter L. Lingle, programme and platform manager at the Southern Presbyterian Summer Conference at Montreat, North Carolina from 1910 to 1924, points out that the seating capacity of the Auditorium at that time was between 2,500 and 3,000. "The auditorium was full when your father spoke," he says. "I learned to know well a good many gifted speakers from both sides of the Atlantic, but in my judgment Dr. Campbell Morgan was the greatest teacher of the Bible and the greatest expository preacher that came to Montreat during those years."

Dr. Lingle has many memories, but an incident which left the most marked impression on his mind took place much later:

"Although I did all the correspondence with him in connection with his coming to Montreat, and looked after his comfort as best I could while he was there, and although I sat on the platform with him every day, I never felt that I got very close to him. There was a certain aloofness about him that I attributed to the fact that he was an Englishman. All the while I felt that there must be a warm heart beneath that English exterior. Fifteen or twenty years passed by, and one of my daughters happened to be in London over Sunday and attended Dr. Morgan's church. After service she went forward and spoke to him. To her utter astonishment he saluted her with a holy kiss, saying, 'For your father's sake'. I didn't know that I had any sake, and had supposed that he had forgotten me long before. You never can tell how much warmth there is in the heart of an Englishman by looking at his seemingly cool exterior."

It was given to Dr. John A. Hutton to strike a note which was pre-eminently fitting in reference to Campbell Morgan. In a tribute on the occasion of his retirement from the active ministry, he wrote: "Morgan always spoke with authority." Therein lies the secret of the success which was so happily to attend these years of itinerant ministry. My father was ever dogmatic, and with good reason, for he also was 'a man under authority', and like the One he served he spoke 'with authority'. And for those of us who were continually separated from him as he went from place to place, it was good to know and realize, as we surely did, that we ourselves were helping him onward. This he was quick and eager to acknowledge, as witness this line from a letter sent home: "I am always conscious that you are all following step by step and helping in prayer." Through all the way his was a trumpet which never gave an uncertain sound.

IN CANADA

By Dr. F. A. Robinson

OVER several years, Dr. Campbell Morgan conducted Dominion-wide campaigns in Canada, promoting the study of God's Word. Letters constantly reach the Toronto office of Missions of Biblical Education telling of the lasting blessing that his visits brought to individuals and congregations, so that one feels like saying that his ministry is, and will still be, active. The late Principal, Clarence Mackinnon, of Pine Hill College, Halifax, once said to the writer that he doubted if anything bigger or more helpful had been done for the Canadian Church than Dr. Morgan's Biblical expositions. Other equally eminent leaders felt that a national service was rendered by his thoughtful expositions relevant to present day problems. I heard him preach and lecture over a thousand times and never once was he dull. Nor was there ever any indication of inadequate preparation. While some of his sermons were long, judged by the desires of to-day's average congregation, yet they were never so long as to prevent people from longing for more. He never preached 'Sermonettes for Christianettes'.

In his Canadian missions he never read a sermon, and I think it would have handicapped his persuasive powers had he done so. What overflowing crowds gathered to hear him! Once in one of the largest theatres in the Maritime Provinces I had to send word to the hotel at 6.30 p.m. telling him the place was packed. People who had attended the afternoon meeting refused to leave, and sat through the subsequent four hours rather than run the risk of not getting a seat! He began to speak three-quarters of an hour before the announced opening of 8 o'clock. Noonday meetings, held for business men in the auditoriums of great hotels, attracted hundreds from offices and stores. Eagerly they listened, and his very helpful blackboard outlines are still cherished in many a notebook.

The minister and officials in a Nova Scotia congregation, hearing that Dr. Morgan was passing through on his westward journey, and knowing that he had one and a half hour's wait between trains, were exceedingly eager to give the community an opportunity of hearing him. They wrote and wired so appealingly that in spite of the necessarily unusual hour, he consented to preach. The service had to be announced for 9.30 p.m. The church was crowded. While it was a rather strenuous extra, Dr. Morgan so appreciated the Committee's enthusiasm and the amazing response at that hour that he had unusual liberty in preaching and perhaps gave the most effective message of that tour.

Although eminently successful in his several pastorates, Dr. Morgan was temperamentally fond of movement and new scenes. He frequently said in private and in public how very happy he was in his peripatetic teaching missions in the United States and Canada.

Others will write more fully of Dr. Morgan's pulpit messages. All I need say is that our correspondence files across the years show that multitudes of burdened and sorrowful ones found in him a God-given tenderness and sympathy and guidance that often dispelled the clouds that had darkened the way. Many wayward and wandering ones were led by his earnest appeals to lay their burden of sin at the foot of Calvary's Cross. His messages were often evangelistic although he only seldom made definite appeals for decision for Christ. He was more concerned to arouse Christians to a deeper sense of their responsibility. He knew that in the main they were not reading the Bible, and he did not hesitate to point out the Biblical illiteracy of the average church member.

He believed in an evangelism that expressed itself in service. If people were going to be good they must be good for something, and they must be good to somebody. The singing of 'Rescue the Perishing' within the glow of stained-glass windows was of little use unless it resulted in action. He made the Gospel poignantly relevant to the perplexing problems of our social conditions. He dealt fearlessly with society's leprous pollutions but, like his Master, he brought a message of love and pardon for the poor wanderer. What a world of compassion and tenderness was revealed as he quoted in prayer: 'If some poor wandering child of Thine have spurned to-day the Voice divine, now, Lord, the gracious work begin'. His nature was deeply sensitive. He stirred his hearers to the depths because he was so deeply stirred himself.

I do not know if Dr. Morgan ever read prayers in the pulpit, but I never knew him to do so during the years of my association with him. He prayed with deep reverence and with the confidence of one who *knew* God. I always felt that he was praying in the atmosphere of our Saviour's words, 'God is a Spirit; and they that worship Him must worship Him in spirit and in truth'. Those words were a controlling thought in all his petitions.

The series of services we arranged on ten different tours covering more than a decade, were for a period of one or two weeks each. Long distances were usually covered between Friday and Saturday nights. He spoke twice daily and refused all invitations for extra meetings, feeling that twelve addresses a week were the limit of what he could effectively do. The daytime meeting would be at noon in a hotel, or at 3 o'clock in a church. Until the last year with us he always used blackboard and chalk for these daytime expositions of the Scriptures. At the beginning of a Mission he would announce that the afternoon meetings would be kept within the hour, and through all the years I never once knew him to fail to keep that promise. "The evening meetings will begin at eight o'clock and will close" (a slight pause and then quickly) "when I'm through." His social engagements were restricted to afternoon tea immediately following his 3 o'clock expository address. This gave opportunity for meeting more intimately leading Christian workers, many of whom discovered for the first time his gentlemanly charm. He was usually back to his hotel room within an hour. His evening meal was at the close of the day's work.

Many ministers were led to commence expository preaching at least once a Sunday through Dr. Morgan's elaborate and illuminating analyses of the Bible. The pastor of a large city church in Central Ontario wrote us that, by adopting Dr. Morgan's technique, the attendance at his mid-week prayer meeting had been trebled. Under his guidance many came to see the joy that is to be found in the regular and prayerful study of God's Word.

Even those who disagreed with his Biblical literalism were in the main greatly and helpfully influenced by his striking and powerful personality and by his clear, confident, and authoritative voice. How that voice would ring out in his proclamation of the Gospel! Few pulpit voices have or had more resonance and music than his. Sometimes there was 'the glorious outburst of winged words'. In Byron's phrase he had an eloquence that was 'the poetry of speech'. His diction was never commonplace. His eloquence was not only in words and tones, but in his eyes and gestures, and in his perfect choice of words. Doubtless the constancy of his Bible reading had much to do with the last named. For over half a century he had saturated his thinking in the pure and sublime language of the Book that he knew as few men did.

He once told us that he read the Book of Exodus through at a sitting forty times before he put pencil to paper for his expository notes thereon. All his sermons had in them a solid basis of Scripture. The Bread of Life was the staple of all his messages. He often spoke of not having found the text, but that the text had 'found' him. He liked to quote from his friend, John A. Hutton: 'A text without its context is only a pretext'.

Dr. Morgan had few topical sermons, and such topics as were used were always dignified and Scriptural. During a recent summer conference for ministers, Professor Edward H. Roberts, D.D., of Princeton Theological Seminary, conducted a sermon clinic. In the course of one address he narrated an incident that is more penetrating and illuminating in regard to Dr. Morgan's reverent handling of the Word than any descriptive passage the writer might attempt. It occurred in a church where the brilliant young pastor drew large audiences by such topics as 'Popping the Question', 'The Price of a Haircut', 'Two Lumps of Sugar, Please', etc. By mistake on the part of the printer the bulletin gave Dr. Morgan's subject as, 'That's My Weakness Now', a topic that was to be the popular young preacher's a week hence.

In introducing Dr. Morgan the youthful pastor smilingly explained that the visitor would not preach on the topic announced, but that he himself would do so on the following Sunday. Amidst the general laughter that the explanation evoked Dr. Morgan stood up and, looking solemnly over the great audience, said with vibrant reverence, "Hear the Word of God." No apology. No pleasantries. The effect was, if I may use one of his own adjectives which he certainly would not have used himself, *tremendous*. Many years have passed since that Sunday morning, but as long as memory lasts, the deathly silence that followed will not be easily forgotten by those who were present. As Dr. Roberts added: "It was an effective rebuke to flippancy."

Dr. Morgan used every avenue of research to gain a complete knowledge of text and context. I recall his search into the formation and meaning of certain rather uncommon architectural terms for a sermon on 'the pillar and ground of truth'. For an Easter sermon his etymological search concerning the word itself took several hours. He studied with prayerful thoroughness and had a reserve of knowledge far beyond what the actual sermon content required. He got so fully into his subject that his subject got fully into him.

He was keenly alive to daily contacts and incidents that might be grist to his homiletic mill. In one of the most famous cherry orchards of south-western British Columbia, Dr. Morgan stood amazed at the abundance and size of the fruit. "Well!" he said to the grower, "anyone can see that cherries are easily grown here." "Dr. Morgan," said the fruit grower, "we are fighting for the life of those cherries 365 days in the year." The reply was turned to telling account in a later message on Christian watchfulness.

Congregations were often profoundly stirred by his dramatic reading of Scripture and hymns. Who that heard him quote stanzas of 'For all the saints who from their labours rest', will ever forget those lines, as with perfect but unstudied elocution he made us see 'the countless host' streaming through the gates of pearl. Even as I write memory brings again the thrill of those moments, and especially the heart-stirring and perfectly musical tone with which he uttered the word, 'singing', in the line 'Singing to Father, Son, and Holy Ghost'.

Then, too, I always felt it was a loss to the congregation when he asked (which was seldom) someone else to read the Scripture lesson. 'The Lord hath rent the kingdom from thee', would not seem to need or provide much in the way of vocal interpretation, but Dr. Morgan put disaster and crash and tragedy into that one word, 'rent'. 'Go tell that fox' (Luke 13. 32) is another example of what he could do with a word. He ferreted out all the possible meanings of words in the original. Although 'fox' was applied to Herod, "the word is in the feminine gender," said Dr. Morgan "—Go tell that vixen!" and that bit of information coloured the stinging tone in the reading.

Dr. Morgan's reading and teaching of the Bible made it a new Book to many thousands. With what appreciative devotion he handled the Book itself! It was, indeed, the Book of books to him personally. He believed the Bible to be its own best interpreter and he gave it first place in the time he allotted to reading. He used to tell of the old coloured mammy who had been given a concordance. Being asked some months later how she liked it, her reply was: "Oh, I likes it all right; the Bible sho does throw a lot of light on dat dere concordance!"

He pleaded with his hearers to give the Bible the place which he knew it should have and assured them of the riches that were therein. To neglect it was to do one's own soul a wrong. He knew that the more it was read the more it would be treasured. He knew from his own studies that 'A glory gilds the sacred page, majestic like the sun; it gives a light to every age; it gives, but borrows none'.*
What light, under God, he caused to gleam and glow from the sacred page!

Dr. Morgan regarded a hymn as 'the uplifting of the soul to God in terms of song'. He constantly encouraged wholehearted congregational singing and set a good example by always taking his full part in it. When desirable he could effectively lead the audience in song. Of much modern music he used to say that the 'rest' was its most enjoyable feature. He used mainly the great hymns of the Church, yet he was fond of the bright choruses and newer gospel hymns that may be classed as evanescent. In our week-night meetings he frequently requested me to teach the congregation 'Shine, shine, just where you are.' It has only four lines, but is very singable by even the unmusical crowd.

*Cowper.

We used it one evening in the First Baptist Church, Calgary, Alberta. Dr. Morgan rose from his pulpit seat and stood alongside me. "Let's sing it as a duet," he said quietly. Neither of us was a 'duettist', but incredible though it may seem, the audience with western cordiality, vigorously applauded! We responded to the encore.

A few weeks later I received a letter from a lady in a remote district of British Columbia: "We were so delighted to hear Dr. Morgan and you sing, 'Shine, Shine'. Enclosed find twenty-five dollars towards your good work." On Dr. Morgan's subsequent visits I naturally enough suggested the singing of our little duet again, but there was no further financial encouragement!

His books had a very large circulation throughout Canada, and several volumes became out of print as a result of the unusual demand that followed his Dominion tours. I was once indiscreet enough to announce that if his autograph were desired on books purchased, Dr. Morgan would be at the pulpit steps at the close of the service. It certainly was desired with a vengeance! I venture to say that that picturesque autograph—if 'picturesque' may be used of an autograph—is treasured in hundreds of homes from the Atlantic to the Pacific, for from that night on there was a line-up of people with books to be autographed, and I never heard him complain about the bother of it all.

During the intimacy of constant travel together, and in frequently occupying adjacent hotel rooms and dining together day after day, I can truthfully say that there was never once any indication of vanity, although he was often almost overwhelmed by the groups that desired to praise him. Yet those who thanked him and praised him were, I believe, thanking and praising God more. He led men to think more of the One of whom he preached than of himself. He valued genuine appreciation, but he was not concerned as to the verbal and other honours men could bestow upon him. Many homes were eagerly desirous of entertaining him, but he restricted the acceptance of invitations to the brief period already mentioned for afternoon tea.

He thoroughly enjoyed himself in a select gathering at such times. Sometimes, however, we were invited to homes of luxury and wealth merely because of Dr. Morgan's eminence as a man, and not because of any special interest in his preaching and teaching missions. While he was a delightful, and at times a merry guest, he was not particularly happy where there was only an insipid sociability.

In one home the object of the boringly fluent and gushing hostess seemed to be to impress us with the cost of the book-bindings in the library. She knew little or nothing of the contents of the books. Even some marble statues of considerable merit only had the monetary value stressed. She was well informed on the cost of everything, but she appeared to know the value of nothing. The honoured guest gave a deep, significant sigh of relief as we passed through the elaborate doorway to the waiting car, and I tried to avoid having him pass through similar ordeals. Ordinarily, such afternoon functions were delightful alike to speaker and invited guests. Frequently there would be members from one of Dr. Morgan's English congregations, and that was always an added joy to him, for wherever he went, and however beautiful and attractive other lands were, he always spoke with deep affection of his 'dear old flowery, showery England'.

When I first met him in Northfield over forty years ago, I confess that I thought he lacked cordiality. Many who met him only casually held the same opinion. It might seem incredible to some, that one facing such audiences as Dr. Morgan did day after day, and meeting all types of people in the sanctuary and in social gatherings could be shy, but I am sure he was, and that shyness often caused people to misjudge him and to accuse him of lacking in courtesy.

He was a gentleman in the highest sense of the word. They say that cranky old King James the First of England, as he scribbled his signature to a courtier's 'patent of nobility', said: "Any monarch can make a nobleman, but only God can make a gentleman." I say with reverent knowledge that God had done good work in completing the cultural side of Dr. Morgan's life.

He was the soul of honour, and would never tolerate anything that appeared to belittle or do an injustice to his fellow-workers. During a series of meetings in the great American Presbyterian Church in Montreal, a sign stretching half-way across the building bore the announcement of the various services. One of his associates was to speak at noon, and Dr. Morgan himself at 3 and 8 o'clock. The name of his associate was in smaller letters than his own. When Dr. Morgan saw it he insisted that the names be equal in size, and the Committee had to make the change.

One of his song leaders had incurred the displeasure of a certain minister in a city to which the Morgan party was to go for two weeks of services. At a ministerial meeting, when final preparations for the visit were being made, the minister referred to said that he would have nothing to do with it and would publicly oppose the meetings if the song leader came. A friend wrote the song leader, stating the facts, expressing the confidence of the entire Ministerial Association in him, but suggesting that it might prevent any unpleasantness if he could be engaged elsewhere during that period.

The song leader discreetly informed Dr. Morgan that he was doing other work and would not go with him to X—. But Dr. Morgan was not convinced by the reasons given, and in a few minutes had ferreted out the cause of the song leader's decision. Nothing more was said and the song leader regarded the matter as settled. Two or three hours later, Miss Howell, Dr. Morgan's secretary, brought the copy of a telegram to the song leader's room, saying that the message had already been sent to X—. It read: "Am greatly surprised at the suggestion of your Ministerial Association that Mr. J— should not accompany me to X—. That such action should be taken in the case of a man of such unimpeachable character and of such ability as Mr. J—, is almost incredible. Unless he accompanies me in his usual capacity please cancel all meetings.' He was not concerned as to what the Committee might think of him, he was only concerned to do the right and honourable thing. That was typical of Dr. Morgan. He had investigated the matter and was convinced of the unfairness of the minister's opposition. The Ministerial Association at once consented to the personnel being as announced. The objecting minister took a two-weeks' holiday visiting friends while the meetings in X— were successfully carried on.

Dr. Morgan's kindly consideration for those who held different opinions or had convictions that were not his, was one of several characteristics of the Christian gentleman he was. How sympathetically he listened to those of us who tried to preach in his presence! He was almost as good a listener as he was a teacher and preacher and expositor. One wellnigh life-long friend tells of being in a great audience at Northfield when Dr. Morgan, using blackboard and chalk, was 'shepherding' his flock as he crossed from one side of the wide platform to the other. Dr. Glenn Atkins, who was as enthralled as every other listener, said without taking his eyes off Morgan, "That man has too much!" So it was not easy to preach when one unexpectedly discovered Dr. Morgan in the pew.

It fell to my lot to be occupying the pulpit of Whitefield's Tabernacle, in London, one summer. As I stood up to announce the first hymn I saw the family of the then minister of the City Temple. My knees grew weak—but they almost folded up when I saw Dr. and Mrs. Morgan and others of his family immediately in front of me. For a moment or two I desired to be back on the American continent, or anywhere else than where I was. Dr. Morgan had a merry twinkle in his eyes, and for a second I looked reprovingly at him, for I knew he was supposed to be out of the city on holiday. He was playful enough to enjoy my obvious embarrassment. At the close he came to the vestry and, placing his hands on my shoulders, spoke words that sent me to my knees that night with tearful eyes and a heart full of humble thanksgiving. As long as memory lasts I shall treasure those heartening words from the man whom I have always regarded as one of God's Greathearts, and who knew how to reach the conscience and teach the Word as few men of his generation.

What stories he could tell of his association with pulpit giants like Joseph Parker, Alexander McLaren, Sylvester Horne, W. L. Watkinson, and many others. They lose much in cold print, for up to the present, with all our inventions, we have not been able adequately to reproduce the tonal qualities of the human voice through the printed page. But when a few of us could get together for an hour or two after the week-night meetings and, as he would laughingly say, when he could be released from my 'benevolent autocracy', and I 'loosed him and let him go'—then his mimicry was perfect.

Of Dr. Watkinson whom he greatly loved, Dr. Morgan had a dozen good stories. Few if any could so perfectly reproduce the high-pitched voice and the sniffling mannerism of Watkinson. One of the stories was of a friend of Dr. Watkinson's who had a faithful dog, a great pet with the entire household. On Watkinson's visit a year later they told him that Rover had died a few weeks before. "We have buried him at the foot of the garden and we are going to erect a little stone. You know how fond we were of him. We wondered if you would suggest some suitable epitaph." Without a moment's hesitation and very soberly Watkinson replied (with a sniffle or two), "Without being dogmatic, I suggest that you put on the stone: 'His bark has reached the other shore'."

Another Watkinson gem referred to a young minister who was, I think, assistant pastor. The Doctor felt the young man was rather too much with the ladies of the congregation, and he ventured a word of warning. Rather glibly the assistant replied: "Oh, well, Dr. Watkinson, there is safety in numbers." "Yes, young man," was the prompt reply, "there is safety in numbers, but there is more safety in exodus."

After the nervous strain of his services he was frequently

hilarious at the freedom from immediate further preparation, and more than once I heard him quote a Scottish preacher who is reported to have said to his wife on the eve of his overdue vacation: "Well, Jean, thank God I ha' na' to preach nor pray for a month."

When he gave his hat a few twists and pulled it down over his forehead, and turned his lower jaw well to the left, and then (when our little group was alone) walked bow-legged along the upstairs hall of the hotel, he was one of the most humorously grotesque figures one could ever expect to look upon!

One of his fellow-workers was fond of mixing up the hats in the cloakroom of a ministerial gathering, and of changing shoes after the occupants of the Pullman car had retired. Dr. Morgan enjoyed the ensuing confusion and vigorous language quite as much as the perpetrator of it all. Any good story that a member of his party could tell had to be repeated again and again for the benefit of those who had not heard it, and Dr. Morgan would laugh heartily and encouragingly every time.

Another of memory's pleasant pictures is of Dr. Morgan and his travelling companion sitting in the rear seat of a day coach of a British Columbia branch line train. Between them was a six-quart basket of cherries—a fruit of which each was exceedingly fond. He had been speaking in that famous fruit district where the finest cherries in Canada are grown. With a newspaper over the knees and a handkerchief tucked under each chin, there was a competition in ingestion. For a considerable time the only pause was for the counting of two little heaps of stones to make sure the consumption was on a fair basis. The boy-like disputing over any possible irregularity, or over the surreptitious putting of more than one at a time into the mouth was a source of great amusement to two friends sitting opposite. What a joy it was to see the boy —the fun-loving boy—in the preacher, prophet, and expositor at whose feet we were daily learning the deeper things of God.

He enjoyed telling his intimate friends this incident relating to his general appearance.

As a number of Conference speakers at Northfield were sitting around the dining-table, Mr. W. R. Moody, the host, passed a book of daily devotions, suggesting that each guest read the text under his birthday date. Dr. Stuart Holden, Dr. F. B. Meyer and others read the verse as suggested, but when Dr. Morgan's turn came he looked up the date, and at once without saying a word, passed the book to the next minister. Moody was curious to know the reason for the silence, especially as he had noticed Morgan's whimsical expression. The verse was, 'Can these dry bones live?' Those who remember Dr. Morgan as he was in those days will appreciate the laughter which followed.

Few evangelistic campaigns and preaching missions are free from financial criticism, and I feel compelled to write briefly on this aspect of our work together. It is no secret to those who knew Dr. Morgan to say that he had a very small portion of acquisitiveness. His income was large compared to that of a city pastor, and he was a very free spender. I never knew him to hesitate over the purchase of anything on account of the price. It was only necessary for one of his loved ones to say that this brooch or that necklace in the jeweller's window would go well with a certain dress worn by a relative or friend, to have it procured.

He dressed immaculately, and carried at considerable cost the equal of two ordinary wardrobes. He once informed me that he had brought along nine suits for our two months' tour from Newfoundland to Victoria. However, one must remember that a journey of that length involves many varying degrees of temperature. On another occasion, in releasing his baggage from the U.S.A. as he came to Toronto, I paid twenty-eight dollars on the excess weight. He could not do without a goodly assortment of books, from works of fiction which he read late at night to Greek lexicons, commentaries, and the latest theological literature. He also carried much other material for the continuous outpouring of his mind and pen.

He preferred having one or more members of his family

journeying with him so that expenditures were large, which in turn placed fairly heavy financial responsibilities on those of us who arranged his many tours. But when he was at his best (as he usually was!) I felt it was worth all the cost financially and physically. Offerings were received at all meetings without high pressure methods. I can still see his erect, slim figure moving near my side when I was announcing the offering as we neared the close of a preaching mission. Whenever there was a danger of a deficit he would say: "May I be permitted to butt in?" After referring to the local committee's obligations he would mention the fact that his own needs were met through the same offerings. "The Lord has taken good care of me"—he paused long enough for the audience to look at his leanness, for people at that time described him as 'awfully skinny'—and then he would add, to the accompaniment of smiles and laughter, "though you may not think I look like it!"

In the generous use of his income he frequently helped friends out of financial difficulties. At times he gave a good lift to some needy work. Then there were individuals who consulted him regarding projects of their own. A book that I edited and put through the press was the fulfilling of a promise made to a dying man. The lady who made the promise had for twenty years been unable to fulfil it. She brought her long-awaiting manuscript to the church one afternoon and told the story of her promise and the subsequent gathering of the needed material for its possible publication. Through Dr. Morgan's financial aid and that of another friend the volume was at last printed and served its purpose. Later he had several conversations with her. The almost ecstatic joy that it brought to the one who had made the promise years before and alongside a dying bed, and the helpfulness of the book itself were ample repayment to Dr. Morgan and his associate in the undertaking.

Dr. Morgan preferred, as most men do, first-class hotels, and knew he could do his best work by declining private hospitality. Hosts and hostesses are usually too anxious to introduce an honoured guest to all their callers, and even go to the trouble of calling in passing friends. Such well-meant geniality would have prevented the honest and uninterrupted study that Dr. Morgan insisted on having. Journeying across the Dominion with over twenty outstanding and overseas preachers, I came to know their characteristics and habits fairly well. A few never seemed to study. One of the most famous could enjoy sightseeing and dining out and social converse until thirty minutes before his evening address, but never once did I see Dr. Morgan neglect his sacred periods of Bible reading and preparation for even the most enticing and attractive social function. The King's business was his all-consuming passion and concern.

His love for human companionship was always manifest. What the friendship of men like D. L. and W. R. Moody, F. B. Meyer, his associate pastors at Westminster Chapel and a number of others meant to him, no one but himself could realize. When he referred to such men as we sat alone, his eyes would fill and his voice become husky.

At one of our summer conferences in Sackville, New Brunswick, he and Dr. Meyer were speakers. Although the closest of friends they had not met for ten years. Meyer arrived a day before Morgan. When I met the latter he at once asked for Meyer. As soon as his baggage had been placed in his room, he said: "Where shall we find him?" I knew the secluded spot under the trees where Meyer was reading his Greek Testament. He did not hear our approach. I called his name. He sprang to his feet. Hands were clasped; neither could say a word for several seconds. To see these two ambassadors of Jesus Christ gazing into each other's eyes with an emotional fervour that comes only to those in whom dwells the Spirit of the Master, made a little picture of Christian love and fellowship that I shall never forget. What hours of blessed reminiscences they had during the days that followed! What experiences had come to each during the long years of separation! But each could say, 'All the way my Saviour leads me'.

What enriching hours we had with these two God-sent messengers! And though both are now absent in the body, the fruitage of their labours is still blessing the Canadian Church.

To Dr. and Mrs. Morgan, and to the members of his family associated with him from time to time, and also to his faithful secretary, Miss Winifred Howell, that same Church owes a debt of gratitude that will not willingly be forgotten.

CHAPTER VIII

1926-1932: 62 to 69 years

CINCINNATI—LOS ANGELES (B.I.O.L.A.)—PHILADELPHIA
—(GORDON COLLEGE, BOSTON)

DURING the years of itinerant ministry in the United States and Canada, 'home' was in Athens, Georgia. Dr. Morgan was well known in Georgia particularly through his many years of association with the Baptist Tabernacle in Atlanta and his long friendship with its renowned pastor, Dr. Len. G. Broughton. Among the many friends in the vicinity were Mr. and Mrs. A. S. Parker, of Athens who, learning that Dr. Morgan was seeking a home base, persuaded him to look with favour upon their town, sixty miles to the south of Atlanta, and the seat of the University of Georgia. Athens, in the peaceful 1920's disseminated that stimulating atmosphere which belongs in a peculiar way to centres of learning and at the same time clung to the traditions of the 'old South' with its air of leisurely well-being and hospitable living. Events in history were dated as 'before the war', and 'after the war'—referring not to the faraway 'world' conflict of 1914-1918, but to the catastrophic upheaval of the War between the States. An Englishman whose schooling had contributed to his background a long succession of wars of which this of 1860-65 was but a paragraph in the history book, was brought up sharply to a consciousness of relative values! But it was a congenial atmosphere among kindly and well-bred folk, proud of their heritage and satisfied with life as it was. Dr. Morgan bought a house in Athens and called it 'Ataraxia'.

The girls, in the manner of easy adaptation to which Morgans had become accustomed, exchanged the austerity of an English boarding school for the luxury (to them) of 'Lucy Cobb Institute', a private school for young ladies, with a headmistress who revered the aristocracy of good manners and a cultural education. They slipped into the elastic rules and regulations with a sigh of content and came home for the week-ends, filling the house with their friends. Their brothers—suddenly, it seemed—had gone out to establish homes of their own. Each as he came to the age of decision had felt the call to the ministry, with no coercion on the part of his parents except that exerted by the example of their lives. The churches they served were of easy access to Athens, and the big, wide-porched house and sheltered garden re-echoed repeatedly to sounds of welcoming voices and the good-natured banter of brothers and sisters who, closely bound by affection, have been separated for a while. 'In-laws' were quickly accepted and comfortably absorbed into the family and, as each small 'outlaw' made his or her noisy appearance, the first visit from home was to 'Grandma's,' in Athens.

From the time he moved into the house on Lumpkin Street in September, 1921, until he took up pastoral residence in Cincinnati, Ohio, in January, 1926, Dr. Morgan himself lived in it for an aggregate of only eight months—never for more than nineteen days at a time. Yet of all his American homes it was here that the roots went deepest. It personified for him all he wanted from life when he was not actively engaged in his work. He enlarged and improved it so that his expanding family could all be together whenever possible, adding more rooms downstairs at the back, and over them a giant-size study which overlooked the garden and the rolling country beyond. It was this study, perhaps, which, being of his own conception and plan, made 'Ataraxia' something special in the way of homes. Its long, high walls were book-lined, the volumes catalogued and filed by Miss Howell whose office adjoined it. Couches and chairs, comfortable and a bit shabby from long usage circled the room, and its centre was dominated by a large billiard table, covered by mahogany 'leaves', making of it an ideal work table—room to spread out books, notes, and outlines. In the evening the study was the gathering place for family and friends. The sound of the balls when a game was in progress was expertly imitated by 'Polly', joining loudly in the laughter she provoked, and murmuring 'Good-night', softly to herself when her cage was covered as a hint that her company was no longer desired. This room was the centre of fun in the summer holidays and at Christmas. On the big table crossword puzzles were solved with the help of 'Murray' and 'Webster'. Family and friends gathered here to hear 'Dad' read aloud; problems were discussed here and decisions made. It was the workshop, the rumpus-room, the confessional, the holy of holies. It stood for all that was meant by 'Ataraxia' —'undisturbedness'. To this room in this house his thoughts must have often turned from hotels, Pullman cars, conference halls and church auditoriums in far distant places. This was 'Home'.

When Kathleen left school she accompanied her father on many of his tours and later Ruth did the same. Thus it continued for four years. Travel did not agree with Mrs. Morgan, and she found that her health depended upon the quiet and routine life of home, rather than on the migratory one of moving from place to place.

Churches in many parts of the United States invited Dr. Morgan to come as their pastor, and in 1926 he knew that if he and Mrs. Morgan were to enjoy their remaining years together he must find a preaching centre. Such a centre was the First Presbyterian Church in Cincinnati, Ohio. Its physical location made it within easy access of many large cities in the Middle West. Dr. Morgan accepted the pastorate of this church for a tentative period of five months, using it as a preaching centre on Sundays and conducting a Bible School on Friday nights. The first part of each week he was to be free to go to other places for Bible conference work. His eldest son, Percy, was to serve as co-pastor and have oversight of all other church activities. Meanwhile 'Ataraxia' was to be retained until time should prove if this move should be permanent.

During this five month period, January till May, 1926, the attendance and tone of the assembled congregations were carefully kept and noted. By the end of March Dr. Morgan was convinced in his own mind that he had not found in this particular church the answer to his quest. Many views might be advanced regarding this decision. The Session was not unanimously in favour of Dr. Morgan's programme, feeling that it was turning the Church into a Bible Institute, whereas they felt that more in the nature of pastoral work was needed. It is distinctly sensed from the comments in his diaries that Dr. Morgan himself was disappointed in the fact that, in a building which accommodated over 700, the average congregation numbered 300 to 400. This disappointment vindicated the critics who insisted that 'Dr. Morgan must have his crowd'. What they could not condone might have been better understood could they have seen the crowds which flocked to hear the messages in other places during the week. In Chattanooga, "the church was crowded and some were turned away." In Grand Rapids—"a hall densely packed." In Toledo, "the night was bitterly cold; notwithstanding this the church was filled in every seat." (At home, the next night, "our congregation was less—224—and no extra bad weather to account for it.") In St. Louis, "the place was packed out by 7.15 so we started the service." In Findley, Ohio, "people were standing wherever they could ... and hundreds were turned away." In Lorain, Ohio, "the place was overcrowded and a mob was outside." In Dayton, Ohio, "a pouring wet night, but the church was crowded." There was the exception, too. "A restless sort of crowd" in one place, which "didn't seem used to my sort of work ... not more than 400 in the building, and at first a listless atmosphere. It improved and on the whole was a good service." This improvement continued and the church was filled before the meetings closed.

Home congregations picked up to a certain extent after it became known that Dr. Morgan's ministry would terminate at the end of May, which explains one reason at least for successful itinerant work. People make the most of what they know will not last. On the other hand it must be said for those who composed the Cincinnati group that the tone of the congregations was of the finest. Other factors may have contributed to the lack of the appearance of success. Within the family circle itself, the father-son co-pastorate was not considered likely to last for any length of time, not because of any friction between them, for there was throughout a oneness of purpose and plan, but simply because the psychological natures of this particular father and son and this particular church did not add up to a total of continuing and satisfactory development.

When Dr. Morgan's decision to terminate the Cincinnati ministry became known, many individual expressions of appreciation and gratitude bore witness to the blessings of this short ministry.

"I am living . . . about 23 miles from the city," wrote a member of the Friday Night Bible School, "and it is quite an effort in the midst of my many duties to attend each week. . . . Last night we discovered at 11.30 p.m. that the bus was not running, so were compelled to look for a medium priced hotel. . . . I am not stating these facts to solicit your sympathy but to say that both my wife and I appreciate the teaching you give and do not mind the inconveniences for we feel well repaid. . . . As long as God makes it possible I expect to make this 46 mile trip on Friday evenings. I do feel the great need of this splendid Bible Class."

"As a minister and as a member of Cincinnati Presbytery," wrote another, "I am greatly distressed over the possibility of your withdrawing from the work in this city where your type of preaching and Bible exposition is so sorely needed. . . . What you are doing is a contribution to every denominational group in the city." Another expressed it thus: "Cincinnati needs more than she realizes the type of spiritual leadership which you can give. . . . To many of us the fact that she is permitting you to leave will always be a source of profound regret."

But the five months of resident ministry would have been eminently worth while had it claimed no other testimony than that contained in a note which is tucked away in the diary pages. It reads in part: "Now that the end has come, may I try to express my gratitude for all your preaching has meant to me. You came just when I was in sore need of help, crushed by sorrow and utterly alone. . . . I felt that I was the special object of God's wrath. As I have heard your beautiful teaching of the Word, my dying faith has been gradually rekindled and I feel that I am still His child. I come away from each service with this feeling in my heart: 'God surely must care for me for He has sent Dr. Morgan to Cincinnati because I needed him so'."

★　★　★　★　★　★

In the summer of 1926, Dr. Morgan went to England for four months, and a wonderful summer it was. He had not been back since he left Westminster in 1919 to make his home in the United States. If he had had any doubts as to whether or not he would be welcomed, or any wonderings as regards what kind of welcome it would be, they were all dispelled from the moment he set foot upon the soil of the homeland.

July 2nd, 1926—"Travelled comfortably to Liverpool Street (London), where Marsh met us. . . . Called at Westminster. . . . Stood for a moment in the old pulpit."

There were less than a dozen witnesses, but they were old friends who remembered, and were able to share in sympathy the moment when he stood there 'in the old pulpit', looking out upon the empty church, so full of memories. Doubtless he was remembering it as it had been in its 'former glory'. This year would be a barometer. Changes had taken place in seven years—there were some he would miss who had passed away, there would be old friends and new, and the never failing stream of summer visitors.

However high his hopes or confident his thoughts, they did not anticipate the overwhelming welcome he was to receive.

"Predictions made last week," reported the *British Weekly*, of the fourth of July Sunday, "that crowds would flock to Dr. Campbell Morgan's ministry during his two months at Westminster were abundantly verified at the first morning service. At 10.45 lines of visitors were waiting in the aisles and the lower gallery was rapidly filling. Half an hour later the only vacant seats were in the back of the upper gallery. The British and American flags were draped in front of the pulpit, and the silver bowl close by overflowed with white roses. As Dr. Morgan entered his old pulpit he may have recalled those strenuous twelve years when he renewed the dilapidated building and, as Dr. Jowett's biographer remarks, 'completely restored the fallen prestige of the old church.' The culminating event of these years—some would say of his life's ministry—was the great service in which he rallied London on the first Sunday evening of the war.

"Unchanged is the tall, slender figure which scarcely fills out the rich gown of silk and velvet. There was always something gracious, attractive, benignant in Dr. Morgan's outward presence, and to-day, with his abundant white hair he looks, as someone said, 'as handsome as a picture.' . . . What is his secret for voice preservation? There was not a harsh note in his utterance, either in prayer or preaching. Healthily tanned by sun and sea-wind, he comes amongst us with energies unimpaired, after long continued wanderings."

To the 'boys' in the States he was writing in a few weeks: "the crowds at Westminster are really wonderful. . . . The stewards know how to handle them—their work is perfectly done. Last night . . . they placed chairs in every available position. I only just had room to stand in the pulpit to preach, and Marsh had to occupy my chair while I did preach."

"To-night (August 29) saw such a crowd as Westminster has never seen—the church packed, and in the neighbourhood of a thousand in all the school halls listening through amplifiers. The service was broadcast, too, so perhaps I addressed the largest congregation of my life."

Neither was it at Westminster alone that Campbell Morgan

was made to feel that his countrymen were glad to have him back. A triumphal tour through more than thirty towns and cities of England and Wales showed how spontaneous and happy was the welcome. In Manchester he records that "hundreds could not get in. I spoke for 1½ hours with freedom." His former church at New Court was "densely packed." Towns in Wales as in former years allowed nothing to hinder attendance. "At Swansea the church was packed in spite of pouring rain."

"I am bound to say to you," he wrote, "and I do so with perfect honesty, that it is amazing. Wherever I go the same thing happens—the buildings are not able to hold the crowds and we are having great times. One thing which is almost overwhelmingly evident is the hunger of the people over here for real constructive Bible teaching and preaching."

An incident occurred in connection with meetings held in a town in England, which shows a side of Campbell Morgan few people ever knew, and those who did, it is likely, never forgot. Soon after concluding a series of meetings at which the offering had been particularly generous (which was not always the case!) Dr. Morgan received the following letter:
"Dear Sir,

"Having recently heard of the cheque you were paid by our treasurer, I wish to point out that to receive over thirteen pounds a day for expounding the Scriptures is a great stumbling block to the ordinary Christian, and still more so to 'the man in the street'.

"One frequently hears that preaching is only a profession like any other, its main object being to get money, and your big fees make me feel that there is a good deal of truth in it.

"Your reputation as one of the greatest Biblical scholars is in my opinion quite justified, and I thank God you use your great gifts to His honour and glory, but your love of money is positively appalling.

"If, as I have been told, you have heavy expenses, my reply is, no Christian is justified in living extravagantly, and no one else that I know of asks or expects such huge fees.

"If I thought that studying the Scriptures produced such fruit as that!—but of course, such a thing is absurd, for its effect should be just the opposite, on a lowly, Christlike life.

"It is the inconsistent lives of Christians that produce such harm. . . .

"Yours sincerely,

————."

To which Dr. Morgan replied:
"Sir,

"I am in receipt of your amazing effusion of Sept.—. It is characterized by impertinence based on ignorance.

"In the course of it you use the expressions, 'big fees', and 'huge fees'. For your enlightenment I may say that I make absolutely no charge for my work, neither does Mr. Marsh, who has made all my arrangements. The amounts which are paid to me are decided by those whom I serve, and it is of the essence of bad manners for anyone outside the interested party to interfere in such arrangements.

"When you speak of 'living extravagantly' you are once more revealing your crass ignorance, and I have no intention of giving you any information as to my methods of life.

"The only kindness you can do me is to let me know how much you contributed toward the gift of love which was handed to me at X—, and allow me the pleasure of sending you a cheque for the same.

"Faithfully yours,

"G. CAMPBELL MORGAN."

No one can afford to be careless regarding what he puts into writing, and Dr. Morgan's statement of the method he followed in the matter of remuneration he received for his services was always meticulously carried out. What he never put into writing, and what was never known to the rank and file was the extraordinary generosity with which he used the 'huge fees' when they came his way. Less than a week after dictating this letter, he was making arrangements to help a friend which involved a long journey and a new start in life, and for this privilege he was footing the bill, not as a loan but as a gift. This side of his character was, it is needless to say, entirely unknown to his explosive correspondent.

★ ★ ★ ★ ★ ★

It was a fairly new daughter-in-law who in 1921 asked a pertinent question. Dr. Morgan wrote in reply: "As to my theology. In the sense in which the words, 'Liberal' and 'Conservative' are used in that connection, I certainly am conservative. About that, there is no question, as any man who calls himself 'Liberal' would tell you if he were talking about me."

These terms of which he spoke are synonymous with the more familiar 'modernist' and 'fundamentalist' in the ecclesiastical vocabulary, and the latter group claim Campbell Morgan as one of their own. His every written and spoken word bears testimony to his belief in the infallibility of the Sacred Writings, and his teaching is rooted and grounded upon the fundamental facts of the Faith. At the same time he was vitally distressed by the schisms in the church, and deplored the bitterness evinced by many fundamentalists.

"I have long felt," he wrote to a son, "that whereas I stand foursquare on the evangelical faith, I have no patience with these people whose supposed fundamentalism consists in watching for heresy and indulging in wicked self-satisfaction because they have an idea that they alone 'hold the truth'—hateful expression! . . . Whereas, in many ways I agree with their theological position I abominate their spirit."

Campbell Morgan never compromised for a moment with a philosophy which denied the tenets of his convictions. He regarded it for the most part with pity for the ignorance from which he felt it came, not untinged with amusement. "He is a good man with a lot of funny ideas," he said of one. "Curious that, in order to square their ideas with their philosophy of God, some of these men prove their ignorance of God's character by the undermining of the authority of the Biblical revelation. . . . It is for those of us who stand on what Gladstone referred to as 'the impregnable rock of Holy

Scripture' to maintain our witness." But his work as he saw it would be injured and hampered by the arguing of controversial issues. His policy was to carry on his own work in his own way, ignoring them as far as possible. Moreover he found it possible to execute this policy and yet compel the attention of both groups. What took place in one middle-western town in the United States is typical of similar experiences elsewhere. "We are really having a good time here," he wrote. . . . "It is a particularly difficult city for my work from the fact that for years it has been a storm centre of theological controversy. The thing that is pleasing me is that both wings are attending my meetings. I hope, therefore, that there will be real value in them along the line of constructive Biblical teaching."

He chose to ignore, also, as far as possible, the personal attacks which his own conservative position inevitably invited, to the keen disappointment and chagrin of those who felt it his duty to defend it. Typical of this attitude is a reply sent to one of his sons, who had expressed indignation over a misrepresentative attack of this nature. "I have seen the cutting you enclose," he wrote in reply, "I feel very much as you do. . . . However, I am not troubled about it. My reputation is in higher Hands than can be affected by this kind of thing. In all my public work I have observed without deviation one rule, and that is never to attempt in the Press to overtake a blunder made by the Press. I could not prepare a statement for the Associated Press. It might raise all manner of questions and lead to controversy. It is far better to let this kind of thing alone. It will all blow over directly, and in the meantime I can get on with my work."

But adverse publicity could not always be ignored, and this was particularly impossible to Campbell Morgan when the assault from one side or the other was directed against a friend, and one whom he felt was unjustifiably charged. Such an issue culminated the next step in his career.

Early in 1927, Dr. Morgan conducted a series of Bible Conferences on the Pacific coast, and while there received an invitation to join the faculty of the Biblical Institute of Los Angeles. In this theological seminary, founded on the conservative doctrines of the Faith, the training ground of prospective ministers and missionaries, Dr. Morgan felt that he had found a field of service after his own heart. He was particularly happy among students, and never so much at home as in the classroom. In the summer he moved into a home in nearby Glendale with Mrs. Morgan, Kathleen and Ruth.

There began a singularly happy experience for he enjoyed equal popularity among students and professors. He had long been known in the coastal cities of Pasadena, Santa Monica, Sacramento, Bakersfield, and others, and these now laid claim to his services when he was not engaged in college lectures and seminars.

Now for the first time the Morgan 'clan' was really scattered. The home in Athens was sold: Percy had gone to Canada; Howard to Indiana; only Jack and Frank remained in Georgia. But if Dad, Mother, and the girls were happy in their new home and could be together for what 'Dad' referred to as "the next step of the journey, most probably the last," all was well. He regretted the separation and felt it as keenly as they did. He used often to say that he wished he could live like the patriarchs of old—having a central tent and all his children and their families encamped about him. "I am sorry we are going to be so far away from all of you," he wrote to Frank from Glendale. "I think you know if I could arrange my own affairs I would be in easy reach of all my children. But as years go on that cannot be —for their sakes as well as for ours. You have all now found your place in life and service, and I am content. For what remains to Mother and me of life this side the veil, we need each other more than ever, and the divine guidance seems to be out here—so I have no alternative."

Dr. Morgan took up his duties at the B.I.O.L.A., in October, 1927. In November, his friend, Dr. J. M. MacInnis, Dean of the Institute, gave him the manuscript of a book he had written, entitled, *Peter, the Fisherman Philosopher*, asking

Dr. Morgan to write a foreword to it. He did so, stating that the greatest value of the book lay in the fact that "it will help many who are bewildered by the conflict and controversies of the days in which we live, to clear thinking upon the really fundamental things of our faith and life." There were some fine points, however, upon which the extreme fundamentalist group, some of whom sat upon the college board of directors, did not see eye to eye with the writer of the foreword, and chose so to interpret them as to make them a matter of altercation and debate. The breath of 'heresy' was fanned into a storm, and when at last, in November, 1928, it became imperative to take sides, Campbell Morgan stood by the friend in whose integrity he believed, drawing the same criticism towards himself. The Board was not unanimous, but straws in the wind pointed to the fact that Dr. MacInnis would be forced to resign. Campbell Morgan had determined in his own mind that, in this eventuality, he also would resign in protest. It might be reiterated to the point of tedium that it was good to be able to call Campbell Morgan one's friend. but there is nothing so final as proof. Proof of this friendship is to be found in two documents which are self-explanatory. The first was written under date, 19th November, 1928:

A STATEMENT.

"I have handed in my resignation from the Faculty of the Bible Institute of Los Angeles, to take effect on December 31st of this year.

"My action has been caused by the fact that my friend, the Rev. John Murdoch MacInnis, D.D., Dean of the Institute, has placed his resignation in the hands of the Board.

"The reason for his doing so is briefly as follows. Last year he published a book entitled, *Peter, the Fisherman Philosopher*. This book has been charged with infidelity to the Evangelical Doctrines of our Faith; and a tendency to what is called 'Modernism'. Those appointed by the Board of the Institute to investigate this matter have declared that there is no trace of anything of the kind in the book, and have put on record their conviction that Dr. MacInnis is absolutely loyal to the fundamental things of the Faith.

"Notwithstanding this fact, by a majority vote they have taken the position that because the attack has cast suspicion upon the Institute, it would be in the interest thereof that Dr. MacInnis' resignation should be accepted.

"Thus the Board virtually says: This man is not guilty, but because some people think he is he must be sacrificed in the supposed interests of an Institution.

"Those who know me will know that I could not continue to work in relation with a Board capable of such an unjust and cruel practice of expediency.

"I return, therefore, to my work on independent lines, as I did it before coming to Los Angeles.

"G. CAMPBELL MORGAN."

The second is found on the dedication page of a book published in 1930, entitled, *Categorical Imperatives of the Christian Faith:*

<blockquote>
To
My Friend,
JOHN MURDOCH MACINNIS, D.D., PH.D.,
Saint and Scholar
True as Steel to the Evangelical Faith, and a Revealer
of the Truth that the Spiritual and Intellectual
are not Incompatible.
</blockquote>

* * * * * *

Again, in 1928, three summer months were spent in England. "The Westminster crowds are as great as they were two years ago," he said. At the age of 64 his health was still seemingly unimpaired, though he was blandly ignoring advice once given to him by a doctor which he was fond of quoting to other ministers: "You must not think that because you are a preacher you can break the laws of God with impunity." He wrote home: "On my itinerary you will find the word 'REST' against August 6. I expect to preach in Stebbing that day. You will find the same word against August 20 and 21. On August 20 I am to be in Bridgewater and on August 21, at Mundesley."

On September 11, on the eve of his return to the United States, a great Thanksgiving Service was held in Westminster Chapel in recognition of 'Dr. G. Campbell Morgan's three months' ministry in Westminster, and his service to the churches in England'. It was a noteworthy occasion in many respects, but primarily because its keynote was the one which consistently followed Campbell Morgan's ministry wherever it went—the catholicity of his message and of his influence among people of all classes and conditions, among all denominations and orders.

★   ★   ★   ★   ★   ★

Christmases in the Athens days had been particularly happy times. Dr. and Mrs. Morgan had slipped so easily into the rôle of grandparents that it was as if it had been written especially for them, and they both acted the part as if they had known no other. It was unfortunate that the toy train and the automobile that came unassembled should be 'too old' for those for whom they were originally intended, but 'Grandpa' had a wonderful time with the train, and the Uncles did a most painstaking job on the automobile. It was 'Grandma' who proved to have an inexhaustible supply of alternative attractions for little Bill, Len, and Nancy.

Now those happy days were past. The girls did all they could with a tree and gifts to make festive the California Christmas, but when Dr. Morgan came to enter up his diary for December 25th, 1928, all he could think of to write was: "We missed the little ones."

It was not time yet, however, to live for long in retrospect. The only reference to his birthday which followed directly upon his resignation from the Biblical Institute was the one word, "Hitherto."* In a sense that verse was like an anthem which sang itself throughout his life, and because he had proved it true he loved its counterpart in the words of the old hymn he so often chose for morning prayers:

> His love in times past forbids me to think
> He'll leave me at last in trouble to sink.

*I Samuel 7, 12.

Already the calendar of another year was filling with activity. December 30 was "my last idle Sunday for some time —and I am glad. I hate them."

★ ★ ★ ★ ★ ★

During the first six months of 1929, Dr. Morgan resumed his independent itinerant work on the West Coast. Then with the summer the Bible Conferences at Cedar Falls, Winona and Northfield brought him back to the East again. The month of September found him in Philadelphia, in Baptist and Methodist churches, and the Tabernacle Presbyterian Church, being without a pastor, extended to him a unanimous invitation, which in due course, he accepted. At the same time he was received into the Presbytery of Philadelphia.

So began Campbell Morgan's only pastorate in the United States, and for the three years of its duration it was a singularly happy one for both pastor and people, though his period of residence in Philadelphia started in a most inauspicious manner.

The Tabernacle Presbyterian Church is architecturally very beautiful, and the manse adjoining it, constructed in the same Gothic stone design, is connected to the church itself by a cloistered walk.

While Dr. Morgan, accompanied by his younger daughter, was holding meetings in Baltimore and Wilmington, Mrs. Morgan and Kathleen were moving into the manse and sleeping there alone, Miss Howell having a room nearby. But undetected leaking gas from the furnace was poisoning the air, and early one morning, Mrs. Morgan woke to the persistent ringing of the door bell, knowing that she was deathly ill and that something was very wrong. Fighting an almost overwhelming drowsiness, she struggled into Kathleen's bedroom only to find her—as she thought—dead. How she managed to get downstairs to the front door where William, the chauffeur, was becoming alarmed at the delay, she never knew. Somehow she managed to unlock it and say: "William, go to Miss Kathleen," before she fell to the floor in a dead faint. The doctor who was summoned said that in a short time the asphyxiating fumes would have been fatal. It never seemed to occur to Mrs. Morgan that she had done anything remarkable. She was thankful for the Providence that had sent help in time, and let it go at that.

The officers of Tabernacle Church had not, for twenty-five years, seen such a congregation as gathered that first Sunday morning. As the crowd streamed out of the building after the service, a member of a Roman Catholic Church nearby who was passing said to someone: "What is the matter here? Has there been a fire?" It was not the kind of fire she meant, but an interest had been kindled that promised well for the future. One of the Trustees, a Professor at the University of Pennsylvania, said to Dr. Morgan in a tone of real appreciation: "You know, you are breaking up a lot of ice around here!" "Yes," replied Dr. Morgan with one of those flashes of wit for which he was famous, "but I am finding the water warm underneath!"

His passion for making the Church sanctuary and its premises as useful and beautiful as possible soon suggested to him changes that needed to be made at 'Tabernacle'. In fact, he had not been pastor for three months when he had launched a scheme of certificates for a loan to liquidate a debt and provide enough to make some necessary renovations. $12,000 was needed, and at one congregational meeting certificates were applied for more than covering this amount. The organ was moved and underwent necessary repairs, this work being made possible by a gift from Mrs. Herbert Halverstadt who, thirty years before, had carried 'Strong's Concordance' up the hill in Northfield on a hot July day and insisted on Dr. Morgan showing her how to use it! She was present in Philadelphia at the time of the dedication of the renovated organ.

During 1930, Dr. Morgan travelled to New York one day each week for a speaking engagement at the John Street M.E. Church, and, in the summer, was approached with an invitation to join the faculty of Gordon College in Boston, continuing from New York there to lecture to the students two days a week. Thus for the third time in his life he was given the opportunity for direct contact with student ministers and missionaries, and with the remembrance of the joy the experience had vouchsafed, both at Cheshunt and in Los Angeles, he accepted it, even though it meant, during the college year, a train journey of 650 miles a week. Undoubtedly the anticipation of seeing all those earnest young faces looking up at him, eager and impressionable and waiting to carry the work and method of teaching in which he believed into the uttermost part of the world, was quite irresistible. It would not be accurate to say that he had not considered his age and health as items which had crossed to the debit side of the ledger. He knew all the arguments on the wisdom of the conservation of physical strength and believed in them thoroughly—for other people. For himself he expressed it thus: "I have never before had to teach or lecture to as keen a crowd of students as I am finding up there (in Boston). I have never done my teaching with a greater sense of freedom. The days are strenuous, but I have got all the arrangements for travel and so on worked out, so as to do it under the most comfortable conditions. How long I shall be able to keep up the pace I don't know, and I am not trying to know. I intend to keep it up as long as I can."

That year his birthday fell on a 'Gordon College' day. "At 9.40," he wrote, "we had quite a celebration, the students presenting me with a desk pen. Then I had a fine time lecturing."

Church meetings at which Dr. Morgan's presence as minister was imperative must now be held on Thursdays and Saturdays. Every day was filled during the College year, and as soon as it ended summer conferences began, and he was off to Iowa, Indiana, Long Island, and North Carolina. In 1931, his four sons filled the Tabernacle pulpit successively while their father was speaking at nine of these conferences.

With less than a week's respite he resumed work at Tabernacle in September, and at Gordon College in October.

All at once the strain began to tell in an occasional attack of amnesia, not lasting for long at a time, but warning of mental fatigue. The doctor told his patient that, if he would avoid a complete breakdown in health, he must face the fact that his physical strength, which considering his physique had been prodigious, had passed its zenith, and that the part of the programme which involved weekly travelling must cease. It was with real regret that the happy relationship with Gordon College, its faculty and students, was terminated in December, 1931.

Meanwhile England was calling for another summer's visit, and as had happened before when it was known that he would go, invitations began coming in almost every mail, including those which said, in one way or another: "Our pulpit is vacant and at your disposal should you desire to settle in England."

To one such cable he replied: "Cannot settle in England this year," and after another glorious summer he returned but this time with a difference. The backward look was, for the first time, stronger than the look ahead.

So many factors had a bearing on this attitude. Not only had Westminster opened her arms to him by arranging a great Bible Conference in July, but had made a happy choice in the other leaders who would share it, for with none did Campbell Morgan feel more closely knit in heart and mind than with Dr. John A. Hutton, Dr. Harris Kirk of Baltimore, Maryland, and Dr. Hubert Simpson, the last now being Westminster's minister. This conference showed by the interest created and the crowds that attended how much they appreciated his return, and in addition it was borne in upon him by the minister himself and by the church officers, that Dr. Simpson's health would not permit him to continue carrying the work alone, but that he would go on if Dr. Morgan would share it with him; suggesting that they preach alternately, and use the week between to rest or accept other engagements as they desired. The organized work of Westminster, though not at such a peak or of such variety as in the days of Mr. Swift's administration, was yet in capable hands. Westminster was admittedly recognized now as a great preaching centre in a world metropolis, and its present need was for a strong, prophetic voice. These were the 1930's. Strange and disquieting voices proclaiming another kind of doctrine were making themselves heard across the Channel in Europe, and on the horizon a small cloud at first ignored was gathering magnitude in ominous proportions. These things had been discussed and considered, and Dr. Morgan was urged to return 'home'.

There were other rather special and intimate experiences of this particular summer that played their part in turning Campbell Morgan's thoughts back to England. If they were but fragile threads of emotional fibres, they formed together a cord which it would take a strong effort to break. There were those with whom he had never failed to renew long friendships and share experiences in previous visits who, it was now evident, were nearing 'the end of the pilgrimage'. Among them was Mr. Samuel Chadwick, of Cliff College, who "looks very frail this year." Others had already 'finished the course'. In Cardiff, Dr. Morgan was requested to unveil a memorial window to the memory of the first boyhood friend he had ever known, Mr. Frank Fifoot. Dr. Morgan was reminded of how, when his sister Lizzie died, his father, realizing his loneliness and need of a friend, had singled out Frank Fifoot, four years his senior. In unveiling the memorial window he said in reminiscence, "From that moment, through the years, we were friends. Although there were stretches of years when we never saw each other, in spirit we were never parted."

Neither Dr. nor Mrs. Morgan ever had any morbid feeling about death, or any other than a Christian attitude about their earthly abiding places. The divine appointing was all that was important to them in determining the locality of their home and their work. A favourite quatrain of Mrs. Morgan's which she expressed a wish at one time to have copied and framed to hang on the walls of their home, was this:

> To me remains nor place nor time,
> My country is in every clime,
> I can be calm and free from care
> On any shore, since God is there.

Even so, when afternoon shadows fall across the pathway, and the day is drawing to a close, it is natural to look with some nostalgic longing to the place we call 'home'. If in God's goodness He should see fit to bring their wandering footsteps back to the dear England they had always thought of as their real earthly home, they would be content.

Letters of affection and appreciation are always among the threads of the cord that draws one back. There was that of the wife of a University professor pleading for the young life of England so greatly in need of "such teaching as you are giving," and another from two little sisters saying that "although we are only schoolgirls we have understood and learned a lot from every one of your services. Our beliefs have been thoroughly strengthened and increased. . . . We have hesitated to write, but feel, perhaps, you would like to know how some young people love and appreciate you."

In the last analysis it is the heart rather than the head which exerts the greatest influence. Westminster had always held his peculiar love and devotion, and this summer its old building had seen the wedding of Kathleen to Donald Shute, the son of two of the most loyal of the old-time members of Westminster, and close family friends. The eldest son, too, in those later years, had united with the Episcopal Church, and returning to England, had taken up residency as a curate in London. As the *Olympic* steamed out of Southampton harbour, Kathleen and Don were waving good-bye, and only Ruth accompanied her parents back to the United States.

Upon his return, Dr. Morgan talked over all these things and many more with his friends, the officers of the Tabernacle Church. They were full of sympathy and understanding, and expressed these along with their own personal desire that he continue to remain in Philadelphia. Meanwhile they had become acquainted with the four sons of their pastor, and when it became evident that Dr. Morgan felt that he now wanted to return to his homeland, a call was immediately extended to Dr. Howard Morgan, the youngest of the four, to succeed his father at the Tabernacle Church.

On Dr. Morgan's last Sunday Howard was present 'to help with the services'. What Dr. Morgan said to his congregation at that time regarding his son's coming to carry on his work among them, has already been told. During the past seventeen years, until this present hour, that pastorate has continued and has been blessed.

The year drawing to its close saw Dr. and Mrs. Morgan and their youngest daughter on board the *Britannic* homeward bound. How many more diaries would there be? What momentous events would they predict and chronicle? What would be the outcome of the 'gathering storm'? If these questions came to Campbell Morgan's mind there is no record of them. 'Hitherto' was enough, and in 'the promises' there was rest.

CHAPTER IX

1933-1945: 69 to 81 years

THE SECOND WESTMINSTER MINISTRY—RETIREMENT
—THE END OF THE PILGRIMAGE

CAMPBELL MORGAN'S second Westminster ministry began and ended in association with others with an interval of four years in which he served alone. Unfortunately Dr. Simpson's health did not improve to any marked degree. After a year of their working together he was forced to retire, but it was sincerely hoped that after a period of rest and treatment the association might be resumed. The Church, therefore, requested Dr. Morgan to assume responsibility for the two Sunday services and the Bible School for 1934. At the close of the year this arrangement was extended into 1935 and then, when it was learned that Dr. Simpson would not be able to return to Westminster, the church asked Dr. Morgan to accept the pastorate officially for the second time.

Most ministers would agree that it is unwise to return to a church one has served before, especially after a long period of time, and when the first ministry has been phenomenally notable as was the case in Dr. Morgan's relationship with Westminster. Not only has a large percentage of the membership been added during the intervening years, and a new generation arisen who 'knew not Joseph', but those left who were active in the past are inclined to lament 'the good old days', and bog down in disillusionment because 'times have changed'. Whereas it was at the invitation of the majority that Campbell Morgan returned, there was a minority group who felt it to be an unwise step. In his inaugural address, Dr. Morgan, with no intolerance or bitterness towards this minority, said: "I want the whole church as now assembled to realize that I am conscious that this minority was as sincere as was the majority, and equally honest. Moreover, that minority had not only the right to have, but also to express its opinion. I am prepared quite frankly to say that if I had been voting as a member I should probably have voted with that minority. Looking at this matter from a purely worldly standard of wisdom I do not know that there is anything more strange or unwise than to ask a man who appears to be in failing health, at 72 years of age, to take oversight of a great centre like this. . . . With regard to that minority, then, I definitely say to them, that, respecting their opinion and their right of expression, the time has now come when they fall into line, and as one body we go forward; or if that is impossible, that they send in their resignation—but I think there are going to be no resignations."

It takes a double portion of wisdom, ingenuity and understanding to gather together living threads of differing texture and quality and unify them into the pattern of sure and successful progress. That Campbell Morgan possessed all this is indicated by the years which followed—bright, constructive years in which the buildings took on new cleanliness and beauty; enriching years of filling the spiritual storehouse; years when the approaching storm drew Christian people around a prophetic leader who could see beyond the clouds; dark years when the world rocked beneath their feet and nothing but the abiding things remained.

There are no means of evaluating the contribution Campbell Morgan brought to London at the close of his life. He did not come back expecting to repeat the programme he had mapped out for himself and the church three decades ago. None was better aware than himself that the physical virility of those years was gone, and that what was left of strength was diminishing. Yet the conviction that there was still work to be done in the place he had never ceased to love and cherish, and that it was the divine Will that he return to do it, was as sure and uncompromising as it had been in 1904. Just before leaving America, in December, 1932, Dr. Morgan wrote to his friend, Dr. McInnis of Los Angeles:

"I have been growingly driven to the conviction during the past few years that my work in the States is really done. My last two visits to England have shown me that what I am now able to do is needed there; and more, that the doors of opportunity for it are wider open than I have ever known them. When the crisis came I found I had no alternative. I dare not refuse the call that came—a combination of calls from Westminster and the country at large."

Those vitally concerned for the welfare of Westminster saw any fears they may have had dispelled, as it became evident that Dr. Morgan had lost none of his skill, his personal magnetism, or his uncanny ability to draw all classes and conditions of people around him and weld them into a united fellowship. Within a month of his return he was writing to his sons in America:

"The start of my work in this country, is full of encouragement. . . . The Friday Night (Bible School) is outstanding. To see two thousand keen, eager people with hundreds among them young is a sight to gladden the heart."

The call from 'the country at large' to which he had referred acceded to a more limited itinerant work between Sundays, but with all the joy of reunion, not only with individual friends but with whole towns and cities who turned out, with mayor and council in some instances, to greet him. There were times when he forgot how many birthdays had gone; certainly he wasted no time speculating upon those which remained; yet he was reminded, sometimes harshly, that the former pace could not be continued. "My programme is a strenuous one," he wrote, "but I am getting through. My meetings in Swansea and Northampton have been wonderful. After Tunbridge Wells I was bowled over and had to cancel Bridgewater. . . . You know how I hate doing this but I could not help it. Fortunately P.C. was able to go down to Bridgewater and he had a wonderful time. A letter from the minister was most enthusiastic. I was in the Potteries last week, and in spite of bitter wintry weather we had great crowds and splendid times."

"I am still running like Charlie's Aunt and I think sometimes fooling as much," he wrote exuberantly, in April, 1933. "I am glad to say that I am keeping fairly well, though I do feel that I shall have to slow up a bit in the future." Thus in his seventieth year, when many in the ministry and out of it are enjoying retirement and leisure, it is characteristic of this man, who had already done enough in his working years to have kept three men active and busy, that he was thinking of the 'slowing up' process as something which must be faced 'in the future'.

He writes of "an amusing little incident" which happened at Bristol. "I was leaving the hall," he says, "when a man I did not know—I think he was a minister—gripped my hand terrifically and said: 'How do you do it? What do you eat and drink?' To which I replied laughingly, 'Very little'. Again shaking my hand and turning on his heel he said, 'That accounts for it! Good-bye!'"

It was at the close of this first year of his return to England that Dr. Morgan gave a sitting to one of London's leading artists in the world of photography, Mr. Howard Coster. Because this likeness is considered to be outstanding by all who knew Dr. Morgan at this time, it is used as the frontispiece of this book.

Campbell Morgan was among those rare individuals who derive great enjoyment from being photographed, dating back, perhaps, to the days of his friendship with the Welfords and the famous 'pose . . . in holiday attire', which Mrs. Welford so graphically describes. In the years between he had been the subject of many studio portraits, good, bad, and indifferent, and the number of amateur cameras that at one time or another clicked before him will never be known. He also sat for artists and sculptors of note, so that he could rightly be called an expert 'sitter', and possessed very definite views on the ways in which he liked and disliked to be reproduced. He referred once in a letter to "that trick of the photographer's to tell you to look away from the camera; but as a rule I have ignored it, and even though he turned my head away I have turned my eyes to look into the camera itself. I like photos that represent the person as looking at you."

But an expert recognizes another expert, and Mr. Coster in prevailing upon Dr. Morgan to 'look away from the camera', produced a profile picture which is a superb example of how light and shade and dimension may be combined to reveal personality.

On a cold, wintry day in December, shortly after his seventieth birthday, Dr. Morgan went to the studio. Indicating a low, deep chair, Mr. Coster asked him to be seated while he prepared his equipment. The visitor, still feeling the cold, raw, outside chill, sank just as he was without removing his overcoat into the comfort of the chair, relaxing in the warmth and quietness of the room. He put one elbow on the chair's arm, and in a way that was all his own rested his chin on his hand, one finger pointed along his cheek. What he did not know as he sat there was that Mr. Coster had prepared that special chair and background for his coming, and had a camera placed so as to get the picture without his being conscious of it. When the 'profile' and other proofs appeared, the 'reclining photo', as it came to be called, drew forth many differences of opinion in the clan. No one was surprised to get a new photo of 'Dad', for this happened with a degree of regularity, but no previous photo had ever been the cause of more varied comment. Dr. Morgan himself jumped into the controversy, enjoying it enough to add his share of fuel to the flames.

"Opinions differ," he wrote to his son, Frank. "Kath dislikes it . . . and declines to have it in her home. Ruth loves it. Personally I don't care for it. . . . If I saw that picture of another man I should think it was a very excellent and suggestive one, but of a man whose work was done, and who has the ability just to take it quietly. . . . I said this to Jack, and, O, my dear sir! you should see the eloquent and forceful homily I have received in reply!"

But he had not said it quite so mildly to Jack. The expres-

THE RECLINING PHOTO

Photo: Howard Coster

Reproduced by permission of The Ministry of Information.

sion in his letter which provoked the storm of protest was that "it is the picture of an old man with his work done, waiting for the Reaper!"

"You misunderstood me a little," he wrote to Jack later. "I did not mean that *I* felt like an old man with his work done. Indeed, it is because I do *not* feel like that that I do not care for this picture which to me seems to suggest that attitude. Perhaps, however, your interpretation is right . . . because your suggested title for it . . . really does reveal the condition of my mind." And there it remained. You love it very much, or you do not like it at all. But if you love it, it is because you agree with Jack in his title for it: 'Peace . . . not as the world giveth'.

★ ★ ★ ★ ★ ★

Since the 'Renovation Scheme,' in 1904, nothing save running repairs to the church fabric had been maintained. An initial action taken at the start of Campbell Morgan's second ministry was an echo—but a most substantial echo— of the first. In the summer of 1933 a 'Restoration Fund' of seven thousand, five hundred pounds was launched for the complete cleaning, redecorating and repairing of the church and school buildings inside and out, including the tower which had become unsafe, refurnishing of the buildings, and a thorough cleaning and restoration of the organ. It was pointed out at this time that the organ in Westminster Chapel was one of the finest in the country, having been built in the 1880's by Father Willis himself. The title implied a patriarchal dignity of fine workmanship, being conferred upon only two master-builders, Father Smith, in the seventeenth century, and Father Willis in the nineteenth.

People marvelled at Dr. Morgan's ability to initiate and achieve large financial schemes, saying that his success in this realm was almost magical. It was rather due to the fact that he always kept his appeals on the high level of Christian obligation and privilege. Then, too, if he believed in a cause he believed in it for himself as well as for others. It is safe to say that he never made a financial appeal of this nature without setting the example of starting it off with his own always generous, and always anonymous contribution.

On the first Sunday in December, 1934, he preached on the theme of giving, and invited the congregation to augment the sum already in hand by making him a birthday gift of one thousand pounds, so that the major part of the work of restoration might be commenced. The response was immediate and enthusiastic. In the week before his birthday the next Sunday the "Birthday Fund" exceeded twelve hundred pounds.

Work began with the new year and the church reopened for worship on the first Sunday in March. "You will see a change when you look at Westminster," Dr. Morgan wrote to his son, Frank, who was coming to England that summer. "The cleaning of the outside walls and repainting have worked wonders. I always thought Westminster was built of red brick. It is not. It is the old London hard yellow brick with certain red brick facings, and it looks an entirely new thing. They wrought well seventy years ago, for the architect tells me they have not discovered a single brick deteriorated, whereas a good deal of the stonework, sills, etc., have. I like the inside, too. It is done in two colours of grey, and we have an entirely new system of lighting."

It was inevitable that with the coming of summer, Campbell Morgan's thoughts should turn towards Mundesley and the Bible Conference. A visit there confirmed his determination to re-establish the Conference and a tent was procured. For the two following summers—1934 and 1935—'Mundesley' again became a reality. They were not the halcyon days of the years that were past. Like Indian summer the Conference was short-lived; like Indian summer too, they were days of richness and beauty. But the leader knew that his own unconquerable spirit was reaching out beyond the limits of his physical strength. "The tent was crowded," he said of that first summer. "The missionary hour . . . a splendid time. . . . Dr. Kirk preached a great sermon. . . . P.C. gave us a splendid sermon. . . . A characteristic sermon from Hutton. . . . A wonderful address from Mildred Cable." But of himself he wrote: "I had a free time but exhausting." . . . "I felt very tired but was helped through" . . . and on the last day. "For the first time I personally had complete liberty."

The teacher knows his limitations when the students are unconscious of them. To others, Dr. Morgan's lectures showed no lessening of ability or force; he seemed rather to bring forth new treasures from his store of wisdom and experience. The group that met at the close was enthusiastically in favour of continuing. "It seems to me that we must arrange for another conference in 1935," he wrote in his diary, and plans were laid accordingly. But in the months between the 'tired feeling', which was more mental fatigue than physical weariness, resulted in slight attacks of vertigo and occasional, though short, spells of amnesia. It was the red flag of danger, but Dr. Morgan refused to become alarmed by it until he began to experience something new and altogether foreign to him—a dread of the pulpit which began in the autumn of 1934. Once he began to preach this phantom of fear was banished and he seemed to become filled with power, appearing to his congregation just as vital and vigorous as ever, but with the approach of the next service it returned. He fought against it with every weapon of determination, but it took toll of his strength and left him utterly exhausted. The doctor ordered a drastic cutting down of pulpit work and a cancelling of outside engagements, but he had an obdurate and strong-willed patient who would only obey under pressure, and when his own bodily weakness underlined and enforced the doctor's instructions.

In answer to a cable from Frank he wrote: "Yes—I do remember that four of you are carrying on. That I never forget, and I thank God upon every remembrance of each one of you. I do not know how long *I* shall carry on. That is not said morbidly but quite cheerfully. I am absolutely careless about it. Whenever the end comes, when I think of you four and these two girls I feel I shall go saying:

> Now Thou art setting free, liberating
> Thy bond-slave, O Despot,
> According to Thy saying, in peace.

Moreover, it has been a gracious Despotism!"

He leaned heavily on this third son in that final Mundesley Conference of 1935. The effort of preparation and execution proved too much for his strength and he had to pull out in the middle of the week to return home. But Frank was there to step into the gap, and the Conference continued, a worthy finish to a long and fruitful branch of Campbell Morgan's service to Westminster and to England.

★ ★ ★ ★ ★ ★

1936 was, in a sense, the climactic year of the second Westminster ministry. Exactly sixty years before, in August, 1876, a lad of thirteen had stood up to preach his first sermon in the schoolroom of the Wesleyan Chapel, in Monmouth. Plans for the Jubilee year included a return to the same little schoolroom during August, and that notable occasion has already been recorded. The desk which was used sixty years before was then given to Westminster to become a part of the Diamond Jubilee Celebration, and on the Sunday preceding Dr. Morgan's birthday it took the place of honour on the rostrum. If the writer of Ecclesiastes had allowed 'a time for pure sentiment', surely it would be now, as early comers, knowing the peculiar significance of this occasion, are thinking of a slim, childish figure behind that desk, barely tall enough to read the notes he has so painstakingly prepared for the country folk of a generation ago. But in the twinkling of an eye that dream is gone, and they are back in 1936 in beautiful Westminster, freshly furnished and painted under the new lights. Only the old desk reminds them of the past for the one standing behind it with the light shining on his silver hair and the scarlet hood of his black pulpit gown bears no resemblance to the child. Nothing but the desk is the same except the Book, and the message, and the child-like spirit of the man. But these are all that really matter; these are the eternal verities.

"It is sixty years since I stood at this very desk. . . . The Methodist Church in Monmouth has been kind enough to send it to me. It will find its place in our Institute Hall. For this day it is here, taking the place of the ordinary desk.

"The sermon of sixty years ago was a boy's sermon . . . delivered to between fifty and a hundred people. . . . I recognize that I took a big subject, indeed, so big that I have never been able to exhaust it.

"The years have passed, and I stand here to-night in the building dearer to me than any other on earth, and my mind goes back to that earliest occasion. I have been careful in announcing my theme ('Salvation') not to say that I am going to preach the same sermon I preached sixty years ago. That would, of course, be impossible, but the theme is the same, and the scheme and outline are the same. . . ."

A major goal of the Jubilee year was to complete the second part of the Restoration Fund amounting to £3,000, for the redecorating and refurnishing of the schools and halls. The amount actually received on December 9 was £3,301 6s., making the total amount raised for the whole of the restoration £10,800 as compared with the £12,000 in 1905. The Renovation Fund began with a gift of twelve penny stamps from a charwoman, and thereafter represented all classes of other consecrated givers. The Restoration Fund was made possible in like manner. Mrs. Andrew Carnegie referred simply to a 'thank-offering' in a letter of congratulation and appreciation to Dr. Morgan for 'happy memories of the past'. Another letter written in the most beautiful copperplate handwriting, said: "I enclose a donation of ten shillings in memory of happy Friday nights . . . about thirty years ago . . . I am a Methodist Church caretaker." A retired missionary to China sent five pounds—"A small contribution as a token of loving gratitude and appreciation of your work. I have followed your method and found much delight in committing to faithful men and women 'the things I heard', and learned, that they may 'teach others also'. Your books have been of immense service to me and to many Chinese." Another letter says: "I have decided to contribute two shillings and sixpence per week out of my Old Age Pension, from 1st June to end of December, 1936, by which time sincerely hope that the required amount will be in hand."

Campbell Morgan had never been one to court adulation, yet no man could be unmoved by such tributes as came at the close of that Jubilee year, especially from those associated with him in the work and service of the ministry. At the great Diamond Jubilee Meeting, held in Westminster, on December 9, Lord Craigmyle took the chair, and addressing the large assembly acknowledged his thanksgiving to God that in his long lifetime of eighty-four years he had been given some of the world's greatest divines to be his dearest friends, "and in these latest happy times yet another in the person of Dr. Campbell Morgan." Dr. John A. Hutton, Dr. Sidney Berry, Rev. C. E. Walters, and Dr. Charles Brown, representing the four great denominations of Protestantism, paid their tributes of love, admiration, and gratitude to the one they delighted to honour.

Dr. Morgan was almost overwhelmed by the number of messages which came to him from all parts of the world. Some were printed in *The Westminster Record*, including those of Miss Jane Stoddart, Assistant Secretary of *The British Weekly*, Dr. T. Ferrier Hulme, ex-President of the Methodist Conference; and Dr. T. Wilkinson Riddle, F.R.S.L., of the Baptist Church in Plymouth. Scanning these for the mountain peaks it is noticed that Miss Stoddart praises his voice—and small wonder! "There have been preachers and politicians whose voice in middle age became so hoarse, raucous and overstrained that audiences ceased to bear with them. Others like Gipsy Smith and Dr. Morgan keep the silver trumpets blowing sweetly as the day declines."

Dr. Hulme called his friend "'the bond-servant of Jesus Christ'—surely the preacher's distinguished service medal of which Paul coveted no greater distinction." He made reference to the founder of his denomination, John Wesley, as being aware of "the distinct advantages of itineration. His preachers became the shooting stars of the ecclesiastical firmament, and others the fixed stars. . . . Campbell Morgan in his ministerial life has proved that there is a happy medium. Whilst always giving precedence to concentration he has still found time for a sane and instructive itinerating evangelism. He appears to believe that the reward of service is more service."

Dr. Riddle spoke of three great qualities that endeared Dr. Morgan to him—his friendship—"once he takes you to his heart you are grappled to him with hoops of steel. Through fair weather and foul you may rely on him"; his amazing charity—"He is swift to praise and slow to blame"; and his generosity—"I have never known a man less conceited. I have proved him to be not only a great encourager but one who lavished extravagant praise upon another's efforts."

A poem by Miss Ivy Marks has this exquisite tribute in one of its verses:

> You lit the lamp which led my youthful feet
> Upward to God, o'er pathways dark and dim,
> You put me right where I had gone astray,
> Through you I gave my heart's young love to Him.

There was ample testimony to the quality of Campbell Morgan's preaching as he passed the three score and ten years. His sermons were brief now, rarely exceeding half an hour, but with an economy of words, they were the cream of a lifetime of devoted study. A reporter for *The Christian World*, of August, 1937, says:

"Dr. Campbell Morgan's doctors say he is a tired man; the strain of fifty years' preaching is beginning to tell. No one would think it to see him in the pulpit at Westminster Chapel. His sermons are the quintessence of virility. Tall and upright in his black and scarlet robes and with his snow-white hair and forceful diction, Dr. Morgan is an arresting figure. For thirteen years before the war and since 1932 he has preached here. And still he fills the church.

" . . . The earnestness of his message and the intensity of his manner communicate themselves to the congregation. From his circular rostrum he dominates his audience. One can 'hear a pin drop' during the service. Dr. Morgan reads the Parable of the Prodigal Son. How he reads it! With such feeling, such understanding! It lives . . . 'for this my son was dead and is alive again; he was lost, and is found.'

"The parable is the theme of the sermon also. Christ received sinners and ate with them. Here was a complete revelation of the function of the Christian Church, a crystallization of the essence of the Gospel. As He received sinners so must the Church, though it cost her suffering and tribulation. But receiving is not enough. We must eat with them. Eating is the sacramental symbol of fellowship. Are we prepared to go to that length? Or are we conscious, deep down in our hearts, of a resentment and anger like that of the elder brother? Dr. Morgan is still doing what he has done for fifty years—bringing people face to face not with new theories, but with the very words and spirit and challenge of Jesus Christ."

★   ★   ★   ★   ★   ★

As the weeks lengthened into months the signs of the approaching catastrophe which was so soon to engulf the world were becoming more and more apparent in Europe. In the last analysis the concern of those who watch and wait is not so much for the fate of nations as for those individuals around whom centre personal affections. To the sons in America the storm clouds were gathering ever nearer those they loved—Dad, Mother, and the girls. Looking back upon those disturbing and ominous years before their consummation in 1939, the picture shows the increasing darkness serving only to high-light the lovely, compensating events and experiences in the lives of their parents which occurred during those years. These are some of the things which are cherished with thankfulness and remembered with joy.

England had never been more beautiful than in those summers of the middle 1930's. Sunshine and showers mingled their warmth and refreshing to draw from the earth its most enchanting delights, as if nature itself was aware that some of the glory was soon to pass for ever, and gave itself generously in benediction. Longer periods of leisure for Dr. and Mrs. Morgan gave their friends the opportunity of entertaining them—and what wonderful friends they had! There were invitations to country houses, a yacht off the Isle of Wight, an old castle in Scotland. Others placed cars at their disposal, asking them only to choose the road and the companions. They 'trundled' about through Devon and Cornwall—Kingsley's and Billy Bray's country, reminiscent of Dr. Morgan's popular lectures; they went to see Tetbury, his birthplace; Staunton, "where Nancie's people came from"; Cardiff, the home of Frank Fifoot, his first friend; Monmouth where he had preached his first sermon; the Wye Valley and Welsh Borderland—scenes of the early adventures of a 'wandering evangelist'; Market Drayton, where a certain wedding had taken place nearly fifty years ago; Stone—"Brown, the butcher's boy," and tea with the Babbs; Rugeley and Birmingham—"What great times we had here!" How they relived the old days with all their joys and sorrows, dipping into the exhaustless treasure chest of memory. Sometimes it was enough to lie back in a long chair and enjoy the garden at Yew Tree, listening to the lazy hum of bees among the sweet william and the clink of spoons against china as tea was being prepared in the house. Everywhere there were familiar faces—in hamlets and cities, Scottish glens and Welsh hills, for these two had the collector's instinct for acquiring friends, Dr. Morgan just by preaching to people, Mrs. Morgan by remembering faces, making mental notes of birthdays, anticipating needs and desires of which no one else was aware.

In this way passed many resting days, enjoyed to the full because of the knowledge that strength was being stored up for more work days ahead, for leisure was to Campbell Morgan, even in these latter years, a means to an end. It was a different joy to be back in the old pulpit again. Two services on Sunday and one on Friday were all the doctor permitted, but it was enough. The dread before preaching gradually grew less. There was more time now for study and reading. As a reward for the painstaking toil of the years the Bible opened up to its student richer and deeper truths for his pulpit and pen. Series which were made and given at this time and eventually appeared in book form are the cream of this patient and diligent study:—*The Answers of Jesus to Job*, *Paul's Corinthian Letters*, and *Notes on the Psalms*. What a word is compensation! It means something so satisfying, or so full of bitterness and remorse, according to how one has merited it. A verse of Scripture which Campbell Morgan had known always began now to be a part of his personal experience. He referred to it publicly and thought upon it, too, for he sometimes jotted down the reference at the head of a letter he wanted to keep—Ecclesiastes 11. 1.

For him the 'bread upon the waters' was sweet 'after many days'. He was seeing himself renewed again in his sons, as each in his own field was carrying on with the teaching and preaching of the Word. Children were growing up in America whose activities gave endless pleasure to the grandparents in England. Their sayings and doings, though normal and sometimes rather boring to others, were always brilliant and wonderful to Grandma and Grandpa. In each experience they saw themselves again as young parents, and were sure that little 'Tats', or David or Dick were just like their daddies when they were young! In 1931, Dr. Morgan had dedicated his book *The Bible and the Child* to

EIGHT GRANDCHILDREN
Don, Bill, Len, David, Nancy, Tats, Patsy,
Dick, and those to follow!

It was well that he was far-sighted enough to add 'those to

follow', for there were still to come Mary, Crossley, Michael, Howdy, and Johnnie in America, and Pam, Barbara and Mary in England. Kathleen's little girls filled a special need in the lives of their grandparents in those days before 1939, for they lived near enough to run in and out, bringing in the sunshine whatever the outside weather might be. In 1938 the first great-grandchild was born—another boy to carry on the name.

In the summer of 1937 Dr. and Mrs. Morgan came to the United States for the last time. It was a visit of three weeks, spent in Philadelphia, and although Dr. Morgan preached and lectured in the Tabernacle Church, the visit was really made for the purpose of seeing the sons and their families. It was a happy reunion as members of the clan gathered round the parents once more, anxious to see them again, and for them to see the new grandchildren. In all these things Dr. and Mrs. Morgan were happy and blest, secure in the affection of their children and their children's children.

In the Tabernacle Church Dr. Morgan lectured on his reminiscences of sixty years of preaching. and at the close he made reference to the word from Ecclesiastes. "I am conscious," he said, "that the sun is westering, the shadows are lengthening, but now I understand as never before the words, 'Cast thy bread upon the waters; for thou shalt find it after many days.' I am constantly receiving messages that tell me of results from my work in years long ago."

Especially gratifying were the letters from missionaries at home and abroad, telling of how much his sermons and his leadership in the study of the Bible had meant to them in their work, and of how Bible Schools 'in the Morgan method' had been established in other lands. Dr. Morgan's interest in missionary work increased with the years, if that were possible, and when he was able to go to only a few gatherings as a speaker, it was often to the missionary meetings, chiefly the three committees or boards in which he was particularly interested—the E.U.S.A. (Evangelical Union of South America), the Ludhiana Mission (for the women of India), and the C.I.M. (China Inland Mission).

Letters from Canada recalled long and happy journeys across the Dominion. In reply he wrote his friend and fellow-traveller, Dr. F. A. Robinson, in September, 1937: "Among the happiest privileges of my life was that of my association with you in the service of the King. . . . I have always said, and with perfect honesty, that among all those who have arranged meetings for me, I never had the thing done as perfectly as in Canada. I feel that my wanderings are over, and the possibility of seeing Canada again does not exist. I am thankful to be able to do what I am, and am going quietly on for this year, all being well."

Out of that large armada of 'ships that pass in the night', one voyager wrote such an understanding and beautiful letter that Dr. Morgan, in sending it to Mrs. Morgan to read, wrote in red ink upon it: "I think you will be interested in this. Read Ecclesiastes 11. 1. I am getting a lot of bread back these days." The writer said:

"Yesterday I opened *The Christian World* and read that you were feeling the strain of fifty years' labours in the Master's service. . . . To myself I said, I must write to Westminster Chapel; surely a letter will find him there.

"A young girl of 16 years, training as a pupil teacher between the years 1894 to 1898 in ——, had occasion to be passing the Congregational Church . . . and popped in to hear a lecture on 'Music'. . . . The lecturer was yourself, and I the unknown girl in the congregation. . . . That evening's ministry coloured my whole life.

"Therefore, whilst feeling the strain of the years, will you not think of many another person similarly blest, and totally unknown to you whom God has richly helped through your labours and messages.

" . . . There was an illustration of a rose upon a mountain in your lecture forty odd years ago. May God grant me the privilege of being that 'rose' to you to-day."

The letter-writer was referring to Dr. Morgan's lecture entitled, *'The Music of Life.' In the early days 'popular

*Published F. H. Revell, 1946

lectures' were often made and given for the purpose of raising money for one cause or another; then in the busy days of conference work they were discontinued. Upon the insistence of one of Dr. Morgan's sons, this lecture was revised in 1944 and printed in booklet form, though Dr. Morgan felt that it did not have enough value to warrant publication. However, many people have received pleasure and inspiration from this simple development of a simple theme which uses the language of music to interpret the span of life in all its major and minor keys, and its various moods and expressions. "When things get a bit thick," writes a friend on her 1949 Christmas card, "I love to read at least a chapter and hear a true chord struck with such a wonderful insight into the needs of human nature."

On August 20th, 1938, Dr. and Mrs. Morgan celebrated fifty years of marriage. For many weeks, plans had been made and carried out to make it a memorable occasion. Mr. Marsh had contacted friends all over the world, obtaining more than a thousand signatures which were placed together in a big blue, leather-bound album and presented as an expression of love and congratulation. In addition there were many personal greetings, some engraved and hand-painted with loving care. A banquet was given for the honourees in the dining room at St. Ermins, the apartment hotel home of Dr. and Mrs. Morgan, for the family and close friends, including Mrs. Donald Newbegin, a witness to the simple ceremony in the church at Market Drayton in 1888. "It was a happy time," Dr. Morgan wrote in his diary, as though the golden moments of its passing were too full of memory for further expression. In revising *The Music of Life* he said of their marriage: " . . . for over half a century we have travelled together over mountains and through valleys sharing our experiences, and there has been music all the way."

As the daily record of activities became shorter that of visitors to St. Ermins became longer. Sometimes it told of friends from America, perhaps Professor and Mrs. Charles R. Erdman from Princeton, Mrs. Will Moody, Mr. and Mrs.

Halverstadt or Dr. F. A. Robinson from Canada. There would be news to exchange and reminiscences to share. Added to the compensations of friendship was deep thankfulness for the measure of strength which remained. Health and the conservation of it was becoming increasingly important now, for it was the arbitrary dictator which decided how much work might be accomplished. At 74 years of age walking was more difficult, and it became an exertion to climb the stairs to the rostrum, but Campbell Morgan's powers in the pulpit were unimpaired as far as his hearers were concerned. Through the kindness of a friend a new set of stairs of much more gradual and easy ascent were constructed to bridge the passage from the floor of the church to the rostrum.

He was glad to be told in a letter that his sermons were reading as well as ever. To this observation he replied: "I am glad you do not find any sense of weariness or weakness in what you read in the *Record*. It is an interesting thing that in my work, both of preparation and delivery, I lose all sense of weariness. I do not know that I have ever enjoyed preaching more than I am doing now. When things are over I am liable to flop, but, of course, that is to be expected!"

He was still drawing the crowds and filling the church, especially on Friday nights, though the blackboard was no longer used in the lectures. It was only two services a week now that he was permitted, making it necessary for a guest-preacher to take the second service on Sundays. In the summer of 1938 it was announced that Dr. Martyn Lloyd-Jones would conduct this second service (sometimes in the morning and sometimes in the evening), for a period of some months.

Dr. Lloyd-Jones had been an eminent Harley Street physician until he left the medical profession for the ministry. Dr. Morgan had first heard and met him in the United States and was impressed by his method and ability. In his whole approach to the Scriptures in study and interpretation, Dr. Lloyd-Jones was a man after his own heart. His coming to

Westminster at the very hour that he did, the dark breathless hour before the war was, above all the compensations, the cause for humble thanksgiving to those who saw in it the directing finger of an Almighty Hand.

★   ★   ★   ★   ★   ★

Those of us whose homes were far away from the lands torn by the rough talons of war can never know what it meant to live beneath shrieking shells and dread the coming of the full moon. The millions of words describing the tragedy almost as it took place were hard to comprehend as we looked out upon a peaceful landscape where children played and windows drew no blackout curtains. As young men donned unaccustomed uniforms and left for unknown destinations our hearts went with them, but there was a point beyond which our minds could not penetrate.

It would be less possible to follow Dr. Morgan into the shadow of war had he not written so much of his impressions of it. He had practised the art of letter-writing all his life, and at its close left a series of pictures of those stormy years, that by their very brevity and simplicity are more moving than eloquence.

During the itinerant years he had sometimes contemplated a return to England, to 'a comparatively quiet place' in which to spend 'the last stretch of the pilgrimage'. He had talked in his letters of 'a little home in the country, perhaps twenty or thirty miles from London,' and of 'doing a quieter sort of work.' But it was not to be. Westminster's call could not be denied, and that acceptance meant living nearby, and an eventual settlement in St. Ermins about two blocks from the church, so that it was here in the city of Westminster itself, close to the Abbey, Buckingham Palace and the Parliament buildings, coveted targets for enemy aircraft, that those last years were to be spent. There was to be no 'quietness' for him except in the inner world of the spirit —and there indeed he and his dear ones found their ataraxia.

Of the Munich crisis in November, 1938, he wrote: ". . . I believe that there are occasions when God orders wars. That is, He compels men to work out their own philosophies when they inevitably issue in war. Nevertheless, I feel that everything ought to be done to avoid it, and I have no sympathy with the view that the action at Munich was a mistake. Personally, I believe very strongly that in this case it was God who averted the catastrophe for us. . . . I confess that I have no confidence in statesmen except as, often in spite of themselves, they are in the grip of God. . . . There are problems ahead, but at any rate we have breathing space. If it should be true as some people say that war is only postponed, I shall still believe that God will overrule. Without any hesitation I say with the Psalmist, 'Though war should rise against me, even then will I be confident.'"

In spite of the averted catastrophe grim preparations were being impelled forward by a government made alert for trouble. "We all went and were measured for gas-masks," says the letter of November, 1938. "Personally, I was disinclined to do so, but felt it right to fall in with Government requirements." In May of 1939, he wrote: "We are living in strange times. From all I can gather we are much quieter and calmer than America seems to be about us. There is a very strong and united feeling that it is necessary to be ready for any eventuality."

As Dr. Morgan was conducting the service on Sunday morning, September 3rd, 1939, a piece of paper was handed to him bearing the news which everyone was expecting and dreading. For the second time it fell to his lot to announce from that pulpit his country's declaration of war. Hardly had he finished speaking than the sirens wailed their warning of enemy aircraft. The congregation was asked to go quietly to the basement of the church. Ruth tells how her mother rose, and turning to the friends in the pew in front of her, inquired after the health of an absent member as though nothing untoward were taking place. It was her overture to the war against 'evil things'. Her smile, her poise, and her utter lack of excitement or panic proclaimed her undaunted conviction: 'The Lord is on my side; I will not fear; what can man do unto me?'

"With regard to ourselves," Dr. Morgan wrote in October, "Mother, Ruth and I are still here (in London) and shall remain. I may say that they have excellent air-raid shelters in the cellars of this building (St. Ermins). We have been down there twice when air raid warnings have been given ... in neither was the alarm fulfilled. Kath and her three girls are at Stebbing with Ted and Edith...*"

Dr. Morgan's daughters have supplemented the record of the war years. It is of interest to note from his own letters and from Ruth that he never lost his independent spirit. He was a nonconformist to the last!

"When the air-raids first started Dad said he would never go down at all to any shelter. However, Mr. L——, the Manager, and Head Warden of our district, told him that, though he couldn't make him go down, it would make his work very much easier if he would go. Dad then consented to go down into the lounge where we used to take up residence for the night. Dad and Mother had a small couch each, and Winnie and I had armchairs. We did this for weeks until the London Transport Building was hit, and we were nearly blown out of the lounge! After this we did go right down to the shelters. Blackie† got two cots for Dad and Mother and I had a 'Lilo' mattress and we were in a small room with two old ladies. I think Winnie must have gone home to sleep about this time, because I cannot remember her in the shelter."

Writing again of conditions in the early part of the war, Dr. Morgan stated: "The thing has played havoc with us at Westminster. It is difficult to account for it, but the difference between this outbreak of war and that of 1914 is very marked. Then people crowded into the churches. Now our congregations are depleted, at least cut in half. ... I suppose the

---

*N.B.—Yew Tree Farm is near Stebbing in Essex.
† Dr. M. G. Blackie.

explanation is that at the beginning of 1914 there was no particular fear of air raids. Now there is that fear. That fear, moreover, has caused the evacuation of children and their teachers, and that has its effect. Because of necessary and proper lighting restrictions we cannot hold evening meetings. Our second Sunday service, therefore, is held at three o'clock. The Friday nights could not be held, but we have transferred the Bible School to Saturday, at 2.30, and all things considered, we are having good companies, that is to say, between six and seven hundred. So we are going on as well as we can."

"Things are exceedingly trying here. The whole situation from the standpoint of international politics is so entirely perplexing. No one can foresee developments from one day to the next. However, there is one thing that can be done, and that is to stand by and carry on. . ."

"I preached on Christmas morning (1939), and we had what I think was an excellent congregation—fully 700 people. I made and preached a new sermon on 'The desirable things of all nations shall come'. I enjoyed it, whether other people did or not! I know you will be wondering how I dealt with it. Well, briefly, in the Hebrew the noun is singular and the verb plural. Thus the Authorized Version is warranted in writing it, 'The desire of all nations', but the revisers have interpreted the values in rendering it 'the desirable things'. I took that as the basis. What are they? Happiness, peace, righteousness; in spite of all appearances these are the things that humanity is seeking. They all came with the coming of our Lord, whose mission was that of proclaiming the Kingdom of God. What is the Kingdom of God? The Kingdom of God is: righteousness, peace, joy; the very things humanity wants. But humanity is seeking them in the wrong order. In the Kingdom of God everything begins with righteousness."

With 1940 the 'phony war' ended and Goering began in earnest to make an end of Hitler's British adversary, wreaking his vengeance far and wide, but concentrating on the seat of the Empire. As the R.A.F. soared to meet the attacks many bombs fell on the open country as enemy planes sped home, so that little Stebbing was not an altogether peaceful refuge for Kathleen and her children. She doubts if it be relevant to include those experiences in a life of her father, merely giving them as a background and explanation for her long absences from her parents during their last years. Yet it is probable that when Dr. Morgan referred in a letter to "the discipline of the more difficult experiences of life," he had in mind among other things this enforced separation from a daughter who had shared so much of his life and work, whom he loved very devotedly, and who loved and understood him. It may be of interest, too, to read of a young mother's attitude to the experiences she had to meet alone.

"I was there (in Stebbing) because, having lived through one war myself already, and having memories of my own absolute terror of those nights at Mundesley when we children went to bed with our winter coats at the bottom of the bed, and our shoes ready under it—I made a vow to myself that if it was humanly possible, my three should *not* go through the agony I suffered. Uncle Ted wanted me to wake up the girls and bring them downstairs to sit with us. I refused to do this. I said I took full responsibility for my decision, but that I would not wake them and bring them down to sit and shiver with fright as I had done as a child. If they woke and wanted to come down that was a different matter. But they never did! I admit that when I got a place of my own it was not easy to sit by myself night after night, wondering what in the world was happening outside, and how near the planes were, but I kept to my resolve, and I know now that I was right. My three children's memories of the war are fading, and I believe it has left no scars. As to the rest; I lived for the girls. I was kept busy with and for them, and so the months and years passed, with, of course, the wonderful red-letter days when Don could be with us. There is a sense in which I shall forever regret that I saw so little of Dad and Mother during this time, but in a greater sense I have always been glad that my memory for the most part goes back before the days of growing weakness and infirmity."

Order and method in the personal affairs of life had always been second nature to Campbell Morgan. Only those who love the beauty of system and regularity can fully understand what it must have meant to have these things suddenly broken into and shattered. Young roots when torn up or diverted from their regular course begin immediately and tenaciously to adapt themselves to a new way of life. But the roots of age have grown deep in habits and customs. When war broke in its full fury and violence in 1940 it was the very old who experienced the most discomfort and hardship. But the house against which the winds blew was still 'Ataraxia', for it was founded upon a rock.

" . . . the situation here is pretty ghastly," wrote Dr. Morgan in June, 1940. "Although I confess it is not easy, I am constantly hearing in my own soul the words: 'In nothing be anxious, but in everything by prayer and supplication with thanksgiving, let your requests be made known unto God'."

On October 8 he wrote: "London is going through a tremendous ordeal. I have not been in bed for six weeks. Down in the lounge we do get some sleep during the night at intervals. and so we are keeping up. As to services. The chapel has been hit three times. . . . That means that last Sunday week we could not hold any services there, but went to Livingstone Hall (in the London Missionary Society Building) which is nigh at hand. Last Sunday we had a morning service in the centre of the church and Dr. Lloyd-Jones preached. We have no shelter in connection with the chapel nor would it be possible to have any there, so we have to be prepared to close down if a raid comes."

Somehow the diary continued to be written. While there are references to air raids early in 1940, they began in earnest in the summer. From August 15 until October 20, when Dr. and Mrs. Morgan left London for a time to get some rest in the country, there were only seven days in August when there was not a raid, and none at all in September and October. Typical entries read as follows:

Sept. 1 (Sunday).—"At 11 started service at Westminster when warning sounded. Closed and came home. All clear by 11.30. Went back and found a number of people so continued service and preached. Lunch at 12.30. Started to rest and again a warning at 2. All clear at 2.30, so finished the rest. Tea at 4. At 6 o'clock took service—a good attendance."

Sept. 2-6.—"Two or three air-raid warnings every day and night."

Sept. 7.—"A daytime raid. They came pretty near. At night the heaviest attack so far on London and coming pretty near us."

Sept. 8 (Sunday).—"Got things in order for possible service. It being National Day of Prayer, at 11 o'clock I gave a brief address and we had prayer. Whole service lasted 45 minutes. Warning at 12.30. All clear at 1.30. Preached again at 6. Warning at 8 so down to the lounge.

Sept. 15 (Sunday).—"Preached in Westminster at 11. As I was uttering the last sentence warning went at 11.52. All clear 12.55. Another warning at 2.12. All clear at 3.20. At 6 to Westminster but very few and no service. Warnings all night."

Sept. 25.—"Went to look at church after incendiary bomb hit it last night. A sad sight."

Sept. 26.—"Looked over possible references for sermon on 'The Voice of the Devil'. Two warnings in the day and at night."

Sept. 27.—"Six warnings to-day. In the intervals I have prepared a rough outline of sermon on Genesis 3. 1."

Sept. 29 (Sunday).—"Westminster not being habitable we had service in Livingstone Hall, about 150 being present. A short service but a good one."

Sept. 30.—"Four warnings to-day. In intervals a few letters and some work on sermon on Job 1. 9."

Oct. 5.—"Three warnings to-day. Sketched outline of Psalm 56. 3, 4."

Oct. 9.—"At about 11.30 p.m. an incendiary bomb struck us. It was promptly dealt with."

Oct. 13 (Sunday).—"Did not go out. Made rough outline of Luke 4. 5-7."

Oct. 14.—"At 11.30 p.m. the Transport Building was hit and windows here shattered. We had to go to the shelter for some hours."

Oct. 20 (Sunday).—"Five warnings during the day. Went to church but had to return."

On October 9 was written a letter from Dr. Morgan, a paragraph of which quoted to an American congregation, found its way into the press. "I am quite convinced in my own mind," it said, "that this is our right place, and it is almost a commonplace of our confidence to say that we are quite sure we are in the hands of God. Of course, if there should be such raids as to produce the devastation of London, which, personally, I do not think will ever take place, we may all be killed. Well, if that news should ever reach you, you will know that we have passed through fire into Light, and reached the place where 'they have no more that they can do'. This is not intended as a sort of stoical indifference, but a statement of the realization of our Christian position."

But there had yet to appear a crisis which Mrs. Morgan did not see as a challenge to her ingenuity. With the same old-time spirit and Ruth's help she made and adapted herself to the new arrangements for sleeping in the shelter. It was here that friends did so much to help, bringing those small comforts which ease conditions and smooth rough places. To everyone's surprise, Dr. Morgan announced one day that he would grow a beard, shaving having become so troublesome and difficult a part of the daily routine. His sense of humour had by no means dimmed. "I am growing a beard," he wrote, "I have very little hope of successfully emulating Lord Armistead at present. In due season I expect you will get a snapshot."

When the snapshot arrived the sons agreed that "he looks just like old Grandpa!" A month later he wrote again: "I have become accustomed to the beard and by no means feel it a nuisance. At any rate it saves me from the Egyptian barbarism of shaving, and that is something to be thankful for!"

Telling of the damage to the church referred to in the entry of September 25, Mr. A. E. Marsh says: "The bombing attacks on London were in three phases. First, the period of the incendiaries scattered all over the city with a view to destruction by fire. Second, the heavy explosion bombs varying in size and weight, the object of which was to destroy the buildings by razing them to the ground. The third phase, which began to operate toward the end of the war, was the flying bomb and the rocket.

"In the early stage the church suffered from many incendiary bombs which were dealt with as a result of there being at least three on duty each night, otherwise the church must have been destroyed by fire. On two occasions fires were started but were put out before they got hold of the building. A good deal of damage was done in this connection. The largest fire led to our being without the use of the church for about two months. (October to December, 1940).

"Some damage was caused in the second stage as a result of bombs falling in the district rather than directly on the building.

"In the third stage very heavy damage was done, principally to the roof, which will require about twenty thousand pounds to put right. This was due to a flying bomb which fell on an adjacent block of flats.

"Temporary repairs were effected to the roof, fractures to the huge timbers and other damage being made secure for the time being by steel bands, etc. All the frames and glass to the windows were filled in with boards.

"The damage to the Institute Hall was on two different dates. First, as the result of a piece of a plane penetrating the roof and the ceiling and falling into the Hall. Then, at the time of the flying bombs when the church was badly damaged. The Institute Hall roof and ceiling were practically destroyed. Temporary repairs were effected to enable continued use of the Hall."

How heart-breaking it must have been to see the beloved building so recently restored to order and beauty, desecrated in a moment of time by the ruthlessness of war! But those who loved it best viewed its scars with pride as well as sorrow, for the British people were one in the sentiment voiced by Mr. Winston Churchill in those dark days of 1940: "We would rather see London in ruins and ashes than that it should be tamely and abjectly enslaved."

When, in 1947, Dr. Harris E. Kirk, who had so often served as guest-minister in Westminster during the summers before the war, saw what the bombs had done to the church, and especially the irreparable damage to the pulpit Bible, he returned home to tell his people in Baltimore about it. The Franklin Street Church, graciously decided to present Westminster Chapel with a new pulpit Bible.

Dr. Walter L. Lingle, in recording the event in the *Christian Observer*, of 7th April, 1948, gives this sidelight of interest:

"It so happened that in connection with the commemoration of the jubilee of King George the Fifth of England, in 1935, two hundred large, handsome Bibles were printed by the Oxford Press. These Bibles were designed by the American typographer, Bruce Rogers. The Franklin Street people were able to secure two of these Bibles, one for their own church and one for Westminster Chapel. The fact that the two churches have similar Bibles is an additional tie that binds.

"The front cover of the Bible (given to Westminster) bears the following inscription: 'Presented to Westminster Chapel by Dr. Harris Elliott Kirk, Minister, and the Congregation of Franklin Street Presbyterian Church of Baltimore, Maryland, U.S.A. We thank God upon every remembrance of you, for your fellowship in the Gospel from the first day until now. God bless you, and strengthen you and forever give you courage.'

"Thus the Bible went from America to England as an ambassador for God, and at the same time an ambassador to promote Christian friendship and fellowship between two great peoples. No more appropriate gift could have been sent to Westminster Chapel, whose ministers have been great expository preachers of the Word of God."

In the latter part of October, 1940, Dr. and Mrs. Morgan were persuaded to go to the country between Sundays in order to get some rest, but he insisted upon returning to town for the services. "Now the church is habitable," he wrote in December, "and by an overwhelming vote on Sunday last the congregation decided that we go back there and attempt to carry on with the new year."

Silver End, a little village in Essex, was chosen as a quiet, unfrequented spot. Unfortunately on the afternoon of their arrival Dr. Morgan fell, hurting and wrenching the muscles in his knees. Mrs. Morgan felt afterwards that he never fully recovered from the shock of that fall. From that time there was increasing weakness and he never walked alone again without a fear of falling.

Mental powers and sheer will and determination were as keen as ever, and there was constant battle between these and physical disability. In July, 1941, Dr. Morgan wrote: "I am still going on on Friday nights and once on Sundays but with almost terrific difficulty. Still there is such a thing as being 'faint yet pursuing! . . . ' We were here (in London) on the night of March 10. We spent the night in the shelter. It was a terrible night but we were kept safe. Incendiary bombs fell on St. Ermins but they were promptly dealt with. The next morning the whole neighbourhood was a scene of charred remains."

With the year's end came the attack on Pearl Harbour, and compared with what had preceded it, a somewhat quieter period for London as far as air raids were concerned. But the long year of danger from the skies, irregular hours, and the suffering and distress which touched every human life had taken their toll, though examinations pronounced

Dr. Morgan physically sound. One doctor told him, "The trouble is A.D.!" which rather amused him. Diary entries confine themselves to the essentials—preaching and health; the former was, for the most part, "exhausting," "difficult," "hard" with references to the "mighty preaching" (a phrase often used) of his colleague, Dr. Martyn Lloyd-Jones.

"I am going on with a growing sense of weakness," he wrote. "Preaching is not what it used to be. I have now just to work my way through my notes and not trust to the inspiration of the moment for anything. . . . However, I mean to keep on as long as I can and am able. I am greatly comforted and helped by my colleague. . . . He is a remarkable preacher and a delightful personality."

In May, the youngest daughter, Ruth, was married to Mr. Bryan Shute, the brother of her sister's husband. Dr. Morgan, assisted by Dr. Lloyd-Jones, officiated at the ceremony.

The three eldest grandsons in the uniforms of the British Army and the Royal Canadian Air Force appeared at unexpected intervals, usually of short duration, at the home of their grandparents, and then there came, from time to time, a number of young men in the uniforms of the United States Army, Navy, Air Force and Marines, introducing themselves as members of one church or another "where your son is the minister." They wrote home of the welcome they received, sometimes adding that Mother's gift was a parting kiss!

Inactivity irked Dr. Morgan more than anything else, all the more so when others around him were active and busy. Assuming annoyance, he was secretly amused by the fact that Mrs. Morgan seemed so little affected by 'A.D.'! In 1942 he wrote: "Mother keeps remarkably well, all things considered. She has had a cold . . . but she is quite alert, and still goes round with a duster! I think she will carry that to heaven with her! . . . I am thankful that so far I am able to keep up two services a week without a break. Winnie remarks, 'It is marvellous!' Well, I suppose it is, but each time I am utterly exhausted. . . . We old folks are just quietly going on. . . . Our Bible School is now moved to Saturdays at 2.30 on account of lighting restrictions. My present subject is 'Gleanings from the Psalms.' . . . Then I propose to take five weeks summarizing the five books (of the Psalms), and after that take a selection of psalms in detail."

★ ★ ★ ★ ★ ★

The one increasing purpose of this full life had been the work of the Bible School and all that term involved. Whether on Friday nights at Westminster, or on weeks and months of itinerant ministry, the unfolding and teaching of the divine literature, setting on fire a love of the Book, creating a hunger to understand it and providing a working plan of study—if in his eyes this purpose had fallen short of some of the high hopes he had set for it, the task had been gloriously accomplished. In April, 1943, when it became physically impossible to continue his leadership of the Bible School, Dr. Morgan handed in his resignation as minister of Westminster also, but Dr. Lloyd-Jones and the officers of the church begged him not to resign as long as he could preach at one service on Sunday.

But the Bible School had been the heart-beat of Campbell Morgan's ministry. When he had to give it up there was no complaint, only the thankfulness that he had been permitted 'a magnificent innings'; but the vital spark had gone out.

"One by one the 'old guard' are going . . . and I shall not go on much longer," he wrote to his sons. Then with a touch of the old Campbell Morgan—"But the Lord remains. . . . I shall go thankful for all of you, glad that I am your father, and being certain of your loyalty to the Word of God to the end."

He wrote to Dr. F. A. Robinson in Toronto: "I am able now to take only one service a week. What a change it seems from the long years in which I took twelve! . . . I am very thankful that I am not a sufferer except from extreme and growing weakness. I have just been reading Mann's *Life of F. B. Meyer*, and have been amazed at all he did, and feel that by comparison I have not done much. . . . On

December 9 I shall reach eighty. I should like to have gone on till then. . . . However, I have had a long innings. Sixty-seven years of preaching is something to be thankful for, at least for the preacher, to say nothing of the hearers!"

He proffered his resignation again in June, 1943, and this time it was reluctantly accepted, the church conferring upon Dr. Morgan the honour of becoming Minister Emeritus. He preached his last sermon as minister on the last Sunday in August. "Fully 2,000 people were there," he said, "and I preached with a good sense of freedom." His daughter, Kathleen, was present at that time and says of it: "It was a most inspiring service in every way. He chose the hymns and readings as he always did with great care. There was to be 'no sadness of farewell' but the onward look. It was the last time I saw him stand in that pulpit, and it was like a most beautiful benediction from start to finish. He preached on the text from the last words in Matthew, 'Lo, I am with you . . .' It was not a long sermon, certainly not as full as I have often heard him on that text, but it said all that was needed, and the emphasis was on the point that though Dad was laying down his ministry at Westminster, God was not leaving Westminster. It was a wonderful end to a wonderful ministry, and when he finished he had that great crowd in the palm of his hand!"

To this Ruth adds: "I also was present at that service, and it was wonderful. Perhaps more especially so to Mother and me, for we had been there all along, watching Dad every Sunday, knowing what a burden preaching had become to him, but on *that* day he was given special strength and admitted that he had enjoyed every minute of it."

While retirement is life's major goal to some, and opens up a vista of attractions to others, it had never held any charms for Campbell Morgan, so that when it was forced upon him he referred to it in the only way it had any meaning for him—"I am on the list of the unemployed." He wrote that he was taking "a busman's holiday" on Sundays, going about, as he was able, to hear other London preachers, especially enjoying any who were old friends or former students. Miss Howell had been ill for some time, but was able to come for a few hours now, two or three times a week, to work on manuscripts. "We are trying to prepare a volume on the Corinthian Letters—reports of Bible School lectures. . . . Ruth keeps me level with correspondence." He wrote to Dr. Robinson again just before his birthday: "I expect you know by this time that I have retired. . . . My action was rendered necessary through extreme and growing weakness and mental tiredness. . . . When I think of Meyer, Luke Wiseman, Scott Lidgett, Ferrier Hulme and others, active well into the eighties, I feel it is rather early. . . . But I have had a long innings and lived a strenuous life. I am thankful for all that is past and can truly say I trust Him for all that is to come. Mrs. Morgan has passed her 78th birthday and is still wonderfully active for her years—far more so than her husband."

Dr. Robinson, in writing of those days, says: "There is extreme pathos in seeing one as active as Dr. Morgan had been, becoming increasingly weary and worn; but it was the weariness of a full day's work well done. At its close he knew there would be the joy of home and rest . . .

> 'I am tired; heart and feet
> Turn from busy mart and street.
> I am tired; rest is sweet.
>
> 'I am tired; I have had
> What has made my spirit glad,
> What has made my spirit sad.
>
> 'I am tired; God is near,
> Let me sleep without a fear,
> Let me die without a tear.
>
> 'I am tired; I would rest
> As the bird within its nest;
> I am tired—Home is best.'

One of Dr. Morgan's greatest joys and causes for satisfaction in the last year of his life lay in attending the morning services at Westminster, and hearing the preaching of his friend, colleague and successor, Dr. Martyn Lloyd-Jones. "I cannot tell you with what pleasure I listen to him. . . . It is mighty preaching, most appropriate for these days" Here was more 'bread upon the waters'. Sons were 'loyal to the Word of God'; former students were studying and teaching it as he had taught them to study and teach, and the church he loved above all others was continuing under the leadership and direction of a man he loved and approved.

The war claimed a casualty in the death of Dr. and Mrs. Morgan's eldest son early in 1945. The duties of an air-raid warden in addition to those of the vicar of a parish on England's south coast 'invasion area' had been strenuous and unremitting, and he had performed them all with the heroism of a true soldier who does not count the cost. He knew his physical limitations and the weakness that had lain dormant since the tubercular condition years before, but he chose to spend nights and days of air raids and their horrible aftermath on the home front. Dr. Morgan was quite unequal to the sixty mile journey by car or train to visit him in the last days, but for Mrs. Morgan it was just another instance of her wonderful reserve of physical and spiritual power that she could and did divide her love and comfort between husband and son.

When the end came for Percy, Dr. Morgan accepted it as one who knows how much nearer is the reunion than had been the last earthly meeting. "For him it is gain," he said, " . . . we sorrow not as those who have no hope, believing as we do that we shall meet him on the other side."

★ ★ ★ ★ ★ ★

Winter yielded to Spring, and V.E. Day came on the eighth day of May. The moon shone down upon the scars of London, but the terror of pilotless planes and rocket bombs was over. The weary, the aged, and the young could sleep unmolested and waken to see flowers appearing in the ruins. Another chapter in history was closed.

The man lying on the couch in St. Ermins was waiting. Each day he grew weaker but there was no anxiety in his heart. He had walked too long beside the Shepherd to doubt His love and wisdom now. If the face of Death was hidden it was because he stood silhouetted in light. His wings were edged with silver and his feet were shod with peace.

Through the window the tower of Westminster Chapel could be seen standing against the sky. The work would go on; the Word would be proclaimed to the generations to come.

On May 16th, 1945, George Campbell Morgan passed peacefully home in the sunset to the ataraxia of the Father's house. The book of his pilgrimage was finished and its last word was

VICTORY

Memorial Services

THE MEMORIAL SERVICES

LONDON

FOLLOWING the cremation at Golders Green, a memorial service was held in Westminster Chapel on Monday, May 28th, 1945. It was fitting that the chairman for this occasion should be Dr. D. Martyn Lloyd-Jones, and that those who brought their tributes were representative of a host of friends in the ministry.

Mr. A. E. Marsh read from 1 Corinthians 15. 20-28 and 35-58. "A meeting like this would have been incomplete," said Dr. Jones, "if Mr. Marsh had not taken some part in it —Dr. Morgan's friend and colleague, one who worked with him probably longer than anyone else and more intimately." Rev. W. H. Aldis, of the Anglican Church, and Chairman of the Keswick Convention Council led in prayer.

In his introductory address the chairman sounded the keynote of the service by stating that "there never was a man, surely, of whom it could be said more truly that he belonged to all the churches as Dr. Morgan," and this note was repeated in one way or another by all the subsequent speakers.

In the first of these tributes, Dr. John A. Hutton said: "Campbell Morgan more than once declared that his sole ambition in life, the thing for which he humbly believed that he had been elected and directed, was to be a *teacher* of the Word of God. . . . 'I am a teacher,' he would say, 'or I am nothing'. His Bible was the whole Book from Genesis to Revelation. . . . He saw quite clearly that the whole revelation of God was given not in texts, not in chapters, not even in separate books! Not in the bright patches only, not only in the heights, but in the dark passages and in the depths . . .

"Morgan was content with the Bible's 'In the beginning God created the heavens and the earth.' If anyone should have claimed for time a million years . . . a hundred million years or even of light years, I believe my old friend with a gay voice would have said, 'Take your own time and welcome! So long as you leave God where the Bible places Him, at the beginning'.

" . . . He was marvellously equipped for his calling as he conceived it to be. . . . I have heard Morgan in moments of sheer vision, of revelation, the very experience of which made a date in one's life forever."

Miss Mildred Cable said that she spoke on behalf of the great missionary bodies all over the world. The 'contagion' of Dr. Morgan's enthusiasm for Bible study, she said, had changed the lives of many of Christ's ambassadors.

"Dr. Morgan had his own peculiar line of Bible teaching. He believed in the Book; the Book was everything to him, and he saw to it that his students loved the Book, too. He never by suggestion or word implied that he thought it wrong to take up a critical study of the Book . . . providing you knew the Book first; and he saw to it that everyone who came to him for teaching knew that Book right through, knew it in and out, and spent time upon it.

"Yes, but it did not end there. As I talk to you now I can see Bible Schools in Central Asia where thirty men and women have given up their time for the winter months while the harvest was in the earth; they have come for teaching; and the textbook is the Analyzed Bible in Chinese. . . .

"We missionaries have lost one who has been to us a teacher and a friend; one who sponsored all our work with prayer and with thought; one who always wrote strong words of encouragement when we needed them; and whenever we committed words to print we always received appreciative letters from him. He had, to an amazing degree, one of the qualities that is curiously absent in Christian communities—the capacity to rejoice wholeheartedly with those who rejoice.

" . . . Speaking for myself I can say that I caught from him that which has been a passion through life, to know this Book by every translation I could buy, every language in which I could read it, to study it in and out in every way. . . .

"What was the secret of his success? He was often asked that by young ministers. He told me once, 'I always say to them the same thing—work; hard work; and again, work'. I suppose most of us know that until quite recent years Dr. Morgan was in his study soon after six in the morning that he might study this Book without interruption. People could not disturb him in the mornings; he was reading and studying the Book—God's Word to man demanded man's best. And Dr. Morgan—he had it. He taught us much, and we missionaries who were bearing the burden of the Church's advance-guard thank God for what he has been to us. 'Wherever the river came there was life'. 'He that believeth on Me from him shall flow rivers of living water.' Rivers have started out, and they have gone to India, to Africa, to Central Asia and to Japan—but the end is not yet!"

Dr. Charles Brown recalled earlier days when Dr. Morgan first came to London. When he came back from America to take up the work at Westminster he was asked to give a series of Bible readings for five consecutive days in the Ferme Park Baptist Church.

"I never heard five expository addresses in my old church on so high an intellectual and spiritual level as those of Dr. Campbell Morgan," said Dr. Brown. "He was a Bible teacher and a Bible preacher. He spoke with dogmatic certitude. He did not go into the pulpit to stretch lame hands of faith and gather dust and chaff. He had fought the battle in his study which was also his oratory, had fought his doubts and gathered strength, and found the light, and he took that light given to him from the inspired page to his congregation, and poured it full flood into their minds and hearts and consciences.

" . . . It is reasonable and inevitable to conclude that, to my friend's conviction and conception of the splendour of the Bible and the greatness of the Christian ministry, may be traced the fact that all his sons went into the Christian ministry. I know of only one other case where that has happened. I think the sharer of all his desires and ambitions, his companion, the dear lady of his chimney-corner, had her share in it. Certainly if it had not been for her influence and the elevated conception of the worthwhile, the sons would never have followed in their father's footsteps. Here they are, three Presbyterian ministers in America. One of them whom God called to higher service was in the Anglican Church in this country.

" . . . I would like to say once more in bearing my tribute of deep affection for Dr. Morgan, that he was never a bigot. He was a man of catholic mind and broad sympathies. If any man loved Jesus Christ and the advancement of His Kingdom, Campbell Morgan gladly had fellowship with him. I thank God with you to-night here in this large company, for his ministry. Blessed be his memory. Blessed be the grace of God that sustained him in his multifarious labours, and blessed be God for his present peace. He is in the great multitude that no man can number who follow the Lamb whithersoever He goeth; and my personal prayer is that I may, by God's mercy and grace, be accounted worthy to meet him again in the life beyond."

Dr. Sidney M. Berry spoke as one representing "a denomination whose boundless limits were able to contain a ministry like that of Dr. Campbell Morgan." But he observed that "the prophets do not fit very well into denominational pens. . . .

" . . . I think it is true to say that he did not come into the ministry in a conventional way. There are some people who might be shy of saying that on an occasion like this. I should glory in it;—but then, you see, I am a Congregationalist! I do not think that any of the rigid rules you lay down are infallible, nor that any of your schemes of preparation for the Christian ministry are necessarily those that God is going to use to send His prophetic servants into the midst of His people. The rules and customs and observances and all the rest of them are, no doubt, very useful and very wise —and what would committees do without them? Yet, if I may say it reverently, Providence in its wisdom plays pranks with all our man-made rules. And our friend of whom we are thinking to-night, and for whom we are thanking God from our hearts—well, there was nothing of the conventional about him, either in the way in which he entered the ministry or in his conception of it. . . . He was of the true race of the prophets.

" . . . Dr. Charles Brown has asked why the Congregational Union did not make him Chairman. Why didn't Dr. Brown try to get him to agree to be Chairman? I once tried, during the period of my Secretaryship, to get him on to the platform of the Congregational Union for one specific purpose—to give an address. But it took a lot of letters and interviews even to do that. And when he got there he was not happy! No, it was not in that sort of way that he made his great and magnificent contribution to the Church universal. Men must be true to their own lights and their own gifts, and they must find, under the guidance of God's Spirit, their own way.

"Dr. Campbell Morgan was a great expositor. This has been said and will be said again. He made the Bible a new and living Book, not only to the congregations who listened to him, but to the vast multitude of people who read his articles and his books. He made the Bible a living Book to countless souls for whom before it was a dead Book. . . . He was more than an expositor, he was a preacher; he soared like an aeroplane. That is the picture that comes into my mind. I travel in my memory to one of those times after a long exposition—the runway—the plane gradually lifted, and you get some flash, a kind of flash from the clouds—the plane was up and he was there, not so much the expositor as the preacher. Surely all true exposition ought to be like that. For the exposition of the Word of God, as that Word has been revealed in human experience through the prophets and saints of old, must lead to the flash of the living Word, illuminating the whole world of to-day. And Campbell Morgan's expositions always did that.

"I think some of the greatest sermons I ever heard him preach were at the beginning of the last war—preached from this pulpit. . . . Out of the very heart of the Word of God Campbell Morgan brought just the strength, the insight, the grasp of principle and truth that was the one need of the nation at that decisive hour.

"I am glad that people have said that he was not a bigot . . . because he was not. He was not a 'Mr. Know-All', and the preachers who are 'Mr. Know-Alls' never really reach the human heart. There was a kind of humility about him in his teaching. Is it not true, those of you who sat under him and gloried in him as a teacher—did he not seem to you to be talking, not from some superior height, but carrying you along a road on which your were all travellers and learners; and he was the greatest learner of all? Can you ever have a great teacher who is not also a great learner?

" . . . We who gather here to-night, his friends, those who really loved him and thank God for every memory of him, we are only just a tiny part of the great company who, under God, owe everything to Campbell Morgan."

Dr. S. W. Hughes sounded the note of optimism that re-echoed through Dr. Morgan's preaching, describing his friend as one who combined "the gift of the seer with the winsomeness of the saint." He said: "We recall with what joy he transmitted theology into the Christian evangel. He taught the Redeemerhood of Christ with the yearning love of his Saviour. He thrilled to the Christian conception of the sovereignty of God. He never floundered amongst the speculations of Humanism hoping that God might reign. Events sometimes saddened him but they never overwhelmed him. He knew that though 'the whole creation groaneth and travaileth in pain together until now' there was something to wait for in the purpose of God. He knew that in Christ all things hold together. He knew that his Redeemer lived, and was 'alive for evermore'. The Bible was his textbook, and Christ the greatest Being knowable. He had a triumphant and contagious faith. . . . He did not win people by rhetoric; he was aflame with God.

" . . . Those of us who were privileged to share his friendship, here and in America, often returned to our work with what a local preacher friend called 'our homiletical reserves greatly replenished'. His home talk often became positively exegetical, so much so that by stealth I sought a pencil to take a note *en route*. He not only taught us how to take texts, but he left us with the impression that we could never really attempt to preach until the text took us. . . . As friend to enquirers many personal contacts became living links with Christ.

" . . . We cherish his memory with affection. To-night in the knowledge of his hallowing home life we pray that lovely memories may mingle with the consolation of our heavenly Father in the sacred thoughts of Mrs. Campbell Morgan and her family. His memory is a benediction and a challenge to us all. . . ."

Dr. D. Martyn Lloyd-Jones closed this memorable service. He reiterated the fact that preaching and teaching were the supreme passion of Dr. Morgan's life. "But the point I want to make about him as a preacher is this," he said, "that we are all agreed that he was God's gift to His Church. He surely was the supreme illustration of the fact that God always gives His gifts at the right time. . . . When did he come upon the scene? It was immediately after those wonderful campaigns of D. L. Moody and Sankey in this country. There had been those great visitations of the Spirit. Men and women had been converted by the thousand. This great evangelistic movement had come into the whole life of the Church, and what was needed above everything else at that point was someone who could teach these converts. And 'a man came from God' whose name was George Campbell Morgan; and he came at the critical moment, at the very right time when all those spiritual emotions and experiences needed to be harnessed and deepened and fostered.

The evangelists had done their work; it was the time for the teacher; and God sent him.

"... It is my privilege as I travel about the country to engage in conversation with ministers, and they always come and talk to me about Dr. Morgan ... and they have told me of the blessing they have received from him. I am amazed at the number of men who have told me that the whole basis of their preaching has been derived from the method adopted by Dr. Morgan. And that is true, not only of Free Church ministers but of Anglican clergymen also. One of the latter said to me: 'I never approach a text without asking myself, What would Campbell Morgan do with this?' And there is this further special point I want to make here. If ever there has been a preacher who has been of untold blessing to lay preachers, it has been Dr. Morgan. They come to me wherever I go and tell me about the help he has been to them.

"... Let me leave the preacher and ... say a word about Dr. Campbell Morgan as a man.... It has been my privilege to meet men in other realms of life besides that of the ministry, and I do not hesitate to say that he was surely the most intelligent man I have ever known. Intellectually alive, and alert, and keen. And that intelligence of his persisted until almost the last moment of his life. I think you would like to share with me one experience. I called to see him on the last day of his life; it was somewhere round about half past twelve, and he was obviously dying. I tried to be natural, and to speak as I always spoke to him, and I left with the impression that I had not revealed in any way my feeling that that was to be our last meeting here on earth. However, a short time afterwards he was visited by his doctor, and he said to her, 'I am dying'. 'What makes you think that?' she asked. 'I saw it in Lloyd-Jones' face'. He was dying; life was ebbing away; but with that flashing eye and that keen intelligence of his he was watching me, and he diagnosed my feelings aright.

"... He was a great individualist.... We are entitled to say with due respect to others of his generation that he seems to have been the last of the great pulpit personalities, the last of that mighty succession of men and masters of assemblies who could control vast gatherings, and impress their personality upon great congregations.

" . . . He did everything in a big way; he painted on a large canvas. How impatient he was with everything that savoured of smallness! . . . But to see the real bigness and largeness of the man you had to look at his heart and observe his marked generosity. How generous he was in his judgment of others; and in his estimate of the preaching of other men he was almost ridiculously generous. He read into a man's sermon what the preacher had often never even imagined. And . . . his bigness and generosity displayed itself with respect to financial matters also. He was so generous and even reckless where there was need and suffering. He would adopt a whole family; he would pay for children's education. The largeness of the man's heart made him unusally sensitive to the need and suffering of others.

"I do want to add one other word and that is concerning his extreme humility. Here was a man who was supremely successful in his ministry. Crowds attended upon him and yet there was never the slightest trace of pomposity. He was natural; he was humble and approachable."

In closing Dr. Lloyd-Jones spoke of Dr. Morgan as a colleague and companion. "I am not referring to him now as a gifted man," he said, "but in a more personal way. There was never the slightest suspicion of difference between us. . . . I shall always have a treasured memory of him as a listener. He was incomparably the greatest listener I have ever known. That mobile face of his let you know exactly what he was thinking; you could see when he appreciated any points that were made; they were registered on his face. He listened as only a man well versed in the Scriptures and with a sympathetic heart could listen.

" . . . I am sorry for those who never met him in private, and who never had the opportunity of listening to his endless fund of stories, and the play of humour. His memory was inexhaustible, and his experience rich and varied; he had worked with so many men. I tried to persuade him to write the story of his life or his memoirs, but he would not do it, and I think we are all the poorer for his refusal. But he was in private and in his home life one of the most interesting and ideal companions anyone could ever choose to have.

"I have spoken of him as a preacher and public man, as a man and as a companion. But I want most emphatically to join with Dr. Brown in saying that even he could not have been what he was were it not for Mrs. Morgan. . . . She was with him through all the long years; she willingly spared him for his larger work, and never grudged his absences from her. It is right and fitting that we should pay our tribute and honour to Mrs. Morgan as we pay our tribute and honour to him to-night.

" . . . We have been thinking of a great man and of a great Gospel that made him what he was. We thank God for him, and we shall all, I am certain, dedicate ourselves anew to the exposition and preaching of the Word of God to which Dr. Campbell Morgan gave himself without measure and without stint through his long and notable ministry."

★ ★ ★ ★ ★ ★

The meeting closed with the playing of Mendelssohn's 'O for the wings of a dove', by the organist, Mr. E. Emlyn Davies, F.R.C.O., and all present stood in silent tribute to the memory of Dr. Campbell Morgan.

PHILADELPHIA

ON Friday, June 15th, 1945, a Memorial Service was held in the Tabernacle Presbyterian Church, Philadelphia, Pennsylvania. At this service Dr. Morgan's three sons, Kingsley John, Frank Crossley and Howard Moody were present, and participated with two guest speakers, Dr. Charles R. Erdman and Dr. Milton Harold Nichols.

Presiding as pastor of the church, Dr. Howard Morgan, in his opening words, sounded the note of Christian triumph:

'Hallelujah; for the Lord our God, the Almighty reigneth. Let us rejoice and be exceeding glad, and let us give the glory to Him.'

His prayer of invocation was concluded with the Lord's Prayer in which the congregation joined. Dr. F. Crossley Morgan read the same Scripture passages as were used at the Memorial Service in London, after which Rev. K. J. Morgan led in a prayer of thanksgiving for the life on earth of their father and for the communion of saints, remembering those far away yet united with them in thought and love.

A cable message of greeting from the congregation of Westminster Chapel was read, and another from Mrs. Morgan which ended with the words: "Am experiencing victory over death."

"Many of you here this evening who remember them both," said Dr. Howard Morgan, "rejoice with us that all God's goodness through so many years has been with them both, and rejoice in our sense of quiet triumph with Mother at this hour."

Representing the churches of Philadelphia, Dr. Milton Harold Nichols recalled the first time he heard Dr. Morgan 'at the turn of the century'; of the friendship that developed through the years, and of his joy in welcoming Dr. Morgan to Philadelphia when later he came as a resident and as the pastor of the Tabernacle Church.

He called Dr. Morgan "a specialist in the interpretation of God's blessed Book." Of his messages he said: "(They) were never little, never trivial, never provocative, no, nor even argumentative. His themes were the great themes of the Book. I think he could list them under the words God, and Christ; Sin, Suffering and Salvation; The Saviour, The Cross, Redemption; The Resurrection and Life Eternal. On those themes you could build the great truths he preached again and again to his congregations. He had a great way of making you feel the truth, of communicating his faith to you who sat in the pew, so that you said, Yes, this is it! Yes, I have it! And you went out again rejoicing in that new-found faith."

Dr. Charles R. Erdman of Princeton, New Jersey, whose friendship with Dr. Morgan covered almost half a century, said in the opening words of his address:

"No more eloquent tribute could possibly have been paid to the life and memory of Dr. Morgan than is embodied here to-night by the presence of his three sons who so worthily are carrying on the work of their father in the father's own way. The work of the father was the work of a preacher, and the way was the way of Bible exposition; and he followed that way so assiduously and so passionately that he became the supreme and peerless expository preacher of his age."

Dr. Erdman recalled the early life of Dr. Morgan, telling how his godly parents, the influences of his childhood, his unconventional entrance into the ministry, his evangelistic work in Hull, were all contributing factors to a great life and ministry. Dr. Erdman was reminded of their first meeting in Northfield's pleasant environment, and of his friend's subsequent contribution to the religious life of two continents.

He made reference to Dr. Morgan's personality and appearance 'at once attracting and arresting the audience, holding it through long discourses'; to his 'marvellous voice' (and to the 'melodious modulated voices of these three sons who at least have inherited this among other things from their father'); to his 'enunciation . . . he could make more out of one word than most men could make out of a sentence or paragraph'; his 'wealth of English, pure and undefiled'; his 'vivid imagination' and his sense of humour. Above all "there was his moral passion, the spiritual unction with which he spoke; and the message to which we always revert—the message of the Holy Scriptures; first, and last and always a man of one Book, but not only of one Book. Of course, one must know human nature and human history, if he is to adapt the message of the Book to the men and women of his age."

Dr. Erdman said in conclusion: "There was in Dr. Morgan's ministry that divine and supernatural element of which one speaks guardedly, with some hesitation though with deep conviction. Dr. Morgan was a gift of the ascended Christ to His Church, ministered by the power of the Holy Spirit, and I mention that in connection with the fourth chapter of Ephesians which Dr. Morgan loved to dwell upon. Before a great group of ministers in the Witherspoon Building he . . . told us that the Apostle insists that the ascended Christ has granted these gifts to men. 'He gave some, apostles; and some, prophets; and some, evangelists; and some, pastors and teachers, for the perfecting of the saints unto the work of ministry unto the upbuilding of the body of Christ'. Dr. Morgan was all four of these, eminently so. Apostolic in his zeal and his fervour, laying down foundations. He was prophetic in his insight and his utterances. Dr. Morgan had peculiar evangelistic gifts; but the great stress of his ministry was in the sphere of the pastor-teacher.

"As we thank God to-night for this great servant of the Master, we do so not to praise his powers, not to analyze the human sources that led to such wide, wise influence, but we do so to thank God for the countless men and women through sixty or seventy years who on both continents thank God they were prepared for their ministry of saints in the home, in the business office, specifically perhaps in the pulpit . . .

"To-night we can almost hear him say to us: 'Preach the Word; be instant in season, out of season; reprove, rebuke, exhort with all long-suffering and doctrine. . . . Make full proof of thy ministry. . . . I have fought a good fight, I have finished my course, I have kept the faith: henceforth there is laid up for me a crown of righteousness, which the Lord, the righteous Judge shall give me at that day: and not to me only, but unto all them also who love His appearing'."

After the singing of the inspiring hymn, 'For all the Saints who from their Labours Rest', the congregation remained standing as the organist, Mrs. Yeakel, played the triumphant music of the Hallelujah Chorus.

Part II

Introduction

'This house of many memories!'

IN the hush of a lovely English summer evening the service in Westminster Chapel was half over, and the guest-preacher was beginning his message. Memories of my own had crowded too much upon me for the concentration that the hour of worship demanded. Through hymns and prayers and the reading of Scripture the old building had been re-enacting for me the scenes of the past. In my imagination those two graceful balconies held once again their full burden of humanity. On the floor of the church people stood against the walls, under the windows and out into the vestibule. Some had drifted in from the streets that wind their tortuous ways around the old building; others were thousands of miles of land and sea from the spot they called home.

With that 'inner eye' I could see again the one who has drawn them together, standing under the light. His silver hair, his tall figure, his beautiful hands upon the Book, the face that proclaims him scholar and mystic, prophet and seer, the voice perfectly modulated so that even a whisper is audible in the upper gallery. I sensed a rustle of expectancy, a shiver of anticipation, for somewhere in that vast crowd was the child I used to be. There are times when memory is stronger than reality, the past nearer than the present.

The picture was so real to me that Sunday evening that even the marks and ravages of seven years of war upon London were blotted out.

Yesterday I had walked through this empty building. I had touched the burned places on the carpet of the dais, witnessing to the incendiary bomb which had fallen through the roof. Mr. Clegg, the old custodian had told us the story of the boy who was passing when it fell. This was his church, he was a member of the Sunday School here. Breaking a window the lad had rushed in, and throwing his coat over the missile, ran with it into the street, thus saving the building from burning.

"The old place needs paint," said the custodian, "cleaning up, and lots of repairs." But this was the summer of 1947, and churches must wait until homes are rebuilt and life for the people made more endurable. This was reality, the other was dreams. It was the past in which I had been wandering, and the past was gone, irrevocably, irretrievably! Yet can the past be dismissed so lightly? I rebelled against the thought that the glory was departed and all the splendour faded. For the present is the fruit of the past and the seed of the future. I knew my own life to be nobler for having learned and grown in this place, and that there were thousands of others to bear the same testimony. I knew, too, that the influence of those who had gone before was marching on through the strong leadership of to-day to a future of continuing service. It is on noble memories that man's spirit rises to achieve its destiny.

Dr. Harris E. Kirk was the guest-preacher for the month of August, 1947. Forty years in the Franklin Street Presbyterian Church of Baltimore have assured him a place in the life of that American city such as that which Dr. Campbell Morgan made for himself in London. There was a note of nostalgia in his voice as he referred to the building in which he stood as "this house of many memories". He reviewed the great personalities who, at one time or another, had filled the pulpit; "Dr. Henry Jowett, Dr. John A. Hutton, Dr. Hubert Simpson, and Dr. Campbell Morgan himself—they were my friends, and I miss them," he said simply.

The speaker unfolded the theme of his sermon; thoughtful and sincere, it revealed mature thinking and quiet power. There was enough here, surely, for any casual passer-by to glean courage for the battle. He spoke of a man's life as being the centre of three concentric circles. There is first the large outer circle, he said, which represents the world in which we live. On its fringes are thousands upon thousands whom we shall never know and who will never know us. Within this circle is another a smaller one, which represents all those whom we touch in a personal way, some only once, some many times, and upon whom we leave our mark for good or ill. Within this circle is another, which Dr. Kirk called 'the inner circle', composed of 'the family' and our very closest and dearest friends. This is the circle 'where we can dare to be ourselves'. In the very centre each one of us stands alone, for there is a place 'where human kinship is not enough, and a man is alone—with God'.

What Dr. Kirk said applied to each individual listener, but to me it applied primarily to one man—Campbell Morgan of Westminster. In a measure he touched the outermost circle of all, and continues to do so. The words which drew the crowds to him are finding their way, through the printed page to lands beyond the sea, and are bringing help to missionaries, to lay-workers, and to Christian people of far-off lands and foreign tongues. I picked up a book one day on a shelf at Westminster, and though I cannot read Dutch I knew it was a copy of *The Great Physician*, translated into the speech of the Netherlands.

How very large was 'the smaller circle of human contact' it is impossible to estimate, for they were drawn to him 'to hear him' wherever he went in the United States and Canada as well as in his native land. The phrase, "I knew your father in—" became something of a joke in the family, as sons and daughters heard it repeated so many times. Yet those who only knew the voice and fell under the spell of the message, felt that God was speaking to them personally through His servant.

Yet simply to know Dr. Morgan the preacher and expositor was to see only one side of a personality with as many facets as a jewel, each glowing with its own peculiar light. There remains the 'inner circle' of those to whom he was 'Chief', 'Rabbi', 'General', 'Governor', 'Doctor', and, most intimately,

'Dad'. These with whom he 'dared to be himself' cherish a fount of memories which is ever fresh and ever stimulating. Like a stream it flows among them whenever two or more get together. One of the greatest compliments that can be paid to this man is that whenever his children congregate there is laughter, and joyous happy memories of Mother, Dad, and home.

But even within the family group those who loved and knew him best recognized a boundary of loneliness 'where human kinship is not enough'. Here was a man who coveted for himself a constant withdrawal from the pressing demands of his busy life, and kept inviolate the sanctity of the early morning vigil of prayer and meditation. Here he breathed the atmosphere of heaven, and daily recharged his spirit with the power that in turn poured out in extravagant measure in the preaching and proclamation of the Word.

The circumstances that led me to Westminster that Sunday evening were many and varied. They involved a journey of more than 5,000 miles and the kindness of many Texas friends who made the journey possible. Last of all was a desire to hear one of America's outstanding preachers in one of London's greatest pulpits. As I thought of all these things I remembered how Dr. Morgan liked to quote the friend who once said to him: "Remember, Morgan, circumstances are sometimes the fingers of God!"

Thus it was that I came again across the years to 'this house of many memories', and there found the plan which forms the background of the second part of this book.

CHAPTER X

The Larger Circle

AS I think it through—this plan—I find that the circumferences of these three circles do not divide but merge, as the ripples on a brook when a stone is thrown into the water. The larger circle suggests mission fields far away; yet those who carried there the spirit of Campbell Morgan and the Westminster method belonged to the inner circle of his friends. If their names appear in reference to these outer fringes of influence it is only because they were privileged to travel further afield, and become identified with them.

"The Christian is the world's Bible," said Mr. D. L. Moody. It was a favourite quotation with Dr. Morgan, and all his life he sought to infuse with missionary zeal those with whom he came into contact. One of Campbell Morgan's primary goals was to maintain Westminster as a missionary church, and whatever else fell below the ideal he had set, this objective was successfully and gloriously accomplished. In faith, at the beginning of his ministry, the officers pledged to give ten per cent. of all the Church's income to missions, and this was never relinquished through good times and bad, in peace and war. The missionary cause was the church's love in action. Lessons learned in the Institute and Sunday School were translated into service and directed towards missions at home and abroad. The ministers and staff set a precedent by pledging themselves to support a native teacher in India. His picture appeared in the *Record*, with an account of his activities. Soon there were two more pictures of native evangelists, these maintained by the Young People's Institute and the Brotherhood. Two little orphan girls in India were supported by the Primary Department.

In 1906 the *Record* proudly announced the arrival in China and South Africa of 'our first missionaries' from Westminster's own membership, in the persons of Dr. Andrew Young and Miss Kathleen Dickenson respectively. Dr. Charlotte Murdoch, a member of the Sisterhood, later went out to China to marry Dr. Young, and a story began more exciting and interesting than many a novel. Charlotte was one of three daughters of a Baltimore dentist, and her sister, Agnes, was a nurse. When their father died, Dr. Morgan sent for the youngest sister, Mary, and she came to London and also joined the Sisterhood. Mary was quiet and retiring, self-effacing and very lovable. When her sisters went to China as Doctor and nurse she went along; someone must mend their clothes and look after them, she said. But she learned the language quicker than they did, and went on itinerating tours alone with a Chinese woman into parts of South China.

Dan Crawford of Africa, Charles Abel of New Guinea, Wilfred Grenfell of Labrador, and Mildred Cable of the China Inland Mission were among the many ambassadors of the Cross in lands beyond the seas whose visits to Westminster were anticipated with eagerness, where they were sure of a welcome for themselves and their message.

When their furloughs were over it was the custom at Westminster to bid farewell to the missionaries of her congregation at a Communion Service, an impressive and inspiring experience, assuring them of the prayers and support of those they represented. During their term of service their letters and activities were circulated through the *Record*, copies of which were mailed to them each month, so that they and those at home might be in constant remembrance of each other. The Mundesley Bible Conference was a rendezvous for all returned missionaries, and their presence and messages were a highlight of those summer gatherings. The Bible School was a training ground for missionary students, those of the China Inland Mission making it a special practice to attend all courses. Dr. Morgan's Biblical Analyses were admirably adapted to field work under varied conditions. As a direct outcome of the Westminster Bible School, similar schools using the Westminster method were set up in many other parts of the world. Groups of students both large and small were organized by those who had caught at Westminster and Mundesley the fire and zeal for systematic Bible Study. A minister in Jamaica gathered together fellow-ministers for periodic Bible Conferences. Another in Bulgaria gave a series of Bible Studies introducing the Westminster method. Another started similar work in Australia. A lady who went to live in Winnipeg, Manitoba, began a Bible School with a group of young people, and another who went out to North-West Canada after studying the Book of Genesis at the Friday Night Bible School, wrote back of the unique way in which she used this teaching. "Opportunities came to me . . . on the trail, as we covered perhaps forty to fifty miles. I had always keen listeners. Those who have driven me have been educated men who once were familiar with the Bible stories, but who have long given up any thought of religion. The prairie is so dreary in bad weather that any lead could be given to the conversation, so as Genesis is my standby, it was generally Genesis I began with, and the eagerness with which they recognize or themselves fit in the parts which were familiar to them was delightful."

Dr. Morgan served in an official capacity on the Governing Board of the London Missionary Society. He was Vice-President of the Board of the Women's Christian Medical College at Ludhiana, in the Punjab, India. He was one of the founders of the Evangelical Union of South America.

He became interested in the Ludhiana Mission through Miss Edith Craske, the 'Sister Edith' of Westminster and New Court, and organizer of the Missionary Sunday Schools in both these churches during Dr. Morgan's ministries.

The Ludhiana Mission was founded in 1894 by Dame Edith Brown, a brilliant Christian physician who had seen a great vision and a great need and determined to pioneer for the medical training of the women of India. Until 1916 the Ludhiana Mission was the only separate medical college for women in all India. Miss Craske visited this field and became its travelling secretary, telling of its work in England,

and later, through Dr. Morgan's help and sponsorship, in the United States, writing of it in a book, *Sister India*, for which he wrote an introduction. When she was asked to tell of his interest in missions she wrote:

"Your dear mother (Sister Freda*) would have been the one best qualified for it. . . . In her day the monthly missionary sermon was one of the pulpit features. Some thought that such sermons would decrease the attendance, but Doctor's masterly presentation and vital understanding of the missionary commission of the Church resulted in a larger, not a smaller attendance.

"He followed, too, with keen interest the work of the Missionary Study Circles which Sister Freda arranged; and at the Saturday night prayer meetings our own Westminster missionaries (whose photos hung on the walls around us) were remembered by name in prayer.

"Hence when I was appointed to the Sunday School work I came into an atmosphere surcharged with the missionary spirit, and thus was able to realize one of my youthful dreams. Never shall I forget how attentively Doctor listened as I outlined my plans for the Missionary Sunday School, and then wholeheartedly gave me a free hand to go right ahead. To my mind the genius of Doctor's leadership lay in the confidence he inspired and the faith he placed in his fellow workers. The Missionary Sunday School was founded in 1911, and during the succeeding seven years of his ministry at Westminster this added department to our Graded Sunday School was a source of perpetual satisfaction to him. In 1915, to Doctor's great joy, he received an invitation to visit India, which he accepted. But restrictions upon women travelling by sea during the first World War did not allow of Mrs. Morgan's accompanying him, and so the project was abandoned.

"When some years later Doctor came to know of my appointment as London Secretary of the Ludhiana Women's Christian Medical College and my visit to India, he wanted

*Mrs. A. M. Gardner.

to hear all about it. I told the story as best I could in *Sister India*, and sent the manuscript to Doctor to read.

"Soon after the book was published I visited America to speak about Ludhiana W.C.M.C. as occasion offered. Through Doctor's introduction there were many opportunities provided. They were strenuous days, crowded with happy memories and generous response.

"In 1938, Doctor had the pleasure of meeting Dame Edith Brown, M.D., the founder of the College, and heard her tell its story for himself. Upon her return to India he presided at her farewell meeting.

"By this time Doctor was completely enamoured with this unique college and hospital, and as Vice-President remained its staunch friend and advocate for the rest of his life."

Mention has already been made of the circumstances which led to the organization of the Evangelical Union of South America in 1911. Its active and consecrated secretary from the beginning, Reverend A. Stuart McNairn, F.R.G.S., writing his reminiscences of Dr. Morgan says:

"South America, the one-time 'Neglected Continent', owes much to Dr. Morgan. Together with many others in the missionary world he was shocked and deeply perturbed by the submission of the organizers of the first great Missionary Conference held in Edinburgh in 1910, to the refusal of the Anglo-Catholic bishops to participate in the Conference, were missionary work in South America to be included; and their threat to withdraw if such work were recognized as truly missionary, their attitude being that South America was 'under the care of our sister Church of Rome', and therefore not a mission field in the terms of the Conference programme.

"This decision came as a severe blow to the missions and missionaries working in South America, several of whom were, at the invitation of Dr. John R. Mott, Chairman of the Conference, preparing material for the various committees. The decision was made, however. But successive World Missionary Conferences held since Edinburgh have seen an ever-growing representation and increasing number of delegates from the 'Neglected Continent'. It was the searchlight thrown on South America by this very exclusion from such a Conference of one-seventh of the land of the globe, as well, perhaps, as the blood-curdling revelations of the rubber-slave-traffic in Amazonia (the heart of this alleged 'Christian Continent'), quickly following the Edinburgh blunder, that opened the eyes of the Christian world to the actual condition of South America, and its importance as a mission field. Dr. Morgan was used of God at this crucial moment to gather up and give expression to the disquiet that this so momentous decision had aroused.

"He immediately got in touch with the leaders of such independent work as was being carried on in South America. He called to his side outstanding leaders of Christian and missionary thought, such as Dr. Stuart Holden, Dr. Len Broughton, Dr. A. C. Dixon and others. Also men with business interests in South America, like Mr. Charles Hay Walker, a member of his own congregation and head of a great engineering firm engaged in extensive construction work in various South American republics. These he formed into a working committee pledged to put South America on the missionary map of the world. Dr. Harry Guinness, of the R.B.M.U., was called into consultation, and agreed to pass over the work of his society in Argentina to the united society in contemplation. Mr. A. Stuart McNairn, a missionary of the R.B.M.U., in Peru, had arrived home on furlough, authorized to speak for his fellow-workers in the negotiations which they had heard were on foot. He agreed, with the consent of Dr. Guinness, that the Peru Mission should also link up with the projected Board. Mr. Bryce Rankin, representative of the South American Evangelical Mission was also approached, and agreed to throw in his lot with the new movement. So came into existence the Evangelical Union of South America, which name was adopted and the new Society brought to birth at Keswick in 1912. In the following year the Help for Brazil Mission linked up with the new Society, and to-day the E.U.S.A. represents the largest, and in some respects the most influential society working from Great Britain in South America.

"Not content with launching such a barque on the troubled waters of missionary controversy, Dr. Morgan accepted the responsibility of pilot, and later, for many years, that of captain, as the Chairman of the E.U.S.A. Board of Directors. Not only so, but for a long period he devoted one evening service every month at Westminster Chapel to a missionary address on South America as a mission field. These notable sermons were no mere emotional appeals for the 'Neglected Continent', but deeply thought-out studies of a great mission field embracing ten republics, with all the reading and research involved. They were printed in the *Westminster Record*, a valuable contribution to the then meagre knowledge of that terra incognita.

"Much might be written as to his deep and unselfish devotion to this long neglected land, and to his wise guidance in the direction of the affairs of the Mission he was so instrumental in bringing into being. One little glimpse will underscore this unselfish devotion. During the first World War, when Mission Boards, like many other organizations, found it extremely difficult to continue their administrative work, and many of the E.U.S.A. directors found it impossible to meet, Dr. Morgan, at that time resident at Mildmay in connection with his work for the Y.M.C.A., added to his almost overwhelming labours by inviting Mr. Stuart McNairn, General Secretary of the E.U.S.A., and Mr. B. A. Glanvill, its treasurer, to come to his home once a week to deal with the ever-pressing business of the young Society. It was in great measure due to the wise guidance of this great missionary statesman, and the courage and help he imparted to the overburdened secretary, that the Mission not only weathered but emerged triumphantly from those dark war years."

Each missionary's work is unique, each one's story a sequel to those written by the noble army that has gone before. In these later days the work of three intrepid travellers merits a page all its own. Mildred Cable, Evangeline French and her sister, Francesca French, have recorded some of their experiences in China, Mongolia and Tibet, often doing their writing 'en route', and under watchful and admiring eyes which had never before seen women behaving and speaking as did these. The strange hieroglyphics of the pencil provoked such observations as "What ability!" "What speed!" "They write in the scholar's flowing style!" "Much learning has destroyed their eyesight. Look, they all wear glasses!" Between them these three representatives of the China Inland Mission have given ninety-eight years to missionary work in the Far East.

Having been a close friend of Dr. Morgan for many years and a member of two of his churches, Miss Cable was asked to tell something of her association with him, and his influence on her life and work.

"It was in the days of his ministry at Tollington Park, North London, that I first met Campbell Morgan. Many people were impressed by the preaching of this remarkable young minister who had recently come to that church, and one Sunday morning I went to hear him. It happened to be a day of national rejoicing and festivity, and most of the preachers lent themselves to the popular attitude of self-complacency which came easily to Victorian England, praising themselves in her achievement in the world, and thanking God for the prosperity with which He had rewarded them. This young man, however, chose as his subject Paul's great challenge to the Church of Christ, 'The Offence of the Cross'. Most daringly he called on his hearers to view afresh the crucified Lord and face all the implications of His Cross and its offence. All who heard him did so with a renewed sense of urgency, and there was a great silence on the congregation when it left the church. Personally I went away realizing a little of the courage it must have taken to speak as he did on such an occasion, and I made up my mind to come and hear him again. I soon learned with great joy that he was shortly to start a course of study which he called a 'Bible School', and I attended one or two of the sessions with keen enjoyment. After my return from the summer vacation I decided that, in view of my hoped-for missionary career, training in the Scriptures was a necessary part of my equipment so, busy as I already was with my ordinary work and study, I decided to become a regular member of the Bible School and do all the work required in connection with it. One of the first courses given was on 'The Symbolism of the Tabernacle' of which a huge model was erected in the church. That proved most interesting but, fascinating as it was, its interest paled beside the teaching given in the next session on 'Books of the Bible'. We were taken through the content of each book, one book an evening. Needless to say that such a comprehensive survey of Holy Scripture entailed a tremendous amount of preparation during the week which elapsed between the lectures. I spent hours of each week in Dr. William's library, in Gordon Square, with my Bible and text-books, for I was determined that so far as in me lay, I would become familiar with each book. In this way Campbell Morgan gave his people an intelligent grasp of what the Bible was about, what was its scope, what its intention, and as we listened to his teaching we all began to see something of the wonder, the breadth and glory of our calling. At the end of each term examination papers were issued and the corrected papers were returned to each candidate. Later on we studied various books of the Bible in more detail. Who of those privileged to be present can ever forget the lectures on 'Acts of Apostles', as he liked to call the book, those on the Gospel of St. John and many others?

"Each of the courses of study was treated seriously, and though there were some who came, listened, enjoyed themselves, but went home forgetful of what they had heard, yet the inner circle of young men and women who were preparing themselves for the work of God knew that they were being offered a unique privilege, and vied with one another in becoming real students of the Word. The outcome of such teaching was to provoke a positively exciting interest in the Bible as its scope and pattern captured the mind. Many who were there caught the infection of their teacher's enthusiasm, and I was one of these, with the result that love of the Bible and a passion for its study has remained with me through life. For this alone I owe Campbell Morgan a lasting debt of gratitude.

"As a preacher he was soon making such a name for himself in London that it became the usual thing to see a long queue waiting for entrance to an already full church each Sunday evening. At the morning service definite Bible exposition was given. It took more than a year to go through St. Matthew's Gospel, passage by passage, and on other occasions he took some such subject as 'Christ's Dealing with Individuals', but the Sunday morning hour was always devoted to worship, to teaching and to meditation. The planning of the Sunday for his own group of young workers still appears to me to be one of the sanest and best that I have ever met. Every popular preacher has to recognize the fact that a large proportion of the crowd which listens to him is composed of 'yes-yes' people who echo his sentiments, love to be soothed by his eloquence, and settle down in the pews to an hour of easy enjoyment as soon as he begins to speak. There certainly were some such at Tollington Park, but the fault was not Campbell Morgan's. In the morning we were all welcomed and expected to profit from the teaching which he gave us, but in the evening two hundred of the young people were detailed to be out on soul-winning business, leaving more space for those who crowded into the church to find a seat. A very large music-hall in a poor part of London was hired, and there, every Sunday evening a children's service was held, and this was followed by an open-air meeting, after which the great hall was packed with men and women brought in from the streets for an evangelistic service. One of the senior deacons had charge of all arrangements, and to me fell the responsibility of sharing in the women's work. We were such a happy band, full of zeal and enthusiasm, our zest for prayer being maintained by thanksgiving for the men and women whom we saw Sunday by Sunday drift into the hall, and so often leave it having had an experience of meeting with Christ Himself and being made new creatures. Such work gave the young people an invaluable experience in Christian service. Nothing was planned on stereotyped lines, and it was up to each one individually to follow, to shepherd, to visit and to guide those who were brought to them, and they did it.

"Those who only knew Dr. Morgan in much later years can scarcely imagine the energy and tact with which he handled this church work. He was sometimes spoken of as unapproachable, and in later years this may have been a fact, but at that time, while it was true that men and women could never break in on his time of writing and preparation, and while he did not encourage personal interviews which would easily have absorbed all his spare time, he reserved every Sunday evening from five o'clock until service time for the group of workers. Each one brought his or her questions and each question was discussed. Together they learned, together they prayed, and together the difficulties were overcome. We all enjoyed that time to the full. He was free and so were we, he was full of interest in our findings and was keen to help us, and being all together under one teacher led to great comradeship and intimacy, strengthened the team spirit and repressed the devotion and adulation of the few.

"In due course my period of training came to an end and I left for China, but by this time Dr. Morgan had already accepted an appointment in America. When we parted he and Mrs. Morgan exacted a promise that on my way through America to Shanghai I would spend some time with them. So when my father, who travelled with me to New York, left me, I went straight to Baltimore to stay with my friends.

"Here I found the whole family keenly enjoying their Christmas holidays, for Dr. Morgan had just brought one of his long tours of Bible teaching to a close and was spending a month at home. He observed his own rigid rule of undisturbed mornings devoted to study, but in the afternoons he was ready for a walk, or a game, or to sit round the fire and talk with the boys. His old father was with us, always full of dry humour and wit, and making his own contribution to the general happiness. From Baltimore they all saw me off on the trans-continental train for the West Coast, and it was many, many years before we met again.

"However, we kept up an intimate correspondence all through the years I was in China, and Dr. Morgan was the one and only person to whom I felt I could write freely and frankly of life as I found it on the mission field. I remember writing to him of a fellow-worker who seemed to me to ring false, like a spurious coin, and who was yet so ready to tell of her wonderful experiences in the realm of the Spirit that she was invariably spoken of as 'so spiritual', an expression which from that day I have disliked intensely. As I heard it used then and on many other occasions it seemed to convey a suggestion of one who was distinctly unbalanced and who lacked the poise of the perfectly equipped man or woman of God's choice. I told him quite frankly about this woman, and asked his advice as to how to deal with a situation which had arisen. Never shall I forget his answer, which was brief, terse and emphatic: 'Trust her with your purse, my dear, but never trust her with your reputation'.

"Seven long years passed before I was back again on furlough, and we next met in London where Dr. Morgan had accepted the charge of Westminster Chapel. On the very first Sunday that I was at home he insisted that I spend the whole day there. The church itself, the Institute and all the buildings connected with it offered great scope to a man with a wide vision and the great gifts of Dr. Morgan. He took me round and showed me with immense joy and pride the various halls, all of which were teeming with young life. He spoke to me of his plans—such dreams he had of what might come to be in the future. 'Do you see these rooms?' he said. 'At present some very old people live there, but they will soon be moving on, and then we are going to have a Bible School, yes, a residential Bible School. We are going to have Westminster Extension, and the students will not only work here in England but scatter all over the world, and carry this Bible teaching tradition far and wide'. He had already collected a fine group of Sisters who superintended different departments in connection with the church, and Friday evening was already beginning to be a 'booked night' for crowds of Christian people who thronged the great building to hear the Bible lecture from the minister who taught with blackboard and chalk. It was grand, but to one who had been a member of that former inner circle it appeared that in fulfilling the wider ministry somehow the personal care and attention formerly given to the few was missing, and these larger audiences contained more of those who came to hear and enjoy it all without fulfilling the responsibilities of Christian service. Again he was taking one whole book each Friday night, but this time he stressed the theme of each book's message rather than its content. My comrades and I felt that we were indeed getting what missionaries so much need, some spiritual food which was not predigested for the easy-going hearer, but which demanded concentrated attention. I always had a place beside Mrs. Morgan, and we enjoyed together many of the little touches which we both knew and understood.

"We also heard of one of the latest schemes which was to hold a summer Bible School at Mundesley in Norfolk. Would we go? Of course we would. Such a spiritual treat was not to be missed, and that week immediately had priority on our programme. What a week of instruction it proved to be! Dr. Morgan lectured daily on the Bible, Dr. John A. Hutton on the Early Church, Dr. Stuart Holden enriched us from a never-failing store of spiritual experience, and the Welsh poet, Elvet Lewis, was at his best in that congenial atmosphere. Again we were being taught, and were not merely asked to listen to fine speeches or to the reiteration of time-worn stories. What an unforgettable evangelistic address

Campbell Morgan gave one night on 'She touched the hem of His garment!' Everyone present bowed before the Lord Who had spoken such words of power, and souls came to Christ that night. Yes, Campbell Morgan was at the very zenith of his power that year at Mundesley. Correspondents still remind me of the fervour, the earnestness, the Christian fellowship of those days, for they constitute a precious memory to many. When Mundesley was over we parted again for long years which I spent in China, and when I next met my friends it was in New York.

"The earlier years of my missionary life were largely devoted to the development of a girl's school in inland China. When I first went there educational facilities for girls were nil and I concentrated my effort on making these available to the daughters of Christian families. The effort was blessed by God and great success attended it. By degrees a staff of young Christian teachers was formed through whose influence a Christian standard was to be established and maintained throughout the school. That Christian standard of thought could only be satisfactorily developed by means of the knowledge of the Word of God and obedience to its commands. By reason of all the help which I had derived from my own Bible training, I was able to help these young Christian women also to become lovers of the Book. My own weekly Bible School with them was the most deeply appreciated class that they attended, and it became their own aim to help their pupils to gain the same love of the Bible as they themselves had found. Thanks to the generosity of friends at Westminster Chapel, rooms were built to accommodate women student-evangelists who devoted the bulk of their time to the study of the Scriptures. In later years this Bible School extension was carried on to oases towns on the border of the Gobi Desert where, in the most unlikely surroundings, men and women gave themselves to this work. Thus, to speak of one direction only, the influence of Campbell Morgan's passion for the Bible extended beyond the scope of human measurement.

"Meanwhile the great European war had come and gone, and as it was still impossible to return to England by Suez, my friends and I travelled home via the States. As soon as we reached New York we saw posters advertising a short-term Bible School to be conducted by Dr. Campbell Morgan. Such an unexpected chance was not to be missed and we promptly arranged to stop off and attend it. We secured rooms in a nearby hotel, and when we had finished the course we felt so spiritually refreshed that if, for nothing else, the journey across the Pacific seemed worth while. To this hour I cannot forget the lecture on our Lord as revealed in the first chapter of Revelation. The Christ lived before us, and the meeting closed in adoration and worship. Such a picture of the King in His beauty can only have been the result of long meditation, thought, and prayer.

"There was, however, a very serious change in my friend. He was more frail and seemed definitely weary. He had lost something of his amazing vitality, and one afternoon he fainted in the pulpit. This occurred just after he had made a statement which to me explained the change I saw in him. He spoke from the pulpit of how cruelly he had been maligned by enemies who accused him of unfaithfulness to his Master in regard to what they were pleased to call 'modernistic tendencies'. I had heard these very rumours on the China mission field which was a happy hunting ground for those who attacked in turn the reputations of F. B. Meyer, Stuart Holden, and Campbell Morgan, by circulating vicious reports accusing them of unfaithfulness in their ministry, and urging the missionary body to have nothing to do with any of these men. These lying accusations had followed Dr. Morgan throughout the States, and his persistent refusal to be drawn into any controversy, but to give himself only to constructive teaching was misinterpreted as a sign of weakness. On this particular afternoon he allowed himself to say publicly: 'You know where I stand. You know that these statements are lying propaganda. Once for all I reassert my loyalty to one Lord, to His Church, and to His Word, and there I leave it.' Alas, it did not so easily leave him, and the collapse which it caused remains a responsibility upon those who dared to fight a soldier of the Cross with weapons which have no place in the warfare of Christ's Kingdom.

"We parted in New York, and when I next saw Dr. Morgan it was many years later, and he was once more at Westminster Chapel. Back in the old place he appeared to be still keen and full of enjoyment in his work and service, but he had passed through another and painful crisis. One of his greatest desires had always been to see the establishment of a Bible College worthy of the name in London. He visualized himself as directing that College, and he confided that hope to a wealthy friend, thinking that he also might catch the vision and become a business partner in the concern. It was a mistake, for the friend refused to have anything to do with it. 'You are too old a man, Dr. Morgan, to become head of a Bible College,' he said brusquely. To a supersensitive temperament it was a mortal blow from which he never quite recovered his normal poise. He spoke to me of this incident several times in later years, and I realized the devastating effect that one man's unconsidered speech could have. Had he consulted a group of men and women of more insight they would, I believe, have rallied round him, and the dream would have become a reality. But the mischief was done and he banished from his mind that long-cherished hope, greatly to the loss of the Christian community in this land, for he could have directed such a concern with unequalled skill and experience.

"All through the long years Dr. Morgan's interest in missionary work was unflagging. Speaking for myself alone, I was conscious that he followed all I was doing in China with the most intense interest, and when I had to make a decision which entailed leaving the work in North China into which I had thrown all my heart's endeavour, to take an unknown path which was going to lead me to the dreary wastes of the Gobi Desert, he understood the depth of my need for guidance, and he was full of understanding and ympathy. He was one of the very few who at that time grasped the sense of urgency which was upon me, and he wrote me a long and most carefully thought-out letter reviewing the whole situation and giving his judgment upon it. As a team we knew that his intelligent understanding of a difficult situation secured for us a true and sympathetic adviser.

"'You will understand with what intense interest and sympathy I have read your letter. It is one of those communications in the presence of which one can only be reverently silent. When a divine call comes to any of the servants of God, others can but take up that attitude of quiet acquiescence and of gladness. It seems to me that there can be no room for any doubt that this is such a divine call. It has been given to you to do a great work in these twenty-one years, and I am perfectly certain you cannot lay it down without some sadness. Such sadness however, can have in it nothing save such as is the outcome of love for the work, and for those who have been gathered round about you. There can be nothing of regret or of resentment merging in your necessary and inevitable sorrow at separation. You must in such a case rest in the assurance that the One Who is calling you out to a new venture—or I would rather say adventure—will not fail to guide and govern in connection with the work which you now lay down.

"'You certainly are being called to one of the difficult outposts of the field, and I think you are justified in looking upon such a call as high honour conferred upon you by the One Who is directing all the affairs of His own work in this world, and moving with inerrant wisdom towards the great consummation. I need say no more on the subject, for I am certain that you and your fellow-workers know the place you have in my heart and thought and prayer. As you go to seek "something lost behind the ranges," it will surely be given you to find also; and both in the seeking, costly though it be, and the finding, glorious as it ever is, you will have fellowship with Him Who came to seek and to save the lost.'

"Referring to a sentence in my letter about the difficulty of guidance where there are many conflicting voices, he advised ignoring them, and went on to say: 'Yes, I do know a good deal about this heresy-hunting method. I am bound to say, however, that I do not see any escape from very real conflict in the coming days. Modernism is aggressive and impertinent in this country. It is assuming a scholarship, and arrogantly treating all those who do not accept its findings as uneducated. One would not care a bit about this as it affects one's personal pride; but one does care tremendously when vast multitudes of our young people are given the impression that all that we, for lack of a better word, call traditional, is obscurantist and unenlightened. I am strongly inclined to believe that the next few years will see a new cleavage, one in which it will be impossible for any public teacher not to take sides. If that comes, and I am in this country, there can be no question as to which side I stand on. Many things are done by the fundamentalists that I do not like; but as to the interpretation of Christian truth, I am with them entirely. So far I have gone quietly on as you know, doing my work without associating myself with any party. To do that will be increasingly difficult, and the difficulty will not be created by the fundamentalists, but by the modernists, and if a man who has taken my position is driven to declare himself there is no doubt as to where I stand.'

"I was back in England when war was declared, and travel across the world became impossible, therefore I was much in London and I saw Dr. Morgan at frequent intervals. There was always the same warm welcome from him and from Mrs. Morgan when I went to St. Ermins, and he always wanted to hear where I had been, what I was doing, and what the reaction was to the messages given. His keenness often surprised me. I remember showing him a letter I had received which bore the simple signature, 'Elijah', and I told him how proud I was to have Elijah's autograph, even though the message it bore was a reproof from some crank telling me that women should keep silence in the Church. 'Let him go up like his namesake, my dear, in a chariot of fire', was his immediate retort. Dr. Morgan had strong ideas on the subject of women's ministry, and I have heard him express the opinion that those who attempted to repress gifts which were undoubtedly bestowed by the Holy Spirit might well find themselves under condemnation as having resisted the Spirit and helped to rob the Church of her heritage. I heard him express himself strongly on this subject on one occasion when Mrs. Bramwell Booth occupied his pulpit, speaking with great power and conviction. Here again, however, he allowed no controversial subject to find a place in his preaching lest it detract from the urgent commission which God had laid upon him. Nothing must interfere with that dominating purpose, though by word and by action he unhesitatingly showed what his own convictions were. At St. Ermins he still worked on, even beyond the limits of his strength, and carried the responsibility of Westminster until it was obvious he could no longer do so. Only then did the Church call Dr. Martyn Lloyd-Jones to the position of co-pastor. Gradually but certainly the day came when Dr. Morgan could do no more, and must perforce leave the teaching and preaching to others while he prepared himself for the journey which lay ahead. His interest was as keen as ever in all that took place both in Westminster and in the particular service of friends who talked with him, and he never seemed to forget the incidents which they told him. The decline, however, was quite evident to all. As he once wrote, he had lived in the presence of Jesus of Nazareth for all the long years of his ministry, had learned from Him and dwelt with Him, and now we all felt that the day when the servant would pass into the King's presence would be a day of great rejoicing. When it came to the last hours and the things of the earth were passing away from his consciousness, that presence must have become more real and certainly more vital. Campbell Morgan was, I believe, a messenger to his generation of the power of the Word of God, of the reality of its message, and of the assurance that the man or woman who would give time and take trouble to dig deeply for its hidden treasure would certainly not fail of great reward."

★ ★ ★ ★ ★ ★

An even wider ministry is that of the pen. Dr. Morgan's books were, almost without exception, sermons and lectures reported first, then edited for publication. The first little volume, *Discipleship*, bears this inscription: 'To my Wife——In whose unobtrusive and consistent discipleship I have found the inspiration of service, and that sense of "sanctuary" in the home which has been largely the strength of service also—I dedicate this, my first book'.

Mr. Fleming H. Revell, a brother of Mrs. D. L. Moody, was a friend of Dr. Morgan from early Northfield days. For more than half a century the company which he founded has published the American editions of the more than seventy books bearing Dr. Morgan's name. They have found their way and brought their message into many homes in many lands, as has the *Westminster Record* bearing his sermons, Bible analyses and lectures. By means of a fund maintained during the Westminster years for the free distribution of Dr. Morgan's books to missionaries, these were circulated far and wide over the globe. Hundreds of letters of appreciation were received for the inspiration brought by these publications. Indeed, Dr. Morgan himself estimated that 'thousands of ministers' had told him by word and letter of help received in this way.

Some of his work was translated into Bulgarian, Dutch, and French, as well as into the dialects of the Far East. In the summer of 1906 Dr. Morgan received the following interesting letter:

"I have read your sermon . . . which you preached on the 9th March at the Westminster Pulpit. This pamphlet containing your sermon was handed to me by a friend of mine. I do praise the Lord for allowing me the privilege of reading this, and for the sweet and edifying message it conveyed to me. It has helped me greatly, and lifted from off my eyes the scales of ignorance and difficulty that have been there before. . . . Now I feel joyous and the darkness dispelled. Your explanations of various things are so explicit, and your illustrations so simple and clear that I fully understand it (through God's Spirit). I believe you will be wondering who I am that thus write to you. I am a Chinese boy of seventeen years, who has been brought to the knowledge and love of God when about five, and during that time to now my knowledge and love to Him increased. I have been an orphan from my very youngest days and have no relative in this world. My foster parents have cared for me to the age of fourteen, and from that time I have been in this world alone to support my own life (through God's love and grace). I have practically been most of my time in a boarding school, and had no fatherly or motherly love and advice. But these are all made up by my Heavenly Father's love and tenderness. . . . I am at present working in the National Bank of China, Hong Kong, and am earning my own living. I will soon be leaving it, and am going to Canton for training to become a medical missionary. I feel that since God has so wonderfully loved and led me I must also do something for Him. I am sure you will pardon me for thus writing you, but I often heard and read of you, and saw your photo in magazines. . . . The more I read of you I am more and more drawn toward you and I feel that I love you. May God bless your labours for Him, and may your sermons and homely talks be helpful to all those who come under its hearing."

The daughter of a minister, troubled because her faith was shaken by her College professors, came across two of Dr. Morgan's books, *The Practice of Prayer*, and *The True Estimate of Life*. They helped her to fight her way through 'college clouds of doubt'. She found in them 'the teacher who to *me* seemed most like Jesus, whose spirit was most like His.'

After a radio broadcast in August, 1926, the British Broadcasting Company sent Dr. Morgan a post card bearing on one side a picture of the beautiful interior of the Groote

Kerk, Preekspoel, Haarlem. It was addressed to 'The Minister whose sermon was sent out by radio last Sunday night, August 29th, by the 'London Calling, Daventry, England'. It read: "Dear Colleague, I hope this card will reach you. Just when I had returned from my church (I preached from the chair you see in the picture. Subject: Shamgar, Judges 3. 31), I heard your excellent and stimulating sermon about the calling of Christ to holiness, hope and heroism. I received it as a voice from heaven. You have strengthened me for my work. What a blessed moment to hear your congregation singing! I felt it to be the communion of saints! Receive the salutations of a brother in Christ. God bless you and your work.

"L. D. POOT."

Letters of appreciation of Dr. Morgan's writings from his fellow-ministers must have brought him much joy as he passed the three score and ten milestone. Typical of these is a short note: "In my early ministry I went carefully through 'John' with the aid of Godet and Alford, and now am repeating the journey with the aid of Morgan, and I want to write and thank you. It is thrilling! You are a seer. You have vision, you have imagination, you have evangelical passion. Ten thousand thanks and then ten thousand more!"

Near and far away the ministry of the pen, and in later days the mystery of radio reached 'beyond the scope of human measurement'. What Dr. Morgan once said of another in reference to this larger circle of influence might appropriately be applied to himself. He called him 'a minister of the grace which is confined to no one channel, but filling and flooding them all reaches seeking souls; and then overflows them, and stretches forth to the waste places where the channels have not yet reached, making them also to blossom as the rose and to be fruitful as Lebanon.'

CHAPTER XI

The Smaller Circle

IN most lives the word 'smaller' is applicable in describing the circle of human contact—those we meet and affect personally during our lifetime. In others the word can be used in a comparative sense only. This smaller circle, in Campbell Morgan's life, was a very large one. It was remarkable not so much in the number of people who actually saw and heard and met him, but in the fact that these people were as widely different from each other as it is possible for people to be. This record has attempted to emphasize the catholicity of his appeal. Campbell Morgan knew how to interpret Christ's Imperial Kingship to the high-born, His demands upon the will to the intellectual, His wisdom to the scholar, His sympathy to the poor, His simplicity to the humble, His chivalry to the young, His mission to the worker, His authority to the leader, His beauty to the child, His skill to the professional man and His answer to every need of humanity. He was, indeed, as was once said of him, 'God's gift to all the churches', but his appeal extended far beyond ecclesiastical boundaries.

His attitude toward those of other faiths was exclusively broad. He had great sympathy with both Roman Catholics and Jews, and the fact that this was so was because he had a deeper understanding than most Protestants of the tenets of their faith, having taken the time and trouble to study and examine them with minute thoroughness. But this broadmindedness excluded the things that make a Romanist a Romanist and a Jew a Jew. There were tenets of faith in which he differed profoundly with the Romanist, and bounds beyond which he would not go. With no rancour in his heart for the Jew he was not willing to say that they had all things in common because they had not. He had no patience with a certain careless and sentimental preaching from the text of 'brotherhood', when that kind of preaching trespassed beyond the New Testament interpretation of that much maligned word.

Yet in spite of these convictions which he was at no pains to conceal—or it might be nearer the truth to say, because of them—his honest and scholarly approach to the Bible drew those of other faiths to hear him, to continue with him through series of lectures and expositions, and to win for him some close friends.

A case in point occurred during the later years of the first Westminster ministry in his contact with a priest in his Bible School congregation. Dr. Morgan's position as it is revealed in this correspondence is typical of his relationship with those of the Roman faith.

Early in 1919 he received the following letter:
"My Dear Master,

"In 1911 at the Kingsway Hall I heard you, and with a kind of youthful enthusiasm and ardour I thought you the greatest preacher in the world. I heard you there last Tuesday, and though the youthfulness is over the enthusiasm remains. I thank you from a full heart for all you have taught me, and for the understanding and love for the Scriptures you wonderfully and almost magically kindled within me. I am a Roman priest, and I could listen to you with attention and pleasure even when you spoke on South America! Isn't that a test of my reverence for you? We do really—we Romans—love Jesus Christ supremely, uniquely and *Risen*, but the Cross is to us the *sign* of the vastness of God's love for us. It is our way of looking at Him. I envy your children who learned from you the Word of God.

"Yours very sincerely,
"R. W——."

Dr. Morgan replied:
"My dear Father W——,

"I am almost ashamed to reply to your extremely kind note . . . after so long an interval, but the delay has been unavoidable. . . . I do thank you most heartily for your words. To have been permitted in any way to be of help to one who is in the vocation of Christian ministry is a high privilege. So far as I am personally concerned I have long felt that, whereas there are tremendous differences between my ecclesiastical convictions and those of such as yourself, there are, in spite of these differences real facts of spiritual union which cannot be destroyed. I shall thank God all my life for a friendship given to me for a period now nearly thirty years ago, with a priest of your order—one Father McC——. He and I had long conversations of the most intimate kind on things of the deepest moment. The result was that while neither of us was moved from our personal convictions, we both came to understand the position of the other better—at least it was so in my case—and for me that was a lasting gain. Yes, I agree that your ability to listen to me on South America was a proof, may I say, of your friendship—if not of reverence. I saw you there—and wished you had not been. Still, enough of that matter. Your face has been familiar to me for some years, both at Westminster and at Leicester. I have refrained in every way from attempting to invade your anonymity, and am the more grateful for this brotherly letter from you. I could wish that we might some day meet, but if that may not be, I, at least, shall look forward to knowing you in that life which lies beyond, and which to me is far more real than the life of to-day.

"I only trust that no word of mine has ever caused pain to the heart of any member of the body of Christ, even when I have spoken under stress of strong conviction of some things which to me have seemed to wrong the Christ Himself. Again thanking you for your letter,
"I am, my dear friend,
"Yours gratefully and sincerely,
"G. CAMPBELL MORGAN."

Three days later came another letter:
"My Dear Master,
"Your letter to me was a very great and unexpected joy, and I thank you for it from the very bottom of my heart. I

am staying in London until Easter fulfilling a number of engagements. I should be so glad to meet you, if only for once in my life, but I know how full your life is, and how many persons have claim on your time while I have none. I wonder if I might come into the vestry for a few minutes after your lecture next Friday evening? All next week I shall be busy all day, but the following week I should be free in the evenings. But should it be difficult for you to arrange a meeting I shall quite understand, and I can quite well live on what you have *done* for me. I know there are aspects of Catholicism which must anger those who are not of my communion, as there are aspects which sadden many who are. But the Church of Rome has produced great saints, and surely she should be judged by her greatest children, as a writer is judged by his best works. . . . I thank you again for all you have taught me for many years now, and for the love of God you so wonderfully nurtured in my soul.

"I remain,
"Yours most sincerely,
"N. W——."

The diary for the following Friday says: "To-night was the last night of the Bible School (for this season) and we had a very large audience. Saw a number of people afterwards including Father W——." They met again during summer visits to England in later years.

The sequel to the story of Father W—— came in a letter which reached Dr. Morgan in London during the summer of 1928.

"Dear Dr. Campbell Morgan,

"Knowing how occupied your time and thought must be I have refrained from troubling you, but lest you should miss a face you may have hoped to see, my loved and only brother, N. W—— passed from us last January.

"He had been a Dominican for thirty years, but some months before he died he returned to Protestantism. He was curate in the Church of England for six months at M——, and afterwards at R——, in the hospital of which town he

died. He was so happy, keen and active. His books that I brought him were mostly your books, and show evidence of careful reading. He greatly valued your friendship, and I thought you might care to know how much your interest and sympathy had at last brought him peace and the comfort of strength . . .
"In deep gratitude,
"M. J——."

In August and September of 1927 there appeared in *The Catholic World* some articles by Mr. Theodore Maynard, the poet. An extract from the August number reads as follows:

"My father was pleased when . . . I began attending Westminster Chapel where the minister filled, Sunday by Sunday, the huge building to overflowing. An hour before the evening service there was a queue waiting for the doors to open. The congregation was not only large but distinguished. Several Cabinet Ministers, including Mr. Lloyd George, were fairly regular attenders. Other members of the congregation were the Spenders of *The Westminster Gazette*, Mr. W. T. Stead, and Gladstone's friend and pall-bearer, old Lord Armistead. . . . What interested me was the enthusiasm of the large number of young men and women.

"The minister of Westminster Chapel at that time, and for some years to come, was Dr. Campbell Morgan. From this preacher, a man of the most extraordinary eloquence and spiritual power, I received so many profound intellectual and spiritual benefits that I am glad of the opportunity of acknowledging them. There followed for me a time of rapid growth, and of a new vision of liberality, for though my minister was what would be called in America a fundamentalist (and as such highly acceptable to my parents), he preached familiar doctrines with an unfamiliar power of imagination, and with a graciousness that was a revelation to me. All his sermons—and each took an hour to deliver—were closely expository of the Scriptures. He preached twice every Sunday, and managed to gather 1,500 people every Friday night for a lecture on the Bible. . . .

"Years afterwards when I had become a Catholic, the Prior of the Dominicans in London told me that he never missed an opportunity of going to listen to Dr. Morgan; and he even instituted lectures on the Bible in the St. Dominics' Church, and followed, to some extent, Dr. Morgan's own method. Some years later still, when I met Dr. Morgan by accident in America, he spoke to me in warm terms of the Dominican Prior—'a great soul', he called him.

"When I had finished my first book of poems I sent a copy to Dr. Morgan from whom I got one of the most appreciative letters ever written to me. 'Your poems,' he wrote, 'will first be treasured by the Church and then by the world'."

A brief quotation from Mr. Maynard in the September number of the same magazine refers to Dr. Morgan in this way:

"Other powerful influences were at work upon me. Rev. R. J. Campbell was stirring my religious world with his New Theology. I was not immediately affected by it because I was devoted to Dr. Morgan who belonged to a very different school."

★ ★ ★ ★ ★ ★

Dr. Morgan's early experiences in the Jewish school in Birmingham and their influence on his life were debts which he appreciated and never forgot. Returning to Birmingham in later years, the diaries make references to visits to Mr. Levy, showing that he not only remembered the schoolmaster, but respected and honoured him. It is not so remarkable that this should be so as it is that the Hebrew youngsters to whom he was Junior Master should remember and honour *him* long years after this early association. These two letters greeted Dr. Morgan after his 79th birthday. There seems nothing to indicate that either of these knew that the other was writing:

"Dear Dr. Morgan,

"I have just learned that you have celebrated your birthday, and feel that I must write you a line to congratulate you on that event, and to express the hope that you may be spared for many years to continue your sphere of service and usefulness.

"It is asking you to look back many years to recall the curly-headed youngster affectionately (I hope!) called 'Sammy' by E. Lawrence Levy, yourself, and my schoolfellows, but I look back to those happy days with many pleasant recollections, and not the least to your own kindliness to us youngsters, and to your inspiration which I can honestly assure you has proved on very many occasions in after years of great help to me in solving life's difficulties. . . .

"Sam J. Levi."

"Dear Dr. Morgan,

"Only on two occasions during the past fifty-five years have I had the opportunity of a few minutes' talk with you —once on New Street Railway Station platform, and the last time about ten years ago after service (and your sermon) at the Free Trade Hall, in Manchester. I can hardly expect, therefore, that you will remember a lad of about eleven years of age whose great joy it was to walk with you from school to your rooms in Great Colmore Street, and then raced home to his own dinner full of joy and pride that he was one of the privileged boys of the school.

"I often wonder if you realized in those days the hero-worship you inspired in all of us. I can only say that so far as my brother Leonard and I were concerned, the great height to which you have attained in the ecclesiastical world has not surprised us. And now, please, accept our very hearty congratulations on your recent birthday, together with the hope of many more years of good health

"Harry Emanuel."

★ ★ ★ ★ ★ ★

No minister had more friends in denominations other than his own than did Campbell Morgan. While he had no zeal for organic union he never lost sight of the fundamental unity of the Spirit, and was at home in any pulpit so long as he could preach the Word without restriction. He believed that the Scriptural form of Church government was congregational, and that the Scriptural form of baptism was by immersion, but would never make an issue of the barriers which divide evangelical groups. He was criticized because he declined more than once to be nominated for the Chairmanship of the Congregational Union of England and Wales. He knew all the arguments and the advantages of leadership in organizational work, the constructive use of the committee and the administrative office. His reluctance to take a part in these things was not because he did not believe in them and what they accomplished for the Kingdom of God in the world, but because he did not believe that he himself was fitted or intended for this work. He saw in it something that would limit his time and restrict his activities and side-track his energies from the 'one thing'—the preaching and teaching of the Bible. If others misunderstood and saw in it a shirking of responsibility he regretted it, but it never swayed his judgment. When a flurry of censure crossed his way his attitude was: "It will blow over. Meanwhile, I go quietly on with my work."

His position was vindicated in that the 'work' to which he referred benefitted churches of all denominations. The itinerant ministry from its beginning in the Potteries to the far-flung journeys through the United States and Canada, was carried on under the auspices of first one and then another. Only the building and its name would be different. The congregation which assembled was universally composed of members from all the denominations—and of none. Of such is the power of the Book. In many places churches would unite in supporting a union meeting asking Dr. Morgan to come. With such groups he was most happily at home. After a meeting in Calgary, Alberta, in May, 1921, in which six denominations united, a resolution of 'grateful and devout appreciation' of Dr. Morgan's ministry was tendered by the representatives of 'the Anglican, Baptist, Congregational, Disciples, Methodist, and Presbyterian Churches of Calgary'.

A custom established during the Westminster days was both interesting and impressive. At Communion services visitors from other lands were asked to stand and tell from whence they came. Dr. Morgan's diary during those years tells so often of these services in which "we welcomed friends from all parts of the world." Other insignia was incidental; they bore His name and sign; for this moment of time 'they came from the east and west and from the north and south' to 'sit down in the kingdom of God'.

At the beginning of every calendar year, in his methodical way, Dr. Morgan went through and destroyed the vast accumulation of correspondence that had accrued during the past twelve months. But a small portion of it was preserved, and it is not difficult to understand why. There is a certain kind of letter which takes a slice out of a life and gives it without reservation to another. It bridges the barriers of age, location, position, and vocation. Dr. Morgan was no sentimentalist, but he was an extremely sensitive person. This sensitivity was not clouded by flattery, but it was responsive to sincere appreciation.

Some of these letters were from people who had been members of his Bible Schools, or had somewhere attended his ministry. Such a letter from London reached him in the United States in 1923.

"Dear Sir,

"This is a 'must be' written letter, for gratitude and thankfulness compel me. . . . I am a London city missioner. We have a Prayer Meeting on Wednesday nights. Having been for all too short a time a member of your B.T.A. I thought, why not make the address at the Prayer Meeting a Bible Study? I did, and we have gone through Matthew and Genesis, taking nearly three years in the study of them. Some time back a number of *Westminster Records* were sent to the Mission house, and the bundle I obtained was for the months containing your expositions of Matthew. While I had other books to help me yours was chief, and I told the people so lest they should think another prophet had arisen!

One day, going along Paternoster Row, I saw paper-bound copies of your *Genesis* and *Analyzed Bible* for sale, very cheap. I plunged, and *Genesis, Romans, Isaiah* (2 vols.) are now among my treasures. . . . Now, Dr. Morgan, what I want to say is, practically all who came, and our numbers grew, nearly everyone spoke of the great help these studies have been. Again and again I heard how different ones have been instructed, helped, encouraged, and to several the Bible has become a new Book. The meetings were times of intense interest and power. For myself, the Master knows how again and again I have looked up in my preparation and thanked Him, yes, and sometimes with tears, sir, of pure joy, and an overflow feeling for such revelation of truth, and for such truly inspired opening up of the precious Book. . . . Please, will you accept this sincere tribute from a few thankful people. I know you give God the praise—so do we—but for all your hours and months of hard study and toil, thank you, sir. . . . God bless you always, everywhere. I wish you were back. "Yours faithfully,

"————————————."

A minister in Yorkshire tells how, as a boy of 14, he heard Dr. Morgan in Birmingham, and felt in that moment a call to the ministry. "Suddenly I lost sight of you," he writes, "and became conscious of the presence of Christ."

The pastor of a large city church in the United States, wrote in 1925: "To me you are . . . the King of Preachers. . . . Your preaching has ever had an immeasurable influence on me. It always moves me to the deepest and most profound depths; the sweep of it, the matchless might of it, the rushing power and resistless beauty of it astound and amaze me."

★   ★   ★   ★   ★   ★

Dr. Morgan had been closely associated with the Salvation Army in its early days. Its founder, General William Booth, had been one of the heroes of his youth, and he welcomed any opportunity to champion the Army's cause and co-operate with its work. During the three wonderful months in England, in 1928, when Dr. Morgan packed Westminster every Sunday and Friday, he received the following letter from a Colonel in the Salvation Army.

"You will never know, my dear Campbell Morgan, the great depth of gratitude and sense of obligation under which you have placed large numbers of Salvationists, and particularly Salvation Army officers. . . . Your congregations at Westminster on Sunday nights include from thirty to forty officers of whose presence you may not be aware because they come in civilian attire, not desiring to attract attention. They have ranged from the Principal of our International Training College, the Vice-Principals on the Men's and Women's side, to missionary officers from Java, India, East Africa, and the West Indies. They speak with reverence of these occasions and with deep affection for yourself. I thought you should know."

In May of 1940, when Dr. Morgan had virtually eliminated all outside engagements, he consented to address a Salvation Army Meeting in Queen's Hall, and in August of 1941, when he rarely attended any meetings or services apart from those at Westminster Chapel, he went to Central Hall to hear General George Carpenter.

The General wrote to Dr. Morgan in February, 1943: "You have been a good deal in my thought and prayers lately, for I have realized . . . how much your heart would lead you into special activities for God at such a time as this, yet you must be content to see the world go by without taking the share that has been your custom for so many years. My heart has been drawn to you also through the re-reading of a precious little book of yours which I bought in New Zealand more than thirty years ago—*The Practice of Prayer*. It has refreshed and stimulated me again and again over the years. . . . The Lord be with you in comfort and strength."

General and Mrs. Carpenter were among the close friends who visited Dr. and Mrs. Morgan in the last months. Truly the link with the Army was life-long and life-strong.

During the General's last illness in Australia, in 1948, Mrs. Carpenter wrote an appreciation of Dr. Morgan to his family:

"General Carpenter did not know Dr. Campbell Morgan intimately until he came to London as world leader of the Salvation Army in 1939. He likes to recall his first sight of Dr. Morgan in about 1912, when your father was giving lunch-hour addresses at Bishopsgate Chapel. The General says: 'His easy approach to the people greatly appealed to me, and as I had opportunity I sought to hear him when I saw his services announced in London.' Often have I heard my husband quote from your father's thoughts on the Lord's Prayer; he also greatly values his books, *The Practice of Prayer*, *The Great Physician*, *The Parables and Metaphors of our Lord*, being among his favourites.

"My husband's leadership commenced just after the war began, and on his arrival in London he sensed a fear on the part of the churches to bring together large companies of people. There seemed to be a danger of the Church—including the Salvation Army—largely closing its doors, though the theatres and public houses showed no similar disposition. Partly as a challenge to this attitude, my husband instituted 'Days with God', throughout the United Kingdom. These meetings were largely attended and proved a powerful incentive to faith, and also gave a distinct lead to spiritual aggressiveness. The General invited Dr. Morgan to at least two such meetings in London. He came with Mrs. Morgan and fully entered into the spirit of the gatherings. Though very frail he gave on one occasion a moving address. . . . Dr. Morgan wrote to General Carpenter that, upon their return from Central Hall, Mrs. Morgan remarked, 'These people (meaning the Salvation Army) are the spiritual power in this country to-day'. The Doctor added, 'I entirely agreed with her'. The General says, 'This expression was received not with any sense of exultation, but in humility before God, praying that I might in some way in keeping with the experience of such honoured servants of God, strengthen faith and confidence in the Divine, and in the joy and power of lives fully surrendered to Christ.'

"My contacts with Dr. Morgan were, perhaps, more intimate. I heard him thirty-five years ago when he lectured on the Bible in Highbury Quadrant Church. . . . I enjoyed and profited by his masterly teaching, and at the close of his address he gave his personal testimony to the power of the Word of God in his own life during a time of wilderness experience. I have held his words as a treasure, and have shared them with others more times than I can recall.

" . . . So dear had Campbell Morgan become to us that when our son, who had been a schoolmaster (in Art) for years, turned from the way of the Cross to the world, I felt I could not bear it, and went to your father to tell him of my sorrow. He listened, full of sympathy and understanding. 'Give him time, give him time,' he counselled. 'Don't hurry him'. And to add to his kindness he saw and spoke with the young artist. . . . That son came voluntarily to turn from earthly honours and pleasures and chose God and His Kingdom. . . . He is a soul-winner to-day.

"The Doctor wrote me a warm commendation of my short life of William Booth.

"You will realize from the foregoing that I remember Campbell Morgan with gratitude for many reasons: for his books, for his testimony to the Word of God and of deliverance in great temptation by the Word of God, for his sympathy with a mother in anxiety for a well-beloved son, and for his generous commendation of my own work.

"I suppose you have heard that in his early years . . . Campbell Morgan asked to see Mrs. Catherine Booth and offered himself for Salvation Army service. Mrs. Booth, with unselfish vision, felt she could only counsel him, 'Go on with the work you are doing'."

★ ★ ★ ★ ★ ★

The same man who could evoke such letters from leaders in the Salvation Army, inspired similar appreciation from those in other branches of the ministry and other walks of life. In 1928 the Assistant Bishop of London wrote: "When I have had a spare moment now and then I have come to sit under you, and never once without getting real inspiration."

During his itinerant ministry in the United States in 1930, Dr. Morgan lectured to the students of the Baptist Theological Seminary in Louisville, Kentucky. Dr. A. T. Robertson, who held the Chair of New Testament Interpretation in the College at that time was, in Dr. Morgan's estimation, the greatest scholar of New Testament Greek of his generation. In a letter to Dr. Morgan, following his visit, he said: "I never heard you preach with more power than last week. You were heard by five hundred preachers, and you left a deep impression of the necessity of studying the Bible seriously and earnestly. . . . You have tremendously strengthened my own work and ideals. My students are seeing that it is really worth while to dig into the Hebrew and the Greek. Blessings on you."

A letter of another year tells how the writer as a boy, neglected, ragged, and often hungry, wandered into a hall and heard Campbell Morgan preach. In that moment he resolved to become a minister, later was accepted by the Methodist denomination, came to the United States, and was serving a Presbyterian Church, sending his children to College, one son training for the ministry. He says: "From that night you became my great human ideal. . . . I think I have read every book you have written. I placed your picture on the fly-leaf of my Bible, and I have never stood up to preach without first turning to look upon it. It somehow helps me more than anything else."

The wife of a University professor expressed her appreciation this way: "You help us to want to give thanks to God with more understanding hearts."

Dr. Morgan's appeal to the business man is revealed in a letter from the chief executive of a large manufacturing company in the Middle East of the United States. As teacher of adult Bible Classes he expressed thanks for the help he had received from Dr. Morgan's ministry. "Your method of analyzing and exposition is so similar to my training in the business world . . . that it has been a most delightful experience." Through the studies in the book of Matthew "has come the crystallization of a life purpose to translate these things of the Kingdom into definite testimony in the business world. . . . It is entirely in the experimental stage but we trust God will ultimately use it, not only for internal testimony, but also in some degree to those without, as to the blessedness of the rule of heaven's King in all our lives."

Physicians were among Dr. Morgan's friends on both sides of the Atlantic, and two at least held official positions in his churches. Dr. Drummond Robinson writes of his association with Dr. Morgan during the Westminster days:

"I look upon my friendship with Dr. Morgan as one of God's greatest and best gifts to me. It started at the beginning of his ministry at Westminster Chapel and lasted for the rest of his life. During the earlier part of this period I was associated with him as one of his church officers.

"He was certainly the most remarkable and gifted man that I have ever known personally, and one of the most interesting and entertaining as well as sympathetic and warm and tender-hearted of my friends.

"He possessed a striking presence. . . . His voice was of pleasing quality, and his reading of the Scriptures or of hymns was arresting. He possessed the qualities which might, I should suppose, have made of him a great actor.

"There was poetry in his blood and music in his voice. He was able to express his thoughts in poetic and beautiful language always apt and illuminating.

"Truly 'our hearts burned within us' as he, like his divine Master, 'opened to us the Scriptures'. His knowledge of the exact meaning of words was great, and he exercised a nice discrimination in their use. How often have I sighed inwardly with regret when he terminated a three-quarter-hour sermon which seemed to have been less than half that length. . . . In dealing with passages of Scripture he displayed an aptitude for analyzing them that would have done credit, in their respective spheres, to an architect or an anatomist.

"What a sense of humour and love of fun was his! He was a prince of companions, full of playfulness and laughter, with a zest for a game of tennis or billiards delightful to his friends.

"And what a sympathetic and large-hearted man he was! And how loving and well-beloved! Even little children loved him. Mine did.

"Though he could not have failed to recognize his own ability he was humble-minded and free from conceit, and he was quick to see ability in others and generous in giving it praise. He seemed to be entirely free from professional jealousy.

"A genius? Yes. But what a delightfully human and altogether lovable genius!"

Another physician, an elder in Dr. Morgan's church in Philadelphia, wrote him in 1930: "Rest assured that unless hindered by my professional duties I cannot afford to miss one of your expositions. It has been a source of constant delight to me to find at last a minister who believes in a supernatural religion and a real Kingdom of God on this planet working and functioning."

A letter from Dr. F. A. Robinson of Toronto, of February, 1943, was written to give Dr. Morgan the following information:

"One of the finest Christian Supervisors of Nurses writing a few days ago says in her letter amongst other things: 'Your reference to Dr. Campbell Morgan took me back over the years. I spent one summer as a young girl at Northfield, and heard him speak to vast audiences, and after one of his addresses on a sweltering summer night, so powerful was the message and so real the glory of the King that it seemed to me the audience stopped breathing. . . . I for one owe him much of spiritual understanding from that night so many years ago. It is such people as Dr. Morgan and yourself who keep the light bright in this stricken world'."

There is usually such a gulf fixed between the man in the pulpit and the child in the pew as can only be spanned by actual personal contact. Did Dr. Morgan stand this test, too? Or was this little writer in California, in 1929, prompted by adults? Since there is no way of knowing, the fact that Dr. Morgan kept the page of childish script shows that, in his eyes at least, it was of value!

"Dear Dr. Morgan,

"I am a little girl, eight years old, but I have been attending your lectures and have enjoyed them so much that they *put me to sleep*. So please accept $1.00 thank offering, and while I know you are *worth more* yet it comes right from my heart."

Letters from former students at Gordon College in Boston, and the Biblical Institute in Los Angeles, were among those which came as 'bread upon the waters'. *The Great Physician* was the book most often cited by these as being most helpful and inspiring. In the war years, when the immediate present was very dark, these candles of love and appreciation threw their beams very far.

All his life Dr. Morgan's habit was to answer each letter personally, but on his eightieth birthday, in 1943, this was impossible because of the number of those who remembered. His way of acknowledging them was characteristic of him both in its manner and in its content. A card was printed and sent to each one. It bore the following message:

9TH DECEMBER, 1943.

"This is my eightieth birthday. I am simply snowed under with love messages. This is not a complaint. I remember that 'He giveth His snow like wool'. Warming to that which is under the snow. For your contribution to this, please accept my sincerest thanks. Believe me, this is a real expression of appreciation due to the fact that I am quite unable to answer all by personal letters.

"G. CAMPBELL MORGAN."

CHAPTER XII

The Inner Circle

'ATARAXIA' was not only the name of a house, but the keynote of the inner circle of Dr. and Mrs. Morgan's family and friends. The 'undisturbedness' in which they moved was shared by those who were privileged to cross the threshold of their home wherever it happened to be, and breathe for a while its invigorating air. It is said that old homes have an aura of their own, but the Morgans lived in many homes, some old, some new, and each became an ataraxia, adopting the personality of those who for a time lent it their presence.

It was an undisturbedness of the spirit, a serenity at the core which had nothing to do with quiet footsteps and muted voices, for the Morgan family was an uninhibited and lusty crowd, and the house hummed with the activities of work and play. Neither did it resound with laughter and singing all day long, for there were times when children cried, brothers and sisters disagreed, servants complained, tempers frayed, and possessions were lost and found, as happens in all large and normal families. But these were surface things, a troubling of the waters that had no power to disturb the calm depths beneath.

Writing objectively of Dr. and Mrs. Morgan in their public and social relationships it is fitting to use the names by which they were known in those circles. But such a formal address would be foreign and stilted in the inner circle of home. If it is permitted for the writer to be personal at all, surely it is in such a chapter as this!

I think it was Mother who was the lodestone of the family rather than Dad. He was such a dynamic and positive person, just as much so at home as on the public platform, and the atmosphere became charged with his presence as soon as he entered the house. While we all adored him and would have changed him not an iota, there was a saying that belonged to certain times—usually of short duration—that 'whatever you say is sure to be wrong!' These periods were accepted philosophically, until suddenly his sense of humour and his inborn courtesy asserted themselves and the family pulse beat normally again. But whatever it was that came to pass Mother was superlative. She never lost her poise nor was she ever shaken in her tranquillity. She taught by her example that most that irks and vexes can be eased by a cup of tea and a few quiet words, that daily strength is given for daily needs, and that no problem will be solved by neglecting the common duties of life. Beds must still be made and meals prepared, and in homely tasks is balm for wounded pride and torn emotions. Her treatment of a hurt child she carried over into the graver and deeper injuries of the spirit—"Take his mind off it, Jill. Gran'ma has a surprise for you, dear. Come and see!" and tears were dried and cut knees bandaged, the pain eased in the delights of a box of buttons or a rosy apple. She found time for a very large correspondence, but would put everything aside for an unhurried and comfortable chat. With her home-spun philosophy she could put together the puzzling pieces of one's life and reduce a mountain of grievance to its mole-hill proportions.

Dad was entirely dependant upon her for she was 'Martha' and 'Mary' to him, and the hub of their universe to her growing boys and girls, in time proving equal to the complicated readjustment of assimilating 'in-laws' and grandchildren into the family circle. In the Athens days when the sons and their families lived near-by, and gathered at the big house for summer holidays and Christmas celebrations, her art of home-making was put to the acid test. The fact that we all look back upon those occasions with pleasure is proof that she handled her task with consummate success. Her servants loved her; she shared their joys and sorrows and was personally concerned in their physical and spiritual welfare. She demanded the best of her staff and scorned shoddy service. I well remember her showing a little maid how to clean the bathroom—'in the corners, too, and under the tub', and if she didn't actually give chapter and verse she left no doubt in her mind that 'the eyes of the Lord are in every place', and therefore, every place must be fit for His inspection! An Englishwoman, living in the 'deep South', the racial problem held no terrors for her, and among those who served her both white and coloured, there was no friction. A little grandson, devoted to William, the chauffeur, unconsciously mirrored his grandmother's attitude when he was heard to say one day: "Willum, why are you black and I'm white?" "Well, Len, I don't know," William replied. "*I* know, Willum," answered the little boy, "it's because God made us that way." The answer satisfied them both.

She had that kind of personality possessed by rare souls which made total strangers lay bare their secrets to her and tell her their family histories. This was especially true of the 'little and lowly people', tradesmen and people who rang the door bell for one reason or another. She entertained many angels unaware, and some, not angels, who went away refreshed and heartened because of a brief contact with her wholesomeness and sanctified common sense.

I remember one such incident which happened in Athens. Returning home for supper we were told of someone who had called and found Mother at home. His name was Stevens, but whether he was selling something, or how he earned his living no one seems to remember. Whatever he hoped to get, he poured out his troubles in Mother's sympathetic ear. He was the father of a young baby who had been very ill and whose life had been saved by no less than Karo syrup! Now, Mother's weakness was this. When she heard of a remedy or a food which had done good to someone else she insisted on doling it out to her long-suffering family. Immediately large quantities of Karo syrup appeared on the table at every meal, and we were told to 'put Karo syrup on your bread', or 'your cereal', or anything else she could think of, always with the added injunction that 'it saved Stevens' baby!' This continued until the family rebelled and laughed it out of existence by anticipating Mother and saying it first. She enjoyed the nonsense as much as anybody, but we knew that before long another cure-all or 'health food' would come to her notice, and the same thing would happen again. To this day I never look at a can of Karo syrup without saying to myself: 'It saved Stevens' baby!'

The Athens home was headquarters during most of the years of the itinerant ministry in the United States and Canada, and Dad's return after one of these great tours was an event to be forever remembered. In anticipation of it, Mother was in her element. It was all the excuse she needed to wash curtains, turn rugs, and give an extra polish to furniture and silver. The big study was her special objective. She seemed to be everywhere at once and thoroughly enjoying it all. On the great day, Esther and Ada Salter, the two sisters who had come out from England to be cook and housemaid, would be busy in the kitchen, Mother's younger brother, Uncle Charlie, trimming the hedge in an already tidy and well-kept garden, and at last the car was dispatched to the station 'to fetch Doctor and Miss Kathleen'.

As soon as Dad walked in at the front door something came alive in the house. It snapped into a sparkling activity different to that of preparation. It is difficult not to overwork the word, 'magnetic', in speaking of him. It was not some quality which just belonged to the pulpit and platform; everything, even the inanimate objects and furnishings of life were accentuated and brightened when he wrote his signature across the day. From long and tiring and triumphant journeys he came home in those days like a schoolboy returning for the holidays. By the first meal he had changed from clerics into a grey or brown suit and brilliant tie and socks, for he dearly loved bright colours. He had a way of making everyone in the house feel included in his pleasure at being home. He would make a play of the food being served: "What's this, Ada?" knowing very well that a dish of baked apples can look like nothing else but baked apples. Poor Ada, whose sister had drilled her to say, 'Sir', 'Ma'am', and

'Miss', when addressing the family, and confused by all the excitement and laughter, stumbled out with, "Sir-r-rapples!" "And what's 'Sir-r-rapples?" he would innocently ask, making her hold the dish while the whole matter was made an issue, and the poor girl, giggling and blushing would at last flee to the kitchen to tell Esther what "Doctor said now!" Everything was admired and commented on in the house, garden, and garage, for he must see this and that, and the changes made somewhere else; renew acquaintance with the dogs, and in a more circumspect way with 'Polly'. Everyone who had had a part in it was made to feel a thousand times repaid for the work that had gone before.

Machinery was set in motion for another departure immediately for his days at home were few, and in a week or two at most he must be off again. Winnie was everywhere, the perfect secretary, quiet, efficient, and quick, looking up trains and checking appointments. Mother was unpacking, sending suits to the cleaners, watching for repairs to clothing and baggage. 'Rest' for Dad was little more than change of activity, but simply to be at home was all he seemed to need to recharge himself for the coming days. He referred once in preaching to "that spot on earth where we feel at home, with no restraint, no keeping up of appearances; at home, in perfect quiet and ease." It may be wondered, at first, if the word, 'quiet', was appropriate; but on second thoughts one remembers times in those busy and exciting days which stand out in even bolder relief than the social hours of fun and gaiety. These times came at the beginning and ending of the day. Before breakfast in the morning the whole family, guests and servants included, gathered in the big living-room for family prayers. To be late was taboo, and to try and slip in by way of the dining-room while the assembled congregation waited in awkward silence for the tardy member was rarely repeated. There was a glance in his or her direction from Dad's eagle eye and enough censure in the way he gave out the number of the hymn! And what singing it was! If Percy was there it was he who played the piano, brilliantly, but like Thor among the thunderbolts, and when a dozen or more voices, from Mother's high soprano to Dad's bass and the little one's obligato, made 'a joyful noise unto the Lord', the sound must have echoed and re-echoed all up and down Lumpkin Street!

Dad himself read the Scripture and led the prayer on the first morning of his home-coming, passing that office to whichever of the boys was there in order of age the following mornings. When the family came to live in the States in 1919, Dad divided the Book of Psalms in such a way as to use a portion of it each day and read the book completely through twice in the year. This practice continued during his lifetime and after, among the members of the family and others of the inner circle, so that wherever they happened to be they knew that each one was reading the same passage each day.

So many people who heard Dr. Morgan in buildings set apart for worship remarked on his voice—that it was worth while to have come just to hear him read the Scriptures. He read at home exactly as he read in the pulpit, and the reverent and unhurried tone and emphasis were even more unforgettable and remarkable in the family circle. It was a short reading usually, but every word was marked and weighed and read with the understanding heart. We kneeled as he led in prayer and may be forgiven a glance at the picture he made as he encompassed a little grandchild in his arm and bore up his brood and his world before the Throne of Grace.

He enjoyed the 'quiet and ease' of home-life, too, when, late at night, after good-nights had been said, he sat alone with his book in the big chair by a lamp in the study. He must have extracted the essence of enjoyment from these moments because they were so rare.

He loved more than anything to have his whole family around him, and in that period when it was practicable he would begin making plans early to gather them in for Christmas.

"Six months to-day is Christmas Day," he wrote round to the clan in June of 1923, " . . . I am particularly anxious that we should all be together on that day. . . . You know that I am not morbid or sentimental, but I do feel that it is impossible to be sure where we may all be a year from that time. . . . Mother, the girls and I may be in Australia. . . . This, then, is a request well ahead that, wherever you may be, you make no arrangements that will interfere with your coming to us for that occasion. I should like to have all my children and their children (in the shell and on foot) round about me on that day."

One of his favourite forms of recreation at these times and throughout the remainder of his life was solving crossword puzzles. For one thing he loved anything to do with words or word study. Then, too, if the crowd were scattered on business of their own, he used this indirect way of demanding their attention and their presence.

Things began calmly enough with, perhaps, one of the girls in attendance. Dad in the big chair, a pencil in one hand and an outsize crossword puzzle in the other, was exceedingly quick in filling in all but the most difficult of the words. But the time always came when something would demand resort to the dictionary. No! that wasn't the right word! Someone passing the door would be hailed and told to get the *Britannica* and look up 'a large quadruped, native of the East Indies, beginning B-A—ten letters', the fifth was R which obviously fitted into the third letter of another ten-letter word *Down*—a town in Azerbaijan, 70 miles S.E. of Tabriz. From then on the fun was fast and furious. Assistants who were busy with the dictionary and the Encyclopædia hunting the quadruped in the East Indies were in no mood to be sidetracked to Tabriz. But never mind, someone else was coming upstairs! "Howard? Ah, come in here a minute, my boy. Get an atlas and find Tabriz—T-A-B-R-I-Z—in the Near East, I believe!" There is great excitement when it is discovered that Tabriz is in Turkey, for the town near by *might* begin T-U-R-K—yes! the K fits Akron (rubber capital of the world). Someone suggests Turkistan. Not enough letters. "Besides, Turkestan is *not* a town, Ruth. Now, Howard, have you found Azerbaijan? What? Oh, my dear boy, is that the best map you can find? Get my big atlas. Where is it? WINNIE! Where is my atlas? Ah, there it is. What's that, Kath? My dear girl, a bobolink is a bird, not a quadruped! Where's Frank? Where's Jack?" So it would go on until all the family was present and the great mahogany table covered with books. This, I am sure, was one reason he loved puzzles—they provided such a wonderful excuse to gather the clan around him. To be in the midst of them all, working, playing, talking, joking, was the utmost he asked for when the long weeks of travelling were over.

The fact that all four of his sons had followed him into the Ministry made a bond of union stronger than all other ties. The sons took full advantage of their father's experience and understanding, constantly seeking his advice as teacher as well as father. Many of these consultations must necessarily be carried on through letters. They knew that wherever he was he would give the most careful attention to their questions and problems, read sermon notes and write immediately his comments and criticisms, assured of a large slice of encouragement and help. That help was often practical as well as advisory. One example represents many. When one of his sons in a small country church launched a scheme to place Bibles throughout the pews, Dr. Morgan wrote at once offering to match Bible for Bible, and this he did at no little expense to himself. When the five could be together in person it was inevitable that they would begin talking 'shop'. A seminary class might well envy the discussions of fine points of interpretation and exegesis, methods of other preachers and gleanings from the great theological minds of the past, as one thought led to another. If occasionally someone went in she might linger a bit to eavesdrop on these conversations; but the listening audience, while always welcome, was at these times completely ignored.

Dr. Morgan said once in preaching: "Fathers are terribly in danger of walking among their children on stilts." While children and young people including his own always respected him, I believe I speak for them in saying that we always felt he was quite natural with us, never on a pedestal, and that he understood our generation. Indeed, one of his gifts was to be able to remember what it felt like to be young. In one of his books he describes the contents of a boy's pockets, and the losing of face that a boy feels in being made to turn them out for public scrutiny. He described a boy's smell as 'Bread, butter, and marbles', and a child's appetite—'Give him another piece of cake. He's got a moreish feeling!' His greatest charm with young people was his way of individualizing each of his young friends. The name of the daughter of his friend, Frank Fifoot, was 'Doris', but "he often called me 'Ethel' which is my second name," she says, "because he said no one else used it." He made up names for people which for some reason he thought suited them better. Sometimes he called me 'Rhoda'. I was aware that it had something to do with Peter knocking on the door, but he never explained why it was appropriate to me! Doris Fifoot says that her brother, Ronald, as a little boy saved up any good stories he heard to tell Dr. Morgan on his next visit. A busy man might be excused for forgetting, but she says that "one of the first things your father would say when he arrived was: 'Well, Ronald, any good ones this time?'"

That he remembered with pleasure those who had been his very young friends is borne out in a letter he wrote to his friend, Mrs. W. R. Moody, as late as August, 1944. Of her girls he said: "I think I knew Betty best, but I well remember Mary when she was very little and went about singing:

> I was lost but Jesus found me
> On the road to Mandalay.

The unconscious humour of children always delighted him, as on the occasion when a grandson was asked by a good Presbyterian deacon if he intended to be a preacher like his grandfather and his daddy and his uncles. "No, sir," came the prompt reply, "I'm going to work!"

The austerity of appearance which sometimes halted older

people had no terrors for those who had once established such a friendship. In her reminiscences, Miss Fifoot continues: "On Sunday, August 11th, 1929, we motored from Vermont where we were staying for the week-end, to Northfield, and called at Mr. Moody's house where Dr. Morgan and Ruth were staying. I remember being told Dr. Morgan wasn't seeing many people. and replying confidently 'He will see *me!*' and overhearing him say when told Miss Fifoot wanted to see him, 'What! Is she here?' and again, 'Not at the door?' because he didn't know I was in the United States."

His fascination for the very young is remembered by Mrs. Leslie Walker, a close friend of the early days who, when asked to write some of her thoughts about Dr. Morgan, referred to the impression he made upon her when she was nine years old. "He would have been about twenty-four when I first saw him. . . . I particularly remember the happy hours spent when the day's work was over, and after supper a few friends were asked in to meet him. . . . Having been banished to bed, I would creep downstairs somehow, and your father always managed to see that I stayed there. . . . I always tried to say good-night to him no matter at what hour he retired, so great was his charm on the opposite sex even at that early age!" She tells of another impression of those early days which must have delighted a child. "This time he was caught out," she says.

"He was taking a service at a remote country chapel on the moors, and, by the way, he had driven us there, Mother and me, I being perched on the back seat of the dog-cart and feeling distinctly nervous as he blithely remarked, 'I am no good with horses, and if this beast bolts I don't know what will happen!' Anyway, we got there safely. The little chapel was packed. . . . When your father got up in the pulpit he almost seemed part of the congregation with the choir packed tight behind him. He gave out the hymn, and as we all rose there was a tremendous blast from four trumpets which shot your father round like a scalded cat to see where the noise was coming from. Mother and I, seeing these instruments being lifted, guessed what was going to be the effect, and hardly knew how to keep from laughing—in fact, we didn't. The look on your father's face was too much. He said afterwards he thought it was the last trump being sounded!"

That Dr. Morgan was a man's man was evidenced by the success of his meetings for men only in many cities, and by the large number of young men who were among his most persistent listeners. At the same time, and with no conscious effort, he had from the earliest years a way of bewitching the opposite sex irrespective of age, as Mrs. Walker has noted. In his altogether satisfying domestic happiness and his abiding affection for his 'Nancie', he behaved toward all women with gentleness and courtesy, and possessed a gift for making a woman feel distinctive and important to which it was impossible not to respond. Young ones loved him for the reason his own daughters did, because he never censured them for being 'modern', or suggested that the virtuous life must wear a long face. Whatever the current fashion, the length of a dress or hair style was never vulgar unless it was abused. The not always 'gentler' sex in his own family recognized his flair for good taste in style. He knew what suited each one, and to have him say, "That's a nice dress. I like it!" meant that the choice was right. He could, and often did, select clothes for his women folk. On a page in one of his later diaries is the amazing statement: "I went into town and bought two hats for Nancie. Hope they will be all right!"

When thoughts turn back to earlier days it is of 'Louie' that the brothers and sisters often speak. "She had an awful time taking care of us," they say, and so she did, for she it was who first appeared upon the scene when the swing crashed through the bannisters and two frightened small boys hung on to the wreckage till help arrived. One gathers that Louie Orgar was devoted to her employers in spite of these trials, and wondered just how she would express her feelings about them. In reply to this query came a letter from New Zealand which might well be representative of the attitude of all who served them. There is no need to moralize on the question of the Christian relationship of employer to employee, for this letter tells it all:

"Dear Mrs. Morgan,

"I had a letter yesterday from Kathleen (or Mrs. Shute, I expect it ought to be, but Kathleen is the name I knew her best by) and she asked me to write a few lines for you as I found the home life at her Father's and Mother's home while I was a maid there. Well, dear, there are a great many things that went to make their home a most happy place for me while I was maid for the four and a half years I was there before I married. Both their lives were a great influence in my life for good and they were both exceedingly good Christian folk. In my own experience, their home and friendship was a thing that I needed in those far away days, and I always felt that I could tell the Doctor and Mrs. Morgan any trouble that I had and was always sure to find a friend and companion. As to the work—well, in my case it was a labour of love, and nothing was too much for me to do to help all I could. I had some real good and happy days while I was there, and at Norwood, and their seaside home at Mundesley were red-letter days for me, and it was a real home life with fun as well as duty, and at times there was sorrow mixed with happiness that they went through, but still there was always that calm and sure confidence awaiting any of us that had trouble. We had only to let them know and there was always a helping hand held out, and even after I married it was always home to me, and I could go whenever I liked and was always welcome, and even when my Cyril was a wee chap they thought such a lot of him, and I can see now the Doctor taking him on his knee at morning worship, and the boy was quite at home, and those are the things that count these days. Well, dear, I do not know you personally, but I know your husband well. This may not help you very much, but you will be able to take what you want of it, and be sure I feel I can never forget the times of help and strength that I received while living with them.

And now they have passed on to Higher Service, but the memory of them still lingers on.

"Yours faithfully,

"LOUIE ORGAR."

The inner circle would be incomplete without additional mention of Uncle Ted and Auntie Edith, who played so large a part in making 'Northfield' the home in England Dad loved the most, and 'Yew Tree' the haven of peace to which he and Mother repaired so often in the later years.

The 'Yew Tree' of to-day is a place of enchantment, wrought by the magic of loving care. The house, so nearly shattered by a German bomb, has covered its scars but bears them proudly as a mark of its sturdiness. The fields have a story to tell of their share in feeding a nation in peace and war. Only the garden is untouched by these things. In another garden, thousands of miles away, the breath of roses brings an exquisite nostalgia. Distance is banished, time rolls back the years, and we are waking on a freshly laundered morning to the scent of roses through the window under the eaves. Afternoons—and there is tea in the garden with an orchestra of birds and bumble bees. Dad sits in a deck chair telling stories, making everybody laugh especially 'Polly', on her perch nearby. Mother and Auntie Edith are deep in conversation in the summerhouse, a revolving structure that can be turned to face the sun or back the wind.

It is good to remember that it was in these surroundings that Mother spent the last months of her life. For her it was a time of waiting—but quiet, restful waiting, loving the birds' call in the dawn and the country sights and sounds that belonged to her youth. How she enjoyed the little church in Stebbing and its young minister, writing to tell us of his messages. Then one morning, as the birds were waking for another day, she woke, too, to the dawning of eternal life and reunion with those she loved.

To us who come from far away, this is 'home'. Whatever we have accumulated of artificiality or complexity, we drop these things at the garden gate. Spiritually we are renewed by this nearness to simplicity and reality. Even the furnishings of the house remind us of other days—the grandfather clock that used to be at Mundesley; the little Estey organ that Dad brought back from America; Mother's desk from which she wrote letters that flew all over the world. The two dear custodians of these treasures are still welcoming us back, and long before we arrive our hearts go ahead of us and anticipate the first sight of the house under the yew trees and the primrose-bordered meadows of 'home'.

Friends who enjoyed the hospitality of the Morgan home were legion. Dr. Morgan had an eagle eye for discovering familiar faces in his congregation, and as long as there was room in his home he would not hear of those who had come miles to hear him staying in a hotel. Ministers and missionaries were often guests. Many of them still cherish memories of that happy home life, and the re-creation they found there, both physical and spiritual. In return they brought blessings of their own for such friendships are mutual springs of refreshment. These members of the inner circle, both in England and America, are to-day held in affectionate remembrance by those who were, in comparison, the younger generation. They were all great in their calling, not less so because they were young in heart. Like their host they carried over into the later years an unshakeable Christian optimism, looking toward a future in which 'the best is yet to be'.

There were times when the Morgans adopted whole families for weeks and months at a time, standing by until they found a new foothold of security or acclimatized themselves to the ways of a new world. It will never be known how many were helped and heartened, blessed and sustained by the Christian hospitality which was not measured by time or counted by cost. It is a famous pastime of human nature to contemplate the good that might be done if the means were available. Dr. and Mrs. Morgan were glorious squanderers of the means at their disposal of bringing joy to others, utterly regardless of social position or advantage.

It is true that among their friends were some who were able to express their affection through gifts of great material value, and these they received with the same graciousness with which they gave to others—a much more difficult accomplishment. But whether accepting or bestowing, Dr. Morgan scorned superficial criticism by outsiders of his way of life. None of these things had any power to move him, for he cared only for the compensation of having learned 'in whatsoever state' to be 'content'.

Though old friends were peculiarly cherished, Dr. and Mrs. Morgan had a way of gathering new friends, and having tried their adoption, they, too, were included in the inner circle, so that at the close of life these two were surrounded by friends, men and women, true as steel, yet younger and more virile in years, who helped to ease the harrowing days of war, so shockingly difficult for those to whom the sunset of life was meant to be peaceful and calm.

* * * * * *

When you begin to analyze it, it is not the big things but the little things which make up the mosaic of the inner circle. Big things belong to the conference hall, the national crisis, the renovation scheme—and these are important. The little things that make up a home atmosphere are important too —so important that words at last must halt and fail. It should have been easy to say: This I was a part of; this I remember.

But there is still one recourse for the expression of that which lies deepest in one's heart. It is summed up in the record of Christian virtues, and in this inner circle I found them all: Love, joy, peace, longsuffering, kindness, goodness, faithfulness, meekness, and self-control.

The Place of Power

'There is a place where human kinship is not enough, and a man is alone with God.'*

IN Campbell Morgan's life that citadel was built in his youth and its strong foundation was a heritage of the past. Agnosticism could not penetrate its walls, and the lure of popularity and notoriety met defeat in its quiet seclusion.

He loved the Bible with a devotion born of intimate knowledge, yet in familiarity he retained a sensitiveness to sacred things. It was a beautiful thing to see him pick it up as he prepared to read. His fingers touched the Book which had been his companion in the place of loneliness with such reverent appreciation as conveyed an unspoken lesson regarding the hallowed nature of the Word of God. The dominant purpose of his life was to make it known and share its wealth with others.

His work bore the hallmark of inspiration, but the spark was fed by the fuel of methodical and perpetual study.

The pointing compass of his life was directed toward the divine Will of God. He was strong-winged in faith.

A balanced standard of values, an adherence to purpose, a sure and authoritative faith, an insatiable desire for knowledge, a prodigious capacity for work—these made up the pattern of Campbell Morgan's life. For their dynamic he depended wholly on the Fortress, the High Tower. Only there could success and failure, ambition and frustration, joy and sorrow, recognition and misunderstanding assume their relative proportions in the light of eternity. He stated his own ideal for life's achievement: "THE GREATEST VICTORY obtainable in this life is that of fulfilling the possibilities of personality, and the greatest defeat is that of failure in this

---

* The quotation at the top of this page is from Dr. Kirk's sermon to which reference is made in the Introduction to Part II

direction. Recognizing that every individual life is a creation of God, having its own peculiar forces and values, we assert that the fulfilling of life consists in realizing to the full the life bestowed. Living includes the active realization of all capacity and its full use within the sphere of divine intention. Full-orbed life admits of no atrophied powers. No more searching words fell upon the listening ear of the seer in Patmos than those spoken by the glorious One amid the lampstands to the Church in Sardis: 'I have found no works of thine fulfilled before my God'. Success consists in living, not in gain; not in the reward of doing, but in the doing."

Let it be the criterion of his own life as we mark its passage and measure its fulfilment.

A LIST OF SOME OF
Dr. G. CAMPBELL MORGAN'S PUBLISHED WORKS

THE WESTMINSTER PULPIT—11 Volumes of Sermons preached in Westminster Chapel.
SEARCHLIGHTS FROM THE WORD.
ACTS OF THE APOSTLES.
THE MESSAGES OF THE BIBLE. Vol. 1.
THE MESSAGES OF THE BIBLE. Vol. 2.
ANALYSED BIBLE.—Outlines of the Books of the Bible:
  Vol. 1—Genesis to Esther.
  Vol. 2—Job to Malachi.
  Vol. 3—Matthew to Revelation.
  Vol. 4—Genesis.
  Vol. 5—Job.
  Vol. 6—Isaiah—Vol. 1.
  Vol. 7—Isaiah—Vol. 2.
  Vol. 8—Matthew.
  Vol. 9—John.
  Vol. 10—Romans.
THE GOSPEL OF MATTHEW.
THE GOSPEL OF MARK.
THE GOSPEL OF LUKE.
THE GOSPEL OF JOHN.
THE CRISES OF THE CHRIST.
THE PROPHECY OF JEREMIAH.
THE GREAT PHYSICIAN.
GREAT CHAPTERS OF THE BIBLE.
PARABLES AND METAPHORS OF OUR LORD.
THE CORINTHIAN, LETTERS OF PAUL.
CATEGORICAL IMPERATIVES OF THE CHRISTIAN FAITH.
THE TEACHING OF CHRIST.
NOTES ON THE PSALMS.
THE SPIRIT OF GOD.
THE LETTERS OF OUR LORD—A First Century Message to Twentieth Century Christians.
GOD'S LAST WORD TO MAN. (HEBREWS)
HOSEA.
THE TEN COMMANDMENTS.
THE TRUE ESTIMATE OF LIFE
THE TRIUMPHS OF FAITH.
THE LIFE OF THE CHRISTIAN.
THE PRACTICE OF PRAYER.
THE BIBLE AND THE CROSS.
SIMPLE THINGS OF THE CHRISTIAN LIFE.
THE STUDY AND TEACHING OF THE ENGLISH BIBLE.

PREACHING.
"BEHOLD, HE COMETH!"
PETER AND THE CHURCH.
THE PARABLE OF THE FATHER'S HEART.
THE BIBLE IN FIVE YEARS.
THE BIBLE AND THE CHILD.
ALPHA AND OMEGA.
THE MUSIC OF LIFE.
TO DIE IS GAIN.
THE CHRIST OF TO-DAY—WHAT? WHENCE? WHITHER?

THE ANALYSED BIBLE

The Revised Version of the Bible, published by The Oxford University Press, interleaved in front of each of the sixty-six Books with the Analysis and Message of the Book by Dr. G. CAMPBELL MORGAN.

BOOKLETS

HIDDEN YEARS AT NAZARETH.
CHRIST AND THE BIBLE.
DIVINE GUIDANCE AND HUMAN ADVICE
THE ROMANCE OF THE BIBLE.
PAUL—WHAT SHALL I DO, LORD?—ONE THING I DO.
THE PURPOSE OF THE INCARNATION.
H.M. THE KING, 1910—1935.
HARMONY OF THE TESTAMENTS.
SIN, RIGHTEOUSNESS AND JUDGMENT.
THE DESIRE OF ALL NATIONS.
"ALL THINGS NEW."

Index

	Page
ABEL, Charles	344
Acton, Lord	156
Adam, Douglas	173
Aitken, Hay	173
Aldis, W. H.	323
Analyzed Bible	164
Archer, T.	53, 125
Armistead, Lord	156, 193, 205, 369
Ataraxia	262, 264, 382
Athens, Ga.	43, 262-63, 273, 276, 383
Atholl, Duchess of	156
Atkins, F. A.	156, 176, 235
Atkins, Glenn	255
Australia	221
BALTIMORE, Md.	118, 312, 340
B.B.C.	363
Bentwick, Countess	193
Berry, Sidney	294, 326
B.I.O.L.A.	273, 381
Bible Teachers' Association	190, 203, 215
Biblical Seminary, N.Y.C.	232
Birmingham	21, 40, 41, 44, 58, 75, 76, 77, 78, 83, 85, 86, 89, 102, 297, 370, 374
Blackie, Dr. Margery	22, 305
Bonner, Carey	173
Booth, Mrs. Bramwell	173, 361
Booth, Mrs. Catherine	377
Booth, General William	57, 67, 374, 377
British Weekly	173, 206, 229, 268, 294
Broughton, Len G.	122, 173, 179, 183, 262, 348
Brown, Charles	106, 173, 294, 325, 327, 332
Brown, Dame Edith	345, 347
Bryan, William Jennings	204
Buchan, John	26, 73
Buckingham Palace	145, 303
Butler, J. L.	26-28, 35, 36, 163, 184, 186, 187, 188
Butler, Mrs. J. L.	29, 188
CABLE, Mildred	291, 324-25, 344, 350-62
Cadman, Parkes	61, 62, 95-6
Campbell, R. J.	370
Cambridge	14, 198
Carnegie, Mr. and Mrs. Andrew	193, 293
Carpenter, General George	375
Carpenter, Mrs. George	376-77
Catholic World, The	369

	Page
Cedar Falls, Ia.	277
Chadwick, Samuel	31, 61, 133, 173, 208-12, 215, 219, 234, 281
Cheltenham, Glos.	26, 36
Cheshunt College	14, 193-94, 204, 213, 218, 279
Chicago	87, 98-9, 124, 125
Chicago Theological Seminary	130
Child, Winifred	86
China Inland Mission	299, 344
Christian Observer, The	241, 312
Christian World, The	295, 300
Churchill, Winston	205, 312
Cincinnati, O.	264-67
Clibborn, Mrs. Booth	173
Collier, Frank	145
Collins Street Congregational Church, Melbourne	221
Congregational Union of England and Wales	372
Coster, Howard	287, 288
Craigmyle, Lord	294
Crake, John	69-70, 71, 72, 81
Craske, Edith	147, 226, 345
Crawford, Dan	344
Cromwell, Oliver	17
Crossley, Frank	102
DALE, R. W.	31, 76-78, 80, 102, 143
Davies, E. Emlyn, F.R.C.O.	332
de Rusett, E. D.	190, 192
Dickenson, Kathleen	344
Dixon, A. C.	348
ECCLESHALL, Staffs.	68, 73, 142
Elliott, Charlotte	240
Erdman, Charles R.	169, 173, 301, 332, 334-35
Erdman, William J.	92
E.U.S.A.	198-99, 203, 299, 345, 347-49
FIFOOT, Doris	390, 391
Fifoot, Frank	25, 133, 281, 297, 390
Fifth Avenue Presbyterian Church, N.Y.C.	110, 115, 128, 183, 225
Fitt, A. P.	120
Forsyth, P. T.	173
Franklin Street Presbyterian Church, Baltimore	312, 340
Free Church Council	177

INDEX

	Page
French, Evangeline	350
French, Francesca	350
Friends, Society of	175
GAMBLE, H. J.	218
Gardner, Mrs. A. M.	146, 346
Gardner, J. Macara	213
George, D. Lloyd	224, 369
Gibson, Monro	173
Girdlestone, R. B.	173
Glendale, Cal.	273
Glover, T. R.	224
Gordon College, Boston	279-80, 381
Grenfell, Wilfred	344
Guernsey	80
Guinness, Harry	348
HALDANE, Viscount	193
Halsbury, Lord	156
Halverstadt, Mrs. H.	122, 278, 302
Harries, John	13-14, 32
Henson, Hensley	173
Hewitt, A. W.	147, 148, 151
Highbury Quadrant Church	224-32, 377
Hiley, D. J.	180
Holden, Stuart	173, 190, 348, 355, 357
Holland, Canon	52
Hopwood, Sir Francis	193
Horn, F. J.	182-83
Horne, Sylvester	256
Howell, Winifred M.	107-109, 112, 115, 119, 146, 226, 254, 261, 263, 277, 305, 317, 386, 389
Hudson, William E.	243-44
Hughes, S. W.	328
Hull,	55-56, 57, 59
Hulme, Ferrier	60, 294, 295, 317
Huntley, Emily	173
Hurndall, W. Evans	139, 140
Hutton, John A.	173, 178-79, 217-18, 234, 235, 245, 249, 280, 291, 294, 323, 340, 355
INTERNATIONAL S.S. Lessons	154
Isle of Man	81
JOHNSON, E. W.	194, 195
Jones, J. D.	71, 173
Jowett, J. H.	102, 173, 223, 225, 238, 340
KELLY, Howard	118
Keswick	15, 172, 323, 348
King George V.	312
Kingsley, Charles	35, 74, 82, 83, 188, 297
LEVY, E. Lawrence	41, 43, 52, 53-55, 370-71
Lewis, Elvet	173, 355
Lever, Sir William	193

	Page
Lidgett, Scott	61, 317
Lightley, J. W.	61
Lingle, Walter L.	244, 312
Liverpool	60
Llandrindod Wells	214
Lloyd-Jones, D. Martyn	121, 302, 308, 314, 315, 318, 323, 329-32, 361
London Missionary Society	105, 146, 198, 345
Lothrop, Nurse	132, 135
Ludhiana Mission	299, 345-47
MACINNIS, J. M.	273-75, 285
Mackinnon, Clarence	245
Manchester	60
Mantle, Gregory,	75, 76, 116, 133, 165, 171, 173
Market Drayton	63, 297
Marsh, Arthur E.	13, 168-69, 203, 267, 268, 270, 301, 311, 323
Martin, Samuel	137, 138-39
Massanetta Springs, Va.	15, 243-44
Maynard, Theodore	269-70
McCormick, Mrs. Cyrus	124
McLaren, Alexander	256
McNairn, Stuart	199, 347-49
McNeill, John	173
Meyer, F. B.	92, 173, 258, 260, 317, 357
Mildmay Institute	222-24, 349
Miller, Amy	147, 191
Monmouth Methodist Chapel	22, 31-34, 292-93
Montreal	99
Montreat, N.C.	15, 244
Moody Bible Institute	98
Moody, D. L.	30-31, 44, 87, 91-95, 98, 109, 114, 118, 120, 121, 140, 260, 329, 343
Moody, Mrs. D. L.	362
Moody, Paul	173
Moody, Will	114, 119, 128, 258, 260
Moody, Mrs. Will	129, 176, 189, 301, 390
Morgan, Annie (Mrs. Campbell Morgan),	14, 22, 62, 63, 64, 65, 66, 83, 84, 100, 103, 107, 109, 115, 118, 119, 134, 159, 162, 184, 187, 200, 203, 221, 224, 264, 273, 277, 278, 281, 283, 297, 299, 300, 301, 304, 305, 308, 310, 313, 314, 316, 317, 318, 333, 346, 382-85, 394, 395
Morgan, Edward	171, 176, 187, 233, 305, 307, 394
Morgan, Mrs. Edward	133, 171, 175, 233, 305, 394
Morgan, Elizabeth Fawn,	24, 117, 192
Morgan, Frank Crossley	30, 107, 118, 120, 126, 129, 132, 184, 186, 187, 223, 228, 229, 273, 288, 291, 292, 332, 333, 389
Morgan, George	23, 24, 60, 117, 118, 192

INDEX 403

Morgan, G. Campbell, birth and boyhood, 23-32; first sermon, 31-32; evangelistic meetings, 36-38, 44-45, 51; year of eclipse, 38-40; teaching, 40-41, 52-55; tent meetings and popular lectures, 45-50; Hull Mission, 55-56; rejection by Wesleyan ministry, 57-60; marriage, 62-64; Stone, 65-73; Rugely, 73-76; Birmingham, 76-87, 101-103; first visit to U.S., 87-101; New Court, Tollington Park, 104-115; Northfield Extension, 117-136; first Westminster ministry, 137-220; Cheshunt College presidency, 193-98; Mildmay, 221-24; Highbury Quadrant, 224-32; itinerant ministry in U.S., 238-45; itinerant ministry in Canada, 245-61; Cincinnati, 264-67; B.I.O.L.A., 271-75; Philadelphia, 277-83; Gordon College, 278-80; second Westminster ministry, 284-316; Diamond Jubilee, 292-96; retirement, 316.

Morgan, Gwendoline May, 73, 80, 81, 83
Morgan, Howard Moody 22, 32, 33, 34, 66, 83, 84, 118, 132, 135, 187, 273, 283, 332, 333, 388
Morgan, Kathleen Annie 127, 132, 264, 273, 277, 282, 288, 299, 305, 307-308, 316, 385, 393
Morgan, Kingsley John 28, 83, 84, 85, 114, 118, 120, 126, 129, 132, 183, 184, 186, 187, 238-45, 273, 288, 289, 332, 333, 389
Morgan, Lizzie .. 24, 31, 81, 281
Morgan, Percival Campbell 66, 107, 120, 128, 132, 184, 187, 199, 200, 204, 264, 273, 286, 291, 318, 386
Morgan, Ruth 184, 264, 273, 288, 304, 305, 314, 316, 317, 388, 391
Morley, Lord 193
Mott, John R. 347
Müller, George 23
Mundesley-on-Sea 15, 92, 169-71, 174, 187-88, 232-33, 275, 290-91, 292, 307, 393, 395
Mundesley Bible Conference 171-80, 189, 191, 197, 214, 344, 345, 355-56
Murdoch, Dr. Charlotte .. 146, 344
Murray, Harold 14-15

New Court Church 101, 104-07, 109-12, 115-17, 131, 140, 142, 269, 345
New Theology, The 236
Niagara Falls 99-100
Nichol, Sir William Robertson .. 173
Nichols, Milton Harold .. 332, 333
Northcliffe, Lord 156

Northfield, Mass. 87, 91, 93, 114, 118, 120, 131, 135, 149, 162, 184, 253, 278, 334, 362, 391
Northfield Bible Conference 88, 92-5, 109, 114-15, 117, 119-20, 122-23, 125-26, 127, 128, 132, 140, 172, 189, 255, 258, 277
Nutton, Samuel 241

Orgar, Louie 392-94
Orr, James 173
Osteopathy 182-83
Ottawa 40

Page, Walter Hines 193
Parker, Joseph 52, 113-14, 115-16, 132, 143, 194, 229, 256
Pattison, F. W. 168, 203
Pearl Harbour Attack 313
Perkins, J. Stanley 195
Pierson, A. T. 140, 173
Plymouth Brethren, The 23
Powell, R. C. 140

Quakers, The 180

Revell, Fleming H. 362
Richmond, Va. 87
Riddle, T. Wilkinson .. 294, 295
Roberts, Edward H. 249-50
Robertson, A. T. 378
Robinson, Dr. Drummond .. 379-80
Robinson, F. A. 17, 245-61, 300, 302, 315, 317, 380
Rome, ... 181
Roosevelt, President Theodore .. 119
Ross, William 200
Rugely, Staffs. 21, 72, 73-6, 84, 297
Ruskin, John 111

Salisbury, Frank 14, 213
Salvation Army 56, 72, 113, 161, 374-77
Sankey, Ira D. 30, 44-45, 92, 93, 121, 329
Sark 80, 101
Scott, Sir Walter 240
Selbie, W. B. 217
Sharman's Orphans' Home 157
Shute, Bryan 314
Shute, Donald 282, 307
Simon, Henry 139
Simpson, Hubert L. .. 280, 284, 340
Smith, David 37-38
Smith, Gipsy 55-57, 61, 62, 116, 176, 294
Song Companion to the Scriptures .. 189
Southport 172
Spender, J. A. 157, 369
Spurgeon, Charles H. .. 52, 194
Stead, W. T. 157, 369
Stephens, J. P. 195-98

INDEX

Stoddart, Jane T. 206, 294
Stone, Staffs. 21, 65-73, 84, 142
Stony Brook, L. I. 15
St. Hellier, Lady 205
Swift, Albert 67, 73, 80, 87, 89, 90, 91, 97, 101, 133-34, 137, 142, 143-44, 145-46, 147, 150, 152, 154, 155, 166-67, 168, 175, 191, 201-03, 214, 281

TABERNACLE, Presbyterian Church, Philadelphia 32-33, 135, 277-78, 279-80, 282-83, 299, 332, 333
Tetbury, Glos. 21, 22
Texas 239, 342
Thomas, W. H. Griffith 173
Titanic, R.M.S. 158
Toronto 15, 99
Tweeddale, Dowager Marchioness of 205

UNION Theological Seminary, Richmond, Va. 240-41

V-E Day 318

WALKER, Charles Hay 348
Walker, Mrs. Leslie 391
Walters, C. E. 294
Wanamaker, John 71
Washington, D.C. 119
Watkinson, W. L. 173, 256
Welford, Mr. and Mrs. Walter D.
45-50, 287

Wesley, John 295
Wesley's Journal 35
West London Mission 146
Westminster Chapel, *Westminster Bible Record* 167, 192; Bible School, 15, 146-47, 149, 159, 162-64, 165, 170, 189, 194, 196, 223, 286, 302, 306, 314-15, 366, 369; Brotherhood, 159; Institute, 150, 153, 155-56, 175, 223, 343; *Westminster Record*, 155, 166, 167, 294, 302, 343, 349, 362, 373; Renovation Scheme, 149-50, 289, 293; Restoration Fund, 289, 293; Sisterhood, 146
Westminster Gazette 157, 369
Westrope, Richard 139-40
White, W. W. 232
Whitefield's Tabernacle 255
Whitehouse, Owen C. 195
Williams, T. Charles 173
Wilson, John 173
Wilson, President Woodrow 204-05, 229, 241
Winona Lake, Ind. 15, 277
Wiseman, Luke 317

YAPP, Sir Arthur 173, 222
Yates, Thomas 173
Yew Tree Farm 297, 394
Young, Andrew 344
Young, Dinsdale 173
Y.M.C.A. 123-24, 173, 222, 223-24, 225, 349

www.ingramcontent.com/pod-product-compliance
Lightning Source LLC
Chambersburg PA
CBHW071229290426
44108CB00013B/1347